# Who's Afraid of MORE C++?

# Who's Afraid of MORE C++?

Steve Heller

AP PROFESSIONAL
AP PROFESSIONAL is a division of Academic Press

San Diego London Boston
New York Sydney Tokyo Toronto

This book is printed on acid-free paper. ∞



ACADEMIC PRESS
525 B Street, Suite 1900, San Diego, CA 92101-4495
http://www.apnet.com

ACADEMIC PRESS
24–28 Oval Road, London NW1 7DX
http://www.hbuk.co.uk/ap/

**Library of Congress Cataloging-in-Publication Data**
Heller, Steve, 1949 Apr. 17–
Who's afraid of more C++ / Steve Heller.
p. cm.
Includes index.
ISBN 0-12-339104-0 (pbk. : alk. paper)
1. C++ (Computer program language) I. Title.
QA76.73.C153H455 1998
005.13'3—dc21 98-20376
CIP

Printed in the United States of America
98 99 00 01 02 CP 9 8 7 6 5 4 3 2 1

# TABLE OF CONTENTS

# *Dedication*

This book is dedicated to Susan Patricia Caffee Heller, the light of my life. Without her, this book would not be what it is; even more important, I would not be what I am: a happy man.

# Acknowledgments

I'd like to thank those readers who read and commented on the early versions of the manuscript for this book, especially Andy Brown, who provided the most detailed feedback.

I'd also like to thank those who posted reviews of my other books on Amazon.com, which gives potential readers an impartial source of information about my work.

I'm also indebted to Michael Andry for his foreword and its clear explanation of my goals for the *Who's Afraid of . . .* series.

Finally, I'd like to thank my mother and father for understanding that I had to do things my own way.

# Letter from a Novice

Who is Steve Heller?

I jumped to the sound of an ominous knock at my front door. A sense of foreboding heightened with every step I made toward the sound. Cracking it open, dark bluish grey clouds revealed themselves as they hung low overhead, threatening to unleash their contents at any moment. The tenseness of the postal worker's expression changed suddenly to an implacable smile as he quickly slipped a large envelope into my unsuspecting hands. Almost as soon as I realized I held the envelope, I looked up again to find the postman gone. The sky began to swirl, though there was only a hint of a breeze on my face. A slow shudder engulfed me as I quickly locked the door.

Half dazed, I was left standing at my doorway, staring at my name on the envelope written in a handwriting nearly identical to my own. Confused, but with a penetrating sense of courage I tore open the mysterious yellow mailer. It in turn seemed to be the catalyst for the rupturing of the sky, and my roof and heart pounded in unison. As the contents of the envelope spilled out on my lap I caught a glimpse of the words "Who's Afraid of C++?" on the looseleaf manuscript. Briefly I was frozen by a paralyzing shiver that gripped my body, as I began to wonder what would become of me. What did this mean? What was C++ and why should I be afraid of it? What was I getting myself into?

That was in March 1995. As I write this in March 1998, I have new insight into these questions. When Steve Heller asked me to help with the writing of *Who's Afraid of More C++?* I felt that shiver down my back again, I groaned, knowing full well this time what I was getting myself into, and wondering if I had the stamina to do it again.

Well, I did and we have a book. I also have the answers to the questions that I asked myself 3 years ago.

I have learned what C++ is. It is a computer programming language. It is an immense language, it is a complicated language, and it is a very powerful language. I learned through the writing of this book that C++ can be molded and shaped to do just about anything you want it to do. It convolutes, twists and turns corners. You can play hide-and-seek with it. Yet, in the hands of an expert, it is amazing to see it come to life.

As Steve and I wrote this book, I became more than a test reader, I also became a usability tester. It was through this I saw just how complicated writing a program was. I had already seen all the source code written to produce the program that Steve wrote for this book, and was amazed to see just this one little screen of words to show for all our efforts. I knew what was underneath that screen, I knew all the hours, the false starts, the redos, the polishing that it took to get to where we were in the program, and I could not believe that so little showed for our efforts.

Just when Steve thought he was done with it, I was quick to inform him that indeed he was not. It didn't take me long to "break" the program, causing more redos. Then there were things I wanted in the program to make it just a little easier, or a just little prettier. Back Steve went to the compiler. Actually, I think this was as much of a lesson on software design as it was on "more C++". There is so much one has to think about when writing a program; it is not only what you want it to do, you also have to program in what you don't want it to do.

I can't say that there is no reason to fear C++. It is a difficult thing to learn, but no more so than any other language including human spoken ones. It takes interest, work, and practice. I think, though, that as with any difficult subject, it can be mastered with the right learning tools and a competent teacher. I believe Steve to be a natural born teacher and through the writing of this book, he has created an excellent learning tool.

As for the other question, "Who is this Steve Heller guy, anyway?": he is now my husband. Even after all the trouble he caused me with C++, I figured anyone who had the same handwriting as I do was destined to be my soulmate.

Susan Patricia Caffee Heller
Dallas, Texas
March, 1998

# Foreword

Those of you who have not read Steve Heller's *Who's Afraid of C++?*, the first book in the *Who's Afraid of . . .* series, are in for a surprise. I am not referring to his inclusion of email communications he had with a novice programmer while writing that book. That was a surprise to its readers, and made his first series book unique in that respect. That beneficial element is also in this book, but that is not the surprise I mean.

No, the surprise that awaits you is really far more fundamental. However, before going any further, let's address a couple of other points: Who I am, and why I am writing the foreword. In covering the second point, we'll start getting into the surprise.

First, I have about ten years experience in programming in xbase languages (dBase, FoxBase, FoxPro). I have made three separate attempts to learn C, and one to learn C++, prior to my getting *Who's Afraid of C++?*. All of those prior attempts to learn C/C++ were abysmal failures. So when it comes to programming, even though I am not a novice programmer, I am a C++ student in the early stages.

Second, a few days after starting on "Who's Afraid of C++?", I sent some email messages to Steve. I didn't know him, and all I knew of him were from some message exchanges I had seen on a CompuServe forum about programming.[1] However, Steve encourages his students emailing him, so I decided to do it. Turns out Steve liked some of the email comments I made. Evidently, I understood something very basic about that book, so he asked me how I would convey my understanding of his book to others. The following comes from my response:

"I would only hope that somehow I would be able to adequately portray the 'image' of the structural integrity with which you write. I am still in Chapter 6, "Taking Inventory", but already I think I am beginning to understand where you were coming from when you wrote the book. You were not just attempting to teach the language of C++. As a matter of fact, you possibly weren't trying to do that at all. What you were trying to do was to take the reader from ground zero to a finished functional structure (i.e, a real-life practical "application"), covering basically all the parameters involved: the computer chip, the interface between that and the keyboard (RAM, ROM, hard drive), and finally the use of C++ to cover both that interface and the one between the keyboard and what the programmer had in mind.

"I read a criticism in a message (I think I saw that message via the Amazon.com internet area) saying that you should have included some stripped-down version of a Borland or Microsoft compiler rather than the one you did include. Again, I'm very ignorant and inexperienced re these matters, but I thank you for what you did do. Included in the documentation for the compiler are various web sites devoted to use of such, downloading of updates, other type files, etc. Again, a reflection of structural integrity: with this approach, the user of the compiler is not out on a limb alone, but instead has ready

1. For those of you who might like to visit this forum, its Compuserve address is CIS:PCPROG.

reference to whatever other paths of interest/need arise from that portion of the application.

"I will be glad to assist you in any way I can. I love learning and I love teaching, and I very much appreciate seeing a method of the latter which is very sound. And I now understand your use of the words, "technical novelist"'. <g>. You really do start the reader on an adventure. I seriously have felt concern that at some point I will finish your book, and if the sequel [this book] isn't ready then, I will feel abandoned. <smile>"

So first, that's who I am, second, in part that's how I got here, and third, to push the envelope just a little, that in essence introduces you to the surprise I am talking about. That is, Steve does not endeavor to teach you C++, but instead to show you how to *develop* and *write* software *using* C++. Not to overstate the obvious, but that point is very important. The books I have used to try to learn the C/C++ language have been of two basic types. One is to only cover very simple concepts, at the end of which there has been no foundation laid for writing a real software project. The other is to try to cover every conceivable code scenario possible, at the end of which assumedly the reader is supposed to go into some type of auto-integrate mode and start spewing out programs. For me, neither approach has been successful. I can't really attribute this to a fundamental lack in my ability to learn complex subjects; I've spent too many years in undergraduate and graduate school to accept that explanation. It seems much more likely that the books I've tried to use to learn C++ were inadequate to the task of teaching this subject.

Steve's *Who's Afraid of . . .* series books are not like other books on C++ (or just about any other subject matter): in Steve's books he is *actively* teaching. In the first book, the email correspondent, Susan, starts out as just that, an email correspondent, and Steve is the author. But soon that changes. Not only does the email correspondent become 'Susan', but Steve is transformed from author to teacher. And you become one of his students.

Steve is a master: these books are *alive*! That transformation of reader to student does not end with the first book. I realized while in the second chapter of the second book that Susan was now a fellow student, and Steve had become the professor. I discovered this after hearing myself say "Thanks, Susan!" when she asked a question that had just entered my mind. While in the first book, in an email to Steve I commented that the book had started something. In reading the second book it is apparent that if that start needed support in any way, the second book provided it in concrete. The first book was the beginning of an extended course in software development using C++; the second is not only continuation, but total endorsement of the first.

Steve begins the second book with a review and outline of the last two chapters of the first book, to reorient students from his first book and to orient new students for his second book. In the first book he led his students through the development of a basic software application by which a corner grocery store could deal with customers and basic inventory items. A primary C++ class of that application was StockItem; consequently, encountering that class once again in the second chapter of the second book was quite refreshing. He then continues on to expand that application and its classes, bringing us along on the journey. Then, to relate to something his students are more likely to have in common and to be able to use for their own purposes, he develops a second application, the "Home Inventory Project". To me, that seems very appropriate for Steve's primary purpose of teaching his students how to develop software, in that such software can be of personal use. The adage "use it or lose it" comes into play here, for not only can this software application be of use to a student: due to its personal nature, a student might be very likely to further expand and develop it after finishing the book. This to me is another instance of the "structural integrity" attribute of Steve's work and commented on above, as are his coverage of ways to safeguard against potentially hazardous use of pointers and arrays, and the practice of defensive programming.

In his foreword to *Who's Afraid of C++?*, Ed Yourdon said ". . . learning a programming language is an intensely personal experience". Steve is well aware of that, and has written these books accordingly. They *are* personal. As described above, you, the reader, become a student, in a classroom with a fellow student. And to even further reinforce this approach, there is an email mailing list available for his students, whos_afraid_cpp@technologist.com, in which code and topics covered in the first book are discussed. There is little doubt the same avenue will be taken by students of his second book.

When Steve Heller asked me to write the foreword for "Who's Afraid of More C++?", I was more than honored. I was also very excited to be even a small part of what Steve is doing— in my opinion Steve is in the process of revolutionizing the way in which instructional programming language books are written!

Michael Andry
Palmdale, CA
March 1998

# CHAPTER 1 Prologue

If you are looking at this book in a bookstore, one of the first questions you will need to answer before deciding to buy it is, "What do I need to know before I start?" The purpose of this prologue is to answer that question.

As simple a question as that might be, however, there are actually several different, but equally valid, ways to describe the knowledge that you should have before you undertake the task of learning and applying the information in this book. First, if you have read and understood the information in either of my two self-teaching books for beginning C++ programmers — *Who's Afraid of C++?* (ISBN 0-12-339097-4) or *The C++ Training Guide* (ISBN 0-12-339102-4) — then you should be all set, as this book takes up exactly where those books leave off.[1] In this case, you will also be quite familiar with my chief novice, Susan, and her role in the learning process.

1. There is one concept that you won't have come across yet if you have an early printing of *Who's Afraid of C++?* or *The C++ Training Guide*: a "member initialization list". However, you don't have to worry about this right now because we will cover it when we get to it in Chapter 2.

Of course, there *are* other books besides those two that are intended to teach elementary C++ concepts and practice, including my classroom textbook, *Introduction to C++* (ISBN 0-12-339099-0), and it's just possible that you've started to learn the language from one of those other books.[2] In that case, you'll need some more information to decide whether this book is the right one with which to continue your study.

Let's start with the ingredient that makes this book (and the other *Who's Afraid of...* books) unique: the participation of an actual, live person who doesn't already know the material, in its preparation. In my case, my "official novice" is Susan Heller, my wife. A main part of her participation is reading every line of the first draft of the book and asking questions, via e-mail, about anything she doesn't understand. I answer her questions, also by e-mail, until both of us are satisfied that she understands the material in question and that the text is clear. After the text is otherwise complete, I extract appropriate parts of the e-mail exchanges, edit them for spelling, punctuation, and so forth, and include them in the text where they will be of most use to the reader.

At this point, I should confess that I have heard from a handful of readers of previous *Who's Afraid of...* books expressing dissatisfaction with the amount of space taken up by these e-mail exchanges. If you want to get the absolute maximum of new information per page, you might want to select another book such as my aforementioned *Introduction to C++* or Bjarne Stroustrup's excellent book, *The C++ Programming Language, 3rd Edition* (ISBN 0-201-88954-4). However, the vast majority of messages I've received from my readers have indicated that they found this

2. These first two chapters will be somewhat repetitious for readers of *Introduction to C++*, as they cover much the same material as in the last two chapters of that book. However, I think the additional reinforcement provided by the participation of my "official novice", Susan, will still be of significant value to you once you start to apply the more advanced concepts covered in those chapters to the main project in the book.

approach very helpful, and I suspect that most readers of this book will feel the same.

Assuming that you don't mind the extra thoroughness that the e-mail exchanges provide, let's see what elements of C++ (and programming in general) you'll need to know before you can absorb the material in this book. We'll start with some general programming concepts:

1. the *array*,
2. the *memory address*,
3. the *pointer*,
4. the idea of *encapsulation*, which means keeping as many details as possible hidden from the user to reduce program maintenance problems.

You'll also need to be familiar with some things that are more specific to C++:

1. the data types int, short, char, and bool,
2. the user-defined data type, or class,
3. the C++ input/output facilities known as iostreams,
4. the fail function of the iostreams classes,
5. user-defined operators, including <, >, ==, !=, and =,
6. constructors,
7. destructors,
8. the friend keyword,
9. the #include preprocessor directive,
10. the C library functions memcpy and memset.

There are also a couple of data types I've provided in a library to aid you in writing programs:

1. the C ++ type vector, which is similar to an array, except that accesses to a vector are checked to make sure that they refer to valid elements,

2. the string class, which allows you to handle variable-length character data in a convenient and safe way.

Although we won't have the opportunity in this book to examine how the vector type works, we will go into detail about how to implement a string class that is reasonably complete in its functionality.

One more thing I should mention before we continue is how the various typefaces are used in the book. Helvetica is used for program listings, for terms used in programs, and for words defined by the C++ language. *Italics* are used primarily for technical terms that are found in the glossary, although they are also used for emphasis in some places. The first time a particular technical term is used, it is in **boldface**; if it is a term defined in the C++ language, it is in **Helvetica Bold**.

Assuming that I haven't scared you off yet by using unfamiliar nomenclature, we're ready to continue with your education in C++, so turn to Chapter 2 and let's get started!

CHAPTER 2

# Stocking Up

We're going to start our investigation of advanced C++ concepts and practices with a simplified inventory control example. We'll begin by defining a class called StockItem and then build on it by using one of the primary organizing principles of C++: **inheritance**. First, let's define this term and a few others that we'll be using in this chapter; then we'll take a look at the objectives.

## *Definitions*

A **normal constructor** is a constructor whose arguments supply enough information to initialize all of the member fields in the object being created.

A **concrete data type** is a class whose objects behave like variables of native data types. That is, the class gives the compiler enough information that objects of that class can be created, copied, assigned, and automatically destroyed just like native variables.

**Inheritance** is the definition of one class as a more specific version of another class that has been previously defined. The newly defined class is called the *derived* (or sometimes *child*) class, and the previously defined class is called the *base* (or sometimes *parent*) class. In this book, we will use the terms *base* and *derived*. The derived class inherits all of the member variables and *regular member functions* from the base class. Inheritance is one of the primary organizing principles of object-oriented programming.

A **regular member function** is a member function that is *not* in any of the following categories:

1. constructor,
2. destructor,
3. assignment operator (i.e., operator =).

A member function in a derived class is said to **override** a base class member function if the derived class function has the same *signature* (name and argument types) as that of the base class member function. The derived class member function will be called instead of the base class member function when the member function is referred to via an object of the derived class. A member function in a derived class with the same name but a different signature from that of a member function in the base class does *not* override the base class member function. Instead, it "hides" that base class member function, which is no longer accessible as a member function in the derived class.

For example, the function Reorder(ostream &) may be defined in a base class (StockItem) and in a derived class (DatedStockItem). When Reorder is called via an object of the base class StockItem, the base class version of Reorder will be called; when Reorder is called via an object of the derived class DatedStockItem, the derived class version of Reorder will be called. This behavior of C++ allows a derived class to supply the same functionality as a base class but implement that functionality in a different way.

A **manipulator** is a special type of member function of one of the iostreams classes. Such a function controls how output will be formatted without itself necessarily producing any output.

A **static member function** is a member function of a class that can be called without reference to an object of that class. Such a function has no this pointer passed to it on entry, and therefore it cannot refer to member variables of the class.

A **buffer** is a temporary holding place where information is stored while it is being manipulated.

**Buffering** is the use of a buffer to store or retrieve information.

## *Objectives of This Chapter*

By the end of this chapter, you should

1. understand how we can use inheritance to create a new class by extending an existing class, and
2. understand how to use manipulators to control the format of iostreams output.

### *Under Control*

Before we get to the details of our inventory control classes — StockItem and its companion class Inventory — let's expand a bit on the first objective as it applies to this case.

There are two reasons to use inheritance. The first is to create a new class that has all of the capabilities of an existing class while adding capabilities that are unique to the new class. In such a case, objects of the new class are clearly not equivalent to objects of the existing class, which means that the user[1] of these classes has to know which class any given object belongs to so that he or she can tell which operations that object can perform. In such a case, it does not make sense to be able to substitute objects of the derived class for objects of the base class. We could call this use of inheritance "inheritance for extension". It's illustrated by one of the Employee class exercises in this chapter.

In the current case, however, we'll be using inheritance to create a new class called DatedStockItem that will be exactly like the StockItem class except that its items will have expiration dates. As a result, the user of this class will be able to use it in exactly the same way as he or she uses the StockItem class as an object of the base class. Of course, to create an object of this class, the expiration date for the object must be provided, but once such an object exists its user can view it exactly as if it were as an object of the base class, which makes this an example of "inheritance for reimplementation". In such a case, it is reasonable to be able to substitute objects of the derived class for those of the base class, and we will see how to do that in the next chapter.

Before we can do that, though, we'll need to learn how to create a new class by derivation from an existing class. In this case, we're going to start with a base class called StockItem, which is intended to represent data for a simplistic but not completely unrealistic inventory management program for a small grocery store. We'll also need to create an initial version of a companion class called Inventory, which we'll use to keep track of all the StockItems in the store.

Of course, before we can inherit from the StockItem class, we have to write it. However, even before that we should see how this class and its companion class, Inventory, are used (Figure 2.1).

**FIGURE 2.1. The initial** StockItem **test program (code\itmtst20.cc)**

```
#include <iostream.h>
```

1. As elsewhere in this book, when I speak of the "user" of a class, I mean the application programmer, who is using objects of the class to perform work in his or her program, not the "end user", who is using the finished program.

```
#include <fstream.h>
#include "vector.h"
#include "string6.h"
#include "item20.h"
#include "invent20.h"

int main()
{
ifstream ShopInfo("shop20.in");
ofstream ReorderInfo("shop20.reo");

Inventory MyInventory;

MyInventory.LoadInventory(ShopInfo);

MyInventory.ReorderItems(ReorderInfo);

return 0;
}
```

This program isn't very complex; it creates an Inventory object to hold the StockItem objects, then loads the inventory data from the input file, and finally calls the ReorderItems member function to determine which items need to be reordered. If you want to see how this program runs, you can compile and step through it using RHIDE. To do this, change to the \whosadv\code directory and type RHIDE itmtst20. When RHIDE starts up, hit F9 to compile the program; then you can use F8 to step through each line of itmtst20. If you want to see how any particular line works, you can use F7 to step into the code that executes that line. When the program terminates, you can look at its output file, shop20.reo, to see what the reorder report looks like.

Now let's start examining how the StockItem class works. Figure 2.2 shows the initial header file for that class.

**FIGURE 2.2. The initial StockItem header file (code\item20.h)**

```
class StockItem
```

```
{
friend ostream& operator << (ostream& os,
  const StockItem& Item);

friend istream& operator >> (istream& is, StockItem& Item);

public:
  StockItem();

  StockItem(string Name, short InStock,
  short Price, short MinimumStock,
  short MinimumReorder, string Distributor, string UPC);

  void FormattedDisplay(ostream& os);
  bool CheckUPC(string ItemUPC);
  void DeductSaleFromInventory(short QuantitySold);
  short GetInventory();
  string GetName();
  string GetUPC();
  bool IsNull();
  short GetPrice();

  void Reorder(ostream& os);

private:
  short m_InStock;
  short m_Price;
  short m_MinimumStock;
  short m_MinimumReorder;
  string m_Name;
  string m_Distributor;
  string m_UPC;
};
```

Here's a rundown on the various member functions of the StockItem class:

1. StockItem(); is the default constructor.

2. StockItem(string Name, written short InStock, short Price, short MinimumStock, short MinimumReorder, string Distributor, string UPC); is the normal constructor.
3. void FormattedDisplay(ostream& os); displays the member variables of a StockItem object with labels so you can tell which value is for which member variable.
4. bool CheckUPC(string ItemUPC); returns true if its argument is the same as the UPC (i.e., the m_UPC member variable) of its StockItem.
5. void DeductSaleFromInventory(short QuantitySold); reduces the inventory (i.e., the value of the m_InStock member variable) by the value of its argument.
6. short GetInventory(); returns the number of items in stock for this StockItem (i.e., the value of the m_InStock member variable).
7. string GetName(); returns the name of the StockItem (i.e., the value of the m_Name member variable).
8. string GetUPC(); returns the UPC of the StockItem (i.e., the value of the m_UPC member variable).
9. bool IsNull(); returns true if this is a "null StockItem". This can happen, for example, when a StockItem is returned as a "not found" value by a search.
10. short GetPrice(); returns the price of the StockItem (i.e., the value of the m_Price member variable).
11. void Reorder(ostream& os); generates a reorder report based on the relationship of the number in stock (m_InStock) versus the minimum desired stock (m_MinimumStock), taking the minimum reorder quantity (m_MinimumReorder) into account.

Here's a brief description of the input/output operators for this class:

1. friend ostream& operator << (ostream& os, const StockItem& Item); sends a human-readable version of the state of a StockItem object to the ostream specified as the left-hand argument to <<. This is analogous to the use of operator << for output of the built-in types.
2. friend istream& operator >> (istream& is, StockItem& Item); creates a StockItem object by reading a human-readable version of the state of the object from the istream specified as the left-hand argument to >>. This is analogous to the use of operator >> for input of the built-in types.

Susan wanted to know why we needed the FormattedDisplay function.

> **Susan:** Do we need the FormattedDisplay to make the data appear on the screen the way we want it? I mean, does the FormattedDisplay function do something that we can't do by just using operator <<?
>
> **Steve:** Yes. It puts labels on the data members so you can tell what they are.

Figure 2.3 shows the initial implementation of the StockItem class.

**FIGURE 2.3. The initial implementation of StockItem (code\item20.cc)**

```
#include <iostream.h>
#include <string.h>
#include "string6.h"
#include "item20.h"

StockItem::StockItem()
: m_InStock(0), m_Price(0), m_MinimumStock(0),
  m_MinimumReorder(0), m_Name(), m_Distributor(),
  m_UPC()
{
```

```
}

StockItem::StockItem(string Name, short InStock,
short Price, short MinimumStock,
short MinimumReorder, string Distributor, string UPC)
: m_InStock(InStock), m_Price(Price),
  m_MinimumStock(MinimumStock),
  m_MinimumReorder(MinimumReorder), m_Name(Name),
  m_Distributor(Distributor), m_UPC(UPC)
{
}

void StockItem::FormattedDisplay(ostream& os)
{
  os << "Name: ";
  os << m_Name << endl;
  os << "Number in stock: ";
  os << m_InStock << endl;
  os << "Price: ";
  os << m_Price << endl;
  os << "Minimum stock: ";
  os << m_MinimumStock << endl;
  os << "Minimum Reorder quantity: ";
  os << m_MinimumReorder << endl;
  os << "Distributor: ";
  os << m_Distributor << endl;
  os << "UPC: ";
  os << m_UPC << endl;
}

ostream& operator << (ostream& os, const StockItem& Item)
{
  os << Item.m_Name << endl;
  os << Item.m_InStock << endl;
  os << Item.m_Price << endl;
  os << Item.m_MinimumStock << endl;
  os << Item.m_MinimumReorder << endl;
  os << Item.m_Distributor << endl;
  os << Item.m_UPC << endl;
```

```
  return os;
}

istream& operator >> (istream& is, StockItem& Item)
{
  is >> Item.m_Name;
  is >> Item.m_InStock;
  is >> Item.m_Price;
  is >> Item.m_MinimumStock;
  is >> Item.m_MinimumReorder;
  is >> Item.m_Distributor;
  is >> Item.m_UPC;

  return is;
}

bool StockItem::CheckUPC(string ItemUPC)
{
  if (m_UPC == ItemUPC)
    return true;

  return false;
}

void StockItem::DeductSaleFromInventory(short QuantitySold)
{
  m_InStock -= QuantitySold;
}

short StockItem::GetInventory()
{
  return m_InStock;
}

string StockItem::GetName()
{
  return m_Name;
}
```

```
string StockItem::GetUPC()
{
 return m_UPC;
}

bool StockItem::IsNull()
{
 if (m_UPC == "")
   return true;

 return false;
}

short StockItem::GetPrice()
{
 return m_Price;
}

void StockItem::Reorder(ostream& os)
{
 short ActualReorderQuantity;

 if (m_InStock < m_MinimumStock)
   {
   ActualReorderQuantity = m_MinimumStock - m_InStock;
   if (m_MinimumReorder > ActualReorderQuantity)
     ActualReorderQuantity = m_MinimumReorder;
   os << "Reorder " << ActualReorderQuantity;
   os <<  " units of " << m_Name;
   os << " with UPC " << m_UPC;
   os << " from " << m_Distributor << endl;
   }
}
```

Susan had a lot of questions about the operator << and operator >> functions for this class as well as about streams in general.

**Susan:** Why do you have to define these functions again?

**Steve:** They have to be defined for every class of objects we want to be able to use them for. After all, every class of objects has different data items in it; how is a stream supposed to know how to read or write some object that we've made up, unless we tell it how to?

**Susan:** What's "is" again? I forgot. :-P

**Steve:** The istream that we're using to get the data for the StockItem.

**Susan:** So, it's just a file? Is it always called is?

**Steve:** No, it's not a file; it's an istream, which is an object connected to a file that allows us to read from the file using >>.

**Susan:** Do you mean any file that has >> or <<? If it is like an istream where does the data end up? Just how does it work? When does the istream start flowing and at what point does the data jump in and get out? What is the istream doing when there is no data to be transported? Where is it flowing? If it is not a file, then where is it stored? So, whenever you read something from an istream, is it always called "is"?

**Steve:** Obviously streams are going to take a lot more explaining, with pictures. We'll get to it later in this chapter.[2]

2. See "stream of Consciousness" on page 63.

## *Taking Inventory*

The StockItem class is designed to keep track of an individual item in the inventory, but we need more than this for our application; we also need a way to keep track of all the StockItems in the store. So let's take a look at the class that serves that purpose in the inventory control application, Inventory. Figure 2.4 shows the initial header file for this class.

FIGURE 2.4. **The header file for the** Inventory class **(code\invent20.h)**

```
class Inventory
{
public:
   Inventory();

   short LoadInventory(istream& is);

   void StoreInventory(ostream& os);

   StockItem FindItem(string UPC);
   bool UpdateItem(StockItem Item);
   void ReorderItems(ostream& os);

private:
   vector<StockItem> m_Stock;
   short m_StockCount;
};
```

Besides the default constructor, this class has several other member functions that we should discuss briefly.

1. LoadInventory reads data from an istream to create StockItem objects for the inventory.
2. StoreInventory writes the current StockItem data out to an ostream to save it for posterity.

3. FindItem locates an item in the inventory by its UPC.
4. UpdateItem updates the data for an item in the inventory.
5. ReorderItems calls each item in the inventory and asks it to generate a line for the reordering report, which tells the user how many of each item need to be reordered from the distributor.

Susan had some questions about the arguments to LoadInventory and StoreInventory:

**Susan:** What are is and os? Why didn't you talk about them?

**Steve:** They're just the names of the reference arguments of type istream and ostream, respectively, as indicated in the header file.

## *Claiming an Inheritance*

Now let's examine the details of the part of this inventory control program that calculates how much of each item has to be ordered to refill the stock. As I mentioned previously, I've chosen the imaginative name ReorderItems for the member function in the Inventory class that will perform this operation. The ReorderItems function is pretty simple. Its behavior can be described as follows:

> 'For each element in the StockItem vector in the Inventory object, call its member function Reorder to generate an order if that StockItem object needs to be reordered.'

Of course, this algorithm is much simpler than what we would need in the real world; however, it's realistic enough to be useful in illustrating important issues in program design and implementation, which is how we will use it.

Before we get to the implementation of the Inventory class, let's see how we use it. Figure 2.5 shows a test program that uses the Inventory class.

**FIGURE 2.5. A test program for the** Inventory class **(code\itmtst20.cc)**

```
#include <iostream.h>
#include <fstream.h>
#include "vector.h"
#include "string6.h"
#include "item20.h"
#include "invent20.h"

int main()
{
ifstream ShopInfo("shop20.in");
ofstream ReorderInfo("shop20.reo");

Inventory MyInventory;

MyInventory.LoadInventory(ShopInfo);

MyInventory.ReorderItems(ReorderInfo);

return 0;
}
```

This shouldn't be too hard to follow. We start by creating an ifstream (i.e., an input stream that can be connected to a file) and an ofstream (i.e., an output stream that can be connected to a file). Then we create an inventory object called MyInventory, load items into it from the ifstream, and call the ReorderItems function to create the reorder report, which is written to the ofstream. Finally, we return 0 to indicate successful completion.

Now let's take a look at how the Inventory class does its work (Figure 2.6).

**FIGURE 2.6. The implementation of the** Inventory class **(code\invent20.cc)**

```
#include <iostream.h>
#include <fstream.h>
```

```
#include "vector.h"
#include "string6.h"
#include "item20.h"
#include "invent20.h"

Inventory::Inventory()
: m_Stock (vector<StockItem>(100)),
  m_StockCount(0)
{
}

short Inventory::LoadInventory(istream& is)
{
  short i;

  for (i = 0; i < 100; i ++)
    {
    is >> m_Stock[i];
    if (is.fail())
      break;
    }

  m_StockCount = i;
  return m_StockCount;
}

StockItem Inventory::FindItem(string UPC)
{
  short i;
  bool Found = false;

  for (i = 0; i < m_StockCount; i ++)
    {
    if (m_Stock[i].GetUPC() == UPC)
      {
      Found = true;
      break;
      }
    }
```

```
 if (Found == true)
   return m_Stock[i];

 return StockItem();
}

bool Inventory::UpdateItem(StockItem Item)
{
 string UPC = Item.GetUPC();

 short i;
 bool Found = false;

 for (i = 0; i < m_StockCount; i ++)
   {
   if (m_Stock[i].GetUPC() == UPC)
     {
     Found = true;
     break;
     }
   }

 if (Found == true)
   m_Stock[i] = Item;

 return Found;

}

void Inventory::StoreInventory(ostream& os)
{
 short i;

 for (i = 0; i < m_StockCount; i ++)
   os << m_Stock[i];
}

void Inventory::ReorderItems(ostream& os)
```

```
{
  short i;

  for (i = 0; i < m_StockCount; i ++)
    m_Stock[i].Reorder(os);
}
```

The ReorderItems function can hardly be much simpler: as you can see, it merely tells each StockItem element in the m_Stock vector to execute its Reorder function. Now let's see what that function, whose full name is void StockItem::Reorder(ostream&), needs to do:

1. Check to see if the current stock of that item is less than the desired minimum.
2. If we are below the desired stock minimum, order the amount needed to bring us back to the stock minimum, unless that order amount is less than the minimum allowable quantity from the distributor. In the latter case, order the minimum allowable reorder quantity.
3. If we are not below the desired stock minimum, do nothing.

To support this Reorder function, StockItem uses the data items m_MinimumStock and m_MinimumReorder to calculate the number of units of the current StockItem object that have to be reordered. Figure 2.7 shows the code for the Reorder function.

**FIGURE 2.7. The** Reorder **function for the** StockItem class **(from code\item20.cc)**

```
void StockItem::Reorder(ostream& os)
{
  short ActualReorderQuantity;

  if (m_InStock < m_MinimumStock)
    {
    ActualReorderQuantity = m_MinimumStock - m_InStock;
```

```
  if (m_MinimumReorder > ActualReorderQuantity)
    ActualReorderQuantity = m_MinimumReorder;
  os << "Reorder " << ActualReorderQuantity;
  os <<  " units of " << m_Name;
  os << " with UPC " << m_UPC;
  os << " from " << m_Distributor << endl;
  }
}
```

Here's the translation of this code:

1. If the number of units in stock is less than the minimum number desired, we calculate the number needed to bring the inventory back to the minimum.
2. However, the number we want to order may be less than the minimum we are allowed to order; the latter quantity is specified by the variable m_MinimumReorder.
3. If the value of m_MinimumReorder is more than we actually needed, we have to substitute the minimum quantity for that previously calculated number.
4. Finally, we display the order for the item. Of course, if we already have enough units in stock, we don't have to reorder anything, so we don't display anything.

Susan had a question about the implementation of this function:

**Susan:** So, are you ordering more than needed in some cases?

**Steve:** Yes, if that's the minimum number that can be ordered.

She also had a question about the type of the argument that the test program supplies to ReorderItems:

**Susan:** In the test program, ReorderInfo, which is an ofstream, is passed as an argument to the ReorderItems member function in the Inventory class. But the ReorderItems(ostream&) function in the

Inventory class expects a reference to an ostream as an argument. I understand the code of both functions, but I don't see how you can pass an ofstream as an ostream. As far as I know, we use fstreams to write to and read from files and istream and ostream to read from the keyboard and write to the screen. So, can you mix these when you pass them on as arguments?

**Steve:** Yes. As we'll see later, this is legal because of the relationship between the ofstream and ostream classes.[3]

## *A Dated Approach*

Now we want to add one wrinkle to this algorithm: handling items that have expiration dates. This actually applies to a fair number of items in a typical grocery store, including dairy products, meats, and even dry cereals. To keep things as simple as possible, we'll assume that whenever we buy a batch of some item with an expiration date, all of the items of that type have the same date. When we get to the expiration date of a given StockItem, we send back all of the items and reorder as though we had no items in stock.

The first question to answer is how to store the expiration date. My first inclination was to use a short to store each date as a number representing the number of days from (for example) January 1, 1990, to the date in question. Since there are approximately 365.25 days in a year, the range of minus 32768 to 32767 days should hold us roughly until the year 2080, which should be good enough for our purposes. Perhaps by that year, we'll all be eating food pills that don't spoil.

However, storing a date as a number of days since a "base date" such as January 1, 1990, does require a means of translating a human-readable date format like "September 4, 1995" into a number of days from the base date and vice versa. Owing to the peculiarities of our

3. See the discussion under the heading "class Interests" on page 55.

Gregorian calendar (primarily the different numbers of days in different months and the complication of leap years), this is not a trivial matter and is a distraction from our goal here.

However, if we represent a date as a string of the form YYYYMMDD, where YYYY is the year, MM is the month, and DD is the day within the month, we can use the string comparison functions to tell us which of two dates is later than the other one.[4] Here's the analysis:

1. Of two dates with different year numbers, whichever has the higher year number is a later date.
2. Of two dates with the same year number but different month numbers, whichever has the higher month number is a later date.
3. Of two dates having the same year and month numbers, whichever has the higher day number is a later date.

Because the string comparison operators compare bytes from left to right and stop when a mismatch is detected, as is needed for alphabetical sorting, it should be clear that dates using the representation YYYYMMDD will have their year numbers compared first, followed by the month numbers if needed, followed by the day numbers if needed. Thus, comparing two strings via string::operator > will produce the result true if the "date string" on the left represents a date later than the "date string" on the right, exactly as we would wish.

Now that we've figured out that we can store the expiration date as a string, how do we arrange for it to be included in the StockItem object? One obvious solution is to make up a new class called, say, DatedStockItem by copying the interface and implementation from

4. In case you're wondering why I allocated 4 digits for the year, it was to ensure that the program will still work after 1999. Unfortunately, not all programmers have been so considerate. Many programs use a 2-digit number to represent the year portion of a date in the form YYMMDD and, as a result, will fail by the year 2000. We'll discuss this problem in some detail later, under the heading "Terror in the Year Zero" on page 241.

StockItem, adding a new member variable m_Expires, and modifying the copied Reorder member function to take the expiration date into account. However, doing this would create a maintenance problem when we had to make a change that would affect both of these classes — we'd have to make such a change in two places. Just multiply this nuisance ten or twenty times, and you'll get a pretty good idea of how program maintenance has acquired its reputation as difficult and tedious work.

Susan had some questions about this notion of program maintenance:

> **Susan:** What kind of change would you want to make? What is maintenance? What is a typical thing you would want to do to some code?
>
> **Steve:** For our purposes here, maintenance includes any kind of change to a program.[5] For example, if we decide that a short isn't the right type of variable to hold the price, then we have to change its definition to some other type.

Since one of the purposes of object-oriented programming is to reduce the difficulty of maintaining programs, surely there must be a better way to create a new class "just like" StockItem but with an added member variable and a modified member function to use it.

### *Ancestor Worship*

Yes, there is; it's called **inheritance**. We can define our new class called DatedStockItem with a notation that it inherits (or derives) from StockItem. This makes StockItem the *base* class (sometimes referred to as the *parent* class) and our new DatedStockItem class the *derived* class (sometimes referred to as the *child* class). By doing this, we are

5. In other contexts, people use "maintenance" to mean fixing bugs rather than adding new features, but that distinction is irrelevant here; all we care about is that the program is being changed.

specifying that a DatedStockItem includes every data member and regular member function a StockItem has. Since DatedStockItem is a separate class from StockItem, when we define DatedStockItem we can also add whatever other functions and data we need to handle the differences between StockItem and DatedStockItem.

Susan wanted to clarify some terms:

**Susan:** Are inheritance and derivation the same thing?

**Steve:** Yes. To say that B inherits from A is the same as saying that B is derived from A.

She also had some questions about the relationship between the notions of friend and inheritance.

**Susan:** How about a little reminder about friend here, and how about explaining the difference between friend and inheritance, other than inheritance being an entirely different class. They kinda do the same thing.

**Steve:** When, in a class definition, you make a function or class a friend of the one you're defining, the friend function or class has access to all members of the class you are defining, disregarding their access specifiers; however, the friend has no other relationship to the class being defined. That is, making class B a friend to class A does *not* make a B object a substitute for an A object.

On the other hand, if B is (publicly) derived from A, then a B object can be used wherever an A object can be used.

I think a picture might help here. Let's start with a simplified version of the StockItem and DatedStockItem classes, whose interface is shown in Figure 2.8. I recommend that you print out the file that contains these interfaces (code\itema.h) for reference as you go through this section of the chapter.

**FIGURE 2.8. Simplified interface for** StockItem **and** DatedStockItem **classes (code\itema.h)**

```
#include "string6.h"

class StockItem
{
public:
 StockItem(string Name, short InStock,
   short MinimumStock);

 void Reorder(ostream& s);

protected:
 string m_Name;
 short m_InStock;
 short m_MinimumStock;
};

class DatedStockItem: public StockItem // deriving a new class
{
public:
 DatedStockItem(string Name, short InStock, short MinimumStock,
 string Expires);

 void Reorder(ostream& s);

protected:
static string Today();

protected:
 string m_Expires;
};
```

Given these definitions, a StockItem object might look as depicted in Figure 2.9.[6]

FIGURE 2.9. A StockItem object

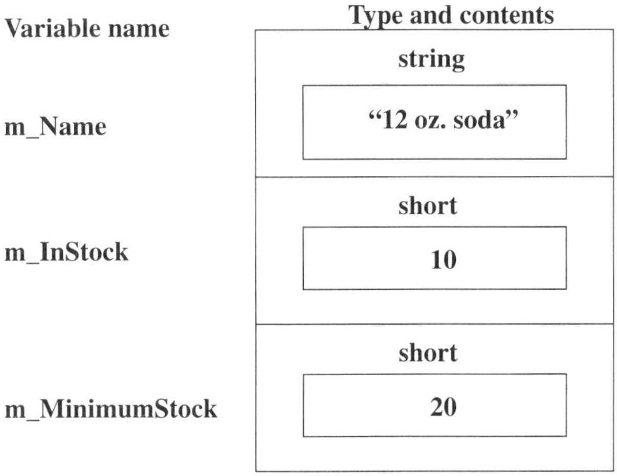


And a DatedStockItem object might look as depicted in Figure 2.10.

As you can see, an object of the new DatedStockItem class contains a StockItem as part of its data. In this case, that *base class part* accounts for most of the data of a DatedStockItem; all we've added is a data member called m_Expires. In fact, a derived class object always contains all of the variables and "regular" member functions in the base class because the derived class object has an object of the base class embedded in it, as indicated in Figure 2.10. We can access those member variables and functions that are part of the base class part of our derived class object exactly as though they were defined in the derived class, so long as their access specifiers are either public or protected. Although the public and private access specifiers have been part of our arsenal of tools for some time, this is our first encounter with the protected access specifier. We'll see

6. I'm simplifying by leaving out the internal structure of a string, which affects the actual layout of the object; this detail isn't relevant here.

shortly that the sole purpose of the protected access specifier is to allow derived class member functions to use member functions and variables of the base class part of an object of that derived class, while protecting those member functions and variables from use by unrelated classes.

**FIGURE 2.10.** A DatedStockItem **object**

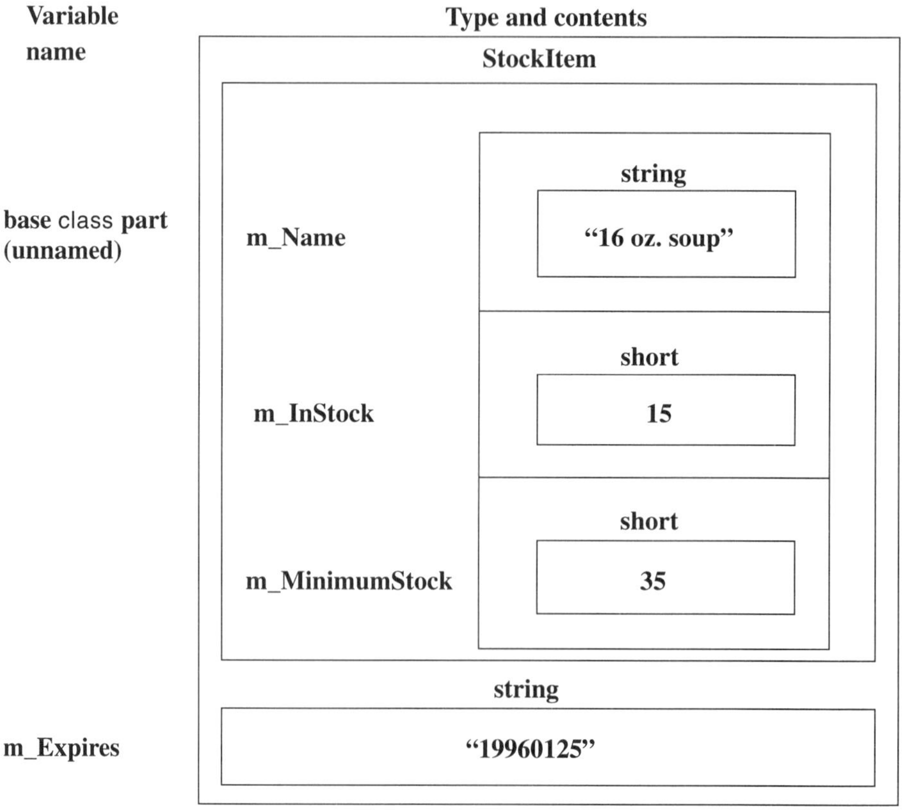


Susan had some interesting comments and questions about the notion of the base class part of a derived class object.

**Susan:** When I look at Figure 2.10 I get the feeling that every DatedStockitem object contains a StockItem object; is this the "base class part of the derived class object"?

**Steve:** Yes.

**Susan:** The word "derived" is confusing: if a DatedStockItem is derived from a StockItem one tends to take a linear approach as in a family tree, which isn't quite right. It would be better to think of DatedStockItem as a fruit like a plum, with the pit being the StockItem, which is the core of the object.

**Steve:** Or maybe an onion, where all the layers are edible, rather than making the distinction between the flesh of the fruit and an inedible pit.

**Susan:** But if so, every member function of the derived class could in fact access every member variable of the base class because "They occur as the base class part of a derived class object".

**Steve:** No, as we'll see, even though private members are actually present in the derived class object, they are not accessible to derived class functions. That's why we need the protected access specifier.

Of course, as noted before, we don't have to rely solely on the facilities we inherit from our base class; we can also add whatever new functions or variables needed to provide the new functionality of the new class. As you will see, we don't want or need to add any public member functions in the present case because our eventual goal is to allow the application programmer to treat objects of the new DatedStockItem class as equivalent to objects of the StockItem class. To reach this goal, these two classes must have the same class interface — that is, the same public member functions.[7]

Instead of adding new public member functions, we will *override* the base class version of Reorder by writing a new version of Reorder for our DatedStockItem class. Our new function, which has the same signature as that of the base class Reorder function, will use the new data member m_Expires. Since the StockItem::Reorder has been overridden by DatedStockItem::Reorder, the latter function will be called whenever the user's program calls the Reorder function of a DatedStockItem.

Susan wasn't sure about the meaning of "overriding" a base class function rather than writing an entirely new one. That discussion led to a more general one about the whole idea of inheritance.

**Susan:** Why is the term "override" used here? The derived class member function is called for an object of the derived class, so I don't see how it "overrides" the base class member function with the same signature.

**Steve:** What would happen if we didn't write the derived class function? Then the base class function would be called. Therefore, the derived class function is overriding the previously existing base class function.

**Susan:** But why do you write a new version of Reorder instead of adding a new public member function?

**Steve:** Precisely because our eventual goal is to allow the user to use stock items with and without dates interchangeably. If StockItem and DatedStockItem had different names for their reordering function, the user would have to call a different function

7. By the way, it's not enough just to have the same names for the member functions in the derived class; they have to have the same meanings as well. That is, the user shouldn't be surprised by the behavior of a derived class function if he knows how the base class function behaves. For example, if the DatedStockItem Reorder function were to rearrange the items in the inventory rather than generate a reorder report, as the StockItem version does, the user would get very confused! So don't do that.

depending on which type the object really was, which would defeat our attempt to make them interchangeable.

**Susan:** But if they (the two versions of Reorder) were exactly the same, couldn't you just declare them public?

**Steve:** If they were *exactly* the same, we wouldn't need two functions in the first place. Reordering works slightly differently for dated than for undated items, so we need two different functions to do the "same" thing in two different ways.

**Susan:** Yes, but if the names were the same couldn't they be used anywhere just by making them public? I thought this was the whole idea: not to have to rewrite these things.

**Steve:** They are public. The point is that StockItem::Reorder and DatedStockItem::Reorder accomplish the same result in different ways, so the user of these classes should be able to just call Reorder and get the correct function executed without having to worry about which one that is.

**Susan:** So is it the expiration date that makes it necessary (?) to make a derived class?

**Steve:** Yes.

**Susan:** Is it impossible to extend our old class so it can handle objects both with and without expiration dates rather than making a new class?

**Steve:** Yes. We need two different classes to handle these two different kinds of objects.

**Susan:** Why can't we just add some new member functions and member variables to a class instead of making a derived class? Are you using inheritance here just to make a point, or is it vital to achieve what we want to achieve?

**Steve:** If you added more functions, then StockItem would not be StockItem as it is and needs to be. You could copy the code for StockItem and then change the copy to handle expiration dates, but that would cause serious maintenance problems later if (when) you had to change the code, because you would have to make the changes in both places. Avoiding such problems was one of the main reasons that C++ was invented.

**Susan:** Okay, so that explains why we shouldn't add more functions to StockItem but not why we shouldn't add any functions to DatedStockItem.

**Steve:** Because a DatedStockItem should act just like a StockItem; this won't be the case if we add new functions.[8] Instead, we'll write new versions of the ones we already have, like Reorder.

**Susan:** I still don't understand why you have to write a new version of Reorder. A DatedStockItem is supposed to act just like a StockItem.

**Steve:** Yes, it is supposed to act "just like" a StockItem. However, that means that it has to do the "same" things differently; in particular, reordering items is different when you have to send things back because their expiration dates have passed. However, this difference in implementation isn't important to the application program, which can treat DatedStockItems just like StockItems.

Before we get into the details of the Reorder function in the DatedStockItem class, I should explain what I mean by "regular member function". A regular member function is one that is *not* in any of the following categories:

8. Actually, this is not strictly true. We can add functions to a derived class without affecting how it appears to users, so long as the functions that we add are either private or protected. We'll see some examples of this later.

1. constructor,
2. destructor,
3. assignment operator (*operator =*).

When we write a derived class (in this case DatedStockItem), it inherits only the regular member functions, not the constructor, destructor, or operator = functions, from the base class (in this case StockItem). Instead, we have to write our own derived class versions of these functions if we don't want to rely on the compiler-generated versions in the derived class.

It may not be obvious why we have to write our own versions of these functions. Isn't that wasteful? The same question occurred to Susan.

**Susan:** So in this case our derived class DatedStockitem doesn't inherit the constructor, destructor, and assignment operator because it takes an object of the Stockitem class and combines it with a new member variable m_Expires to make an object of the derived DatedStockItem class. But if the only differences between the two classes are in the implementation of the "regular member functions" then the default constructor, after the inheritance of the base class, should have no problem making a new derived class object because it won't contain any new member variables.

**Steve:** You're right: that would be possible in such a case, but it's not the way the language works. However, the code in the base class functions isn't wasted because the base class constructor, destructor, and operator = functions are used automatically in the implementation of the corresponding derived class functions.

**Susan:** But what if they are similar to the derived class functions that do the same thing? Can't you use them then?

**Steve:** In the case of the base class constructor and destructor, you actually do use them indirectly; the compiler will always call a base class constructor when a derived class constructor is executed, and it will always call the base class destructor when the derived class destructor is executed.[9] Similarly, the derived class assignment operator will call the base class assignment operator to copy the base class part of the derived class object. However, any new member variables added to the derived class will have to be handled in the derived class functions.

**Susan:** So, anything not derived that is added to a derived class has to be handled as a separate entity from the stuff in the base class part of the derived class? UGH!

**Steve:** Yes, but just the newly added data has to be handled separately; the inherited data from the base class can be handled by the base class functions. After all, *someone* has to write the code to handle the new member variables; the compiler can't read our minds!

This means that we won't be wasting any effort when writing the derived class versions of the constructors, destructor, and assignment operator, because the base class versions of these functions are called automatically to construct, destroy, and assign the base class part of the derived class object. Therefore, we can concentrate on the newly added parts of that class. We'll see exactly how and when these base class functions are called as we go through the corresponding derived class functions.[10]

---

9. When we write a derived class constructor, the base class default constructor is called to initialize the base class part of this class if we don't say which base class constructor we want; however, we can tell the compiler explicitly to call a different base class constructor.

10. It may seem that this automatic calling of base class functions for the constructor, destructor, and assignment operator is a type of inheritance. However, it really isn't because those functions are applied to the base class part of the derived class object, not to the derived class object itself. In the same way, you can refer to base class functions explicitly by qualifying the function name with the class name. This is also not a case of inheritance because these functions are applied only to the base class part.

For the moment, we won't have to define any of these derived class functions except two new constructors. Since the member variables and the base class part of DatedStockItem are all concrete data types, the compiler-generated versions of the destructor and assignment operator, which call the destructors and assignment operators for those member variables (and the base class part), work perfectly well.

Susan didn't let this "compiler-generated" stuff slip by without a bit of an argument:

**Susan:** About this statement that "compiler-generated versions of the destructor and assignment operators work perfectly well": Since when were destructors compiler-generated? I thought only assignment operators could be compiler-generated. You are holding out on me.

**Steve:** Every class, by default, has a default constructor, copy constructor, assignment operator, and destructor. Any of these that we don't mention in our interface will be generated by the compiler.

She also had some objections to my cavalier mention of concrete data types:

**Susan:** Aren't the member variables of a class always concrete data types (i.e., variables that act like native data types)? I thought a concrete data type was "a class whose objects behave like native data types".

**Steve:** Well, if every class defined a concrete data type, we wouldn't need a separate name for that concept, would we? As this suggests, it's entirely possible to have member variables that aren't concrete data types. In particular, *pointers* aren't concrete data types, because copying them doesn't actually copy their data, only the address of the data to which they refer. That's what makes them so tricky to work with.

Before we can use StockItem as a base class, however, there is one change we have to make to our previous definition of StockItem to make it work properly in that application; namely, we have to change the access specifier for its member variables from private to protected. By this point, you should be familiar with the meaning of private: Any member variables or member functions that are marked private can be referred to only by member functions of the same class; all other functions are denied access to them. On the other hand, when we mark member functions or member data of a class as public, we are specifying that any function, whether or not a member function of the class in question, can access them. That seems to take care of all the possibilities, so what is protected good for? I hope the following definitions will help clear this up.

## *More Definitions*

The **base class part** of a derived class object is an unnamed component of the derived class object whose member variables and functions are accessible as though they were defined in the derived class so long as they are either public or protected.

The keyword **protected** is an access specifier. When present in a base class definition, it allows derived class functions access to members in the base class part of a derived class object while preventing access by other functions outside the base class.

## *Protection Racket*

Member variables and member functions that are listed in a protected section of the interface definition are both treated as though they were private, with one important exception: Member functions of derived classes can access them when they occur as the base class part of a derived class object.

In the current case, we've seen that a DatedStockItem is "just like" a StockItem with one additional member variable and some other additions and changes that aren't relevant here. The important point is that every DatedStockItem contains everything that a StockItem contains. For example, every DatedStockItem has a m_MinimumStock member variable because the StockItem class has a m_MinimumStock member variable, and we're defining DatedStockItem as being derived from StockItem. Logically, therefore, we should be able to access the value of the m_MinimumStock member variable in our DatedStockItem. However, if that member variable is declared as private, we can't. The private access specifier doesn't care about inheritance; since DatedStockItem is a different class from StockItem, any private member variables and functions that StockItem might contain wouldn't be accessible to member functions of DatedStockItem, even though the member variables of StockItem are actually present in every DatedStockItem! That's why we have to make those variables protected rather than private.

Susan had some questions about this new concept of protected members:

> **Susan:** I don't understand why, if DatedStockItem has those member variables, it wouldn't be able to access them if they were specified as private in the base class.
>
> **Steve:** Because the compiler wouldn't let DatedStockItem member functions access them; private variables are private to the class where they are defined (and its friends, if any) even if they are part of the base class part of a derived class object. That's why protected was invented.

**Susan:** Well, friend lets a class or a function access something in another class, so what's the main difference between protected and friend?

**Steve:** They're used in different situations. You can use friend when you know exactly what other class or function you want to allow to access your private or protected members. On the other hand, if all you know is that a derived class will need to access these members, you make them protected.

In other words, a protected variable or function is automatically available to any derived class, as it applies to the base class part of the derived class object. To make a class or function a friend to a class being defined, you have to name the friend class or friend function explicitly.

**Susan:** What do you mean by "base class part of the derived object"? I'm fuzzy here.

**Steve:** Every DatedStockItem (derived class) object contains a StockItem (base class) object and can use all of the non-private member functions of StockItem, because DatedStockItem is derived from StockItem. This is what allows us to avoid having to rewrite all the code from the base class in the derived class.

**Susan:** I don't get this. I need some pictures to clear up these base class and derived class things.

**Steve:** Okay, I'll give it a shot. Take a look at Figure 2.11, where I've used a dashed-dotted line around the base class, StockItem, to indicate its boundaries as a base class part. I've also used different line types to indicate level of access to member variables and functions — a solid box to indicate private members, a dashed box to indicate protected members, and a dotted box to indicate public members.

As I told Susan, Figure 2.11 illustrates a hypothetical DatedStockItem class. Here, class, m_Name, m_Price, and m_InStock are protected base class member variables, whereas m_UPC is a private member variable and GetPrice() is a public member function.[11]

FIGURE 2.11. **A derived** class **object with its base** class **part**

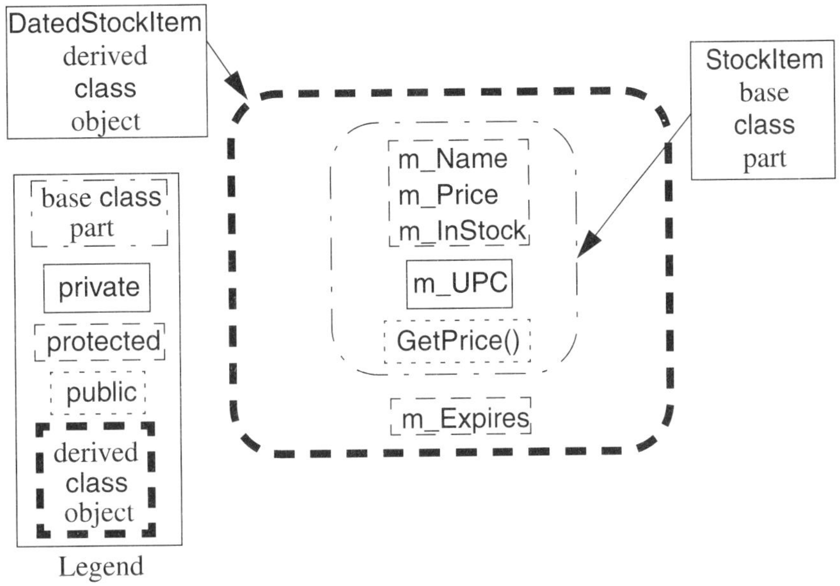


According to this scenario, the derived class member functions can access m_Name, m_Price, and m_InStock. Of course, any member function can access any public member of any other class, so GetPrice is accessible to DatedStockItem member functions as well. However, with this setup member functions of DatedStockItem cannot access m_UPC, even though this member variable is actually present in the base class part of a DatedStockItem.

Now that we've cleared up that point (I hope), we have to consider the question of when to use protected versus private variables. The private member variables of the base class cannot be

11. Of course, because m_Expires is a member of DatedStockItem, all DatedStockItem member functions can access it freely regardless of its access specifier.

accessed directly by derived class member functions. This means that when we define the base class, we have to decide whether we want to allow any derived classes to access some of the member variables of the base class part of the derived object. If we do, we have to use the protected access specifier for those member variables. If we make them private and later discover that we need access to those variables in a derived class, we then have to change the definition of the base class so that the variables are protected rather than private. Such changes are not too much trouble when we have written all of the classes involved, but they can be extremely difficult or even impossible when we try to derive new classes from previously existing classes written by someone else.

However, protected functions (and especially protected variables) have some of the drawbacks of public variables and functions. Anyone can define a new derived class that uses those variables or functions, and any changes to those base class variables or functions will cause the code in the derived class to break. Hence, making everything protected isn't an unalloyed blessing.

As we saw in an earlier discussion of public member variables versus public member functions, the drawbacks of protected variables are more serious than those of protected member functions, which at least don't commit you to specific implementation details. Therefore, it might be better to use protected member functions to allow access to private member variables in the base class rather than to use protected member variables for the same purpose. I haven't investigated this approach enough to render a definitive opinion, but at first glance it appears to be as workable as using protected variables while being less likely to cause maintenance problems down the road.

The moral of the story is that it's easier to design classes for our own use and derivation than for the use of others. Even though we can go back and change our class definitions to make them more flexible, that alternative may not be available to others. The result may be that our classes will not meet others' needs.

Susan didn't think this conclusion was so obvious.

**Susan:** I don't get your moral of the story. Sorry.

**Steve:** The moral is that when designing classes that may be used by others as base classes, we have to know whether those others will ever need access to our member variables. If we are in charge of all of the classes, we can change the access specifiers easily enough, but that's not a very good solution if someone else is deriving new classes from our classes.

**Susan:** Okay, I guess. But what does that have to do with using protected variables or private ones with protected member functions?

**Steve:** Only that if we used private variables with protected member functions to access them, we could allow the derived class to use the member variables in our base class in a controlled way rather than an uncontrolled one, and therefore could keep some say in how they are used. Unfortunately, this solution still requires us to figure out how the derived class member functions may want to use our member variables, so it isn't a "silver bullet".

**Susan:** I still don't understand why we need to worry about who else is going to use our classes; who are these other people?

**Steve:** One of the main advantages claimed for object-oriented programming is that it allows "division of labor"; that is, some programmers can specialize in building classes while others can specialize in writing application programs. This can increase productivity greatly, just as it does in medicine (e.g., general practitioners, specialists, nurses, and lab technicians).

**Susan:** Okay, but what does that have to do with access specifiers? Why don't we just make everything public and avoid all this stuff?

**Steve:** If we are going to let others use our classes, we have to design them to be easy to use correctly and hard to use incorrectly. That's one of the main reasons we use private and protected: so we can determine where in our program an error might be caused. If we notice that one of our private member variables is being changed when it shouldn't be, we know where to look: in the code that implements the class. Because the member variable is private, we don't have to worry that it's being changed somewhere else. This is not the case with a public member variable, which can be modified anywhere in the program. If you'd ever had to try to find out where a variable is being modified in a gigantic program in C or another language that doesn't have private variables, you would know exactly what I mean!

## *Stock Footage*

After that excursion into the use of the protected access specifier and its impact on class design, let's look at the revised test program in Figure 2.12.

**FIGURE 2.12. The revised inventory control test program** (code\itmtst21.cc)

```
#include <iostream.h>
#include <fstream.h>
#include "vector.h"
#include "string6.h"
#include "item21.h"
#include "invent21.h"

int main()
{
ifstream ShopInfo("shop21.in");
ofstream ReorderInfo("shop21.reo");

Inventory MyInventory;

MyInventory.LoadInventory(ShopInfo);

MyInventory.ReorderItems(ReorderInfo);
```

```
return 0;
}
```

The new test program, Itmtst21.cc, is exactly the same as its predecessor, itmtst20.cc, except that it #includes the new header files item21.h (shown in Figures 2.13) and invent21.h and uses different input and output file names.[12] If you want to see how this program runs, you can compile it and step through it using RHIDE. To do this, change to the \whosadv\code directory and type RHIDE itmtst21. When RHIDE starts up, hit F9 to compile the program; then you can use F8 to step through each line of itmtst21. If you want to see how any particular line works, you can use F7 to step into the code that executes that line. When the program terminates, you can look at its output file, shop21.reo, to see what the reorder report looks like; if you do, you will see that it includes instructions to return some expired items.

Now that we've seen the results of using the new versions of our inventory control classes, let's take a look at the interface definitions of StockItem and DatedStockItem (Figure 2.13) as well as the implementation of those classes (Figure 2.15). I strongly recommend that you print out the files that contain these interfaces and their implementation for reference as you go through this section of the chapter; those files are code\item21.h and code\item21.cc, respectively.[13]

Susan had some questions about where the new class interface and implementation were defined:

12. The reason that I am not listing either the header file or the implementation file for invent21 (the new version of the inventory class) is that they are essentially identical to the previous versions except that they use DatedStockItem rather than StockItem to keep track of the inventory items.

13. After looking at the interface file, you may wonder why I have two protected access specifiers in the DatedStockItem class. The reason is that I like to explicitly state the access specifiers for functions and for data separately to clarify what I'm doing. This duplication doesn't mean anything to the compiler, but it makes my intention clearer to the next programmer.

**Susan:** So you just write your new class right there? I mean you don't start over with a new page or something; shouldn't it be a different file or coded off all by itself somewhere? How come it is where it is?

**Steve:** We could put it in another file, but in this case the classes are intended to be used interchangeably in the application program, so it's not unreasonable to have them in the same file. In other circumstances, it's more common to have the derived class in a separate file. Of course, sometimes you don't have any choice, such as when you're deriving a new class from a class that you didn't create in the first place and may not even have the source code for; in that case, you *have* to create a separate file for the derived class.

**FIGURE 2.13. Full interface for StockItem and DatedStockItem (code\item21.h)**

```
class StockItem
{
friend ostream& operator << (ostream& s,
  const StockItem& Item);

friend istream& operator >> (istream& s, StockItem& Item);

public:
  StockItem();
  StockItem(string Name, short InStock,
  short Price, short MinimumStock,
  short MinimumReorder, string Distributor, string UPC);
  bool CheckUPC(string ItemUPC);
  void DeductSaleFromInventory(short QuantitySold);
  short GetInventory();
  string GetName();
  string GetUPC();
  bool IsNull();
  short GetPrice();
  void Reorder(ostream& s);
  void FormattedDisplay(ostream& s);
```

```
protected:
  short m_InStock;
  short m_Price;
  short m_MinimumStock;
  short m_MinimumReorder;
  string m_Name;
  string m_Distributor;
  string m_UPC;
};

class DatedStockItem: public StockItem
{
friend ostream& operator << (ostream& s,
  const DatedStockItem& Item);

friend istream& operator >> (istream& s, DatedStockItem& Item);

public:
  DatedStockItem();
  DatedStockItem(string Name, short InStock, short Price,
  short MinimumStock, short MinimumReorder,
  string Distributor, string UPC, string Expires);
  void FormattedDisplay(ostream& s);
  void Reorder(ostream& s);

protected:
static string Today();

protected:
  string m_Expires;
};
```

**FIGURE 2.14. Latest version of inventory class (code\invent21.h)**

```
class Inventory
{
public:
```

```
Inventory();

short LoadInventory(ifstream& is);

// the following function was added for inventory update
void StoreInventory(ofstream& OutputStream);

DatedStockItem FindItem(string UPC);
bool UpdateItem(DatedStockItem Item);
void ReorderItems(ofstream &OutputStream);

private:
vector<DatedStockItem> m_Stock;
short m_StockCount;
};
```

Before we get to the new implementation for these classes in item21.cc, I should mention the new header file #included in item21.cc: dos.h. This header file defines a data type needed by the Today function, which we'll get to in a little while.

If you're writing programs to run under another operating system such as Unix™, I should warn you that dos.h, as its name suggests, is specific to MS-DOS™. Therefore, this program won't compile in its current form under other operating systems. While this is a soluble problem, the solution is outside the scope of this book.

**FIGURE 2.15. Implementation for StockItem and DatedStockItem (code\item21.cc)**

```
#include <iostream.h>
#include <iomanip.h>
#include <strstream.h>
#include <string.h>
#include "string6.h"
#include "item21.h"
#include <dos.h>

StockItem::StockItem()
```

```
: m_InStock(0), m_Price(0), m_MinimumStock(0),
  m_MinimumReorder(0), m_Name(), m_Distributor(),
  m_UPC()
{
}

StockItem::StockItem(string Name, short InStock,
  short Price, short MinimumStock, short MinimumReorder,
  string Distributor, string UPC)
: m_InStock(InStock), m_Price(Price),
  m_MinimumStock(MinimumStock),
  m_MinimumReorder(MinimumReorder), m_Name(Name),
  m_Distributor(Distributor), m_UPC(UPC)
{
}

void StockItem::FormattedDisplay(ostream& os)
{
  os << "Name: ";
  os << m_Name << endl;
  os << "Number in stock: ";
  os << m_InStock << endl;
  os << "Price: ";
  os << m_Price << endl;
  os << "Minimum stock: ";
  os << m_MinimumStock << endl;
  os << "Minimum Reorder quantity: ";
  os << m_MinimumReorder << endl;
  os << "Distributor: ";
  os << m_Distributor << endl;
  os << "UPC: ";
  os << m_UPC << endl;
}

ostream& operator << (ostream& os, const StockItem& Item)
{
  os << Item.m_Name << endl;
  os << Item.m_InStock << endl;
  os << Item.m_Price << endl;
```

```
  os << Item.m_MinimumStock << endl;
  os << Item.m_MinimumReorder << endl;
  os << Item.m_Distributor << endl;
  os << Item.m_UPC << endl;

  return os;
}

istream& operator >> (istream& is, StockItem& Item)
{
  is >> Item.m_Name;
  is >> Item.m_InStock;
  is >> Item.m_Price;
  is >> Item.m_MinimumStock;
  is >> Item.m_MinimumReorder;
  is >> Item.m_Distributor;
  is >> Item.m_UPC;

  return is;
}

bool StockItem::CheckUPC(string ItemUPC)
{
  if (m_UPC == ItemUPC)
    return true;

  return false;
}

void StockItem::DeductSaleFromInventory(short QuantitySold)
{
  m_InStock -= QuantitySold;
}

short StockItem::GetInventory()
{
  return m_InStock;
}
```

```
string StockItem::GetName()
{
 return m_Name;
}

string StockItem::GetUPC()
{
 return m_UPC;
}

bool StockItem::IsNull()
{
 if (m_UPC == "")
   return true;

 return false;
}

short StockItem::GetPrice()
{
 return m_Price;
}

void StockItem::Reorder(ostream& os)
{
 short ActualReorderQuantity;

 if (m_InStock < m_MinimumStock)
   {
   ActualReorderQuantity = m_MinimumStock - m_InStock;
   if (m_MinimumReorder > ActualReorderQuantity)
     ActualReorderQuantity = m_MinimumReorder;
   os << "Reorder " << ActualReorderQuantity;
   os <<  " units of " << m_Name;
   os << " with UPC " << m_UPC;
   os << " from " << m_Distributor << endl;
   }
}
```

```
DatedStockItem::DatedStockItem()
: m_Expires()
{
}

string DatedStockItem::Today()
{
 date d;
 short year;
 char day;
 char month;
 string TodaysDate;
 strstream FormatStream;

 getdate(&d);
 year = d.da_year;
 day = d.da_day;
 month = d.da_mon;

 FormatStream << setfill('0') << setw(4) << year <<
  setw(2) << month << setw(2) << day;
 FormatStream >> TodaysDate;

 return TodaysDate;
}

DatedStockItem::DatedStockItem(string Name, short InStock,
 short Price, short MinimumStock, short MinimumReorder,
 string Distributor, string UPC, string Expires)
: StockItem(Name, InStock, Price, MinimumStock,
 MinimumReorder, Distributor, UPC),
 m_Expires(Expires)
{
}

void DatedStockItem::Reorder(ostream& os)
{
 if (m_Expires < Today())
  {
```

```
    os << "Return " << m_InStock;
    os << " units of " << m_Name;
    os << " with UPC " << m_UPC;
    os << " to " << m_Distributor << endl;
    m_InStock = 0;
    }

  StockItem::Reorder(os);
}

void DatedStockItem::FormattedDisplay(ostream& os)
{
  os << "Expiration Date: ";
  os << m_Expires << endl;
  StockItem::FormattedDisplay(os);
}

ostream& operator << (ostream& os, const DatedStockItem& Item)
{
  os << Item.m_Expires << endl;
  os << Item.m_Name << endl;
  os << Item.m_InStock << endl;
  os << Item.m_Price << endl;
  os << Item.m_MinimumStock << endl;
  os << Item.m_MinimumReorder << endl;
  os << Item.m_Distributor << endl;
  os << Item.m_UPC << endl;

  return os;
}

istream& operator >> (istream& is, DatedStockItem& Item)
{
  is >> Item.m_Expires;
  is >> Item.m_Name;
  is >> Item.m_InStock;
  is >> Item.m_Price;
  is >> Item.m_MinimumStock;
  is >> Item.m_MinimumReorder;
```

```
  is >> Item.m_Distributor;
  is >> Item.m_UPC;

  return is;
}
```

Now let's get to the interface definition for DatedStockItem. Most of this should be pretty simple to follow by now. We have to declare new versions of operator << and operator >>, which will allow us to write and read objects of the DatedStockItem class as we can already do with the normal StockItem. As before, the friend specifiers are needed to allow these global input and output functions to access the internal variables of our class.

Susan wanted to know why we had to write new operators << and >> for the DatedStockItem class when we had already written them for its base class, StockItem.

> **Susan:** Why can't DatedStockItem use the same >> and << that StockItem uses? If it's derived from StockItem, it should be able to use the same ones. I don't get it.
>
> **Steve:** It can't use the same ones because a DatedStockItem has a new member variable that the StockItem I/O operators don't know about.
>
> **Susan:** But why can't the compiler do it for us?
>
> **Steve:** Because the compiler doesn't know how we want to display the data. Should it put an endl after each member variable or run them all together on one line? Should it even display all of the member variables? Maybe there are some that the user of the class doesn't care about. In some cases, the real data for the class isn't even contained in its objects, as we'll see in Chapter 3. Therefore, we have to write operator << ourselves.

Then we have the default constructor, DatedStockItem(), and the "normal" constructor that supplies values for all of the member variables. We also have to declare the Reorder function we are writing for this class.

Although all of the preceding function declarations should be old hat by now, there are a couple of constructs here that we haven't seen before. The first one is in the class header: DatedStockItem: public StockItem. I'm referring specifically to the expression : public StockItem, which states that the new class being defined, in this case DatedStockItem, is publicly derived from StockItem. We have discussed the fact that deriving a new class from an old one means that the new class has everything in it that the old class had in it. But what does the public keyword mean here?

### *class Interests*

It means that we are going to allow a DatedStockItem to be treated as a StockItem; that is, any function that takes a StockItem as a parameter will accept a DatedStockItem in its place. As this implies, all of the public member functions and public data items (if there were any) in the base class (StockItem in this case) are publicly accessible in an object of the derived class (DatedStockItem in this case) object as well. This is called, imaginatively enough, public inheritance.

The relationship between a base class and a publicly derived class is commonly expressed by saying that the derived class "isA" base class object.[14]

14. By the way, this is the reason it's all right to provide an ofstream variable where an ostream is expected, as I told Susan in the discussion on page 24. Because ofstream is publicly derived from ostream, an ofstream "isAn" ostream. This means that you can provide an ofstream wherever an ostream is specified as an argument or return type.

### private *Bequest*

You might be wondering whether there are other types of inheritance besides public. The answer is that there is one that is sometimes useful: private. If we wrote : private StockItem rather than : public StockItem as the base class specification for DatedStockItem, DatedStockItem member functions would still be able to use the protected and public member variables and member functions of StockItem in their implementation, just as with public inheritance. However, the fact that DatedStockItem is derived from StockItem would not be apparent to any outside function. That is, if we specified private rather than public inheritance, a DatedStockItem would not be an acceptable substitute for a StockItem; alternatively, we could say that DatedStockItem would not have an "isA" relationship with StockItem. There aren't very many applications for private inheritance, and we won't be seeing any in this book.

Susan had a number of questions about the uses of inheritance.

**Susan:** I don't understand this idea of substituting one type of object for another. Why don't you decide which kind of object you want and use that one?

**Steve:** The StockItem and DatedStockItem classes are a good example of why we would want to be able to substitute one type of object for another: To the user of these classes, they appear the same, except that DatedStockItem requires one more item of information (the expiration date) and produces a slightly different reordering report. Therefore, being able to treat them in the same way makes it much easier to write a program using these two classes, because the user doesn't need a lot of code saying, "if it's a DatedStockItem, do this; if it's a StockItem, do something else".

**Susan:** Okay, but if you use : private StockItem, then how come it can use the protected and public parts of StockItem and not just the private parts? I just don't get this at all.

**Steve:** That's understandable because this is another confusing case of C++ keyword abuse: The private keyword in the class declaration line means something different from its meaning in the class definition. In the class declaration line, it means that no user of the class can treat an object of the derived class being declared as a substitute for a base class object. In other words, what is private is the inheritance from the base class, not the variables in the base class. It's sort of like an unrecognized child; the derived class has the DNA of the base class, but can't claim parentage in public.

This substitutability of an object of a publicly derived class (e.g., a DatedStockItem) for an object of its base class (e.g., StockItem) extends to areas where its value is somewhat questionable. In particular, a derived class object can be assigned to a base class object; for example, if x is a StockItem and y is a DatedStockItem, the statement x = y; is legal. The result will be that any member variables that exist in the derived class object but not in the base class object will be lost in the assignment. In our example, after the statement x = y;, x will contain all the member variables of y except for m_Expires, which is not present in the base class. This "partial assignment" is called *slicing*, and it can be a serious annoyance because the compiler won't warn you that it's taking place. After all, since a DatedStockItem "isA" StockItem, it's perfectly legal to assign an object of the former class to an object of the latter class, even if that isn't what you had in mind. However, you shouldn't worry about this problem too much; as we'll see in the next chapter, we can solve it by using more advanced techniques.

Before we get into the implementation of the DatedStockItem class, let's take a look at the other new construct in its interface: a static member function. I'll give you a hint as to its meaning: In the grand old C/C++ tradition of keyword abuse, the meaning of static here is almost but not quite entirely unlike its meaning for either local or global variables.

### *Getting static*

Give up? Okay. When we declare a member function to be static, we don't have to specify an object when we call the member function. Thus, we can refer to the static member function Today by just its name followed by empty parentheses to indicate a function call. Within DatedStockItem member functions, writing "Today();" is sufficient. Of course, if Today were public, and we wanted to call it from a nonmember function, we would have to refer to it by its full name: DatedStockItem::Today. Either of these calls differs from the normal use of a member function, where we specify the function along with the object to which it applies—for example, in the expression "soup.GetInventory();".

That explains what the static modifier does, but why would we want to use it? Because some member functions don't apply to any particular object, it is convenient to be able to call such a function without needing an object to call it for. In the case of the Today function, the value of today's date is not dependent on any DatedStockItem object; therefore, it makes sense to be able to call Today without referring to any object of the DatedStockItem class.

At this point, Susan had a cognition about the utility of static member functions:

**Susan:** I just realized that this way of writing functions is sort of like writing a path; it tells the compiler where to go to find things — is that right?

**Steve:** Right. The reason that we make this a member function is to control access to it and to allow it to be used by this class, not because it works on a particular class object (as is the case with non-static member functions).

**Susan:** So, is using this static thing like making it a default?

**Steve:** Sort of, because you don't have to specify an object for the function to act on.

Of course, we could also avoid having to pass an object to the Today function by making it a global function. However, the advantages of using a static protected member function rather than a global one are much the same as the advantages of using private rather than public member variables. First, we can change the interface of this function more easily than that of a global function, as we know that it can be accessed only by member functions of DatedStockItem and any possible derived classes of that class, not by any function anywhere. Second, we don't have to worry that someone else might want to define a different function with the same signature, which could be a problem with a global function. The full name of this function, DatedStockItem::Today, is sufficient to distinguish it from any other Today functions that belong to other classes, or even from a global function of that name, should another programmer be so inconsiderate as to write one!

There's one other thing here that we haven't seen before: Today is a protected member function, which means that it is accessible only to member functions of DatedStockItem and its descendants, just as a protected member variable is. We want to keep this function from being called by application programs for the same reason that we protect member variables by restricting access: to reserve the right to change its name, return value, or argument types. Application code can't access this function and therefore can't depend on its interface.

Susan had some questions about changing the Today function as well as about the more general idea of many programmers working on the same program.

**Susan:** Why would we want to change the Today function? It seems like it would work fine the way it is.

**Steve:** Well, we might decide to make it return a number rather than a string, if we changed the way we implemented our date comparisons. But the point is more general: The fewer people who know about a particular function, the easier it will be to make changes to its interface.

**Susan:** Who are these other people you're always talking about? I thought a programmer wrote his own programs.

**Steve:** That all depends. Some small projects are done by a single programmer, which might seem to make access specifiers redundant. But they really aren't, even in that case, because a lone programmer puts on different "hats" while writing a significant program. Sometimes he's a class designer and somctimes an application programmer.

But where these design considerations are *really* important is in big projects, which may be written by dozens or even hundreds of programmers. In such cases, the result of letting everyone access every variable or function can be summed up in one word: chaos. Such free-for-alls have led to a lot of buggy software and even to the Year 2000 fiasco, which we'll discuss in Chapter 4.

Figure 2.16 is the implementation of the protected static member function DatedStockItem::Today.

**FIGURE 2.16.** DatedStockItem::Today() **(from code\item21.cc)**

```
string DatedStockItem::Today()
{
 date d;
 short year;
 char day;
 char month;
 string TodaysDate;
 strstream FormatStream;

 getdate(&d);
 year = d.da_year;
 day = d.da_day;
 month = d.da_mon;

 FormatStream << setfill('0') << setw(4) << year <<
  setw(2) << month << setw(2) << day;
 FormatStream >> TodaysDate;
```

```
  return TodaysDate;
}
```

Here's where we use the date type defined in the line #include <dos.h> in Figure 2.15. As its name suggests, a date is used to store the components of a date (i.e., its month, day, and year). Now that we've gotten that detail out of the way, let's look at this Today function. First, we have to call the getdate function (whose declaration is also in dos.h) to ascertain the current date; getdate handles this request by filling in the member variables in a variable of type date. Note that the argument to the getdate function is the address of the date variable (i.e., &d) rather than the variable itself. This is necessary because the getdate function is left over from C, which doesn't have reference variables. Since all C arguments are value arguments, a C function can't change any of its arguments. C handles this limitation by giving the called function the address of the variable to be modified; then the called function uses that address as a pointer to the actual variable. Happily, we don't have to concern ourselves about this in any more detail than what I've just mentioned.

By the way, this is a good example of the difference between calling a member function and calling a nonmember function: We have to specify the address of the date variable d as an argument when calling getdate because getdate isn't a member function of the date type. Since getdate is a leftover from C, which doesn't have member functions, we have to supply the address of the variable on which the function should operate. Of course, with a member function, the compiler automatically supplies the this pointer to every (non-static) member function as a hidden argument, so we don't have to worry about it.

After we call getdate, the current year is left in the da_year member variable of the date variable d, and the current day and month are left in the other two member variables, da_day and da_mon. Now that we have the current year, month, and day, the next step is to produce a string that has all of these data items in the correct order and format. To do this, we use some functions from the iostreams library that we haven't seen before. However, to do this, we need a stream of some sort to apply the functions to.

So far, we've used istream and ostream objects, but neither of those will do the job here. We don't really want to do any input or output at all; we just want to use the formatting functions that streams provide. Since this is a fairly common requirement, the inventors of the iostreams library have anticipated it by supplying the strstream class.

A strstream is a stream that exists entirely in memory rather than as a conduit to read or write data. In this case, we've declared a strstream called FormatStream, to which we'll write our data. When done, we'll read the formatted data back from FormatStream.

This discussion assumes that you're completely comfortable with the notion of a stream, which may not be true. It certainly wasn't for Susan, as the following indicates:

> **Susan:** I don't understand your definition for strstream. What does the str part stand for? Why is FormatStream a part of strstream instead of just from the iostream library? When does it exist in memory? When is it called to work? How is it different from the "conduit" type of streams? I am *not* understanding this because I told you that I don't understand what a stream really is. So what does strstream really do?
>
> **Steve:** You know, you ask a lot of questions for someone from Plano, Texas.

Let's see if we can answer her (and possibly your) questions by taking a closer look at streams.

## *stream of Consciousness*

A stream is a facility that allows us to use various input and output devices more or less uniformly. There are a number of variants of this data type, which are related by inheritance so that we can substitute a more highly specialized variant for a more basic one. So far we've encountered istream, ostream, ifstream, ofstream, and of course most recently strstream. The best place to start a further investigation of this family of classes is with one of the simplest types, an ostream. We've used a predefined object of this type quite a few times already: Of course, I'm referring to cout. Take a look at the program in Figure 2.17.

**FIGURE 2.17. A simple** stream **example (code\stream1.cc)**

```
#include <iostream.h>

int main()
{
   short x;
   char y;

   x = 1;
   y = 'A';

   cout << "Test " << x;
   cout << " grade: " << y;
   cout << endl;

   return 0;
}
```

At the beginning of the program, cout looks something like Figure 2.18.

FIGURE 2.18. **An empty** ostream **object**

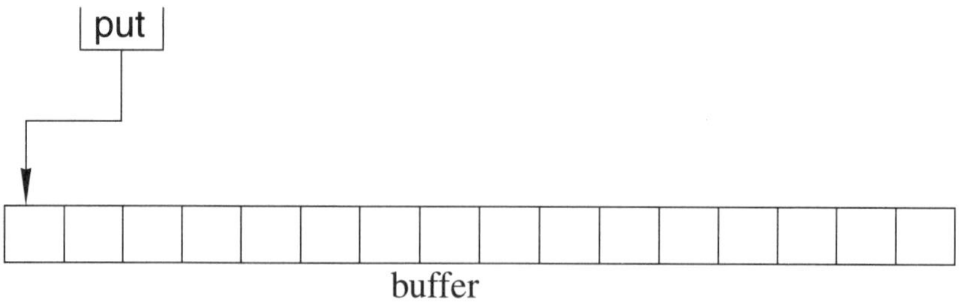


What is the purpose of the buffer and the put pointer? Here's a breakdown:

1. The buffer is the area of memory where the characters put into the ostream are stored.
2. The put pointer holds the address of the next byte in the output area of the ostream — that is, where the next byte will be stored if we use << to write data into the ostream. Please note that the type of the put pointer is irrelevant to us, as we cannot ever access it directly. However, you won't go far wrong if you think of it as the address of the next available byte in the buffer.

At this point, we haven't put anything into the ostream yet, so the put pointer is pointing to the beginning of the buffer. Now, let's execute the line cout << "Test " << x;. After that line is executed, the contents of the ostream looks something like Figure 2.19.

**FIGURE 2.19. An** ostream **object with some data**

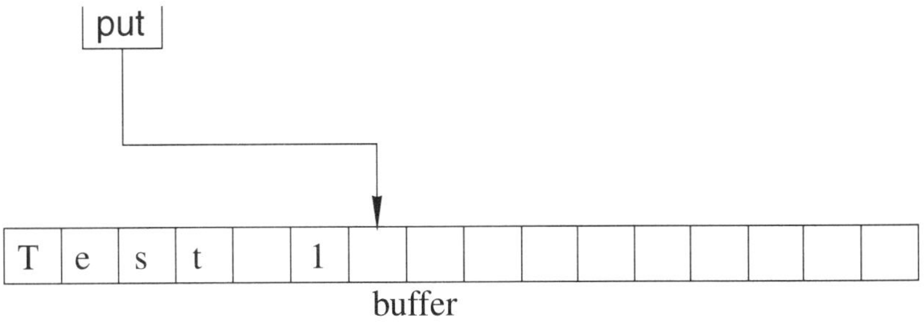


As you can see, the data from the first output line has been put into the ostream buffer. Now let's look at the next statement, which is cout << " grade: " << y;. After this statement is executed, the ostream looks like Figure 2.20.

**FIGURE 2.20. An** ostream **object with some more data.**

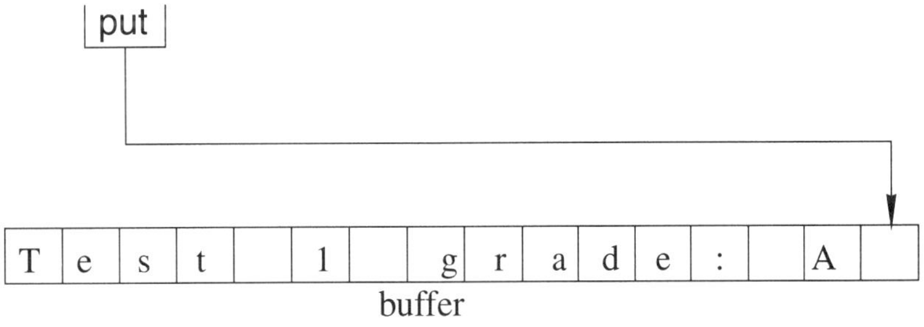


Now we're ready for the final output statement, cout << endl;. Once this statement is executed, the ostream looks like Figure 2.21.

**FIGURE 2.21.** **An empty** ostream **object**

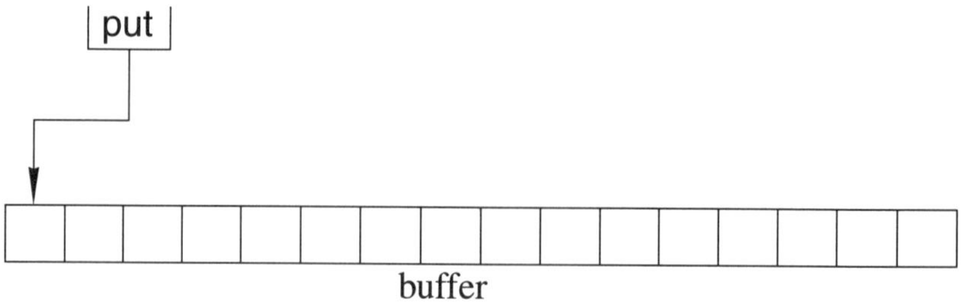


By now, you're probably wondering what happened to all the data we stored in the ostream. It went out to the screen because that's what endl does (after sticking a newline character on the end of the buffer). Once the data has been sent to the screen, we can't access it anymore in our program, so the space that it took up in the buffer is made available for further use.

## *We All* stream *for* strstream

Now it's time to get back to our discussion of strstream. A strstream (short for *string stream*) allows us to write data to its buffer and then read the resulting data back into a variable. An example is the program shown in Figure 2.22, which uses a strstream object to combine a year, month, and day number to make one string containing all of those values.

**FIGURE 2.22.** **A** strstream **formatting example (code\stream2.cc)**

```
#include <iostream.h>
#include <strstream.h>
#include "string6.h"
```

```
int main()
{
   strstream FormatStream;
   string date;

   short year = 1996;
   short month = 7;
   short day = 28;

   FormatStream << year;
   FormatStream << month;
   FormatStream << day;

   FormatStream >> date;

   cout << "date: " << date << endl;

   return 0;
}
```

A strstream is very similar to an ostream, except that once we have written data to a strstream, we can read it from the strstream into a variable just as though we were reading from a file or the keyboard. Figure 2.23 shows what an empty strstream looks like.

We've discussed the put pointer and the buffer, but what about the get and end pointers? Here's what they're for:

1. The get pointer holds the address of the next byte in the input area of the stream, or the next byte we get if we use >> to read data from the strstream.

2. The end pointer indicates the end of the strstream. Attempting to read anything at or after this position will cause the read to fail because there is nothing else to read.

FIGURE 2.23. **An empty** strstream **object**

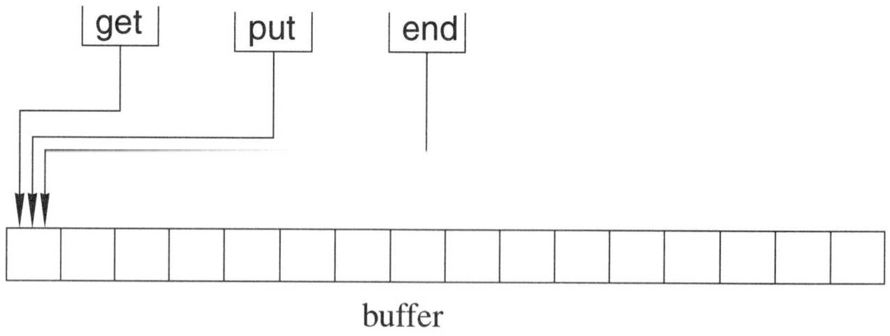


You probably won't be surprised to learn that Susan wasn't that thrilled with all these new kinds of pointers, or with streams in general for that matter.

**Susan:** The only thing that can be worse than pointers is different kinds of pointers. How are get and end different from other kinds of pointers? Ick.

**Steve:** They are effectively the addresses of the current places in the buffer where characters will be read and written, respectively. Since they are not directly accessible to the programmer, their actual representation is irrelevant; all that matters is how they work.

**Susan:** You just have no idea how much trouble this stream stuff is to me. It's all just a vague mess that I have to trust is doing something. I just don't get it.

**Steve:** Why is it any more vague than cout? It's just the same, except that the actual destination may vary.

**Susan:** No, there is no cout word when we're using these other streams.

**Steve:** Yes, but that's the only difference between writing to a strstream and writing to cout, which never bothered you before.

**Susan:** But I can see the screen; I can't see these other things.

**Steve:** Yes, but you can't see the stream in either case. Anyway, I drew all those diagrams so you could "see" the stream. Don't they help?

**Susan:** Yes, they help but it still isn't the same thing as cout. Anyway, I'm not really sure at any given time exactly where the data really is; it just seems to be in some area of memory that is somewhat vague. Where are these put, get, and end pointers stored?

**Steve:** They're stored in the strstream object as part of its member data, just as m_Name and the other member variables are stored in a StockItem object.

**Susan:** Okay, but what about the buffer?

**Steve:** That's in an area of memory allocated for that purpose by the strstream member functions. The streams classes use the get and put pointers to keep track of the exact position of the data in the buffer, so we don't have to worry about it.

**Susan:** I still don't like it. It's not like cout.

**Steve:** Yes, but cout is just an ostream, and a strstream is just like an ostream and an istream combined; you can write to it just like an ostream and then read back from it just like an istream.

**Susan:** I still think streams are going to be my downfall. They're just too vague and there seem to be so many of them. I know you say that they are good, and I believe you, but they are still a little mysterious. This is not going to be the last you've heard of this.

**Steve:** It seems to me that you've managed to survive lots of other new concepts pretty well. I suspect streams won't be any exception.

After the statement FormatStream << year;, the strstream might look like Figure 2.24.

**FIGURE 2.24. A strstream object with some contents**

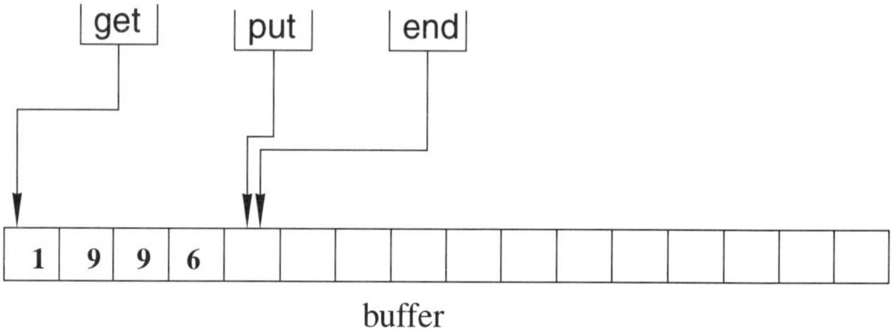


The put pointer has moved to the next free byte in the strstream, but the get pointer hasn't moved because we haven't gotten anything from the strstream.

The next statement is FormatStream << month;, which leaves the strstream looking like Figure 2.25.

FIGURE 2.25. A strstream **object with some more contents**

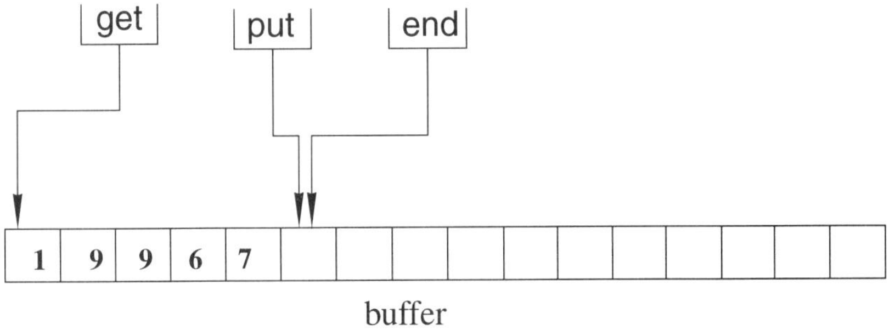


After we execute the statement FormatStream << day;, the strstream looks like Figure 2.26.

FIGURE 2.26. A strstream **object with even more contents**

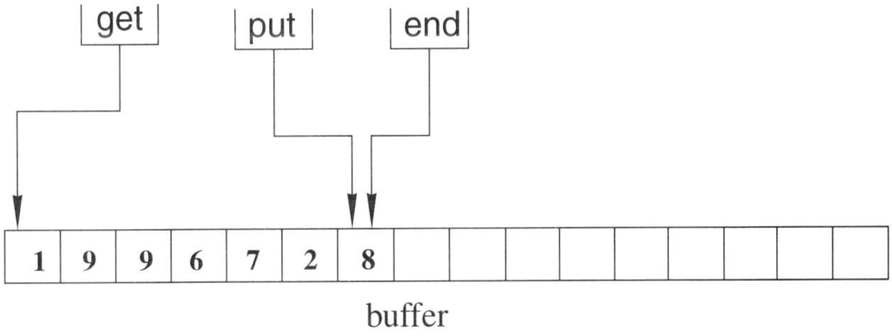


Now it's time to get back what we put into the strstream. That's the job of the next statement, FormatStream >> date;. Afterward the variable date has the value "1996728" and the strstream looks like Figure 2.27.

FIGURE 2.27. **A** strstream **object after reading its contents**

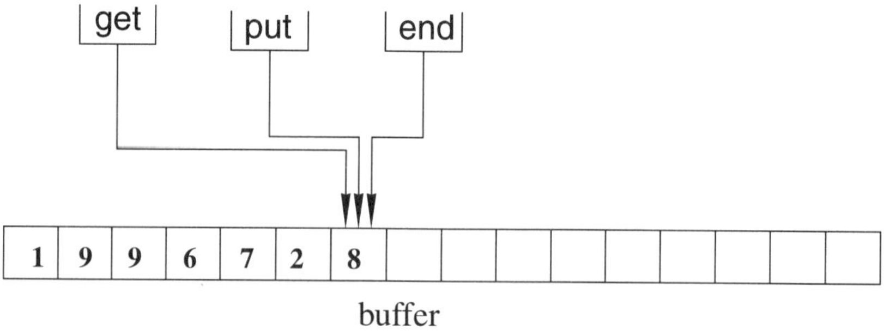


In other words, we've read to the end of the strstream, so we can't read from it again until we "reset" it. This shouldn't seem too strange, as it is exactly analogous to what happens when we've read all of the data in a file through an ifstream, which causes the next read to "fail".[15]

In these diagrams, the end and put pointers always point to the same place, so why do we need both? Because we can reset the put pointer to any place in the strstream before the current end pointer and write over the data already written. We don't make use of that facility in this book, but it's there when needed.

## *Use It or Lose It*

Now let's get back to the problem of converting a date to a string so that we can compare it with another date. You might think that all we have to do is write each data item out to the strstream and then read the resulting formatted data back in, as in the program in Figure 2.22. However, it's a bit more complicated than that because in order to

15. This is covered in *Who's Afraid of C++?*, in the section "References Required" in Chapter 6.

compare two of these values correctly, we need to control the exact format in which the data will be written. To see why this is necessary, consider the program shown in Figure 2.28.

**FIGURE 2.28. Default formatting example (code\coutdef1.cc)**

```
#include <iostream.h>
#include <strstream.h>
#include "string6.h"

int main()
{
  strstream FormatStream1;
  strstream FormatStream2;
  string date1;
  string date2;

  short year1 = 1996;
  short month1 = 12;
  short day1 = 28;

  short year2 = 1996;
  short month2 = 7;
  short day2 = 28;

  FormatStream1 << year1 << month1 << day1;
  FormatStream1 >> date1;

  FormatStream2 << year2 << month2 << day2;
  FormatStream2 >> date2;

  cout << "date1: " << date1 << ", date2: " << date2 << endl;

  if (date1 < date2)
   cout << "date1 is less than date2" << endl;
  else if (date1 == date2)
   cout << "date1 is the same as date2" << endl;
  else
```

```
    cout << "date1 is greater than date2" << endl;

  return 0;
}
```

The output of that program is shown in Figure 2.29.

**FIGURE 2.29. Output of default formatting example (code\coutdef1.out)**

```
date1: 19961228, date2: 1996728
date1 is less than date2
```

What's wrong with this picture? Well, the string comparison of the first value with the second shows that the first is less than the second. Clearly, this is wrong, since the date the first string represents is later than the date the second string represents. The problem is that we're not formatting the output correctly; what we have to do is make month numbers less than 10 come out with a leading 0 (e.g., July as 07 rather than 7). The same consideration applies to the day number; we want it to be two digits in every case. Of course, if we knew that a particular number was only one digit, we could just add a leading 0 to it explicitly, but that wouldn't work correctly if the month or day number already had two digits.

To make sure the output is correct without worrying about how many digits the value has, we can use iostreams member functions called *manipulators*, which are defined not in iostream.h but in another header file called iomanip.h. This header file defines setfill, setw, and a number of other manipulators that we don't need to worry about at the moment. These manipulators operate on fields; a field can be defined as the result of one << operator. In this case, we use the setw manipulator to specify the width of each field to be formatted, and the setfill manipulator to set the character to be used to fill in the otherwise empty places in each field.

Susan had some questions about why we're using manipulators here.

**Susan:** Why are manipulators needed? Why can't you just add the 0 where it is needed?

**Steve:** Well, to determine that, we'd have to test each value to see whether it was large enough to fill its field. It's a lot easier just to use setw and setfill to do the work for us.

Let's change our example program to produce the output we want, as shown in Figure 2.30.

**FIGURE 2.30. Output of controlled formatting example (code\coutdef2.out)**

```
date1: 19961228, date2: 19960728
date1 is greater than date2
```

## *Manipulative Behavior*

The new program is shown in Figure 2.31. Let's go over how it works. To start with, setfill takes an argument specifying the char that will be used to fill in any otherwise unused positions in an output field. We want those unused positions to be filled with 0 characters so that our output strings will consist entirely of numeric digits.[16]

**FIGURE 2.31. Controlled formatting example (code\coutdef2.cc)**

```
#include <iostream.h>
#include <strstream.h>
#include <iomanip.h>
#include "string6.h"

int main()
```

16. Actually, our comparison functions would work correctly even if we left the fill character at its default value of "space", but the date strings would contain spaces instead of zeroes for day and month numbers less than 10, and they would look silly that way!

```
{
  strstream FormatStream1;
  strstream FormatStream2;
  string date1;
  string date2;

  short year1 = 1996;
  short month1 = 12;
  short day1 = 28;

  short year2 = 1996;
  short month2 = 7;
  short day2 = 28;

  FormatStream1 << setfill('0') << setw(4) <<
  year1 << setw(2) << month1 << setw(2) << day1;

  FormatStream1 >> date1;

  FormatStream2 << setfill('0') << setw(4) <<
  year2 << setw(2) << month2 << setw(2) << day2;

  FormatStream2 >> date2;

  cout << "date1: " << date1 << ", date2: " << date2 << endl;

  if (date1 < date2)
   cout << "date1 is less than date2" << endl;
  else if (date1 == date2)
   cout << "date1 is the same as date2" << endl;
  else
   cout << "date1 is greater than date2" << endl;

  return 0;
}
```

The setfill manipulator is "sticky"; that is, it applies to all of the fields that follow it in the same output statement. However, this is not true of setw, which sets the minimum width (i.e., the minimum number of characters) of the next field. Hence, we need three setw manipulators, one for each field in the output. The year field is four digits, while the month and day fields are two digits each.

Now let's get back to our DatedStockItem::Today function. Once we understand the manipulators we're using, it should be obvious how we can produce a formatted value on our strstream, but how do we get it back?

That turns out to be easy. Since the get pointer is still pointing to the beginning of the strstream, the statement FormatStream >> TodaysDate; reads data from the strstream into a string called TodaysDate just as if we were reading data from cin or a file.

Susan had a question about the statement that reads the data back from the strstream.

> **Susan:** How do you know that FormatStream >> TodaysDate will get your data back?
>
> **Steve:** Because that's how strstreams work. You write data to them just like you write to a regular ostream, then read from them just like you read from a regular istream. They're really our friends!

## *Baseless Accusations?*

Now that we've taken care of the new function, Today, let's take a look at some of the other functions of the DatedStockItem class that differ significantly from their counterparts in the base class StockItem, the constructors and the Reorder function.[17]

We'll start with the default constructor, which of course is called DatedStockItem::DatedStockItem() (Figure 2.32). It's a very short function, but there's a bit more here than meets the eye.

17. There are other functions whose implementation in DatedStockItem is different from the versions in StockItem, but we'll wait until later to discuss them. These are the input and output functions FormattedDisplay, operator >>, and operator <<.

**FIGURE 2.32. Default constructor for DatedStockItem (from code\item21.cc)**

```
DatedStockItem::DatedStockItem()
: m_Expires()
{
}
```

A very good question here is what happens to the base class part of the object. This is taken care of by the default constructor of the StockItem class, which will be invoked by default to initialize that part of this object.

Susan had some questions about this notion of constructing the base class part of an object:

**Susan:** I don't understand your good question. What do you mean by base class part?

**Steve:** The base class part is the embedded base class object in the derived class object.

**Susan:** So derived classes use the default constructor from the base classes?

**Steve:** They always use *some* base class constructor to construct the base class part of a derived class object. By default, they use the default constructor for the base class object, but you can specify which base class constructor you want to use.

**Susan:** If that is so, then why are you writing a constructor for DatedStockItem?

**Steve:** Because the base class constructor only constructs the base class part of a derived class object (such as DatedStockItem). The rest of the derived class object has to be constructed too, and that job is handled by the derived class constructor.

The following is a general rule: Any base class part of a derived class object will automatically be initialized when the derived object is created at run time, by a base class constructor. By default, the default base class constructor will be called when we don't specify which base class constructor we want to execute. In other words, the code in Figure 2.32 is translated by the compiler as though it were the code in Figure 2.33.

**FIGURE 2.33. Specifying the base class constructor for a derived class object**

```
DatedStockItem::DatedStockItem()
: StockItem(),
  m_Expires()
{
}
```

The line : StockItem(), specifies which base class constructor we want to use to initialize the base class part of the DatedStockItem object. This is a construct called a *base class initializer*, which is the only permissible type of expression in a *member initialization list* other than a member initialization expression. In this case, we're calling the default constructor for the base class, StockItem.

Susan wanted a refresher on the idea of a member initialization list.

**Susan:** What's a member initialization list again? I forget.

**Steve:** It's a set of expressions that you can specify before the opening { of a constructor. These expressions are used to initialize the member variables of the object being constructed. A member initialization list has much the same effect as a list of variable declaration statements that initialize the variables has, except that it applies only to member variables and (in the case of a derived class object) the base class part of the object. If we weren't going to use a base class initializer, we could achieve much the same effect by including a list of statements in the constructor to initialize the member variables, but using a member initialization list is more efficient and therefore preferable even in that case.

After clearing that up, Susan wanted to make sure that she understood the reason for the base class initializer, which led to the following exchange:

**Susan:** Okay, let me see if I can get this straight. The derived class will use the base class default constructor unless you specify otherwise.

**Steve:** Correct so far.

**Susan:** But to specify it, you have to use a base class initializer — is that right?

**Steve:** Right. If you don't want the base class part to be initialized with the base class default constructor, you have to use a base class initializer to specify which base class constructor you want to use. *Some* base class constructor will always be called to initialize the base class part; the only question is which one.

**Susan:** It just doesn't "know" to go to the base class as a default unless you tell it to?

**Steve:** No, it always goes to the base class whether or not you tell it to; the question is which base class constructor is called.

**Susan:** OK, then say that the base class initializer is necessary to let the derived class know which constructor you are using. This is not clear.

**Steve:** Hopefully, we've clarified it by now.

Whether we allow the compiler to call the default base class constructor automatically, as in Figure 2.32, or explicitly specify that base class constructor, as in Figure 2.33, the path of execution for the default DatedStockItem constructor is as illustrated in Figure 2.34.

**FIGURE 2.34. Constructing a default DatedStockItem object**

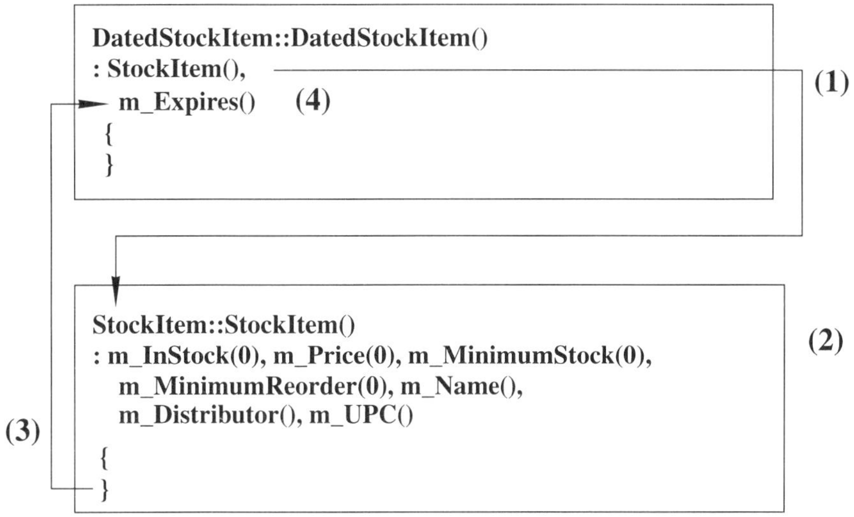
DatedStockItem::DatedStockItem()
: StockItem(),
m_Expires()
(4)
{
}
(1)
StockItem::StockItem()
: m_InStock(0), m_Price(0), m_MinimumStock(0),
m_MinimumReorder(0), m_Name(),
m_Distributor(), m_UPC()
{
}
(2)
(3)

At step 1, the DatedStockItem constructor calls the default constructor for StockItem, which starts in step 2 by initializing all the variables in the StockItem class to their default values. Once the default constructor for StockItem is finished, in step 3, it returns to the DatedStockItem constructor. In step 4, that constructor finishes the initialization of the DatedStockItem object by initializing m_Expires to the default string value (which happens to be "").

This is fine as long as the base class default constructor does the job for us. However, if it doesn't do what we want, we can specify which base constructor we wish to call, as shown in the "normal" constructor for the DatedStockItem class (Figure 2.35).

**FIGURE 2.35. Normal constructor for DatedStockItem (from code\item21.cc)**

```
DatedStockItem::DatedStockItem(string Name, short InStock,
```

```
  short Price, short MinimumStock, short MinimumReorder,
  string Distributor, string UPC, string Expires)
: StockItem(Name, InStock, Price, MinimumStock,
  MinimumReorder, Distributor, UPC),
  m_Expires(Expires)
{
}
```

As before, we're using a member initialization list (in this case : StockItem(Name, InStock, Price, MinimumStock, MinimumReorder, Distributor, UPC),) to specify which base class constructor will be used to initialize the base class part of the DatedStockItem object. This base class initializer specifies that we want to call the "normal" constructor for the base class, StockItem. Thus, the StockItem part of the DatedStockItem object will be initialized exactly as though it were being created by the corresponding constructor for StockItem. Figure 2.36 illustrates how this works.

At step 1, the DatedStockItem constructor calls the "normal" constructor for StockItem, which starts in step 2 by initializing all the variables in the StockItem class to the values specified in the argument list to the constructor. Once the "normal" constructor for StockItem is finished, in step 3, it returns to the DatedStockItem constructor. In step 4, that constructor finishes the initialization of the DatedStockItem object by initializing m_Expires to the value of the argument Expires.

As you can see by these examples, using a base class initializer allows us to use an appropriate base class constructor to initialize the base class part of an object, which in turn means that our derived class constructor won't have to keep track of the details of the base class. This is an example of one of the main benefits claimed for object-oriented programming: We can confine the details of a class to the internals of that class, which simplifies maintenance efforts. In this case, after specifying the base class initializer the only remaining task for the DatedStockItem constructor is to initialize the member variable m_Expires.

**FIGURE 2.36.** Constructing a DatedStockItem object

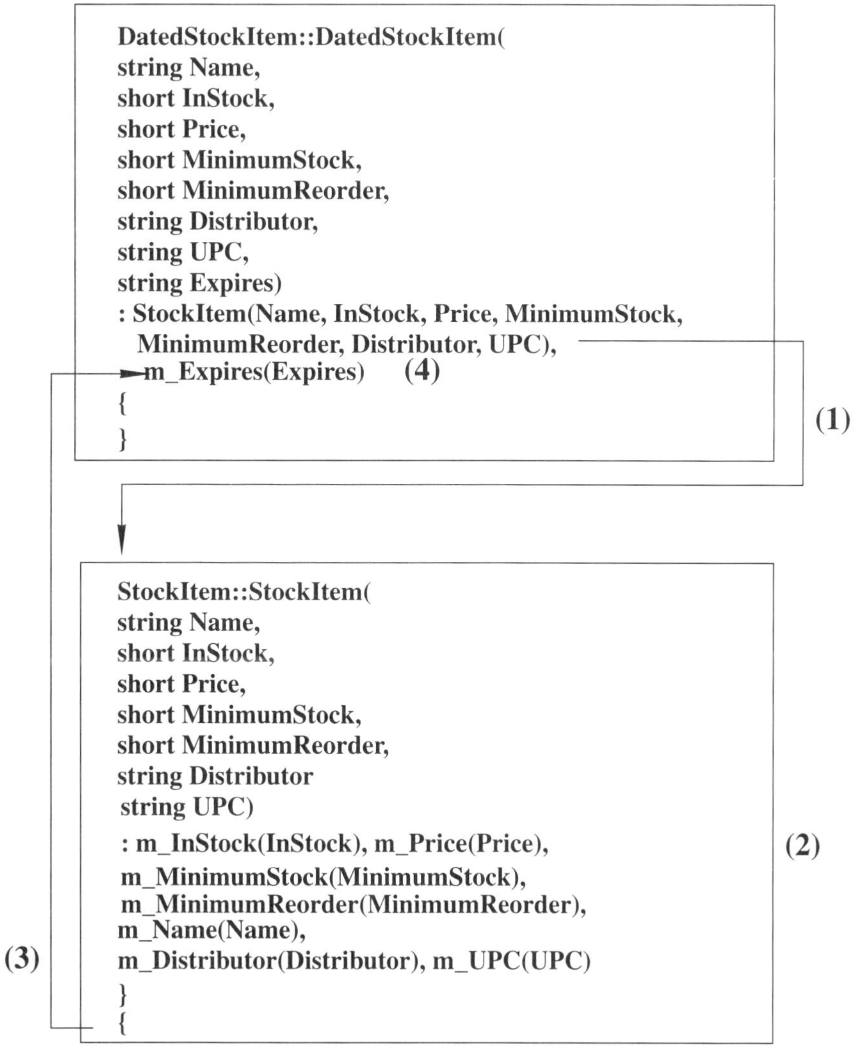
DatedStockItem::DatedStockItem(
string Name,
short InStock,
short Price,
short MinimumStock,
short MinimumReorder,
string Distributor,
string UPC,
string Expires)
: StockItem(Name, InStock, Price, MinimumStock,
MinimumReorder, Distributor, UPC),
m_Expires(Expires)
(4)
{
}
(1)
StockItem::StockItem(
string Name,
short InStock,
short Price,
short MinimumStock,
short MinimumReorder,
string Distributor
string UPC)
: m_InStock(InStock), m_Price(Price),
m_MinimumStock(MinimumStock),
m_MinimumReorder(MinimumReorder),
m_Name(Name),
m_Distributor(Distributor), m_UPC(UPC)
}
{
(2)
(3)

Susan wasn't immediately overwhelmed by the simplicity of this notion, so we discussed it:

**Susan:** How does all the information of step 3 get into step 4? And exactly what part of the code here is the base class initializer? I don't see which part it is.

**Steve:** The information from 3 gets into the derived class DatedStockItem object in the upper part of the diagram because the DatedStockItem object contains a base class part consisting of a StockItem object. That's the object being initialized by the call to the base class constructor caused by the base class initializer, which consists of the following two lines:

```
: StockItem(Name,InStock,Price,MinimumStock,
MinimumReorder, Distributor,UPC)
```

There's another reason besides simplicity for using a base class initializer rather than trying to initialize the member variables of the base class part of our object directly: It's much safer. If we initialized the base class variables ourselves, and if the base class definition were later changed to include some new variables initialized according to arguments to the normal constructor, we might very well neglect to modify our derived class code to initialize the new variables. On the other hand, if we used a base class initializer, and its arguments changed (as they presumably would if new variables needed to be initialized), a derived class constructor that called that initializer would no longer compile. That would alert us to the change we'd have to make.

## *Reordering Priorities*

Now that we have dealt with the constructors, let's take a look at the Reorder function (Figure 2.37).

**FIGURE 2.37.** Reorder **function for** DatedStockItem **(from code\item21.cc)**

```
void DatedStockItem::Reorder(ostream& os)
{
```

```
 if (m_Expires < Today())
  {
  os << "Return " << m_InStock;
  os << " units of " << m_Name;
  os << " with UPC " << m_UPC;
  os << " to " << m_Distributor << endl;
  m_InStock = 0;
  }

 StockItem::Reorder(os);
}
```

We have added a new piece of code that checks whether the expiration date on the current batch of product is before today's date; if that is the case, we create an output line indicating the product to be returned. But what about the "normal" case already dealt with in the base class Reorder function? That's taken care of by the line StockItem::Reorder(os);, which calls the StockItem::Reorder function, using the class name with the membership operator :: to specify the exact Reorder function we want to use. If we just wrote Reorder(os), that would call the function we're currently executing, a process known as *recursion*. Recursion has its uses in certain complex programming situations, but in this case, of course, it would not do what we wanted, as we have already handled the possibility of expired items. We need to deal with the "normal" case of running low on stock, which is handled very nicely by the base class Reorder function.

We shouldn't pass by this function without noting one more point: The only reason that we can access m_InStock and the other member variables of the StockItem base class part of our object is that those member variables are protected rather than private. If they were private, we wouldn't be able to access them in our DatedStockItem functions, even though every DatedStockItem object would still have such member variables.

Susan didn't care for that last statement, but I think I talked her into accepting it.

**Susan:** I can't picture the statement "even though every DatedStockItem object would still have such member variables."

**Steve:** Well, every DatedStockItem has a StockItem base class part, and that base class part contributes its member variables to the DatedStockItem. Even if we can't access them because they're private, they're still there.

Now we have a good solution to the creation of stock items with dates. Unfortunately, it's not possible to have a vector of dissimilar types — that is, our current solution can't handle a combination of StockItem and DatedStockItem objects. On the other hand, it is possible to have a vector of pointers that can refer to either StockItem or DatedStockItem objects, by making use of the characteristic of C++ that a pointer to a base class object can point to a derived class object.

However, using a vector of StockItem*s to point to a mixture of StockItem and DatedStockItem objects won't give us the results we want with the current definitions of these classes. To be precise, if we call Reorder through a StockItem*, the wrong version of Reorder will be called for DatedStockItem objects. To help explain why this is so, I've drawn a number of diagrams that show how C++ determines which function is called for a given type of pointer.

Before we get to the first diagram, there's one new construct that I should explain: the use of operator new for an object of a class type. The first example of this usage is the statement SIPtr = new StockItem("beans",40,110);. In this statement, we're creating a StockItem via the expression new StockItem("beans",40,110)[18] and then assigning the address returned by new to the variable SIPtr (whose name is supposed to represent "StockItem pointer"). It should be fairly obvious why we have to use operator new here: to allocate memory for the newly constructed object, just as we did when we used operator new to allocate memory for an array of chars when

18. The examples in this section use simplified versions of the StockItem and DatedStockItem classes to make the diagrams smaller; the principles are the same as with the full versions of these classes.

creating an object of our string class.[19] The only difference from that usage is that when we use operator new with a class object, we have to choose a constructor to create the object. Here we're specifying the arguments for the name, price, and number in stock. Since the "normal" constructor will accept such types of arguments, it's the one that will be called. On the other hand, if we hadn't supplied any arguments — for example, by writing SIPtr = new StockItem; — we'd get the default constructor.

Now that I've explained this use of new, let's look at Figure 2.38, which shows how a normal function call works when Reorder is called for a StockItem object through a StockItem pointer.

**FIGURE 2.38. Calling** Reorder **through a** StockItem **pointer, part 1**

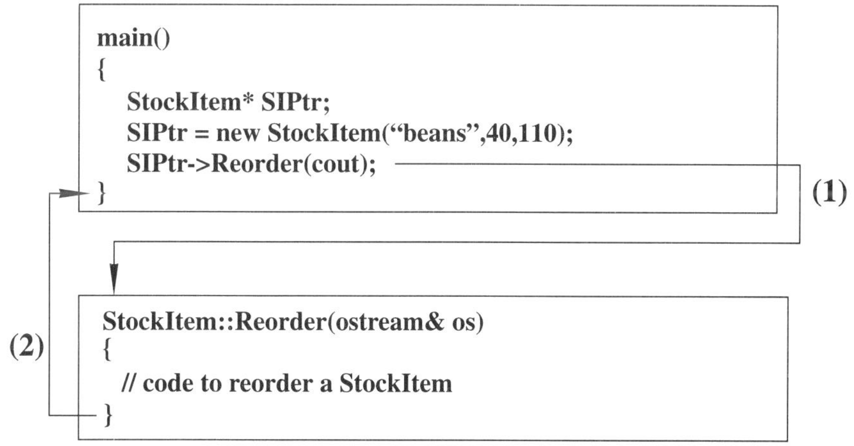
main()
{
StockItem* SIPtr;
SIPtr = new StockItem("beans",40,110);
SIPtr->Reorder(cout);
}
(1)
(2)
StockItem::Reorder(ostream& os)
{
// code to reorder a StockItem
}

Step 1 calls StockItem::Reorder via the StockItem* variable named SIPtr. When StockItem::Reorder finishes execution, it returns to the main program (step 2); since there isn't anything else to do in the main program, the program ends at that point.

19. This was covered in *Who's Afraid of C++?* and *The C++ Training Guide.*

Susan had a question about the syntax of the line SIPtr->Reorder(cout);.

**Susan:** What does that -> thing do?

**Steve:** It separates a pointer to an object (on its left) from a member variable or function (on its right). In this case, it separates the pointer SIPtr from the function Reorder, so that line says that we want to call the function Reorder for whatever object SIPtr is pointing to. In other words, it does for pointers exactly what "." does for objects.

So far, so good. Now let's see what happens when we call Reorder for a DatedStockItem object through a DatedStockItem pointer (Figure 2.39).

**FIGURE 2.39. Calling** Reorder **through a** DatedStockItem **pointer**

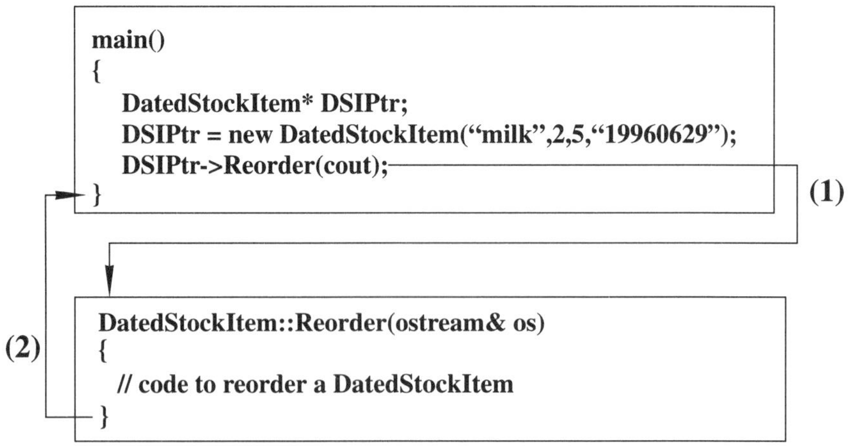
main()
{
DatedStockItem* DSIPtr;
DSIPtr = new DatedStockItem("milk",2,5,"19960629");
DSIPtr->Reorder(cout);
}
(1)
(2)
DatedStockItem::Reorder(ostream& os)
{
// code to reorder a DatedStockItem
}

In Figure 2.39, step 1 calls DatedStockItem::Reorder via DSIPtr, a variable of type DatedStockItem*. When DatedStockItem::Reorder finishes execution, it returns to the main program (step 2); again; since there isn't anything else to do in the main program, the program ends at that point. That looks okay, too. But what happens if we call Reorder for a DatedStockItem object through a StockItem pointer, as in Figure 2.40?

Unfortunately, step 1 in Figure 2.40 is incorrect because the line SIPtr->Reorder(cout) calls StockItem::Reorder whereas we wanted it to call DatedStockItem::Reorder. This problem arises because when we call a normal member function through a pointer, the compiler uses the declared type of the pointer to decide which actual function will be called. In this case, we've declared SIPtr to be a pointer to a StockItem, so even though the actual data type of the object it points to is DatedStockItem, the compiler thinks it's a StockItem. Therefore, the line SIPtr->Reorder(cout) results in a call to StockItem::Reorder.

**FIGURE 2.40. Calling** Reorder **through a** StockItem **pointer, part 2**

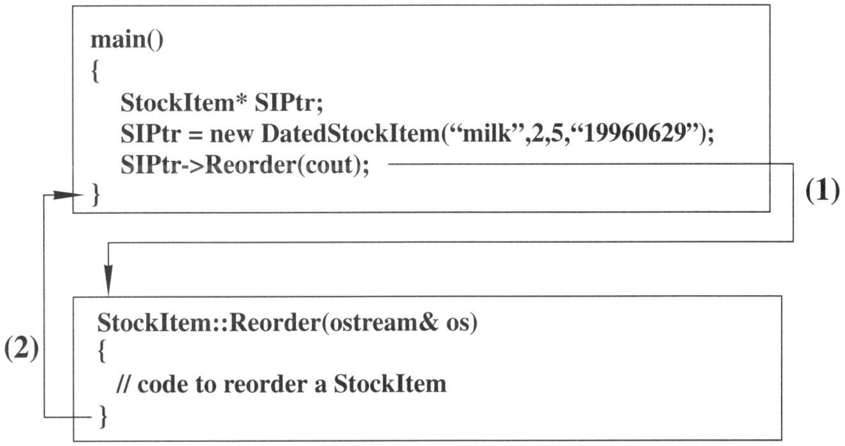
main()
{
StockItem* SIPtr;
SIPtr = new DatedStockItem("milk",2,5,"19960629");
SIPtr->Reorder(cout);
}
(1)
StockItem::Reorder(ostream& os)
(2)
{
// code to reorder a StockItem
}

Before we see how to fix this problem, we should look at a test program that actually uses these versions of the Reorder functions with the simplified versions of our StockItem and DatedStockItem classes we've been using for this discussion. Figure 2.41 shows the test program, Figure 2.42 shows the output of the test program, and Figure 2.43 shows the implementation of the classes.[20] (You may very well want to print out the files that contain this interface and its implementation, as well as the test program. Those files are code\itema.h, code\itema.cc, and code\nvirtual.cc, respectively.).

**FIGURE 2.41. Function call example (code\nvirtual.cc)**

```
#include <iostream.h>
#include "itema.h"

int main()
{
  StockItem StockItemObject("soup",32,100);
  StockItem* StockItemPointer;
  DatedStockItem DatedStockItemObject("milk",
   10,15,"19950110");

  DatedStockItem* DatedStockItemPointer;

  StockItemObject.Reorder(cout);
  cout << endl;
  DatedStockItemObject.Reorder(cout);
  cout << endl;

  StockItemPointer = new StockItem("beans",40,110);
  StockItemPointer->Reorder(cout);
  cout << endl;

  DatedStockItemPointer = new DatedStockItem("ham",
   22,30,"19970110");
  DatedStockItemPointer->Reorder(cout);
  cout << endl;

  StockItemPointer = new DatedStockItem("steak",
   90,95,"19960110");
  StockItemPointer->Reorder(cout);
```

20. The interface for these simplified StockItem and DatedStockItem classes was shown in Figure 2.8

```
  cout << endl;
}
```

**FIGURE 2.42. Function call example output (code\nvirtual.out)**

```
StockItem::Reorder says:
Reorder 68 units of soup

DatedStockItem::Reorder says:
Return 10 units of milk
StockItem::Reorder says:
Reorder 15 units of milk

StockItem::Reorder says:
Reorder 70 units of beans

StockItem::Reorder says:
Reorder 8 units of ham

StockItem::Reorder says:
Reorder 5 units of steak
```

**FIGURE 2.43. Simplified implementation for** StockItem **and** DatedStockItem classes **(code\itema.cc)**

```
#include <iostream.h>
#include <iomanip.h>
#include <strstream.h>
#include <string.h>
#include "itema.h"
#include <dos.h>

StockItem::StockItem(string Name, short InStock,
short MinimumStock)
: m_InStock(InStock), m_Name(Name),
  m_MinimumStock(MinimumStock)
{
```

```
}

void StockItem::Reorder(ostream& s)
{
short ActualReorderQuantity;

if (m_InStock < m_MinimumStock)
{
ActualReorderQuantity = m_MinimumStock - m_InStock;
s << "StockItem::Reorder says:" << endl;
s << "Reorder " << ActualReorderQuantity << " units of ";
s <<  m_Name << endl;
}
}

string DatedStockItem::Today()
{
  struct date d;
  unsigned short year;
  unsigned short day;
  unsigned short month;
  string TodaysDate;
  strstream FormatStream;

  getdate(&d);
  year = d.da_year;
  day = d.da_day;
  month = d.da_mon;

  FormatStream << setfill('0') << setw(4) << year <<
    setw(2) << month << setw(2) << day;
  FormatStream >> TodaysDate;

  return TodaysDate;
}

void DatedStockItem::Reorder(ostream& s)
{
short ReturnQuantity = 0;

if (m_Expires < Today())
```

```
{
s << "DatedStockItem::Reorder says:" << endl;
ReturnQuantity = m_InStock;
m_InStock = 0;
s << "Return " << ReturnQuantity <<  " units of ";
s << m_Name << endl;
}

StockItem::Reorder(s);
}

DatedStockItem::DatedStockItem(string Name, short InStock,
short MinimumStock, string Expires)
: StockItem(Name, InStock,MinimumStock),
  m_Expires(Expires)
{
}
```

There shouldn't be anything too surprising in this program. When we call the Reorder function for an object, we get the function for that type of object, and when we call the Reorder function through a pointer to an object, we get the function for that type of pointer. However, what we really want is to have the DatedStockItem version of Reorder called if the object in question is a DatedStockItem even if the pointer is of type StockItem*. We'll see how to solve that problem in the next chapter.

## *Review*

We started the chapter by defining a simple inventory control example that used a StockItem class and an Inventory class, including a function called ReorderItem that can be called for an Inventory object to produce a reordering report. This function calls a Reorder function for each StockItem in its StockItem vector to calculate the quantity of that StockItem to be ordered based on the desired and current stock.

Then we built on that StockItem class by adding an expiration date. Rather than copying all of the old code and class definitions, we made use of a concept that is essential to the full use of C++ for object-oriented programming — *inheritance*. Inheritance is a method of constructing one class (the derived class) by specifying how it differs from another class (the base class) rather than writing it from scratch. We used inheritance to create a new DatedStockItem class that had all of the capabilities of the StockItem class, adding the ability to handle items with expiration dates.

In the process, we wrote a new Reorder function with the same signature as that of the base class function of the same name. This is called *overriding* the base class function. When the function with that signature is called via an object of the base class, the base class function will be called. On the other hand, when the function with that signature is called via an object of the derived class, the derived class function will be called. This allows a derived class to supply the same functionality as that of a base class but to implement it in a different way.

A derived class object can do anything that a base class object can do because a derived class object actually contains an object of the base class, called the base class part of the derived class object. This base class part is very similar to a member variable in the derived class, but it is not the same for two reasons:

1. A member variable always has a name, whereas the base class part does not.
2. The base class definition can give derived class member functions privileged access to some member variables and functions of the base class part of an object of the derived class, by marking those member variables and functions protected.

In the process of writing the new Reorder function for the DatedStockItem class, we saw how we could store a date as a string that allowed comparison of two dates to see which was later. This required us to create a formatted string representing the date as

YYYYMMDD — that is, a four-digit year number, a two-digit month number, and a two-digit day number. Getting the current date wasn't too hard; we used the date variable type along with its associated getdate function to retrieve the year, month, and day of the current date. However, once we had this information, we still had to combine the parts of the date into a formatted string. One way to do this is to use the strstream data type, which is a stream that exists only in memory as a formatting aid. This topic led to a discussion of how we can specify the formatting of data rather than accept the default formatting, as we did previously; it also led to the related discussion of using the strstream class to generate formatted output.

After delving into the general topic of streams in more detail, we returned to the more specific issue of strstreams, which allowed us to solve our formatting problem by combining the << operator with the *manipulators* setw and setfill to control the width and *fill characters* of the data we wrote to the strstream.

Once we had used << to write the data to the strstream in the required YYYYMMDD format, we used >> to read it back into a string for comparison with the expiration date stored in a DatedStockItem object (see Figures 2.30 and 2.31).

After discussing the formatting of the date string, we continued by examining the default constructor of the DatedStockItem class. While this is an extremely short function, having only one member initialization expression and no code in the constructor proper, there is more to it than meets the eye. The default constructor deals only with the newly added member variable, m_Expires, but behind the scenes the base class part of the DatedStockItem object is being initialized by the default constructor of the base class — StockItem::StockItem(). The rule is that a base class constructor will always be called for the base class part of a derived class object. If we don't specify which base class constructor we want, the default constructor for the base class will be used. To select the constructor for the base class part, we can use a construct known as a base class initializer in the member initializer list in the derived class constructor. In our "normal" constructor for DatedStockItem, we used this construct to call the corresponding constructor for the base class (see Figures 2.35 and 2.36).

Then we looked at the Reorder function for the DatedStockItem class, which includes code to request the return of any items that are past their expiration date and calls the base class Reorder function to handle the rest of the job.

At that point, we had a working DatedStockItem class, but we still couldn't mix StockItem and DatedStockItem objects in the same vector. However, it was possible to create a vector of pointers to StockItems; once we did that, we could make any of those pointers point to a DatedStockItem, employing the C++ feature that a base class pointer can also point to an object of a derived class. After seeing how to use operator new to allocate StockItem and DatedStockItem variables, we discovered that just using a base class pointer doesn't do what we wanted. As these classes are currently defined, the version of the Reorder function called through a StockItem pointer is always the base class version, rather than the correct version for the actual type of the object the pointer refers to.

## *Exercises*

1. Suppose that the store using our inventory control program adds a new pharmacy department. Most of their items are nonprescription medications that can be handled with the DatedStockItem class we already created, but their prescription drug items need to be handled more carefully. This means that the DeductSaleFromInventory member function has to ask for a password before allowing the sale to take place. Create a new DrugStockItem class that enforces this new rule without using inheritance.

2. The store also needs some way to keep track of its employees' hours so it can calculate their pay. We'll assume that the employees are paid their gross wages, ignoring taxes. These wages are calculated as follows:

   a. Managers are paid a flat amount per week, calculated as their hourly rate multiplied by 40 hours.

   b. Hourly employees are paid a certain amount per hour no matter how many hours they work (i.e., overtime is not paid at a higher rate).

   Write an Employee class that allows the creation of Employee objects with a specified hourly wage level and either "manager" or "hourly" salary rules. The pay for each object is to be calculated via a CalculatePay member function that uses the "manager" or "hourly" category specified when the object was created. Use the double data type to keep track of the pay rate and the total pay.[21]

3. Rewrite the DrugStockItem class from Exercise 1 using inheritance from the DatedStockItem class.

4. Rewrite the Employee class from Exercise 2 as two classes: the base Exempt class and an Hourly class derived from the base class. The CalculatePay member function for each of these classes should use the appropriate method of calculating the pay for each class. In particular, this member function doesn't need an argument specifying the number of hours worked for the Exempt class, while the corresponding member function in the Hourly class does need such an argument.

5. Rewrite the Employee class that you wrote in Exercise 2 as two classes: the base Exempt class and an Hourly class derived from the base class. To maintain the same interface for these two classes,

21. This data type is just like a short, except that it can handle larger numbers, including those with fractional parts. See the Glossary for details on this data type.

the CalculatePay member function in both classes should have an argument specifying the number of hours worked. The implementation of the Exempt class will ignore this argument, while the Hourly implementation will use it.

6. Write an essay comparing the advantages and disadvantages of the two approaches to inheritance in the previous two exercises.[22]

7. Reimplement the DatedStockItem class to use a long variable of the form YYYYMMDD, rather than a string, to store the date.[23] Is this a better approach than using a string? Why or why not?

8. Rewrite the operator << functions for DatedStockItem and StockItem so that the former function uses the latter to display the common data items for the two classes, rather than display all the data items itself.

## *Conclusion*

In this chapter, we defined a StockItem class and then extended the functionality provided in that class by deriving a new class, DatedStockItem, based on StockItem.

However, we have not yet seen how objects of these two classes can be used interchangeably. Although we can use base class pointers to point to objects of both base and derived types, we can't yet arrange for the correct function to be called based on the actual type of the object to which the pointer refers. In Chapter 3, we will see how to overcome this barrier.

22. If you'll e-mail this essay to me, I might put it on my WWW page!

23. A long is just like a short, except that it can hold larger numbers. See the Glossary for details on this type.

CHAPTER 3

# Pretty Poly

By the end of the previous chapter, we had created a DatedStockItem class by inheritance from the StockItem class, adding an expiration date field. This was a fine solution to the problem of creating a new class based on the existing StockItem class without rewriting all of the already functioning code in that class. Unfortunately, however, it didn't allow us to mix objects of the original StockItem class in the same vector with those of the new DatedStockItem class and still have the correct Reorder function called for the derived class object. So far, we've been using the first two major organizing principles of object-oriented programming: *encapsulation* and *inheritance*. Now our requirement of mixing base and derived class objects leads us to the third and final major organizing principle: *polymorphism*. Once we have defined some terms, we'll get right to using polymorphism to solve our problem of freely interchanging StockItems and DatedStockItems in our application programs.

## *Definitions*

**Static typing** means determining the exact type of a variable when the program is compiled. It is the default typing mechanism in C++. Note that this has no particular relation to the keyword static.

**Dynamic typing** means delaying the determination of the exact type of a variable until run time rather than fixing that type at compile time, as in static typing.

**Polymorphism**, one of the major organizing principles in C++, allows us to implement several classes with the same interface and treat objects of all these classes as though they were of the same class. Polymorphism is a variety of *dynamic typing* that maintains the safety factor of *static type-checking*, because the compiler can determine at compile time whether a function call is legal even if it does not know the exact type of the object that will receive that function call at run time. *Polymorphism* is derived from the Greek *poly*, meaning "many", and *morph*, meaning "form". In other words, the same behavior is implemented in different forms.

Declaring a function to be **virtual** means that it is a member of a set of functions having the same signatures and belonging to classes related by inheritance. The actual function to be executed as the result of a given function call is selected from this set of functions dynamically (i.e., at run time) based on the actual type of an object referred to via a base class pointer (or base class reference). This is the C++ *dynamic typing* mechanism used to implement polymorphism, in contrast to the *static typing* used for nonvirtual functions, which are selected at compile time.

**Reference counting** is a mechanism that allows one copy of an object to be shared among a number of users while arranging for the automatic disposal of that object as soon as no one is using it.

## *Objectives of This Chapter*

By the end of this chapter, you should

1. understand how we can use polymorphism to allow objects of different classes to be treated interchangeably by the user of these classes,
2. understand how to create a polymorphic object that allows polymorphism to be used safely in application programs without exposing the class user to the hazards of pointers, and
3. understand how to use *reference counting* to allow one data item to be safely shared among several users.

## *Polymorphism*

To select the correct function to be called based on the actual type of an object at run time, we have to use polymorphism. Polymorphic behavior of our StockItem and DatedStockItem classes means that we can (for example) mix StockItem and DatedStockItem objects in a vector and have the right Reorder function executed for each object in the vector.

Susan had a question about the relationship between base and derived classes:

> **Susan:** What do the base and derived classes share besides an interface?
>
> **Steve:** The derived class contains all of the member variables of the base class and can call any of the member functions of the base class. Of course, the derived class can also add whatever new member functions and member variables it needs.

Susan also had a question about this idea of mixing objects of two different types:

**Susan:** Why would you want to handle several different types of data as though they were the same type?

**Steve:** Because the objects of these two classes perform the same operation, although in a slightly different way, which is why they can have the same interface. In our example, a DatedStockItem acts just like a StockItem except that it has an additional data field and produces different reordering information. Ideally, we would be able to mix these two types in the application program without having to worry about which class each object belongs to except when creating an individual item (at which time we have to know whether the item has an expiration date).

However, there is a serious complication in using polymorphism: We have to refer to the objects via a pointer rather than directly.[1] While C++ does have a "native" means of doing this, it exposes us to all the dangers of pointers, both those that you're already acquainted with and others that we'll get to later in this chapter.

Susan wanted more details on why pointers are dangerous; here's the first installment of our discussion of this point.

**Susan:** You keep saying that pointers are dangerous; what do they do that is so dangerous?

**Steve:** It's not what they do but what their users do: mostly, create memory leaks and dangling pointers (which point to memory that has already been freed).

**Susan:** So pointers are dangerous because it is just too easy to make mistakes when you use them?

**Steve:** Yes.

---

1. We could also use a reference, as we'll see in the implementation of the << and >> operators. However, that still wouldn't provide the flexibility of using real objects.

The ideal solution to this problem is to confine pointers to the interior of classes we design so that we can keep track of them ourselves and let the application programmer worry about getting the job done. As it happens, this is possible; thus, we can obtain the benefits of polymorphism without exposing the application programmer (as opposed to the class designers; i.e., us) to the hazards of pointers. We'll see how to do that later in this chapter.

But before investigating that more sophisticated method of providing polymorphism, we need to understand the workings of the native polymorphism mechanism in C++. As we saw in Chapter 2, the address of a derived class object can be assigned to a pointer of its base class. While this does not by itself solve the problem of calling the correct function in these circumstances, there is a way to get the behavior we want. If we define a special kind of function called a virtual function and refer to it through a pointer (or a reference) to an object, the version of that function to be executed will be determined by the actual type of the object to which the pointer (or reference) refers, rather than by the declared type of the pointer (or reference). This implies that if we declare a function to be virtual, when a function with that signature is called via a base class pointer the actual function to be called is selected at run time rather than at compile time, as happens with nonvirtual functions. Clearly, if the actual run-time type of the object determines which version of the function is called, the compiler can't select the function at compile time.

Because the determination of the function to be called is delayed until run time, the compiler has to add code to each function call to make that determination. This code uses a construct called a vtable to keep track of the locations of all the functions for a given type of object so that the compiler-generated code can find the right function when the call is about to be executed.

As you might imagine, Susan had some questions about this notion of virtual function calls.

**Susan:** I don't understand how the function to be executed is selected.

**Steve:** The mechanism depends on whether it is a virtual function. If not, the linker can figure out the exact address of the function when it is linking the program, because the type of the pointer (which is known at compile time) is used. On the other hand, with a virtual function declaration, the function to be executed depends on the actual type of the object pointed to rather than the type of the pointer to the object; since that information can't be known at compile time, the linker can't do it. Therefore, in such cases the compiler sticks code in the executable program that figures it out at run time by consulting the vtable for the particular type of object the base class pointer refers to.

## virtual *Certainty*

But exactly how does this help us with our Reorder function? Let's see how a virtual function affects the behavior of our final example program from Chapter 2 (nvirtual.cc, Figure 2.41). Figure 3.1 shows the same interface as before, except that StockItem::Reorder is declared to be virtual.[2] Because the current test program (virtual.cc) and implementation file (itemb.cc) are almost identical to the final test program (nvirtual.cc) and implementation file (itema.cc) in Chapter 2, differing only in that the new ones #include itemb.h rather than itema.h, I haven't reproduced the new versions of those files here.

If you printed out the corresponding files from the previous chapter, you might just want to mark them up to indicate these changes. Otherwise, I strongly recommend that you print out the files that contain this interface and its implementation, as well as the test

2. You will notice that the virtual declaration for Reorder is repeated in DatedStockItem — this is optional. Even if you don't write virtual again in the derived class declaration of Reorder, it's still a virtual function in that class; the rule is "once virtual, always virtual". Even so, I think it's clearer to specify that the derived class function is virtual, so that's how I will show it in this book.

program, for reference as you go through this section of the chapter; those files are itemb.h, itemb.cc, and virtual.cc, respectively.

**FIGURE 3.1. Dangerous polymorphism: Interfaces of StockItem and DatedStockItem with virtual Reorder function (code\itemb.h)**

```
// itemb.h

#include "string6.h"

class StockItem
{
public:
StockItem(string Name, short InStock, short MinimumStock);
virtual void Reorder(ostream& s);

protected:
string m_Name;
short m_InStock;
short m_MinimumStock;
};

class DatedStockItem: public StockItem // deriving a new class
{
public:
DatedStockItem(string Name, short InStock, short MinimumStock,
string Expires);

virtual void Reorder(ostream& s);

protected:
static string Today();

protected:
string m_Expires;
};
```

Figure 3.2 shows the output of the new test program.

**FIGURE 3.2.** virtual **function call example output (code\virtual.out)**

```
StockItem::Reorder says:
Reorder 68 units of soup

DatedStockItem::Reorder says:
Return 10 units of milk
StockItem::Reorder says:
Reorder 15 units of milk

StockItem::Reorder says:
Reorder 70 units of beans

StockItem::Reorder says:
Reorder 8 units of ham

DatedStockItem::Reorder says:
Return 90 units of steak
StockItem::Reorder says:
Reorder 95 units of steak
```

Notice that the output of this program is exactly the same as the output of the previous test program except for the last entry. With the nonvirtual Reorder function in the previous program, we got the following output:

```
StockItem::Reorder says:
Reorder 5 units of steak
```

whereas with our virtual Reorder function, we get this output:

```
DatedStockItem::Reorder says:
Return 90 units of steak
StockItem::Reorder says:
Reorder 95 units of steak
```

According to our rules, the correct answer is 95 units of steak because the stock has expired, so the program that uses the virtual Reorder function works correctly while the previous one didn't. Why is this? Because when we call a virtual function through a base class pointer, the function executed is the one defined in the class of the actual object to which the pointer points, not the one defined in the class of the pointer.

To see how this works, let's start by looking at the way in which the layout of an object with virtual functions differs from that of a "normal" object. First, Figure 3.3 shows a possible memory representation of a simplified StockItem without virtual functions.

**FIGURE 3.3. A simplified StockItem object without virtual functions**

| Address | Name | |
|---|---|---|
| 12340000 | m_Name | "soup" |
| 12340004 | m_InStock | 0005 |
| 12340006 | m_MinimumStock | 0008 |

StockItem member functions

| Address | Name |
|---|---|
| 12350000 | StockItem(string, short, short) |
| 12351000 | Reorder(ostream&) |

One of the interesting points about this figure is that there is no connection at run time between the StockItem object and its functions. Such a connection is unnecessary because the compiler can tell exactly which function will be called whenever a function is referenced for this object, whether directly or through a pointer.

The situation is different if we have virtual functions. In that case, the compiler can't decide exactly which functions will be called for an object pointed to by a StockItem* because the actual object may be a descendant of StockItem rather than an actual StockItem. If so, we want the function defined in the derived class (e.g., DatedStockItem) to be called even though the pointer is declared to point to an object of the base class (e.g., StockItem).

Since the actual type of the object for which we want to call the function isn't available at compile time, another way must be found to determine which function should be called. The most logical place to store this information is in the object itself because, after all, we need to know where the object is in order to call the function for it. In fact, an object of a class for which any virtual functions are declared does have an extra data item in it for exactly this purpose. So whenever a call to a virtual function is compiled, the compiler translates that call into instructions that use the information in the object to determine at run time which version of the virtual function will be called.

As you might imagine, virtual functions were a major point of discussion with Susan. Here's the first installment of that discussion:

> **Susan:** So, is a virtual function polymorphism?
>
> **Steve:** No. You need virtual functions to implement polymorphism in C++, but they're not the same thing.
>
> **Susan:** Where in the definition of Reorder does it say it's virtual? The implementation file is the same as it was before.
>
> **Steve:** It's in the declaration of Reorder in the interface of the StockItem class in the itemb.h header file: virtual void Reorder(ostream& os);. I've also repeated it in the derived class function declaration even though that's not strictly necessary. After a function is declared as virtual in a base class, we don't have to say it's virtual in the derived class or classes; the rule is "once virtual, always virtual".

If every object needed to contain the addresses of all its virtual functions, objects might be a lot larger than they would otherwise have to be. However, this is not necessary because all objects of the same class have the same virtual functions. Therefore, the addresses of all of the virtual functions for a given class are stored in a virtual function address table, or vtable for short, and every object of that class contains the address of the vtable for that class.

Given this description of the vtable, if we make the Reorder function virtual, a StockItem object will look like Figure 3.4.[3]

**FIGURE 3.4. Dangerous polymorphism: A simplified StockItem object with a virtual function**

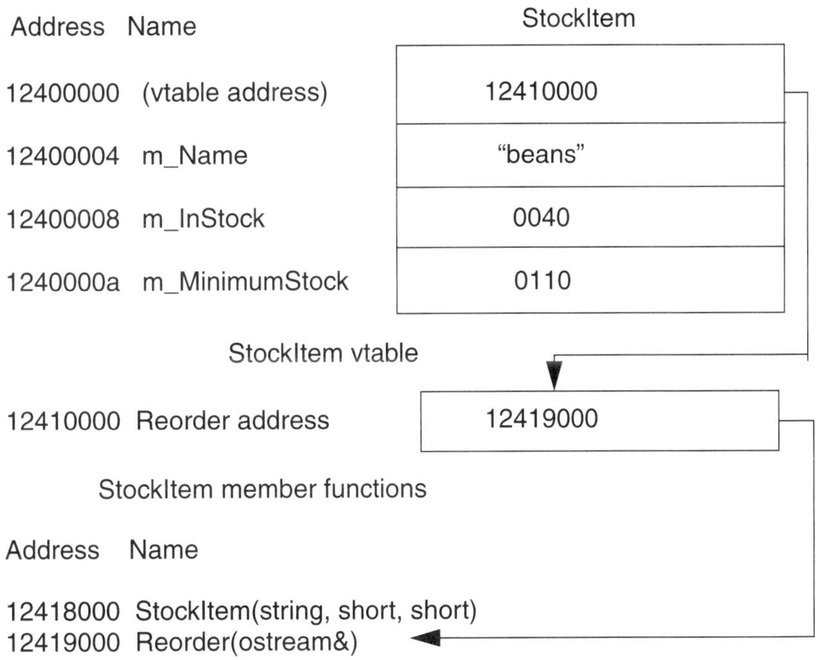


On the other hand, a DatedStockItem will look something like Figure 3.5.

3. Please note that the layout of this figure and other similar figures has been simplified by the omission of the details of the m_Name field, which actually contains a pointer to the data of the string value of that field.

**FIGURE 3.5. Dangerous polymorphism: A simplified** DatedStockItem **object with a** virtual **function**

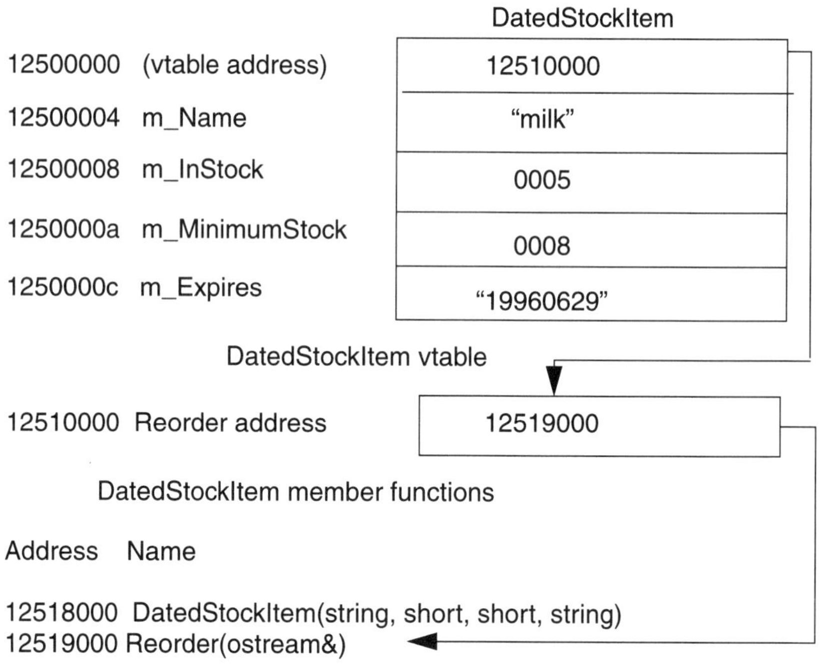


Susan had some more questions about vtables, and I had some more answers:

**Susan:** Are vtables customized for each class?

**Steve:** Yes.

**Susan:** Where do they come from, how are they created, and how do they do what they do?

**Steve:** The linker creates them based on instructions from the compiler after the compiler examines the class definition. All they do is store the addresses of the virtual functions for that class so that the compiler can generate code that will select the correct function for the object being referred to at run time.

**Susan:** How is this stuff different from derivation?

**Steve:** It's part of making derivation work correctly when we want to use pointers to the base class and mix base and derived class objects in our program.

**Susan:** I don't get this vtable stuff. Does it just point the Reorder function in the proper direction at run time?

**Steve:** Exactly!

**Susan:** This stuff is beyond "UGH!". It is just outrageous, and I can't believe that you understand this stuff.

**Steve:** It wasn't that easy for me either. Acquiring a full understanding of virtual functions is one of the major milestones in learning C++, even for programmers with substantial experience in other languages.

Now that we have declared Reorder as a virtual function, let's see how this affects the operation of the function call examples we saw in Chapter 2 (Figures 2.38 through 2.40). First, Figure 3.6 shows how a virtual (i.e., dynamically determined) function call works when Reorder is called for a StockItem object through a StockItem pointer such as SIPtr.

Next, Figure 3.7 shows how a virtual (i.e., dynamically determined) function call works when Reorder is called for a DatedStockItem object through a DatedStockItem pointer.

Finally, Figure 3.8 shows how a virtual (i.e., dynamically determined) function call works when Reorder is called for a DatedStockItem object through a StockItem pointer.

**FIGURE 3.6. Dangerous polymorphism: Calling a** virtual Reorder **function through a** StockItem **pointer to a** StockItem **object**

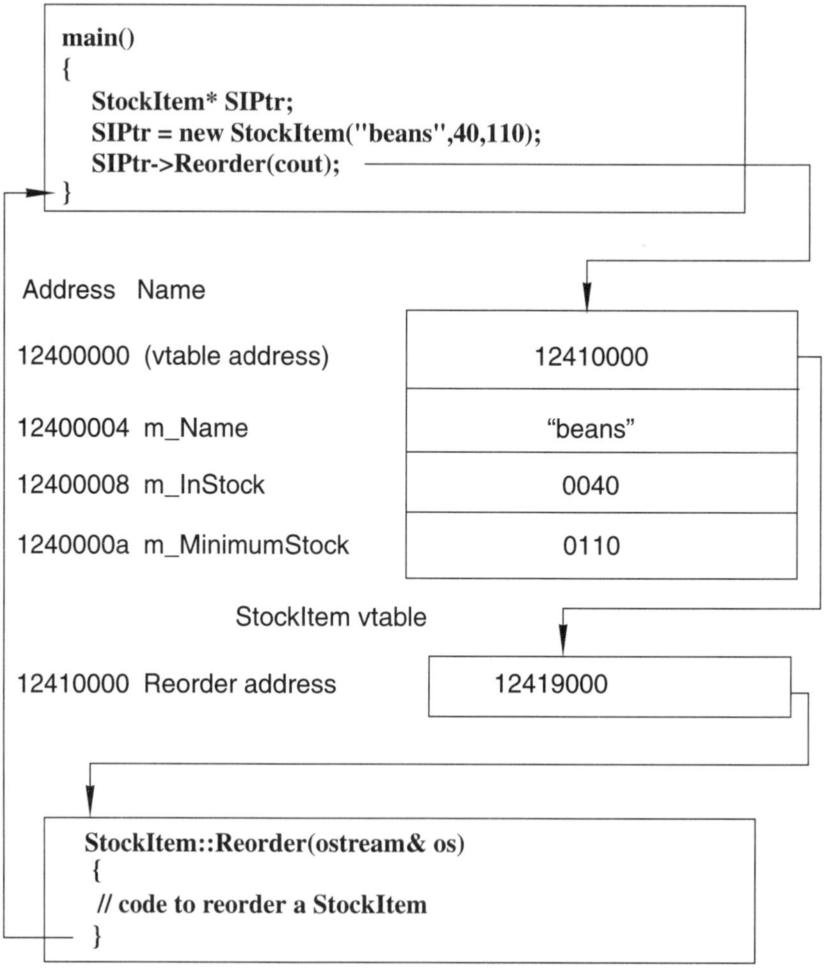


The net result of the call illustrated in Figure 3.6 is the same as that illustrated in Figure 2.38 — StockItem::Reorder is called. As before, this is what we want in this situation.

FIGURE 3.7. **Dangerous polymorphism: Calling a** virtual Reorder **function through a** DatedStockItem **pointer to a** DatedStockItem **object**

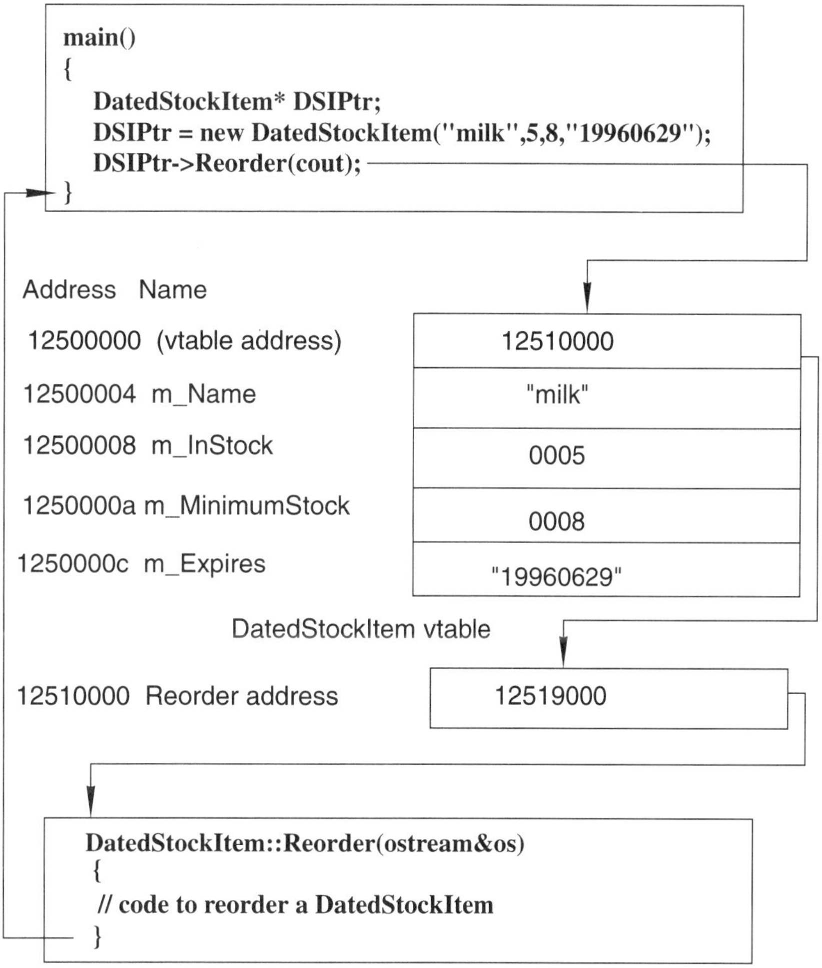


Again, the net result of the call illustrated in Figure 3.7 is the same as that illustrated in Figure 2.39 — DatedStockItem::Reorder is called. This is correct in this situation.

**FIGURE 3.8. Dangerous polymorphism: Calling a** virtual Reorder **function through a** StockItem **pointer to a** DatedStockItem **object**

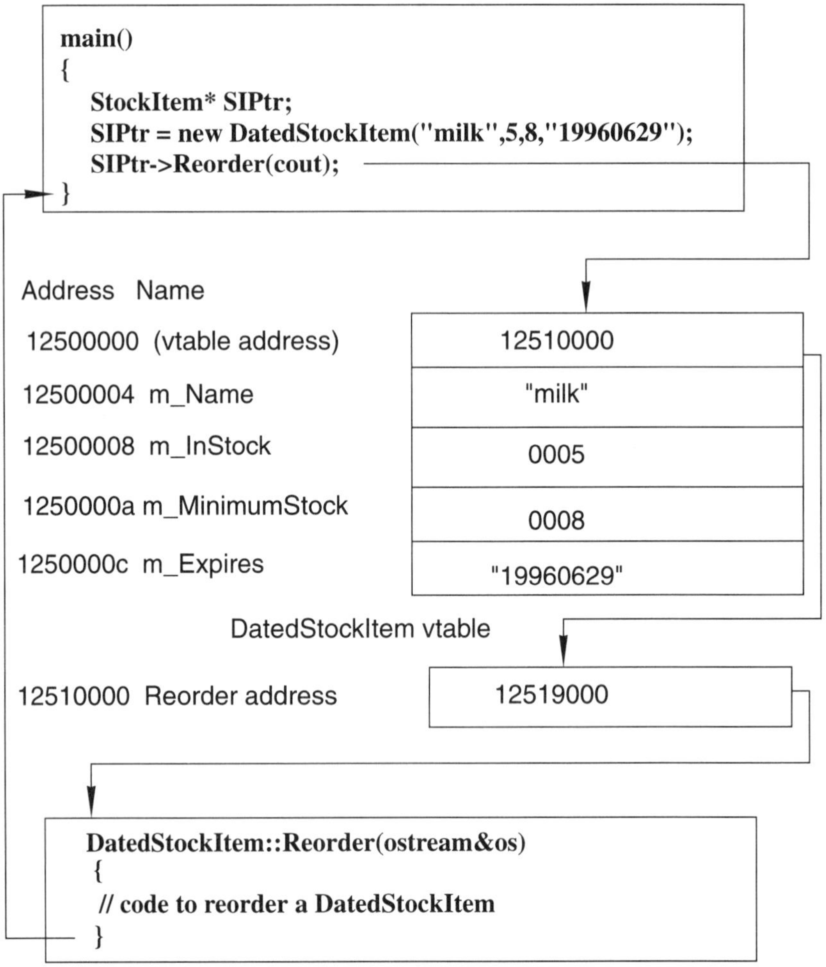


Figure 3.8 is where the virtual function pays off. The correct function, DatedStockItem::Reorder, is called even though the type of the pointer through which it is called is StockItem*. This is in contrast to the result of that same call with the non-virtual function, illustrated

in Figure 2.40. In that case, StockItem::Reorder rather than DatedStockItem::Reorder was called.

What happens if we add another virtual function, say Write, to the StockItem class after the Reorder function? The new virtual function will be added to the vtables for both the StockItem and DatedStockItem classes. Then the situation for a StockItem object might look like Figure 3.9.

**FIGURE 3.9. Dangerous polymorphism: A simplified StockItem object with two virtual functions**

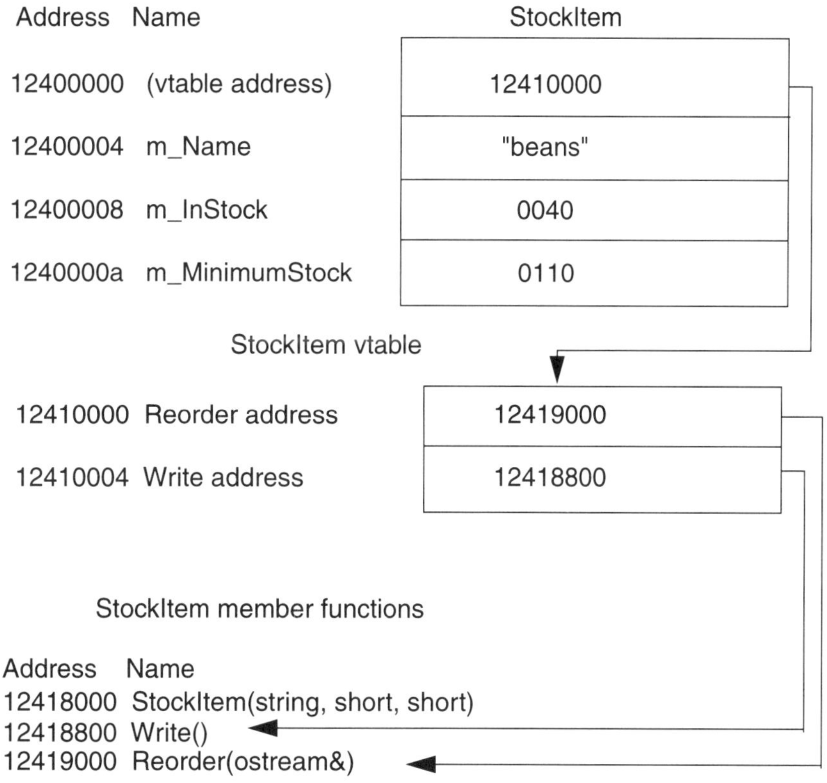


And the situation for a DatedStockItem might look like Figure 3.10.

**FIGURE 3.10. Dangerous polymorphism: A simplified DatedStockItem with two virtual functions**

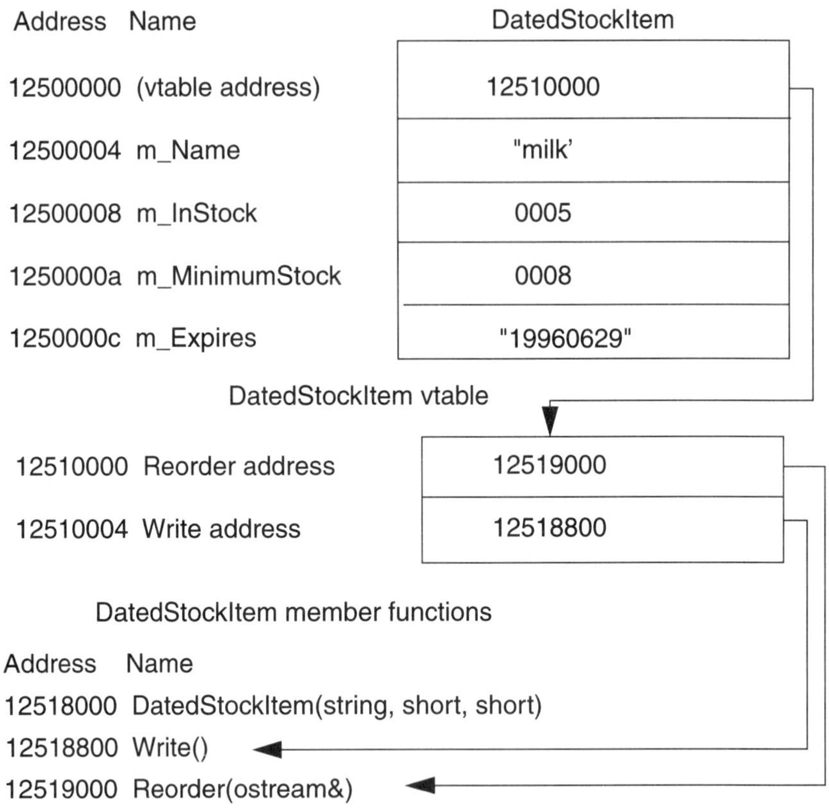


As you can see, the new function has been added to both vtables, so a call to Write through a base class pointer will call the correct function.

To translate this virtual function mechanism into what I hope is understandable English, we can express the call to the virtual function Write in the line SIPtr->Write(cout); as follows:

1. Get the vtable address from the object whose address is in SIPtr.
2. Since we are calling Write through a StockItem*, and Write is the second defined virtual function in the StockItem class, retrieve the address of the Write function from the second function address slot in the vtable for the actual object that the StockItem* points to.
3. Execute the function at that address.

By following this sequence, you can see that while both versions of Write are referred to via the same relative position in both the StockItem and the DatedStockItem vtables, the particular version of Write executed depends on which vtable the object refers to. Since all objects of the same class have the same member functions, all StockItem objects point to the same StockItem vtable and all DatedStockItem objects point to the same DatedStockItem vtable.

Susan had some questions about adding a new virtual function:

> **Susan:** What do you mean by "added to both vtables"? Do StockItem and DatedStockItem each have their own?
>
> **Steve:** Yes.
>
> **Susan:** How does the vtable get the address for the new StockItems?
>
> **Steve:** It's the other way around. Each StockItem, when it's created by the constructor, has its vtable address filled in by the compiler automatically.

## *A Pointed Reminder*

Unfortunately, it's not quite as simple to make polymorphism work for us as this might suggest. As is so often the case, the culprit is the use of pointers. To see how pointers cause trouble with polymorphism, let's start by adding the standard I/O functions, operator << and operator >>, to our simplified interface for the

StockItem and DatedStockItem classes. Figure 3.11 shows a test program illustrating how we can use these new functions, Figure 3.12 shows the output of the test program, and Figure 3.13 shows the new version of the interface. I strongly recommend that you print out that header file and the test program for reference as you leaf through this section of the chapter; the latter file is polyioa.cc.

**FIGURE 3.11. Dangerous polymorphism: Using** operator << **with a** StockItem* **(code\polyioa.cc)**

```
#include <iostream.h>
#include "vector.h"
#include "itemc.h"

int main()
{
  vector <StockItem*> x(2);

  x[0] = new StockItem("3-ounce cups",71,78);

  x[1] = new DatedStockItem("milk",76,87,"19970719");

  cout << "A StockItem: " << endl;
  cout << x[0] << endl;

  cout << "A DatedStockItem: " << endl;
  cout << x[1] << endl;

  delete x[0];
  delete x[1];

  return 0;
}
```

FIGURE 3.12. **Result of using** operator << **with a** StockItem* **(code\polyioa.out)**

```
A StockItem:
0
3-ounce cups
71
78

A DatedStockItem:
19970719
milk
76
87
```

FIGURE 3.13. **Dangerous polymorphism:** StockItem **interface with** operator << **and** operator >> **(code\itemc.h)**

```
#include "string6.h"

class StockItem
{
friend ostream& operator << (ostream& os, StockItem* Item);
friend istream& operator >> (istream& is, StockItem*& Item);

public:
   StockItem(string Name, short InStock, short MinimumStock);
virtual ~StockItem();

virtual void Reorder(ostream& os);
virtual void Write(ostream& os);

protected:
   string m_Name;
   short m_InStock;
   short m_MinimumStock;
};
```

```
class DatedStockItem: public StockItem
{
public:
   DatedStockItem(string Name, short InStock,
    short MinimumStock, string Expires);

virtual void Reorder(ostream& os);
virtual void Write(ostream& os);

protected:
static string Today();

protected:
   string m_Expires;
};
```

Susan had some questions about the StockItem::~StockItem destructor declared in this latest version of the interface.

**Susan:** Why do we need a destructor for StockItem now, when we didn't need one before?

**Steve:** The reason we haven't needed a destructor for the StockItem class until now is that the compiler-generated destructor works fine as long as two conditions are both present. First, the member variables of the class must all be of concrete data types (which they are here). Second, the class must have no virtual functions, which of course isn't true for StockItem anymore. We've discussed the reason for the first condition: If we have member variables that aren't of concrete data types (e.g., pointers), they won't clean up after themselves properly. We'll find out exactly why the second condition is important as soon as we get through looking at the output of the sample program.

**Susan:** Okay, I'm sure I can wait. But why is it virtual?

**Steve:** We'll cover that at the same time.

The first item of note in the test program in Figure 3.11 is that we can create a vector of StockItem*s to hold the addresses of any mixture of StockItems and DatedStockItems, because we can assign the addresses of variables of either of those types to a base class pointer (i.e., a StockItem*). Once we have the vector of StockItem*s, we use operator new to acquire the memory for whichever type of object we're creating. This allows us to access these objects via pointers rather than directly and thus to use polymorphism. Once we finish using the objects, we have to make sure they are properly disposed of by calling operator delete at the end of the program; otherwise, a memory leak results.

The calls to delete in Figure 3.11 also hold the key to Susan's question about why we needed to write a destructor for this new version of the StockItem class. You see, when we call operator delete for an object of class type, delete calls the destructor for that object to do whatever cleanup is necessary at the end of the object's lifespan. For this reason, it is very important that the correct destructor is called. If a base class destructor instead of a derived class destructor were called, the cleanup of the fields defined in the derived class wouldn't occur. However, when we delete a derived class object through a base class pointer, as we are doing in the current example program, the compiler can't tell at compile time which destructor it should call when the program executes. What do we do when we need to delay the determination of a function call until run time? We use a virtual function. Therefore, whenever we want to call delete on an object through a base class pointer, we need to make the destructor for that object virtual.[4]

But that still doesn't explain exactly why we need a virtual destructor whenever we have any other virtual functions. The reason

4. There's one more fine point that I should address here: If a base class destructor is virtual, the destructors in all classes derived from that class will also automatically be virtual, so we don't have to make them virtual explicitly.

for that rule is that there isn't much point in referring to an object through a base class pointer if it doesn't have any virtual functions, because the correct function will never be called in that case! Therefore, although the strict rule is "the destructor must be virtual if there are any calls to delete through a base class pointer", that amounts to the same thing as "the destructor must be virtual if there are any other virtual functions in the class", and that's easier to remember and follow.

Now let's take a look at the new implementation of the StockItem class, which is shown in Figure 3.14. This code is in code\itemc.cc if you want to print it out for reference.

**FIGURE 3.14. Dangerous polymorphism:** StockItem **implementation with** operator << **and** operator >> **(code\itemc.cc)**

```
#include <iostream.h>
#include <iomanip.h>
#include <strstream.h>
#include <string.h>
#include "itemc.h"
#include <dos.h>

StockItem::StockItem(string Name, short InStock,
short MinimumStock)
: m_InStock(InStock), m_Name(Name),
  m_MinimumStock(MinimumStock)
{
}

StockItem::~StockItem()
{
}

void StockItem::Reorder(ostream& os)
{
  short ReorderAmount;

  if (m_InStock < m_MinimumStock)
```

```
    {
    ReorderAmount = m_MinimumStock-m_InStock;
    os << "Reorder " << ReorderAmount << " units of " << m_Name;
    }
}

ostream& operator << (ostream& os, StockItem* Item)
{
    Item->Write(os);
    return os;
}

void StockItem::Write(ostream& os)
{
    os << 0 << endl;
    os << m_Name << endl;
    os << m_InStock << endl;
    os << m_MinimumStock << endl;
}

istream& operator >> (istream& is, StockItem*& Item)
{
    string Expires;
    short InStock;
    short MinimumStock;
    string Name;

    is >> Expires;
    is >> Name;
    is >> InStock;
    is >> MinimumStock;

    if (Expires == "0")
        Item = new StockItem(Name,InStock,MinimumStock);
    else
        Item = new DatedStockItem(Name,InStock,
        MinimumStock,Expires);

    return is;
```

```
}

void DatedStockItem::Reorder(ostream& os)
{
   if (m_Expires < Today())
      {
      os << "DatedStockItem::Reorder says:" << endl;
      os << "Return " << m_InStock <<  " units of ";
      os << m_Name << endl;
      m_InStock = 0;
      }

   StockItem::Reorder(os);
}

string DatedStockItem::Today()
{
  struct date d;
  unsigned short year;
  unsigned short day;
  unsigned short month;
  string TodaysDate;
  strstream FormatStream;

  getdate(&d);
  year = d.da_year;
  day = d.da_day;
  month = d.da_mon;

  FormatStream << setfill('0') << setw(4) << year <<
   setw(2) << month << setw(2) << day;
  FormatStream >> TodaysDate;

  return TodaysDate;
}

DatedStockItem::DatedStockItem(string Name, short InStock,
short MinimumStock, string Expires)
: StockItem(Name, InStock,MinimumStock),
```

```
  m_Expires(Expires)
{
}

void DatedStockItem::Write(ostream& os)
{
   os << m_Expires << endl;
   os << m_Name << endl;
   os << m_InStock << endl;
   os << m_MinimumStock << endl;
}
```

Susan had some questions about the test program and how it relates to the implementation.

**Susan:** Why do you need the same headers in the test program as you do in the implementations?

**Steve:** Because otherwise the compiler doesn't know how to allocate memory for a StockItem or what functions it can perform.

**Susan:** I didn't know that the use of headers also allocates memory.

**Steve:** It doesn't. However, the compiler needs the headers to figure out how large every object is so it can allocate storage for each object.

**Susan:** How does it figure that out?

**Steve:** It adds up the sizes of all the components in the object you're defining. For example, if you've defined a StockItem to contain three shorts and two strings, then the size of a StockItem object will be equal to the size of three shorts plus the size of two strings, with possibly some additional space for other stuff the compiler knows about, such as a vtable pointer.

**Susan:** Why do you have to allocate storage anyway? I mean, why can't you just tell the compiler how much memory you have left and let it use as much as it wants until the memory is used up? Then you know you're done. <g>

**Steve:** It does use as much memory as it needs, but it has to know how much of the memory to set aside for each object that you create.

**Susan:** So, if you have a string class in the implementation of a program and you intend to use it in the interface, then it has to be included in both because they both get compiled separately?

**Steve:** Sort of. An interface (i.e., a header file) doesn't get compiled separately; it's #included wherever it's needed.

**Susan:** Yes, but why does it need to be in both places; why isn't one place good enough?

**Steve:** Because each .cc file is compiled separately; when the compiler is handling any particular .cc file, it doesn't know about any header file that isn't mentioned in that file. Therefore, we have to mention every header in every .cc file that uses objects defined in that header.

**Susan:** So they are compiled separately. How are they ever connected, and if they do become connected, why is it necessary to write them twice?

**Steve:** They are connected only by the linker.

**Susan:** If they are included in the implementations, aren't they included in the test programs?

**Steve:** No, because the test program is compiled separately from the implementations. In fact, the writer of the test program may not even have the source code for the implementations.

**Susan:** And if they are needed, then why aren't the other header files needed in the test programs or any other programs for that matter?

**Steve:** You only have to include those header files that the compiler needs to figure out the size and functions of any object you use.

**Susan:** Yes, but then if they're necessary for the implementation, then they should be needed for the test programs, I would think. I still don't get it.

**Steve:** Each header file is needed only in source files that refer to the objects whose classes are defined in that header file.

**Susan:** Well, if you're writing an implementation for a program, then I think that every source file that uses the class needs to include all the header files, no?

**Steve:** Yes, except that sometimes you have objects that are used only inside the implementation of a class, as we'll see later in this chapter.

Let's start our analysis of the new versions of the I/O functions with the declaration of operator <<, which is friend ostream& operator << (ostream& os, StockItem* Item);. The second argument to this function is a StockItem* rather than a StockItem because we have to refer to our StockItem and DatedStockItem objects through a base class pointer (i.e., a StockItem*) to get the benefits of polymorphism. Although operator << isn't a virtual function (since it's not a member function at all), we will see that it still makes use of polymorphism to do its work.

Susan wanted to know why we were going over the I/O functions again:

**Susan:** Why are you explaining >> and << again? Why won't the old ones do?

**Steve:** Because the old ones can use StockItems directly, whereas the new ones have to operate on StockItem*s instead. This is part of what is wrong with the standard method of using virtual functions to achieve polymorphism.

**Susan:** Why aren't you showing how polymorphism is done with real data instead of these stupid >> and << things again?

**Steve:** This *is* how polymorphism is done with real data, if we expose the pointers to the application program.

**Susan:** Do you have to write *everything* that you see in your classes? Do you even have to define your periods?

**Steve:** No, as a matter of fact, the "." operator is (unfortunately) one of the few operators that can't be redefined.

The next point worthy of discussion is that we can use the same operator << to display either a StockItem or a DatedStockItem even though the display functions for those two types are actually different. Let's look at the implementation of this version of operator <<, shown in Figure 3.15.

**FIGURE 3.15. Dangerous polymorphism: The implementation of** operator << **with a** StockItem* **(from code\itemc.cc)**

```
ostream& operator << (ostream& os, StockItem* Item)
{
  Item->Write(os);
  return os;
}
```

This implementation looks pretty simple, as it merely calls a function called Write to do the actual work. In fact, this code looks too simple: How does it decide whether to display a StockItem or a DatedStockItem?

## *The Old Switcheroo*

This is an application of polymorphism: operator << doesn't have to decide whether to call the version of Write in the StockItem class or the one in the DatedStockItem class because that decision is made automatically at run time. Write is a virtual function declared in the StockItem class; therefore, the exact version of Write called through a StockItem* is determined by the run-time type of the object that the StockItem* actually points to.

To complete the explanation of how operator << works, we'll need to examine Write. Let's look at its implementation for the simplified versions of our StockItem (Figure 3.16) and DatedStockItem (Figure 3.17) classes.

**FIGURE 3.16. Dangerous polymorphism:** StockItem::Write **(from code\itemc.cc)**

```
void StockItem::Write(ostream& os)
{
  os << 0 << endl;
  os << m_Name << endl;
  os << m_InStock << endl;
  os << m_MinimumStock << endl;
}
```

**FIGURE 3.17. Dangerous polymorphism:** DatedStockItem::Write **(from code\itemc.cc)**

```
void DatedStockItem::Write(ostream& os)
{
  os << m_Expires << endl;
  os << m_Name << endl;
  os << m_InStock << endl;
  os << m_MinimumStock << endl;
}
```

The only thing that might not be obvious about these functions is why StockItem::Write writes the "0" out as its first action. We know that there's no date for a StockItem, so why not just write out the data that it does have? The reason is that if we want to read the data back in, we need some way to distinguish between a StockItem and a DatedStockItem. Since "0" is not a valid date, we can use it as an indicator meaning "the following data belongs to a StockItem, not to a DatedStockItem". In other words, when we read data from the inventory file to create our StockItem and DatedStockItem objects, any set of data that starts with a "0" will end up as a StockItem while any set of data that starts with a valid date will end up as DatedStockItem.[5]

If this still isn't perfectly clear, don't worry. The next section, which covers operator >>, should clear it up.

## *It's Not Polite to Point*

First, let's examine the header of the operator >> function:

```
istream& operator >> (istream& is, StockItem*& Item)
```

Most of this should be familiar by now, but there is one oddity: The declaration of the second argument to this function is StockItem*&. What can that mean?

It's a reference to a pointer. Now, before you decide to throw in the towel, recall that we use a reference argument when we need to modify a variable in the calling function. In this case, that variable is a StockItem* (a pointer to a StockItem or one of its derived classes), and we are going to have to change it by assigning the address of a

5. By the way, the use of "0" to mean "never" is safe because "0" is easily distinguishable from any real date. This is not true of actual dates in the year 1999, such as 1/1/99, 9/9/99, or 12/31/99, which have been used to signify "never" in old programs written in the last 30 years. Such a misuse of a date field is contributing to the Year 2000 problem, which is just starting to get some public attention as I write this. We'll discuss this problem in some detail in Chapter 4.

newly created StockItem or DatedStockItem to it. Hence, our argument has to be a reference to the variable in the calling function, and since that variable is a StockItem*, our argument has to be declared as a reference to a StockItem*, which we write as StockItem*&.

Having cleared up that point, let's look at how we would use this new function (Figure 3.18). In case you want to print out the file containing this code, it is polyiob.cc.

**FIGURE 3.18. Dangerous polymorphism: Using** operator >> **and** operator << **with a** StockItem* **(code\polyiob.cc)**

```
// polyiob.cc

#include <iostream.h>
#include <fstream.h>
#include "vector.h"
#include "itemc.h"

int main()
{
   StockItem* x;
   StockItem* y;

   ifstream ShopInfo("polyiob.in");

   ShopInfo >> x;

   ShopInfo >> y;

   cout << "A StockItem: " << endl;
   cout << x;

   cout << endl;

   cout << "A DatedStockItem: " << endl;
   cout << y;

   delete x;
```

```
    delete y;

    return 0;
}
```

Susan wanted to know what the argument to the ifstream constructor was:

**Susan:** What is polyiob.in?

**Steve:** It's the data file we're going to read the data from.

Before we continue to analyze this program, look at Figure 3.19, which shows the output it produces.

**FIGURE 3.19. Dangerous polymorphism: The results of using** operator >> **and** operator << **with a** StockItem* **(code\polyiob.out)**

```
A StockItem:
0
3-ounce cups
71
78

A DatedStockItem:
19970719
milk
76
87
```

Now let's get back to the code. You alert readers will have noticed something odd here: How can we assign a value to a variable such as x or y without allocating any memory for it? For that matter, how can we call operator delete for a pointer variable that hasn't had memory assigned to it? These aren't errors but consequences of the way we have to implement operator >>. To see why this is so, take a look at that implementation, as shown in Figure 3.20.

**FIGURE 3.20. Dangerous polymorphism: The implementation of** operator >> **(from code\itemc.cc)**

```
istream& operator >> (istream& is, StockItem*& Item)
{
  string Expires;
  short InStock;
  short MinimumStock;
  string Name;

  is >> Expires;
  is >> Name;
  is >> InStock;
  is >> MinimumStock;

  if (Expires == "0")
    Item = new StockItem(Name,InStock,MinimumStock);
  else
    Item = new DatedStockItem(Name,InStock,
    MinimumStock,Expires);

  return is;
}
```

This starts out reasonably enough by declaring variables to hold the expiration date (Expires), number in stock (InStock), minimum number desired in stock (MinimumStock), and name of the item (Name). Then we read values for these variables from the istream supplied as the left-hand argument in the operator >> call, which in the case of our example program is ShopInfo. Next, we examine the variable Expires, which was the first variable to be read in from the istream. If the value of Expires is "0", meaning "not a date", we create a new StockItem by calling the normal constructor for that class and assigning memory to that new object via operator new. If the Expires value isn't "0", we assume it's a date and create a new DatedStockItem by calling the constructor for DatedStockItem and assigning memory for the new object via operator new. Finally, we return the istream that we started with so it can be used in further operator >> calls.

The fact that we have to create a different type of object in these two cases is the key to why we have to allocate the memory in the operator >> function rather than in the calling program. The actual type of the object isn't known until we read the data from the file, so we can't allocate memory for the object until that time. This isn't necessarily a bad thing in itself; the trouble is that we can't free the memory automatically because the calling program is in charge of the vector of StockItem pointers and has to remember to call delete to free the memory allocated to those pointers when the objects are no longer needed.

While it is legal (and very common) to write programs in which memory is allocated and freed in this way, it isn't a good idea. The likelihood of error in any large program that uses this method of memory management is approximately 100%. Even if the original programmers get it right, the first time someone tries to maintain the program, he or she will very likely mess up the memory management in one way or another. Besides the problem of forgetting to free memory or using memory that has already been freed, we also have the problem that copying pointers leaves two pointers pointing to the same data, which makes it even more likely that the data will either be freed prematurely or not freed at all when it is no longer in use.

Susan had some questions about the exact dangers of using pointers in this way:

**Susan:** Are you saying that the programmer forgets to free memory?

**Steve:** Yes.

**Susan:** Don't you only have to write the code to free the memory once?

**Steve:** Yes, unless you ever change the program.

**Susan:** Or can these bad things happen on their own even if the program is written properly?

**Steve:** Yes, that can happen under certain circumstances, but luckily we won't run into any of those circumstances in this book.

We'll begin to solve these pointer-related problems right after the following exercises.

## *Exercises, First Set*

1. Rewrite the DrugStockItem class that you wrote in Chapter 2 as a derived class of DatedStockItem, using virtual functions to allow DrugStockItem objects to be used in place of StockItem objects or DatedStockItem objects, just as you can use DatedStockItem objects in place of StockItem objects.
2. Rewrite the Employee class that you wrote in Chapter 2 as three classes: a base Employee class, an Exempt class and an Hourly class. The latter two classes will be derived from the base class. The virtual CalculatePay member function for each of these derived classes should use the appropriate method of calculating the pay for each class so that an Exempt object or an Hourly object can be substituted for an Employee class object. The Employee class CalculatePay function should display an error message, as that class does not have a method of calculating pay. Note that unlike the first Employee exercise in Chapter 2, you *must* maintain the same interface for the CalculatePay function in these classes because you are using a base class pointer to access derived class objects.

## *Pretty Polly Morphic*

As we have just seen, the "standard" method of adding polymorphism to our programs is, to use a technical term, *ugly*; that is, it is error prone and virtually impossible to maintain. As soon as we get some more definitions out of the way, we're going to see how to fix these problems with an advanced technique I refer to as *polymorphic objects*.

## *More Definitions*

A **polymorphic object** is a C++ object that presents the appearance of a simple object that behaves polymorphically, but without the hazards of exposing the user of the polymorphic object to the pointers used within its implementation. The user does not have to know about any of the details of the implementation, but merely instantiates an object of the single visible class (the manager class). That object does what the user wants with the help of an object of a worker class, which is derived from the manager class.

The **manager/worker idiom** is a mechanism that allows the effective type of an object to be determined at run time without requiring the user of the object to be concerned with pointers.[6]

The **reference-counting idiom** is a mechanism that allows one object (the reference-counted object) to be shared by several other objects (the client objects); thus, a copy needn't be made for each of the client objects.

6. *Manager/worker* is my name for what James Coplien calls the *envelope/letter idiom* in his book, *Advanced C++: Programming Styles and Idioms* (Addison-Wesley Publishing Company, Reading, Mass., 1992). Warning: As its title indicates, his is not an easy book; however, it does merit study by those who have a solid grasp of C++ fundamentals.

## *Paging Miss Management*

You may be wondering what an "idiom" is in programming. Well, in English or any other natural language, an idiom is a phrase whose meaning can't be derived directly from the meanings of its individual words. An example would be "to make good time", which actually means "to proceed rapidly". Similarly, the manager/worker idiom used to implement polymorphic objects has effects that aren't at all obvious from a casual inspection of its components.

I should tell you that many, if not most, professional C++ programmers don't know about this method of making polymorphism safe and easy to use for the application programmer. Why then am I including it in a book for relatively inexperienced programmers?

Because I believe it is the best solution to the very serious problems caused by dynamic memory allocation when using polymorphism. For that reason, every serious C++ programmer should know this idiom and understand how to apply it to real-life problems.

At this point, Susan was ready to give this new idea a shot, as the following exchange indicates:

> **Susan:** Okay, I feel I have followed you fairly well up to the point of the big thing you're going to do here with the polymorphic objects. I think that stuff is going to take some real thinking time. I hope it goes well.
>
> **Steve:** I hope so too. Otherwise, we'll see lots of "ughs".

Assuming that I have impressed the importance of this technique on you, how does it work? The most elementary answer is that it involves creating a set of classes that work as a team to present the appearance of a simple object that has the desired polymorphic behavior. The user of the class (i.e., the application programmer) doesn't have to know about any of the details of this idiom; he or she merely defines an object of the single visible class, and that object does what the user wants with the help of an object of another class. James Coplien calls these two kinds of classes *envelope* and *letter*, respectively, but I'm going to call them *manager* and *worker*. I think these names are easier to remember because the outside world sees only objects of the manager class, which take credit for everything done by the polymorphic object even though most of the work is actually done by objects of the worker classes.

As usual, all of the intricacies of the implementation are the responsibility of the class designers (us).[7] However, before we get into the details of how a polymorphic object works, let's see how it affects the way we use the StockItem class. For reference, Figure 3.21 shows the way we used the old StockItem class in Chapter 2, and Figure 3.22 shows how we will use the new StockItem class; note the lack of deletes and the fact that the variables in Figure 3.22 are StockItems rather than StockItem pointers.[8]

**FIGURE 3.21. Dangerous polymorphism: Using** operator >> **and** operator << **with a** StockItem* **(code\polyiob.cc)**

```
// polyiob.cc

#include <iostream.h>
#include <fstream.h>
#include "vector.h"
#include "itemc.h"

int main()
{
   StockItem* x;
```

7. If you are interested in reading *Who's Afraid of C++ Class Design?*, let me know and I'll mention it to my editor.

8. If you were wondering why the file name is different in these two figures, it's because the program in Figure 3.22 is using the "real" version of the StockItem class rather than the simplified one used by the program in Figure 3.21. Therefore, it needs more input to fill in the extra member variables.

```
   StockItem* y;

   ifstream ShopInfo("polyiob.in");

   ShopInfo >> x;

   ShopInfo >> y;

   cout << "A StockItem: " << endl;
   cout << x;

   cout << endl;

   cout << "A DatedStockItem: " << endl;
   cout << y;

   delete x;
   delete y;

   return 0;
}
```

**FIGURE 3.22. Safe polymorphism: Using** operator >> **and** operator << **with a polymorphic** StockItem **(code\polyioc.cc)**

```
#include <iostream.h>
#include <fstream.h>
#include "vector.h"
#include "itemp.h"

int main()
{
   StockItem x;
   StockItem y;

   ifstream ShopInfo("shop22.in");

   ShopInfo >> x;
```

```
    ShopInfo >> y;

    cout << "A StockItem: " << endl;
    cout << x;

    cout << endl;

    cout << "A DatedStockItem: " << endl;
    cout << y;

    return 0;
}
```

I strongly recommend that you print out the files that contain the interface and the implementation of the polymorphic object version of StockItem, as well as the test program, to refer to as you go through this section of the chapter. Those files are itemp.h (StockItem interface in Figure 3.23), itempi.h (UndatedStockItem and DatedStockItem interfaces in Figure 3.24), itemp.cc (UndatedStockItem and DatedStockItem implementation in Figure 3.25), and polyioc.cc (test program in Figure 3.22). By the way, the line class string; at the beginning of itemp.h merely tells the compiler that string is the name of a class, so that it won't complain when we try to use string as an argument type in our function declarations for the StockItem class.

You must be happy to see that we've eliminated the visible pointers in the new version of the example program, but how does it work? Let's start by looking at Figure 3.23, which shows the interface for the manager class StockItem. As we've discussed, this is the class of the objects that are visible to the user of the polymorphic object.

**FIGURE 3.23. Safe polymorphism: The polymorphic object version of the StockItem interface (code\itemp.h)**

```
// itemp.h

class string;
```

```
class StockItem
{
friend ostream& operator << (ostream& os,
  const StockItem& Item);

friend istream& operator >> (istream& is, StockItem& Item);

public:
  StockItem();
  StockItem(const StockItem& Item);
  StockItem& operator = (const StockItem& Item);
virtual ~StockItem();

  StockItem(string Name, short InStock,
  short Price, short MinimumStock,
  short MinimumReorder, string Distributor, string UPC);

  StockItem(string Name, short InStock,
  short Price, short MinimumStock,
  short MinimumReorder, string Distributor, string UPC,
  string Expires);

virtual bool CheckUPC(string UPC);
virtual void DeductSaleFromInventory(short QuantitySold);
virtual short GetInventory();
virtual string GetName();

virtual void Reorder(ostream& os);
virtual void FormattedDisplay(ostream& os);
virtual void Write(ostream& os);

protected:
  StockItem(int);

protected:
  StockItem* m_Worker;
  short m_Count;
```

```
};
```

Unlike the classes we've dealt with before, where the member functions deserved most of our attention, possibly the most interesting point about this new version of the StockItem class is its member variables, especially the variable named m_Worker. It's a pointer, which isn't all that strange; the question is, what type of pointer?

It's a pointer to a StockItem — that is, a pointer to the same type of object that we're defining! Assuming that is useful, is it even legal?

### *We'll Manage Somehow*

Yes, it is legal, because the compiler can figure out how to allocate storage for a pointer to any type whether or not it knows the full definition of that type. However, this doesn't answer the question of why we would want a pointer to a StockItem in our StockItem class in the first place. The answer is that, as we saw in the discussion of polymorphism earlier in this chapter, a pointer to a StockItem can actually point to an object of any class derived from StockItem via public inheritance. We're going to make use of this fact to implement the bulk of the functionality of our StockItem objects in the classes UndatedStockItem and DatedStockItem, which are derived from StockItem.

Susan didn't think this use of a pointer to refer to a worker object was very obvious. Here's the discussion we had about it.

> **Susan:** Ugh. What is m_Worker? Where did it come from, and why is it suddenly so popular? Don't tell me it's a pointer. I want to know exactly what it does.

> **Steve:** It points to the "worker" object that actually does the work for the StockItem, which is why it is called m_Worker.

In essence, we're renaming the old StockItem class to UndatedStockItem and creating a new StockItem class that will handle the interaction with the application programmer. Objects of this new StockItem class will pass on the actual class-specific operations to an object of either the UndatedStockItem or the DatedStockItem class as appropriate.

Now that we have an overview of the structure of the classes we're designing, Figure 3.24 shows the interfaces for the worker classes UndatedStockItem and DatedStockItem.

**FIGURE 3.24. Safe polymorphism: The** UndatedStockItem **and** DatedStockItem **interfaces for the polymorphic version of** StockItem **(code\itempi.h)**

```
class UndatedStockItem : public StockItem
{
public:
  UndatedStockItem();

  UndatedStockItem(string Name, short InStock,
    short Price, short MinimumStock, short ReorderQuantity,
    string Distributor, string UPC);

virtual bool CheckUPC(string UPC);
virtual void DeductSaleFromInventory(short QuantitySold);
virtual short GetInventory();
virtual string GetName();

virtual void Reorder(ostream& os);
virtual void FormattedDisplay(ostream& os);
virtual ostream& Write(ostream& os);

protected:
  short m_InStock;
  short m_Price;
  short m_MinimumStock;
  short m_MinimumReorder;
  string m_Name;
  string m_Distributor;
  string m_UPC;
```

```
};

class DatedStockItem : public UndatedStockItem
{
public:

  DatedStockItem(string Name, short InStock,
    short Price, short MinimumStock, short MinimumReorder,
    string Distributor, string UPC, string Expires);

virtual void Reorder(ostream& os);
virtual void FormattedDisplay(ostream& os);
virtual ostream& Write(ostream& os);

protected:
static string Today();

protected:
  string m_Expires;
};
```

And Figure 3.25 shows the implementation of these classes.

**FIGURE 3.25. Safe polymorphism: The implementation of the** UndatedStockItem **and** DatedStockItem classes (**code\itemp.cc**)

```
#include <iostream.h>
#include <iomanip.h>
#include <strstrea.h>
#include <string.h>
#include "string6.h"
#include "itemp.h"
#include "itempi.h"
#include <dos.h>


//friend functions of StockItem

ostream& operator << (ostream& os, const StockItem& Item)
```

```
{
 return Item.m_Worker->Write(os);
}

istream& operator >> (istream& is, StockItem& Item)
{
 string Expires;
 string Name;
 short InStock;
 short Price;
 short MinimumStock;
 short MinimumReorder;
 string Distributor;
 string UPC;

 is >> Expires;
 is >> Name;
 is >> InStock;
 is >> Price;
 is >> MinimumStock;
 is >> MinimumReorder;
 is >> Distributor;
 is >> UPC;

 if (Expires == "0")
  {
  Item = StockItem(Name, InStock, Price, MinimumStock,
     MinimumReorder, Distributor, UPC);
  }
 else
  {
  Item = StockItem(Name, InStock, Price, MinimumStock,
     MinimumReorder, Distributor, UPC, Expires);
  }

 return is;

}
```

```
// StockItem member functions

StockItem::StockItem()
: m_Count(0), m_Worker(new UndatedStockItem)
{
 m_Worker->m_Count = 1;
}

StockItem::StockItem(const StockItem& Item)
: m_Count(0), m_Worker(Item.m_Worker)
{
 m_Worker->m_Count ++;
}

StockItem& StockItem::operator = (const StockItem& Item)
{
 if (&Item != this)
  {
  m_Worker->m_Count --;
  if (m_Worker->m_Count <= 0)
   delete m_Worker;
  m_Worker = Item.m_Worker;
  m_Worker->m_Count ++;
  }
 return *this;
}

StockItem::~StockItem()
{
 if (m_Worker == 0)
  return;

 m_Worker->m_Count --;
 if (m_Worker->m_Count <= 0)
  delete m_Worker;
}

StockItem::StockItem(string Name, short InStock, // Undated
```

```
  short Price, short MinimumStock, short MinimumReorder,
  string Distributor, string UPC)
: m_Count(0),
  m_Worker(new UndatedStockItem(Name, InStock, Price,
  MinimumStock, MinimumReorder, Distributor, UPC))
{
  m_Worker->m_Count = 1;
}

StockItem::StockItem(int)
: m_Worker(0)
{
}

StockItem::StockItem(string Name, short InStock, // Dated
  short Price, short MinimumStock, short MinimumReorder,
  string Distributor, string UPC, string Expires)
: m_Count(0),
  m_Worker(new DatedStockItem(Name, InStock, Price,
  MinimumStock, MinimumReorder, Distributor, UPC, Expires))
{
  m_Worker->m_Count = 1;
}

bool StockItem::CheckUPC(string UPC)
{
  return m_Worker->CheckUPC(UPC);
}

short StockItem::GetInventory()
{
  return m_Worker->GetInventory();
}

void StockItem::DeductSaleFromInventory(short QuantitySold)
{
  m_Worker->DeductSaleFromInventory(QuantitySold);
}
```

```
string StockItem::GetName()
{
 return m_Worker->GetName();
}

ostream& StockItem::Write(ostream& os)
{
 exit(1); // should never get here
}

void StockItem::Reorder(ostream& os)
{
 m_Worker->Reorder(os);
}


void StockItem::FormattedDisplay(ostream& os)
{
 m_Worker->FormattedDisplay(os);
}


// UndatedStockItem member functions

UndatedStockItem::UndatedStockItem()
: StockItem(1),
  m_InStock(0),
  m_Price(0),
  m_MinimumStock(0),
  m_MinimumReorder(0),
  m_Name(),
  m_Distributor(),
  m_UPC()
{
}

UndatedStockItem::UndatedStockItem(string Name,
  short InStock, short Price, short MinimumStock,
  short MinimumReorder, string Distributor, string UPC)
```

```
: StockItem(1),
  m_InStock(InStock),
  m_Price(Price),
  m_MinimumStock(MinimumStock),
  m_MinimumReorder(MinimumReorder),
  m_Name(Name),
  m_Distributor(Distributor),
  m_UPC(UPC)
{
}

void UndatedStockItem::FormattedDisplay(ostream& os)
{
  os << "Name: ";
  os << m_Name << endl;
  os << "Number in stock: ";
  os << m_InStock << endl;
  os << "Price: ";
  os << m_Price << endl;
  os << "Minimum stock: ";
  os << m_MinimumStock << endl;
  os << "Reorder quantity: ";
  os << m_MinimumReorder << endl;
  os << "Distributor: ";
  os << m_Distributor << endl;
  os << "UPC: ";
  os << m_UPC << endl;
  os << endl;
}

ostream& UndatedStockItem::Write(ostream& os)
{
  os << 0 << endl;
  os << m_Name << endl;
  os << m_InStock << endl;
  os << m_Price << endl;
  os << m_MinimumStock << endl;
  os << m_MinimumReorder << endl;
  os << m_Distributor << endl;
```

```
 os << m_UPC << endl;

 return os;
}

void UndatedStockItem::Reorder(ostream& os)
{
 short ReorderAmount;

 if (m_InStock < m_MinimumStock)
  {
  ReorderAmount = m_MinimumStock-m_InStock;
   if (ReorderAmount < m_MinimumReorder)
    ReorderAmount = m_MinimumReorder;
  os << "Reorder " << ReorderAmount;
  os << " units of " << m_Name << " with UPC ";
  os << m_UPC << " from " << m_Distributor << endl;
  }
}

bool UndatedStockItem::CheckUPC(string UPC)
{
 return (UPC == m_UPC);
}

short UndatedStockItem::GetInventory()
{
 return m_InStock;
}

void UndatedStockItem::DeductSaleFromInventory(
short QuantitySold)
{
 m_InStock -= QuantitySold;
}

string UndatedStockItem::GetName()
{
 return m_Name;
```

```
}

// DatedStockItem member functions

DatedStockItem::DatedStockItem(string Name, short InStock,
short Price, short MinimumStock, short MinimumReorder,
string Distributor, string UPC, string Expires)
: UndatedStockItem(Name,InStock,Price,MinimumStock,
  MinimumReorder,Distributor,UPC),
  m_Expires(Expires)
{
}

ostream& DatedStockItem::Write(ostream& os)
{
  os << m_Expires << endl;
  os << m_Name << endl;
  os << m_InStock << endl;
  os << m_Price << endl;
  os << m_MinimumStock << endl;
  os << m_MinimumReorder << endl;
  os << m_Distributor << endl;
  os << m_UPC << endl;

  return os;
}

void DatedStockItem::FormattedDisplay(ostream& os)
{
  os << "Expiration date: ";
  os << m_Expires << endl;
  os << "Name: ";
  os << m_Name << endl;
  os << "Number in stock: ";
  os << m_InStock << endl;
  os << "Price: ";
  os << m_Price << endl;
  os << "Minimum stock: ";
```

```
 os << m_MinimumStock << endl;
 os << "Reorder quantity: ";
 os << m_MinimumReorder << endl;
 os << "Distributor: ";
 os << m_Distributor << endl;
 os << "UPC: ";
 os << m_UPC << endl;
 os << endl;
}

string DatedStockItem::Today()
{
  struct date d;
  unsigned short year;
  unsigned short day;
  unsigned short month;
  string TodaysDate;
  strstream FormatStream;

  getdate(&d);
  year = d.da_year;
  day = d.da_day;
  month = d.da_mon;

  FormatStream << setfill('0') << setw(4) << year <<
    setw(2) << month << setw(2) << day;
  FormatStream.seekg(0);
  FormatStream >> TodaysDate;

  return TodaysDate;
}

void DatedStockItem::Reorder(ostream& os)
{
 if (m_Expires < Today())
   {
   os << "Return " << m_InStock << " units of " << m_Name;
   os << " with UPC " << m_UPC;
   os << " to " << m_Distributor << endl;
```

```
    m_InStock = 0;
    }

  StockItem::Reorder(os);
}
```

Let's start our examination of this new StockItem class by looking at the implementation of operator << in Figure 3.26.

**FIGURE 3.26. Safe polymorphism: The implementation of** operator << **for a polymorphic** StockItem **(from code\itemp.cc)**

```
ostream& operator << (ostream& os, const StockItem& Item)
{
  return Item.m_Worker->Write(os);
}
```

At first glance, this isn't particularly complicated. It just calls a function named Write via the StockItem* member variable m_Worker and returns the result from Write to its caller. But what does that m_Worker pointer point to?

This is the key to the implementation of polymorphic objects: The pointer m_Worker points to either an UndatedStockItem or a DatedStockItem depending on whether the object was created with or without an expiration date. Since the type of object that m_Worker points to is determined during program execution rather than when the program is compiled, the actual version of the Write function called by operator << varies accordingly, as it does with any type of polymorphism. The difference between this version of StockItem and the one described earlier in this chapter is that the pointer is used only in the implementation of StockItem rather than being accessible to the user of the class. This allows us to prevent the plague of memory allocation errors associated with pointer manipulation in the application program.

Susan had a question about the syntax of the call to the Write function.

**Susan:** What does the -> mean in that line?

**Steve:** It means to call the function on the right of the -> for the object pointed to by the pointer on the left of the ->. It's exactly like the . operator, except that operator has an object on its left instead of a pointer.

Before we get into the details of creating an object of this new version of StockItem, we'll look at a couple of diagrams of the StockItem variables from the example program in Figure 3.22 to see exactly how this "internal polymorphism" works. First, Figure 3.27 shows a possible layout of the StockItem object, x, which is the argument to operator << in the statement cout << x;.

Let's trace the execution of the statement return Item.m_Worker->Write(s); from operator << (Figure 3.26) when it is executed to display the value of the StockItem x (as a result of the statement cout << x; in the example program in Figure 3.22). In step 1, the pointer m_Worker is followed to location 12321000, the address of the beginning of the UndatedStockItem worker object that will handle the operations of the StockItem manager class object. This location contains the address of the vtable for the worker object. In this case, the worker object is an UndatedStockItem object, so the vtable is the one for the UndatedStockItem class.

**FIGURE 3.27. Safe polymorphism: A polymorphic StockItem object with no date**

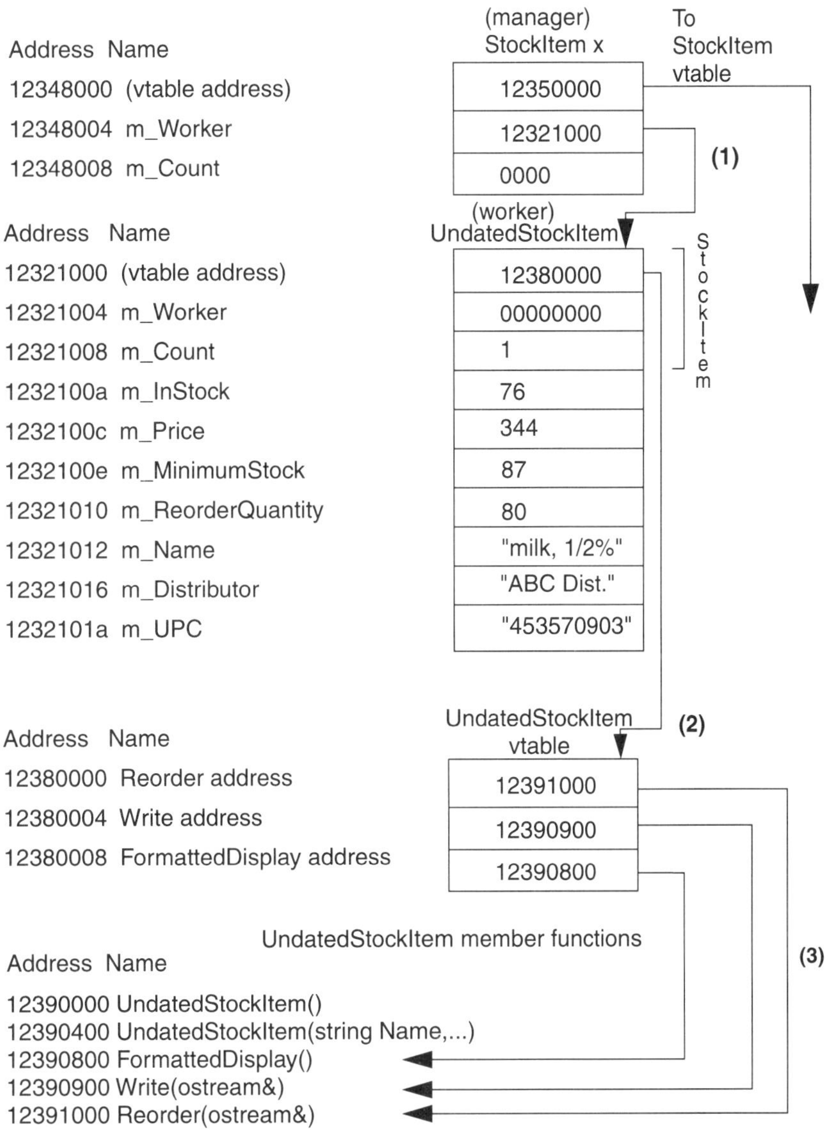
(manager)
StockItem x
To
StockItem
vtable
Address Name
12348000 (vtable address)
12348004 m_Worker
12348008 m_Count
12350000
12321000
0000
(1)
(worker)
UndatedStockItem
Address Name
12321000 (vtable address)
12321004 m_Worker
12321008 m_Count
1232100a m_InStock
1232100c m_Price
1232100e m_MinimumStock
12321010 m_ReorderQuantity
12321012 m_Name
12321016 m_Distributor
1232101a m_UPC
12380000
00000000
1
76
344
87
80
"milk, 1/2%"
"ABC Dist."
"453570903"
StockItem
UndatedStockItem
vtable
(2)
Address Name
12380000 Reorder address
12380004 Write address
12380008 FormattedDisplay address
12391000
12390900
12390800
UndatedStockItem member functions
(3)
Address Name
12390000 UndatedStockItem()
12390400 UndatedStockItem(string Name,...)
12390800 FormattedDisplay()
12390900 Write(ostream&)
12391000 Reorder(ostream&)

In our diagram, that vtable is at location 12380000, so in step 2 we follow the vtable pointer to find the address of the Write function. The diagram makes the assumption that the Write function is the second virtual function defined in the StockItem class, so in step 3 we fetch the contents of the second entry in the vtable, which is 12390900. That is the address of the Write function that will be executed in this case.

Figure 3.28 shows a possible layout of the StockItem object y that is the argument to operator << in the statement cout << y;.

Susan had a number of questions about Figure 3.28.

**Susan:** What in Figure 3.28 is the StockItem? I can't tell exactly what it is supposed to be, just the vtable address, m_Worker, and m_Count? That's it, huh?

**Steve:** Yes.

**Susan:** What are all those member functions in step 3 supposed to be? I don't know where they're coming from.

**Steve:** They're from the class interface for the new version of StockItem, which is listed in Figure 3.23.

**Susan:** Why is there an UndatedStockItem listed along the side of the DatedStockItem thingy?

**Steve:** Because DatedStockItem is derived from UndatedStockItem; therefore, every DatedStockItem has an UndatedStockItem in it, just as every UndatedStockItem has a StockItem in it because UndatedStockItem is derived from StockItem.

**FIGURE 3.28.** **Safe polymorphism: A polymorphic** StockItem **object with a date**

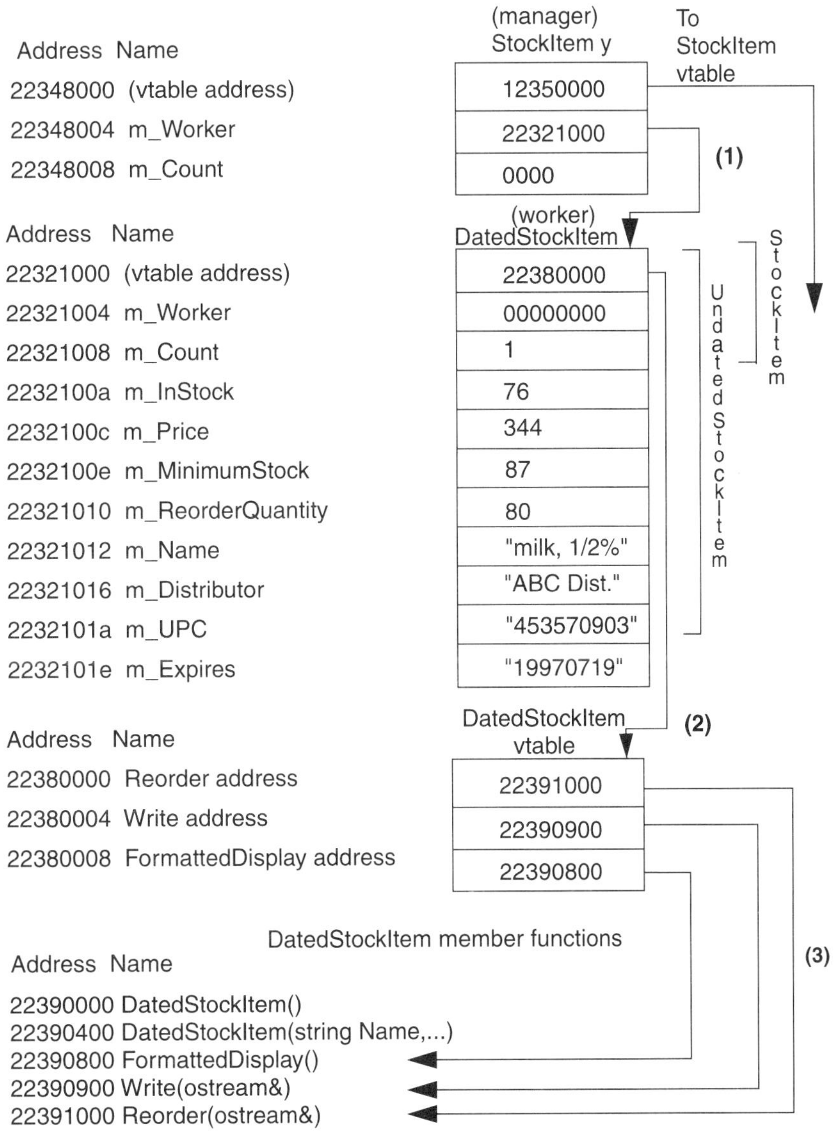

**Susan:** Where is the UndatedStockItem now?

**Steve:** The only UndatedStockItem in Figure 3.28 is the base class part of the DatedStockItem worker object.

**Susan:** I still can't see how these objects look.

**Steve:** I think we need a diagram here. Take a look at Figure 3.29 and let me know if that helps.

**Susan:** Yes, it does.

FIGURE 3.29. **A simplified version of the structure of a** DatedStockItem **object**

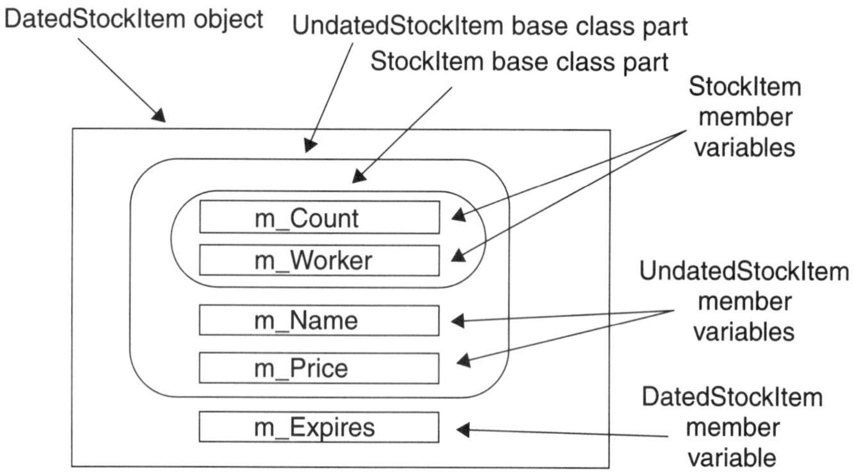


Now that we've cleared that up, let's trace how the line return Item.m_Worker->Write(s); is executed to display the value of the StockItem y (as a result of the statement cout << y; in the example program in Figure 3.22). In step 1, the pointer m_Worker is followed to location 22321000, the address of the worker object that will handle the operations of the StockItem manager class object. This location contains the address of the vtable for the worker object. In this case, the worker object is a DatedStockItem object, so the vtable is the one for the DatedStockItem class. In our diagram, that vtable is at location 22380000, so in step 2 we follow the vtable pointer to find the address of the Write function. As before, the diagram makes the assumption that the Write function is the second virtual function defined in the StockItem class, so in step 3 we fetch the contents of the second entry in the vtable, which is 22390900. That is the address of the Write function that will be executed in this case.

## *Setting the Standard*

We have seen how a polymorphic object works once it is set up, so let's continue our examination of the StockItem class by looking at the "standard" member functions — that is, the ones that are necessary to make it a concrete data type. As you may remember, these are the default constructor, the copy constructor, the assignment operator (operator =), and the destructor.

It may occur to you to wonder why we have to rewrite all these functions; what's wrong with the ones we've already written for StockItem? The answer is that these functions create, copy, and destroy objects of a given class. Now that we have changed the way we want to use the StockItem class and the way it works, we have to rewrite these functions to do the right thing in the new situation.

Susan wanted to make sure she understood where we were going with this:

> **Susan:** Okay, then this is the new StockItem, not the old one. This is your manager StockItem that tells the worker what to do; the DatedStockItem is the worker, right?
>
> **Steve:** Yes, this is the new type of StockItem. By the way, besides a DatedStockItem, an UndatedStockItem is also qualified to be a worker.

Let's start with the default constructor for this new StockItem class, shown in Figure 3.30.

**FIGURE 3.30. Safe polymorphism: The default constructor for the polymorphic** StockItem class **(from code\itemp.cc)**

```
StockItem::StockItem()
: m_Count(0), m_Worker(new UndatedStockItem)
{
 m_Worker->m_Count = 1;
}
```

The first member initialization expression in this function merely initializes m_Count to 0. We won't actually be using this variable in a StockItem object, but I don't like leaving variables around without initializing them.

The second member initialization expression, however, looks a bit odd. Why are we creating an UndatedStockItem object here when we have no data to put in it? Because we need some worker object to perform the work of a default-constructed StockItem. For example, if the user asks for the contents of the StockItem to be displayed on the screen with labels (by calling FormattedDisplay), we want the default values displayed with the appropriate labels, which can only be done by an object that has a working FormattedDisplay function. The StockItem class itself doesn't have any data except for the StockItem* and the m_Count variable (which we'll get to later). Therefore, all of the functionality of a StockItem has to be handed off to the worker object, which in this case is the newly created UndatedStockItem.

Let's see what a default-constructed StockItem might look like (Figure 3.31).

**FIGURE 3.31. Safe polymorphism: A default-constructed polymorphic StockItem object**

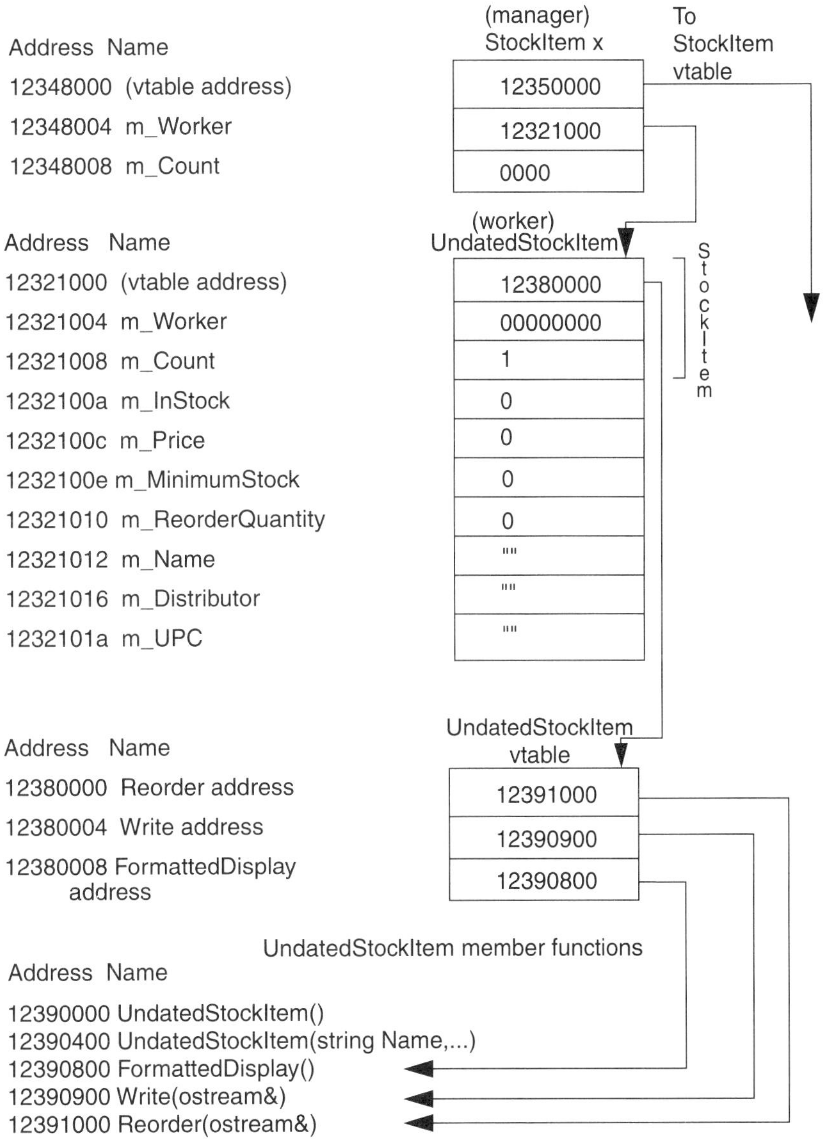

Susan didn't think the need for a valid object as the worker object in a default-constructed manager object was intuitively obvious.

**Susan:** I don't get why you say that we can only call the FormattedDisplay function with an object that has a working version of that function. That doesn't mean anything to me.

**Steve:** Well, what would happen if we called the FormattedDisplay function via a pointer that didn't point to anything? It wouldn't work, that's for sure.

In particular, any attempt by the user to call a virtual function through a pointer to a nonexistent object will fail, because there won't be a valid vtable address in that missing object. The most likely result will be a crash when the code tries to use a vtable entry that contains random garbage.

I still haven't explained exactly what the member initialization expression, m_Worker(new UndatedStockItem), actually does. On the surface, it's pretty simple: It creates a new UndatedStockItem object via the default constructor of that class and uses the address of the resulting object to initialize m_Worker.

However, there are some tricks in the implementation of the constructor of a worker class, and now is the time to see how such a constructor actually works. Figure 3.32 shows the code for the default constructor for the UndatedStockItem class.

**FIGURE 3.32. Safe polymorphism: The default constructor for the UndatedStockItem class (from code\itemp.cc)**

```
UndatedStockItem::UndatedStockItem()
: StockItem(1),
  m_InStock(0),
  m_Price(0),
  m_MinimumStock(0),
  m_MinimumReorder(0),
  m_Name(),
  m_Distributor(),
```

```
  m_UPC()
{
}
```

Most of the code in this constructor is standard: All we're doing is initializing the values of the member variables to reasonable default values. But there's something a bit unusual about that base class initializer, StockItem(1). Before we get into exactly what the argument 1 means, it's important to understand why we *must* specify a base class initializer here.

As we saw in Chapter 2 in the discussion of Figure 2.35, we use a base class initializer when we want to specify which base class constructor will initialize the base class part of a derived class object. If we don't specify any particular base class initializer, the base class part will be initialized with the default constructor for that base class. In the example in Chapter 2, we needed to call a specific base class constructor to fill in the fields in the base class part of the UndatedStockItem object, which should seem reasonable enough. But that can't be the reason we need to specify a base class constructor here because the StockItem object doesn't have any data fields that need to be initialized in our UndatedStockItem constructor. So why can't we just let the compiler use the default constructor for the base class part of an UndatedStockItem?

## *Base Instincts*

We can't do that because the default constructor for StockItem calls the default constructor for UndatedStockItem — that is, the function that we're examining right now. Therefore, if we allow the StockItem default constructor to initialize the StockItem part of an UndatedStockItem, that default constructor will call our UndatedStockItem default constructor again, which will call the StockItem default constructor again, and the program will eventually use up all the stack space and die.

To avoid this problem, we have to make a special constructor for StockItem that doesn't create an UndatedStockItem object and therefore avoids an indefinitely long chain of constructor calls. As no one outside the implementation of the StockItem polymorphic object knows anything about classes in this idiom other than StockItem, they don't need to call this constructor. As a result, we can make it protected.

Susan didn't see why we need a special constructor in this case, so I explained it to her some more:

> **Susan:** So, how many default constructors are you going to need for StockItem? How do you know when or which one is going to be used? This is confusing.
>
> **Steve:** There is only one default constructor for each class. In this case, StockItem has one, DatedStockItem has one, and UndatedStockItem has one. The question is how to prevent the StockItem default constructor from being called from the UndatedStockItem one, which would be a big booboo, since the UndatedStockItem default constructor was called from the StockItem default constructor. This would be like having two mirrors facing one another, where you see endless reflections going off into the distance.

Okay, so how do we declare a special constructor for this purpose? As was shown in Figure 3.23, all we have to do is to put the line StockItem(int); in a protected section of the class definition. The implementation of this function is shown in Figure 3.33.

**FIGURE 3.33. Safe polymorphism: Implementing a special** protected **constructor for** StockItem **(from code\itemp.cc)**

```
StockItem::StockItem(int)
: m_Worker(0)
{
}
```

How can a function that doesn't have any code inside its { } be complicated? In fact, this apparently simple function raises three questions. First, why do we need any entries in the argument list when the function doesn't use any arguments? Second, why does the list contain just a type and no argument name instead of a name and type for each argument, as we had in the past? And third, why are we initializing m_Worker to the value 0? We'll examine the first two of these questions now and put off the third until we discuss the destructor for the StockItem class.

The answers to the first two questions are related: The reason we don't need to specify a name for the argument is that we aren't going to use the argument in the function. The only reason to specify an argument list here is to make use of the *function overloading* mechanism, which allows the compiler to distinguish between functions with the same name but different argument types. In this case, even though all the constructors for the StockItem class have the same name — StockItem::StockItem — the compiler can tell them apart so long as they have different argument types. Therefore, we're supplying an argument we don't need to allow the compiler to pick this function when we want to use it. Here, when we call the function from the worker object's constructor, we supply the value 1, which will be ignored in the function itself but will tell the compiler that we want to call this constructor rather than any of the other constructors.

Susan wanted to know exactly where the 1 was going to come from and how I decided to use that value in the first place:

**Susan:** Where are you supplying the 1 value?

**Steve:** In the base class initializer in the default constructor for UndatedStockItem. This is needed to prevent the infinite regress mentioned just above.

**Susan:** But why 1? Why not any other number, like 0?

**Steve:** Actually, the value 1 is fairly arbitrary; any number would work. However, it's a good idea to avoid using 0 where you just need any old number, because 0 is a "magic number" in C++; it's a legal value for any type of built-in variable as well as any type of pointer. This "multiple identity" of 0 can be a bountiful source of confusion and error in C++, which it's best to avoid whenever possible.

Of course, there's nothing to stop us from giving the argument a name even though we aren't going to use it in the constructor. It's better not to do this, however, to avoid confusing both the compiler and the next programmer to look at this function. The compiler may give us a warning message if we don't use an argument we've declared, while the next programmer to look at this function may think we forgot to use that argument. We can solve both of these problems by not giving it a name, which makes it clear that we weren't planning to use it in the first place.

So now we've followed the chain of events down to the initialization of the base class part of the UndatedStockItem object that was created as the worker object inside the default constructor for StockItem. The rest of Figure 3.32 is pretty simple. It merely initializes the data for the UndatedStockItem class itself. When that's done, we're ready to execute the lone statement inside the {} in Figure 3.30, which is m_Worker->m_Count = 1;. Clearly, this sets the value of m_Count in the newly created UndatedStockItem object to 1, but what might not be as clear is *why* we need to do this.

## *References Count*

The reason we have to set m_Count to 1 in the UndatedStockItem variable pointed to by m_Worker is that we're going to keep track of the number of StockItems that are using that UndatedStockItem worker object, rather than copy the worker object every time we copy a StockItem that points to it. This is called *reference counting*.

The general idea of reference counting is fairly simple, as most great ideas are (after you understand them, at least). It's inefficient to copy a lot of data whenever we set one variable to the same value as that of another; copying a pointer to the data is much easier. Even so, we have to consider how we will know when we can delete the data being pointed to, which will be when no one needs the data anymore. If we don't take care of this requirement, we'll have a serious problem with memory management: When one of the StockItem objects that refers to the worker object goes out of scope and is destroyed, the destructor can do either of the following, neither of which is correct:

1. free the memory where the data is kept, via delete,
2. fail to free the memory.

The first of these is incorrect because there may be other StockItems that still want to use the data in question, and they will now be referring to memory that is no longer allocated to that data. Therefore, at any time the data in that area of memory may be overwritten by new data. The second is also incorrect because when the last StockItem that was using the shared data goes away, a memory leak results. In other words, although the data used by the StockItem can no longer be accessed, the memory it occupies cannot be used for other purposes because it has not been released back to the system via operator delete.[9]

The correct way to share data in such a situation is to write the constructor(s), destructor, and assignment operator to keep track of the number of objects using a particular set of data, and, when that set of data has no more users, to free the memory it occupies.[10] Let's see how reference counting works with our StockItem class.

9. For those of you who have read *Who's Afraid of C++?*, this is the same problem we saw with the compiler-generated copy constructor and the compiler-generated assignment operator for the string class. This is covered in Chapter 8 of that book, starting in the section "For Reference Only".

## *Starring Sharon Sharalike*

Suppose that we have the example program in Figure 3.34 (which is contained in the file refcnt1.cc if you want to print it out).

**FIGURE 3.34. Safe polymorphism: An example program for reference-counting with StockItems (code\refcnt1.cc)**

```
#include <iostream.h>
#include "string6.h"
#include "itemp.h"

int main()
{
   StockItem item1("cups",32,129,10,5,"Bob's Dist.",
      "2895657951"); // create an undated object

   StockItem item2("Hot Chicken",48,158,15,12,"Joe's Dist.",
      "987654321", "19960824"); // create a dated object

   StockItem item3 = item1; // copy constructor
   item1 = item2; // assignment operator

   item1.FormattedDisplay(cout); // display an object with labels

   return 0;
}
```

This program doesn't do anything very useful, except to illustrate the constructors and assignment operator, as follows. First, it creates two StockItems, item1 and item2, with specified contents (via the

10. There is actually another requirement for correct sharing of data in this situation: We mustn't make changes to the data in a shared worker object that has more than one user. In the current application, we don't have that problem, but it's something we'll have to deal with in Chapter 4, when we develop a polymorphic object type whose objects can be changed after creation.

"normal" constructors for undated and dated items, respectively). Then it creates another StockItem, item3, with the same value as that of item1, via the copy constructor. Then it assigns the value of item2 to item1 using the assignment operator.

The line StockItem item1("cups",32,129,10,5,"Bob's Dist.", "2895657951"); calls the constructor illustrated in Figure 3.35 to create a StockItem whose m_Worker points to an UndatedStockItem, because the arguments "cups", 32, 129, 10, 5, "Bob's Dist.", and "2895657951" match the argument list for that constructor.

FIGURE 3.35. **Safe polymorphism: A normal constructor to create a** StockItem **without a date (from code\itemp.cc)**

```
StockItem::StockItem(string Name, short InStock,
  short Price, short MinimumStock, short MinimumReorder,
  string Distributor, string UPC)
: m_Count(0),
  m_Worker(new UndatedStockItem(Name, InStock, Price,
  MinimumStock, MinimumReorder, Distributor, UPC))
{
  m_Worker->m_Count = 1;
}
```

Susan had some comments about this normal constructor for the new version of the StockItem class as well as about the other normal constructor (in Figure 3.37):

> **Susan:** I don't get how this can be a normal constructor if it has m_Worker in it. The normal ones are the ones you wrote before this. I am confused. Same thing with Figure 3.37; these are not normal constructors for StockItem.

> **Steve:** The implementation of the constructor doesn't determine whether it is "normal". A "normal" constructor is one that creates an object with specified data in it, as opposed to a default constructor (Figure 3.32) or a copy constructor (Figure 3.39).

Immediately after the execution of the line StockItem item1("cups",32,129,10,5,"Bob's Dist.","2895657951");, the newly constructed StockItem object and its UndatedStockItem worker object look something like the diagram in Figure 3.36.[11]

**FIGURE 3.36. Safe polymorphism: A polymorphic StockItem object with an UndatedStockItem worker**

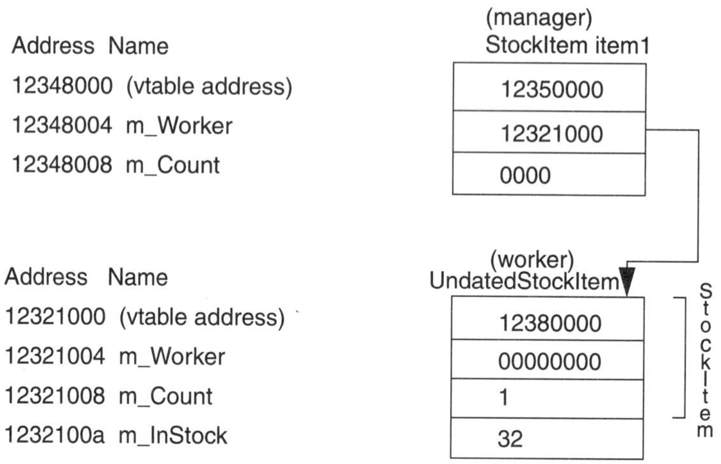


The next line in Figure 3.34 on page 168, StockItem item2("Hot Chicken", 48, 15, 12, "Joe's Dist.","987654321", "19960824");, calls the constructor shown in Figure 3.37, which creates a StockItem whose m_Worker member variable points to a DatedStockItem. As you can see, this is almost identical to the previous constructor, except, of course, that it creates a DatedStockItem as the worker object rather than an UndatedStockItem.

After the statement StockItem item2("Hot Chicken", 48, 158, 15, 12, "Joe's Dist.", "987654321", "19960824"); is executed, the newly

11. In this and the following diagrams, I've omitted a number of the data elements to make the figure fit on the page.

constructed StockItem object and its DatedStockItem worker object looks something like the diagram in Figure 3.38.

**FIGURE 3.37. Safe polymorphism: A normal constructor that constructs a** StockItem **having a date (from code\itemp.cc)**

```
StockItem::StockItem(string Name, short InStock,
  short Price, short MinimumStock, short MinimumReorder,
  string Distributor, string UPC, string Expires)
: m_Count(0),
  m_Worker(new DatedStockItem(Name, InStock, Price,
  MinimumStock, MinimumReorder, Distributor, UPC, Expires))
{
  m_Worker->m_Count = 1;
}
```

**FIGURE 3.38. Safe polymorphism: A polymorphic** StockItem **object with a** DatedStockItem **worker**

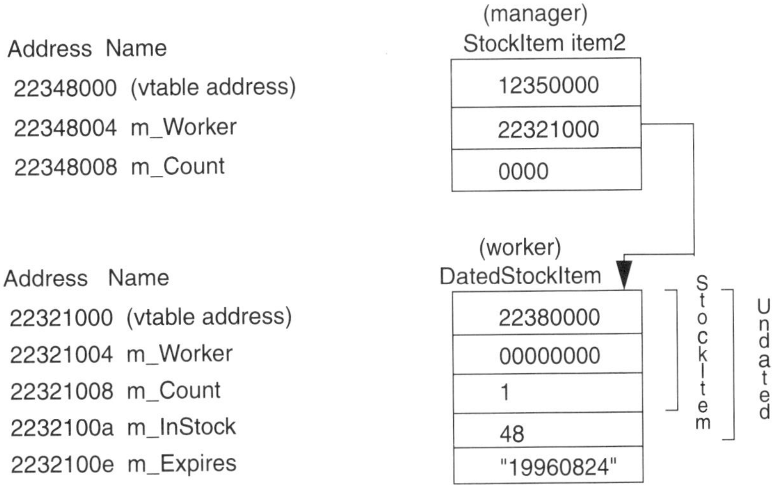


Now let's take a look at what happens when we execute the next statement in Figure 3.34 on page 168, StockItem item3 = item1;. Since we are creating a new StockItem with the same contents as an existing StockItem, this statement calls the copy constructor, which is shown in Figure 3.39.

**FIGURE 3.39. Safe polymorphism: The copy constructor for StockItem (from code\itemp.cc)**

```
StockItem::StockItem(const StockItem& Item)
: m_Count(0), m_Worker(Item.m_Worker)
{
 m_Worker->m_Count ++;
}
```

Susan wanted to know why we would want to create a new StockItem with the same contents as an existing one.

**Susan:** Why would you want to create a new StockItem just like an old one? Why not just use the old one again?

**Steve:** The most common use for the copy constructor is when we pass an argument by value or return a value from a function. In either of these cases, the copy constructor is used to make a new object with the same contents as an existing one.

**Susan:** I still don't see why we need to make copies rather than using the original objects.

**Steve:** In the case of a value argument, this is necessary because we don't want to change the value of the caller's variable if we change the local variable.

In the case of a return value, it's necessary to make a copy because an object that is created inside the called function will cease to exist at the end of the function, before the calling function can use it. Therefore, when we return an object by value we are actually asking the compiler to make a copy of the object; the copy is guaranteed to last long enough for the calling function to use it.

This copy constructor uses the pointer from the existing StockItem object (Item.m_Worker) to initialize the newly created StockItem object's pointer, m_Worker, so that the new and existing StockItem objects will share a worker object. Then we initialize the value of m_Count in the new object to 0 so that it has a known value. Finally, we increment the m_Count variable in the worker object because it has one more user than it had before.

After this operation, the variables item1 and item3, together with their shared worker object, look something like Figure 3.40.

**FIGURE 3.40. Safe polymorphism: Two polymorphic StockItem objects sharing the same UndatedStockItem worker object**

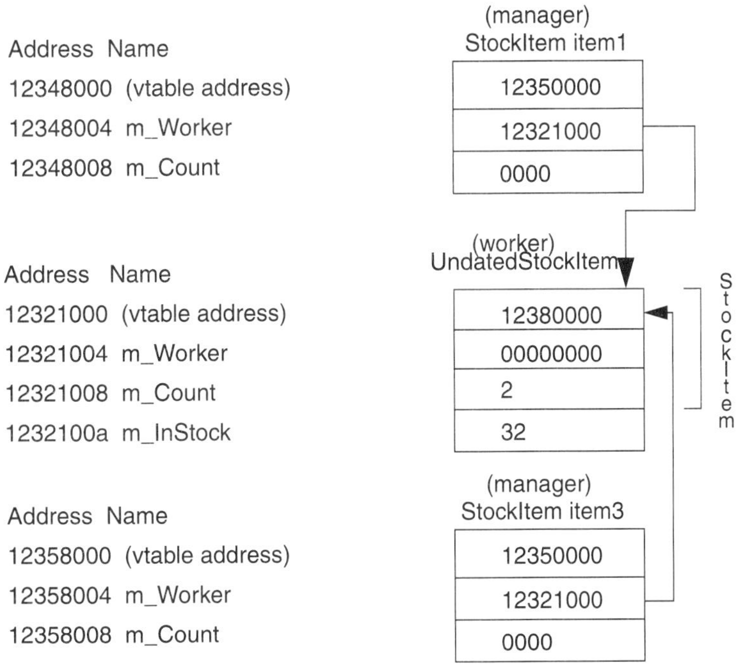


Why is it all right to share data in this situation? Because we have the m_Count variable to keep track of the number of users of the

worker object so that our StockItem destructor will know when it is time to delete that object. This should be abundantly clear when we get to the end of the program and see what happens when the destructor is called for the StockItem variables.

Now let's continue by looking at the next statement in Figure 3.34 on page 168: item1 = item2;. As you may have figured out already, this is actually a call to the assignment operator (operator =) for the StockItem class.

In case that wasn't obvious to you, don't despair; it wasn't to Susan either:

> **Susan:** No, I didn't figure out that this is a call to the assignment operator. It seems to me that you are setting item2 to item1. I see that operator = has to be called to do this, but I don't see how the program is intentionally calling it.
>
> **Steve:** Whenever we assign the value of one object to another existing object of the same class, we are calling the assignment operator of that class. That's what "=" means for objects.

The code for that operator is shown in Figure 3.41.

**FIGURE 3.41. Safe polymorphism: The assignment operator** (operator =) **for** StockItem **(from code\itemp.cc)**

```
StockItem& StockItem::operator = (const StockItem& Item)
{
 if (&Item != this)
  {
  m_Worker->m_Count --;
  if (m_Worker->m_Count <= 0)
   delete m_Worker;
  m_Worker = Item.m_Worker;
  m_Worker->m_Count ++;
  }
 return *this;
}
```

This function starts out with the line if (&Item != this), which implements the standard test to see if the source object and the target object are actually the same object, in which case it doesn't have to (and doesn't) do anything. In the example program, the source object is item2 and the target object is item1, which are different objects. So we continue with the next statement in the code for operator =, m_Worker->m_Count--;, which decrements the count in the worker object pointed to by the target object (item1). If you look at Figure 3.40, you'll see that the previous value of that variable was 2, so it is now 1, meaning that there is one StockItem that is still using that worker object. Therefore, the condition in the next line, if (m_Worker->m_Count <= 0), is false, which means that the controlled statement of the if statement — delete m_Worker; — is not executed. This is correct because as long as there is at least one user of the worker object, it cannot be deleted.

The next statement in the code for operator = is m_Worker = Item.m_Worker;, which sets the worker object pointer in the target object (item1) equal to the pointer in the source object (item2), which was the main point of the whole operation in the first place. Now item1 and item2 are sharing a worker object, so they are effectively the same. Then the statement m_Worker->m_Count ++; increments the count of users of the shared worker object (in this case to 2). Again, this is necessary so that we know when it's safe and appropriate to delete the worker object and reclaim the memory it occupies. Finally, as is standard with assignment operators, we return to the calling function by the statement return *this;, which returns the object to which we have assigned a new value.

When all this has been done, item1 and item2 will share a DatedStockItem, while item3 will have its own UndatedStockItem. The manager variables item1 and item2, together with their shared worker object, look something like Figure 3.42, and item3 looks pretty much as shown in Figure 3.43.

**FIGURE 3.42. Safe polymorphism: Two polymorphic StockItem objects sharing the same DatedStockItem worker object**

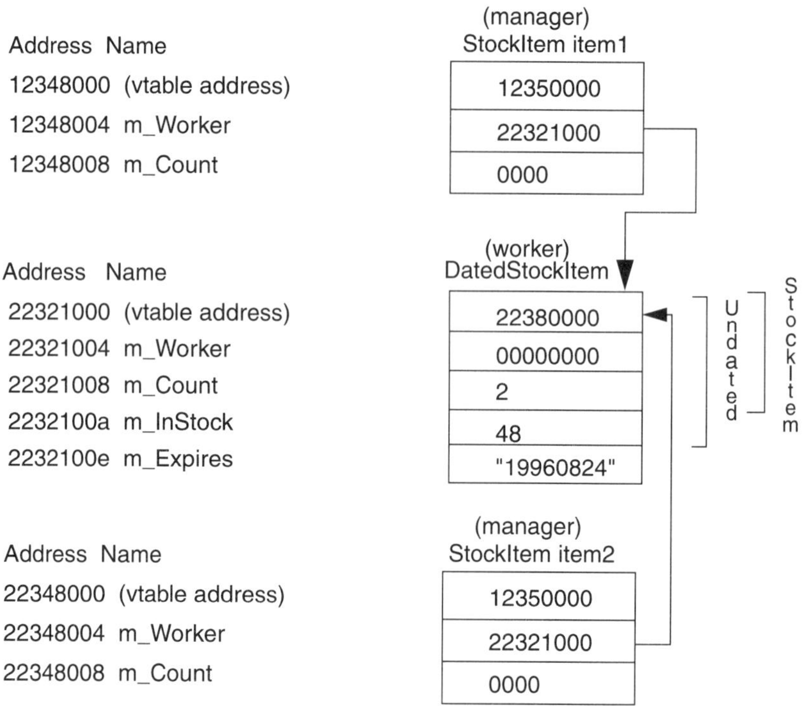


You should note that item1 has effectively changed its type from UndatedStockItem to DatedStockItem as a result of the assignment statement. This is one of the benefits of using polymorphic objects: The effective type of an object can vary not only when it is created but at any time thereafter. Therefore, we don't have to be locked in to a particular type when we create an object, but can adjust the type as necessary according to circumstances. By the way, this ability to change the effective type of an object at run time also solves the *slicing* problem referred to in Chapter 2, where we assigned an object of a derived class to a base class object with the result that the extra fields from the derived class object were lost.

**FIGURE 3.43. Safe polymorphism: A polymorphic StockItem object**

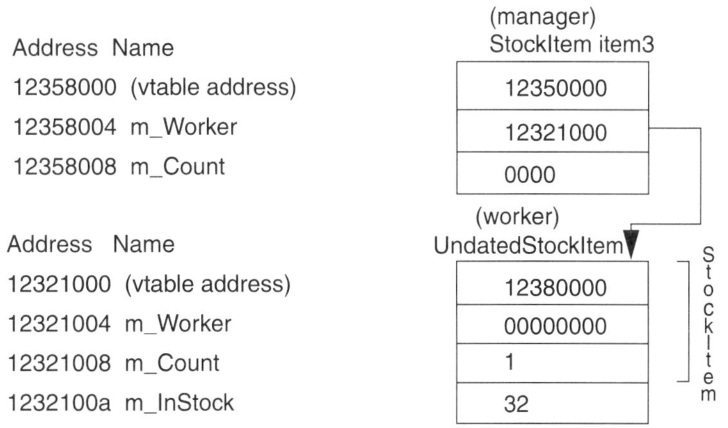


Susan and I had quite a discussion about the implementation of this version of operator =:

> **Susan:** If this is an assignment operator, then how come it has the code for reference counting in it? What does that have to do with anything?
>
> **Steve:** It needs code for reference counting because it has to keep track of how many users of its worker object (pointed to by m_Worker) still remain. The following line does that:
>
> ```
> m_Worker->m_Count --;
> ```
>
> If there aren't any more users of that worker object, then it can (and indeed must) be deleted. That's the purpose of the lines:
>
> ```
> if (m_Worker->m_Count <= 0)
>   delete m_Worker;
> ```
>
> Then it has to copy the pointer to the worker object from "Item", like so:

```
m_Worker = Item.m_Worker;
```

**Susan:** Wait a minute. I don't understand what this part does.

**Steve:** It makes the current object (the one pointed to by this) share a "worker" object with the manager object on the right of the =, which we refer to here as Item.

**Susan:** Okay.

**Steve:** Finally, it has to increment the number of users of the worker object from "Item", since that worker object is now being used by "our" object (i.e., the one pointed to by this). That's taken care of by the line:

```
m_Worker->m_Count ++;
```

**Susan:** So, do we have pointers pointing to pointers here?

**Steve:** Not exactly: We have one object containing a pointer to another object.

## *The Last Shall Be First*

Now let's take a look at what happens when the StockItem objects are destroyed at the end of the main program. As the C++ language specifies for the destruction of auto variables, the last to be created will be the first to be destroyed. Thus, item3 will be destroyed first, followed by item2, and finally item1. Figure 3.44 shows the code for the destructor for StockItem.

**FIGURE 3.44. Safe polymorphism: The destructor for the** StockItem class **(from code\itemp.cc)**

```
StockItem::~StockItem()
{
  if (m_Worker == 0)
    return;

  m_Worker->m_Count --;
  if (m_Worker->m_Count <= 0)
    delete m_Worker;
}
```

Before we get into the details of this code, I should mention that whenever any object is destroyed, all of its constituent elements that have destructors are automatically destroyed as well. In the case of a StockItem, the string variables are automatically destroyed during the destruction of the StockItem.

Susan had some questions about the destructor. Here's the first installment:

**Susan:** Why are you doing reference counting again in the destructor? Is that where it belongs? So, you have to reference-count twice, once for when something is added and again, with different code for when something is subtracted?

**Steve:** Close. Actually, it's a bit more general: Every time a worker object acquires another user, we have to increment its count, and every time it loses one of its users, we have to decrement its count. That way, when the count gets to 0, we know there aren't any more users, and we can therefore use delete to free the memory occupied by the worker object.

**Susan:** So with this reference counting, the whole point is to know when to use delete?

**Steve:** Yes.

**Susan:** How does the delete operator automatically call the destructor for that variable?

**Steve:** That's a rule in C++: Calling delete for a variable that has a destructor always calls the destructor for that variable.

The first if statement in the destructor, if (m_Worker == 0), provides a clue as to why our special StockItem constructor (Figure 3.33 on page 164) had to set the m_Worker variable to 0. We'll see exactly how that comes into play shortly. For now, we know that the value of m_Worker in item3 is not 0, as it points to an UndatedStockItem (see Figure 3.43 on page 177), so the condition in the first if statement is false. Therefore, we move to the next statement, m_Worker->m_Count--;. Since, according to Figure 3.43, the value of m_Count in the UndatedStockItem to which m_Worker points is 1, this statement reduces the value of that variable to 0, making the condition in the statement if (m_Worker->m_Count <= 0) true. This means that the controlled statement of the if statement, delete m_Worker;, is executed. Since the value of m_Count is 0, no other StockItem variables are currently using the UndatedStockItem pointed to by m_Worker. Therefore, we want that UndatedStockItem to go away so that its memory can be reclaimed, and we use the delete operator to accomplish that goal.

Susan had a question about why I used <= as the condition in the if statement.

**Susan:** Why did you say <= 0? How could the count ever be less than 0?

**Steve:** If the program is working correctly, it can't. This is a case of "defensive programming": I wanted to make sure that if, by some error, the count got below 0, the program wouldn't hang onto the memory for the worker object forever. In a production program, it would probably be a good idea to record such an "impossible" condition somewhere so the maintenance programmer could take a look at it.

This is not quite as simple as it may seem, however, because before the memory used by a UndatedStockItem can be reclaimed, the destructor for that UndatedStockItem must be called to allow all of its constituent parts (especially the string variables it contains) to expire properly. As I've mentioned, when we call the delete operator for a variable that has a destructor, it automatically calls the destructor for that variable. Therefore, the next function called is the destructor for the UndatedStockItem being deleted.

Before going into the details of this function, I should explain why it is called in the first place. Remember, we're using StockItem*s to refer to either DatedStockItem or UndatedStockItem objects. How does the compiler know to call the right destructor?

Just as it does with other functions in the same situation: We have to make the destructor virtual so that the correct destructor will be called, no matter what the type of the pointer through which the object is accessed. This answers the earlier question of why we had to define a destructor and declare it to be virtual in Figure 3.13. As a general rule, destructors should be virtual if there are any other virtual functions in the class, as we have to make sure that the right destructor will be called via a base class pointer. Otherwise, data elements that are defined in the derived class won't be destroyed properly, possibly resulting in memory leaks or other undesirable effects.

At this point, Susan had some questions on virtual destructors and the nature of reality (as it applies to C++, at least) :

**Susan:** How are destructors virtual? Do they have a vtable?

**Steve:** They're in the vtable if they're declared to be virtual, as the one in the final version of StockItem is.

**Susan:** With all this virtual stuff going on, what is really real? What is the driving force behind all this? It seems like this is a fun house of smoke and mirrors, and I can't tell any more what is really in control.

**Steve:** The StockItem object is the "manager", who takes credit for work done by a "worker" object; the worker is either a DatedStockItem or an UndatedStockItem. Hopefully, the rest of the discussion will clarify this.

We don't have to write a destructor for UndatedStockItem because the compiler-generated one does the job for us. But what exactly does that compiler-generated destructor do?

It calls the destructor for every member variable in the class that has a destructor. This is necessary to make sure that those member variables are properly cleaned up after their scope expires when the object they're in goes away. In addition, just as the constructor for a derived class always calls a constructor for its embedded base class object, so a destructor for a derived class always calls the destructor for the base class part of the derived class object. There are two differences between these situations, however:

1. The constructor for the base class part of the object is called *before* any of the code in the derived class constructor is executed; the base class destructor is called *after* the code in the derived class destructor is executed. Here, of course, this distinction is irrelevant because we haven't written any code in the derived class destructor.
2. There is only one destructor for a given class.

This second difference between constructors and destructors means that we can't use a trick similar to the "special base class constructor" trick used to prevent the base class constructor from calling the derived class constructor again. Instead, we have to arrange a way for the base class destructor to determine whether it's being asked to destroy a "real" base class object (a StockItem) or the embedded base class part of a derived class object (the StockItem base class part of an UndatedStockItem or DatedStockItem). In the latter case, the destructor should exit immediately, since the StockItem base class part of either of those classes contains nothing that needs special handling by the destructor. The special constructor called by the UndatedStockItem constructor to initialize its StockItem part (Figure 3.33 on page 164) works with the first if statement in the StockItem destructor (Figure 3.44 on page 179) to solve this problem. The special StockItem constructor sets m_Worker to 0, which cannot be the address of any object, during the initialization of the base class part of an UndatedStockItem. When the destructor for StockItem is executed, a 0 value for m_Worker is the indicator of a StockItem that is the base class part of a derived class object. This allows the StockItem destructor to distinguish between a real StockItem and the base class part of an object of a class derived from StockItem by examining the value of m_Worker and bailing out immediately if it is the reserved value of 0.

## *Going, Going, Gone*

Now it's time to go into detail about what happens when item3, item2, and item1 are destroyed. They go away in that order because the last object to be constructed on the stack in a given scope is the first to be destroyed, as you might expect when dealing with stacks.

Figure 3.45 is another listing of the destructor for the StockItem class (StockItem::~StockItem()), for reference as we trace its execution.

**FIGURE 3.45. Safe polymorphism: The destructor for the** StockItem class **(from code\itemp.cc)**

```
StockItem::~StockItem()
{
 if (m_Worker == 0)
  return;

 m_Worker->m_Count --;
 if (m_Worker->m_Count <= 0)
  delete m_Worker;
}
```

At the end of the main program, item3 (Figure 3.43 on page 177), which was the last StockItem to be created, is the first to go out of scope. At that point, the StockItem destructor is automatically invoked to clean up. Since the value of m_Worker in item3 isn't 0, the statement controlled by the first if statement isn't executed. Next, we execute the statement m_Worker->m_Count--;, which reduces the value of the variable m_Count in the UndatedStockItem pointed to by m_Worker to 0. Since this makes that variable 0, the condition in the second if statement is true, so its controlled statement, delete m_Worker;, is executed. As we've seen, this eliminates the object pointed to by m_Worker, calling the UndatedStockItem destructor in the process.

As before, calling this destructor does nothing other than destroy the member variable that has a destructor (namely, the m_Expires member variable, which is a string), followed by the mandatory call to the base class destructor.

At that point, the first if statement in StockItem::~StockItem comes into play along with its controlled statement. These two statements are

```
if (m_Worker == 0)
  return;
```

Remember the special base class constructor StockItem(int) (Figure 3.33 on page 164)? That constructor, which is called from our UndatedStockItem default and normal constructors, initializes m_Worker to 0. Thus, we know that m_Worker will be 0 for any object that is actually an UndatedStockItem or a DatedStockItem, because all of the constructors for DatedStockItem call one of those two constructors for UndatedStockItem to initialize their UndatedStockItem base class part. Therefore, this if statement will be true for the base class part of all UndatedStockItem and DatedStockItem objects. Since the current object being destroyed is in fact an UndatedStockItem object, the if is true, and so, the destructor exits immediately, ending the destruction of the UndatedStockItem object. Then the destructor for item3 finishes by freeing the storage associated with that object.

Next, the StockItem destructor is called for item2 (Figure 3.42 on page 176). Since m_Worker is not 0, the condition in the first if in Figure 3.45 on page 183 is false, so we proceed to the next statement, m_Worker->m_Count--;. As you can see by looking back at Figure 3.42, the previous value of that variable was 2, so it is now 1. As a result, the condition in the next if statement, if (m_Worker->m_Count <= 0), is also false. Thus, the controlled statement that uses delete to get rid of the DatedStockItem pointed to by m_Worker is not executed. Then the destructor for item2 finishes by freeing the storage associated with that object.

Finally, item1 (Figure 3.42 on page 176) dies at the end of its scope. When it does, the StockItem destructor is called to clean up its act. As before, m_Worker isn't 0, so the controlled statement of the first if statement in Figure 3.45 on page 183 isn't executed. Next, we execute the statement m_Worker->m_Count--;, which reduces the value of the variable m_Count in the DatedStockItem pointed to by m_Worker to 0. This time, the condition in the next if statement is true, so its controlled statement, delete m_Worker;, is executed. We've seen that this eliminates the object pointed to by m_Worker, calling the appropriate destructor for the worker object, which in this case is DatedStockItem::~DatedStockItem. As with the UndatedStockItem destructor, the compiler-generated destructor for DatedStockItem calls all the destructors for the member variables and base class part, which in this case is an UndatedStockItem. Therefore, we don't have to write this destructor ourselves.

Lastly, the call to the StockItem destructor occurs exactly as it did in the destruction of item3, except that there is an additional step because the base class of DatedStockItem is UndatedStockItem, and the destructor for that class in turn calls the destructor for its base class part, which is a StockItem. Once we get to the destructor for StockItem, the value of m_Worker is 0, so that destructor simply returns to the destructor for UndatedStockItem, which returns to the destructor for DatedStockItem. Then the destructor for item1 finishes by freeing the storage associated with that object.

If you find the above explanation clear, congratulations. Susan didn't:

> **Susan:** How do you know that the m_Worker can never be 0 in a real StockItem and is always 0 in a StockItem that is a base class part of a derived class object?
>
> **Steve:** Because I set m_Worker to 0 in the special StockItem constructor called from the base class initializer in the default and normal constructors for UndatedStockItem. Therefore, that special constructor is always used to set up the base class part of an UndatedStockItem, and since DatedStockItem derives from UndatedStockItem, the same will be true of a DatedStockItem.

## *For the Benefit of Posterity*

Now it's time to clear up a point we've glossed over so far. We have already seen that the member initialization expression m_Count(0), present in the constructors for the StockItem object, is there just to make sure we don't have an uninitialized variable in the StockItem object — even though we won't be using m_Count in a StockItem object. While this is true as far as it goes, it doesn't answer the question of why we need this variable at all if we're not using it in the StockItem class. The clue to the answer is that we are using that member variable in the object pointed to by m_Worker (i.e., m_Worker->m_Count). But why don't we just add the m_Count variable when we create the UndatedStockItem class rather than carry along extra baggage in the StockItem class?

The answer is that m_Worker is not an UndatedStockItem* but a StockItem*. Remember, the compiler doesn't know the actual type of the object being pointed to at compile time; all it knows is the declared type of the pointer, which in this case is StockItem*. It must therefore use that declared type to determine what operations are permissible through that pointer. Hence, if there's no m_Count variable in a StockItem, the compiler won't let us refer to that variable through a StockItem*.

Susan wasn't sure of what I was trying to say here:

**Susan:** What do you mean, if there were no m_Count variable in a StockItem, we wouldn't be able to access it through a StockItem pointer?

**Steve:** The only member variables and member functions that you can access through a pointer are ones that exist in the class it's a pointer to, no matter what type the pointer may really be pointing to. This is a consequence of C++'s "static type checking"; if we were allowed to refer to a member variable or function that might theoretically not be present in an object at run time, the compiler would have no way of knowing whether what we were trying to do was legal. Therefore, if we want to access a member variable called m_Count through a StockItem*, there has to be a member variable called m_Count in the StockItem class, even if we don't need it until we get to a class derived from StockItem.

This also brings up another point that may or may not be obvious to you: The workings of the polymorphic StockItem object don't depend on the fact that the DatedStockItem class is derived from UndatedStockItem. So long as both the UndatedStockItem and DatedStockItem classes are derived directly or indirectly from StockItem, we can use a StockItem* to refer to an object of either of these classes, UndatedStockItem or DatedStockItem, which is all that we need to make the idiom work.

## Review

We started this chapter with the DatedStockItem class from Chapter 2, which extended the StockItem class by adding an expiration date field to the member variables that DatedStockItem inherited from the StockItem class. While this was a fine solution to the problem of creating a class based on the StockItem class without having to rewrite all the functioning code in the latter class, it didn't solve the bigger problem: how to create a vector of objects that might or might not have expiration dates. That is, we wanted to be able to mix StockItem objects with DatedStockItem objects in the same vector, which can't be done directly in C++.

Part of this difficulty was solved easily enough by making a vector of StockItem*s (i.e., pointers to StockItems), rather than StockItems, to take advantage of the fact that C++ allows us to assign the address of an object of a derived type to a pointer of its base class (e.g., to assign the address of a DatedStockItem to a pointer of type StockItem*). Creating such a vector of StockItem*s allowed us to create both StockItems and DatedStockItems and to assign the addresses of these objects to various elements of that vector. Even so, this didn't solve the problem completely: When we called the Reorder function through a StockItem pointer, the function that was executed was always StockItem::Reorder. This result may seem reasonable, but it doesn't meet our needs. When we call the Reorder function for an object, we want to execute the correct Reorder function for the actual type of the object the pointer is referring to even though the pointer is declared as a StockItem*.

The reason the StockItem function is always called in this situation is precisely that when we make a base class pointer (e.g., a StockItem*) refer to a derived class object (e.g., a DatedStockItem), the compiler doesn't know what the actual type of the object is at compile time. By default, the compiler determines exactly which function will be called at compile time, and the only information the compiler has about the type of an object pointed to by a StockItem* is that it's either a StockItem or an object of a class derived from

StockItem. In this situation, the compiler defaults to the base class function.

The solution to this problem is to make the Reorder function virtual. This means that when the compiler sees a call to the Reorder function, it generates code that will call the appropriate version of that function for the actual type of the object referred to. In this case, StockItem::Reorder is called if the actual object being referred to through a StockItem* is a StockItem, while DatedStockItem::Reorder is called if the actual object being referred to through a StockItem* is a DatedStockItem. This is exactly the behavior we need to make our StockItem and DatedStockItem objects do the right thing when we refer to them through a StockItem*.

To make this run-time determination of which function will be called, the compiler has to add something to every object that contains at least one virtual function. What it adds is a pointer to a vtable (virtual function table), which contains the addresses of all the virtual functions defined in the class of that object or in any of its ancestral classes. The code the compiler generates for a virtual function call uses this table to look up the actual address of the function to be called at run time.

After going over the use of virtual functions, we looked at the implementation of the usual I/O functions, operator << and operator >>. Even though these can't be virtual functions, as they aren't member functions at all, they can still use the virtual mechanism indirectly by calling virtual functions that provide the correct behavior for each class. However, while this solves most of the problems with operator <<, the implementation of operator >> is still pretty tricky. It has to allocate the memory for the object it is creating because the actual type of that object isn't known until the data for the object has been read. The real problem here, though, is not that operator >> has to allocate that memory, or even that it has to use a reference to a pointer to notify the calling function of the address of the allocated memory. The big difficulty is that after operator >> allocates the memory, the calling function has to free the memory when it is done with the object. Getting a program written this way to work properly is very difficult; keeping it working properly after later changes is virtually impossible. Unfortunately, there's no solution to this problem as long as we require the user program to use a vector of StockItem*s to get the benefits of polymorphism.

As is often the case in C++, though, there is a way to remove that requirement. We can hide the pointers and the consequent memory allocation problems from the user by creating a *polymorphic object* using the *manager/worker idiom*. With these idioms, the user sees only a base class object, within which the pointers are hidden. The base class is the manager class, which uses an object of one of the worker classes to do the actual work.

Possibly the most unusual aspect of the manager/worker idiom is that the type of the pointer inside the manager object is the same as the type of the manager class. In the current case, each StockItem object contains a StockItem* called m_Worker as its main data member. This may seem peculiar, but it makes sense. The actual type of the object being referred to is always one of the worker classes, which in this case means either UndatedStockItem or DatedStockItem. Since we know that a StockItem* can refer to an object of any of the derived classes of StockItem, and because we want the interface of the StockItem class to be the same as that of any of its derived classes, declaring the pointer to the worker object as a StockItem* is quite appropriate.

We started our examination of this new StockItem class with operator <<, whose header indicates one of the advantages of this new implementation of StockItem. Rather than taking a StockItem*, as the previous version of operator << did, it takes a const reference to a StockItem. The implementation of this function consists of a call to a virtual function called Write. Since Write is virtual, the exact function that will be called here depends on the actual type of the object pointed to by m_Worker, which is exactly the behavior we want.

After going into more detail on how this "internal polymorphism" works, we looked at how such a polymorphic object comes into existence in the first place, starting with the default constructor for

StockItem. This constructor is a bit more complicated than it seems at first. When it creates an empty UndatedStockItem to perform the duties of a default-constructed StockItem, that newly constructed UndatedStockItem has to initialize its base class part, as is required for all derived class objects. That may not seem too unusual, but keep in mind that the base class for UndatedStockItem is StockItem; therefore, the constructor for UndatedStockItem will necessarily call a constructor for StockItem. We have to make sure that it doesn't call the default constructor for StockItem, as that is where the UndatedStockItem constructor was called from in the first place! The result of such a call would be a further call to the default constructor for UndatedStockItem, then to the default constructor for StockItem, and so on forever (or at least until we had run out of stack space). The solution is simple enough: We have to create a special constructor for StockItem, StockItem::StockItem(int), that we call explicitly via a base class initializer in the default and normal constructors for UndatedStockItem. This special constructor doesn't do anything but initialize m_Worker to 0, for reasons we'll get to later, and then return to its caller. Since it doesn't call any other functions, we avoid the potential disaster of an infinite regress.

This simple function, StockItem::StockItem(int), does have a couple of other interesting features. First, I declared it protected so that it couldn't be called by anyone other than our member functions and those of our derived classes. This is sensible because, after all, we don't want a user to be able to create a StockItem with just an int argument. In fact, we are using that argument only to allow the compiler to tell which constructor we mean via the *function overloading* facility. This also means that we don't need to provide a name for that argument, since we're not using it. Leaving the name out tells the compiler that we didn't accidentally forget to use the argument, so we won't get "unused argument" warnings when we compile this code. Any programmers who may have to work on our code in the future will also appreciate this indication that we weren't planning to use the argument.

Then we examined the use of *reference-counting* to keep track of the number of users of a given DatedStockItem or UndatedStockItem object, rather than copying those objects whenever we copied their manager objects. As long as we keep track of how many users there are, we can safely delete the DatedStockItem or UndatedStockItem as soon as there are no more users left. To keep track of the number of users, we use the m_Count member variable in the StockItem class.

To see how this works in practice, we went through the actions that occur when StockItem objects are created, copied, and destroyed. This involves the implementation of the assignment operator, which copies the pointer to the worker object contained in the manager object. We can do this because we are using the *reference-counting idiom* to keep track of the number of users of each object, so memory is freed correctly when the objects are destroyed at the end of the function where they are created.

The destructor for the StockItem class has a number of new features. First, it is virtual, which is necessary because the derived class object pointed to by the StockItem object must be destroyed when it no longer has any users, but the type of the pointer through which it is accessed is StockItem*. To allow the compiler to call the correct destructor — the one for the derived class object — we must declare the base class destructor virtual. This is the same rule that applies to all other functions that have to be resolved according to the run-time type of the object for which they are called.

Second, the StockItem destructor has to check whether it has been called to destroy the base class part of a derived class object. Just as in the case of the constructor for StockItem, we have to prevent an infinite regress in which the destructor for StockItem calls the destructor for DatedStockItem, which calls the destructor for StockItem, which calls the destructor for DatedStockItem again, and so on. In fact, in this case we can't avoid the first "round trip" because the destructor for DatedStockItem must call the destructor for StockItem; we don't have any control over that. However, the first if statement in the StockItem destructor cuts off the regress right there, as m_Worker will be 0 in the base class part of a derived class object.

That's why we initialized m_Worker to 0 in the special constructor for StockItem that was used to construct the base class part of an object of a class derived from StockItem.

We finished by examining the exact sequence of events that occurs when the objects in the example program are destroyed. We also determined the reason that we had to include m_Count in the base class when it was never used there: The type of the pointer we use to access m_Count is a StockItem*, so there has to be an m_Count variable in a StockItem. If there were no such variable in the StockItem class, the compiler couldn't guarantee that it would exist in the object pointed to by a StockItem pointer and therefore wouldn't let us access it through such a pointer.

## *Exercises, Second Set*

3. Rewrite the DrugStockItem class that you wrote earlier in this chapter as a derived class of DatedStockItem, adding the new class to the polymorphic object implementation based on the StockItem class. The Reorder member function of the DrugStockItem class will be inherited from DatedStockItem, and the member function DeductSaleFromInventory will have to be made a virtual function in StockItem so that the correct version will be called via the StockItem* in the StockItem class. The resulting set of classes will allow the effective type of a StockItem object to be any of UndatedStockItem, DatedStockItem, or DrugStockItem.

4. Rewrite the Employee, Exempt, and Hourly classes that you wrote earlier in this chapter as a set of classes implementing a polymorphic object type. The base class will be Employee, with an Exempt class and an Hourly class derived from the base class. The resulting set of classes will allow the effective type of an Employee object to be either Exempt or Hourly, with the CalculatePay function producing the correct result for either type. To distinguish the effective types, you will need to write two different versions of

the constructor for the Employee class. Do this by adding an additional argument of type float in the constructor that creates an Hourly worker object, specifying the multiplier used to calculate overtime pay. For example, a value of 1.5 specifies the standard "time-and-a-half for overtime" multiplier. Note that you *must* maintain the same interface for the CalculatePay function in these classes because you are using a base class pointer to access derived class objects.

## *Conclusion*

Now that we have enough tools to work with, it's time to tackle a more realistic project. That's what we'll do in the next chapter, where we start to develop a home inventory system.

CHAPTER 4

# The Home Inventory Project

Now that we have enough tools to start working on a somewhat more realistic project, what sort of project should that be? I've spent some time thinking that question over and have come up with what I think is a good way to hone our skills as well as advance them: a "home inventory program" to keep track of the myriad objects, technically known as "stuff", that we have lying around in our houses or apartments. When you consider that insurance companies are a lot happier and quicker to pay after a loss if you have an up-to-date list of your possessions, with any luck this program may actually be useful as well as instructive! Of course, before we start we need to define some terms and establish some objectives for this chapter.

## Definitions

**Aliasing** is the practice of referring to one object by more than one "name"; in C++ these names are actually pointers.

The **aliasing problem** is a name for the difficulties caused by altering a shared object.

An **enum** is a way to define a number of unchangeable values, which are quite similar to consts. The value of each successive name in an enum is automatically incremented from the value of the previous name (if you don't specify another value explicitly). The term enum is short for "enumeration", which is a list of numbers.

The **switch** statement is functionally equivalent to a number of if/else statements in a row, but is easier to read and modify. The keyword switch is followed by a *selection expression* (in parentheses), which specifies an expression used to select an alternative section of code. The various alternatives to be considered are enclosed in a set of curly braces following the selection expressions and are marked off by the keyword case followed by the (constant) value to be matched and a colon.

An **array initialization list** is a list of values that are used to initialize the elements of an *array*. The ability to specify a list of values for an array is built into the C++ language and is not available for user-defined data types such as the vector.

## *Objectives of This Chapter*

By the end of this chapter, you should

1. understand how to create a more realistic application using the tools we already have,
2. know how to use the switch statement to select among a number of alternatives,
3. know how to use the enum data type to give names to constant values that will be used to refer to items in a list,

4. understand the advantages of creating variables at the point of use rather than at the beginning of a function,
5. know how to find or change the size of a vector dynamically when necessary, and
6. understand how to use virtual functions for implementation purposes within a polymorphic class hierarchy.

## *Homing In*

What information will we need to store for the various types of objects in our home inventory? No matter what type of object we are recording, we will want to store the following data:

1. type of object,
2. date of acquisition,
3. price,
4. description,
5. category (e.g., office furniture, kitchen appliance).

While we'll have to maintain the above data for every object, we'll also need to keep track of other infomation on some types of objects. Of course, the exact form of that extra information will depend on each object's type. After some thought, I have come up with the following types of objects that we might want to keep track of (in no particular order):

1. "Basic" objects, for which the above data are sufficient;
2. "Music" objects (e.g., CDs, LPs, cassettes);
3. computer hardware;
4. computer software;

5. other electric and electronic appliances;
6. books;
7. kitchen items such as plates and flatware;
8. clothes and shoes.

Of course, each of these types has different additional information, which is why we need the individual types in the first place.

Undoubtedly you can think of a number of other kinds of objects that don't fit exactly into one of the listed types. However, I think most of these other kinds are close enough to one of the above types that we can use one of those listed without too much strain. For example, what about jewelry and art objects? It seems to me that the "Basic" type is fine for both of these, as we have to keep track of the basic information needed for all objects (value, date of acquisition, description, and category) and not much else.

### *What It Is, Mama!*

This brings us to a very important point in the design of any program, especially an object-oriented one: deciding how to fit the nearly infinite possibilities of real-world entities into a necessarily limited number of categories in the program. I wish there were a hard-and-fast rule I could give you so you wouldn't have to make this decision for every program you write; unfortunately, however, this isn't possible precisely because there are so many possibilities in the real world. The best I can do is give guidelines and examples.

Consider the example of LP records or cassette tapes. In this case, I think it's pretty obvious that an LP or a cassette tape is similar enough to a CD that using the "Music" type for either of these other types of sound recording is appropriate.[1] How did I make this determination?

1. The *purpose* of a CD is to contain music or speech. This is also the purpose of an LP or cassette.
2. The *information* that we might want to store about a CD includes artist, title, and track names. These are also appropriate for an LP or cassette.

Note that the storage medium and other surface similarities among objects aren't significant in this analysis. In fact, a CD-ROM, which uses exactly the same storage medium as a music CD does, is a completely different type of object from a music CD, and needs to be categorized under "computer software". That's because the purpose of the objects and the information we need to store about these two different kinds of CDs are completely different.[2]

What about rare coins or stamps? If you had only a couple of either of these objects, you might very well use the "Basic" type to keep track of them. However, if you had an extensive collection, you probably would want to keep track of their condition, year of minting or printing, denomination, and possibly other data of interest to collectors. To handle this extra information, you would need to add a "Coin/Stamp" type or even two separate types, if you happened to collect both. This merely illustrates the rule that the handling of data has to be based on the use to which it will be put, not on its intrinsic characteristics alone.

1. Of course, if you still have 8-track tapes, you probably also need a "lava lamp" category.
2. This is an oversimplification because both music CDs and CD-ROMs can be stored in the same "CD holder", whereas cassettes and LPs each need their own type of holders. Therefore, for purposes of figuring out how much storage you need for each type of object, the physical form of the object is indeed important. As always, the question is how you will use the information, not merely what information is available.

Now that we've developed a general outline of these classes and the data that they need to keep track of, let's start designing the interface they will present to the application program that uses them.

## *Interface R Us*

Why do I say "the interface" rather than "the interfaces"? Because we're going to implement these classes to give the appearance of a single type of object that can change its behavior; in other words, we're going to use the *manager/worker idiom* again to implement another type of *polymorphic object*. This will enable us to write a main program that allows access to an object of any of these types in a uniform manner. Of course, the implementation of the member functions will be somewhat different in each class, to take account of the peculiarities of each class, but the structure of the program will be essentially the same for any number of types once we've made provisions to handle more than one. For this reason, we'll use just the "Basic" and "Music" types in the text; handling the other types will be left as an exercise. Figure 4.1 shows the initial version of the HomeItem interface.

**FIGURE 4.1. The initial interface for the** HomeItem **manager** class **(code/hmit1.h)**

```
// hmit1.h

#include "string6.h"
#include "vector.h"

class HomeItem
{
friend ostream& operator << (ostream& os,
  const HomeItem& Item);

friend istream& operator >> (istream& is, HomeItem& Item);
```

```
public:
 HomeItem();
 HomeItem(const HomeItem& Item);
 HomeItem& operator = (const HomeItem& Item);
virtual ~HomeItem();

// Basic: Art objects, furniture, jewelry, etc.
 HomeItem(string Name, double PurchasePrice,
 long PurchaseDate, string Description, string Category);

// Music: CDs, LPs, cassettes, etc.
 HomeItem(string Name, double PurchasePrice,
 long PurchaseDate, string Description, string Category,
 string Artist, vector<string> Track);

virtual void Write(ostream& os);

protected:
 HomeItem(int);

protected:
 HomeItem* m_Worker;
 short m_Count;
};
```

If you think this looks familiar, you're right. It's almost exactly the same as the polymorphic object version of the StockItem interface we saw in Chapter 3. This is not a coincidence: Every polymorphic object interface is going to look very similar to every other one. Why is this?

## *Deja Vu All Over Again*

They all look alike because the objects of every polymorphic object manager class do very similar things: managing the "real" objects of classes derived from the manager class. The only differences between the interfaces of two polymorphic object types are in the member functions that the user of the polymorphic objects sees. In this case, we don't have a Reorder function as we did in the StockItem class, for the very simple reason that we don't have to figure out how many HomeItem objects to reorder from our distributors.

Before we get into the worker classes for the HomeItem polymorphic object, let's go over the similarities and differences between the StockItem and HomeItem interfaces; after all, they have to be *somewhat* different or they wouldn't be different types of objects!

1. The operators << and >>, as well as the default constructors, copy constructors, assignment operators, and destructors, have exactly the same interfaces in the StockItem class and the HomeItem class except, of course, for their names and the types of their arguments (if applicable). This also applies to the "special" constructor used to prevent an infinite loop during construction of a worker object as well as to the Write function used to create a human-readable version of the data for an object.

2. The "normal" constructors that create objects for which the initial state is known are the same in these two classes except, of course, for the exact arguments, which depend on the data needed by each object. One point we'll cover later is the use of a vector as an argument to the second "normal" constructor.

3. The GetName, GetPrice, and other class-specific member functions of StockItem don't exist in HomeItem because it is a different class with different requirements from those of StockItem.[3]

4. The member data items for the two classes are the same except, again, for the type of m_Worker, which is a pointer to a HomeItem rather than to a StockItem.

---

3. As we'll see, HomeItem will eventually have its own version of GetName. Many classes need the ability to retrieve the name of an item; using a function called something like GetName is a fairly common way to handle this requirement.

Of course, this class doesn't really do anything by itself; as with all polymorphic objects, we also need the worker classes to get the job done. Figure 4.2 shows the interfaces for HomeItemBasic and HomeItemMusic.

**FIGURE 4.2. The initial interface for the** HomeItemBasic **and** HomeItemMusic **worker** classes **(code\hmiti1.h)**

```
// hmiti1.h

class HomeItemBasic : public HomeItem
{
public:
  HomeItemBasic();

  HomeItemBasic(string Name, double PurchasePrice,
  long PurchaseDate, string Description, string Category);

virtual void Write(ostream& s);

virtual string GetType();

protected:
  string m_Name;
  double m_PurchasePrice;
  long m_PurchaseDate;
  string m_Description;
  string m_Category;
};

class HomeItemMusic : public HomeItemBasic
{
public:

  HomeItemMusic(string Name, double PurchasePrice,
  long PurchaseDate, string Description, string Category,
  string Artist, vector<string> Track);
```

```
virtual void Write(ostream& s);

virtual string GetType();

protected:
  string m_Artist;
  vector<string> m_Track;
};
```

Susan had a question about having two interface files.

**Susan:** Why do we need two different interface files again?

**Steve:** The first one (hmit1.h) is for the user of these classes; the second one (hmiti1.h) is only for our use as class implementers. The user never sees this second interface file, which means that we can change it if we need to without forcing the user to recompile everything.

As we did with the manager classes, let's take a look at the similarities and differences between the HomeItem and StockItem worker classes.

1. The default constructors, copy constructors, assignment operators, and destructors have exactly the same interfaces in the StockItem worker classes and the HomeItem worker classes except, of course, for their names and the types of their arguments (if applicable). This also applies to the Write function used to create a human-readable version of the data for an object.[4]
2. The "normal" constructors that create objects for which the initial state is known are the same in all of these classes except, of course, for the exact arguments, which depend on the data needed

4. In case you were wondering, we don't have to state that the destructors are virtual because that is guaranteed by the fact that the base class destructor is virtual. I've added the virtual keyword to the declaration of the derived class destructors solely for clarity.

by each object. Again, we'll go into what it means to have a vector argument when we cover the implementation of the "normal" constructor for the HomeItemMusic class.

3. The HomeItem worker classes have a GetType member function that the StockItem class doesn't have. The purpose of this function is to allow the proper storage and display of objects of various types. In the StockItem class, we depended on the value of the expiration date ("0" or a real date) to give us this information.
4. The GetName, GetPrice, and other class-specific member functions of the StockItem worker classes don't exist in the HomeItem worker classes, as explained above.
5. The member data items for the HomeItem worker classes are as needed for these classes, as is the case with the HomeItem worker classes.
6. We are using the long data type for the m_PurchaseDate member variable rather than the string data type that we used for a similar field in DatedStockItem.
7. We are using the double data type for the m_PurchasePrice member variable rather than the short data type that we used for price information in the StockItem classes.

The first of the differences between the StockItem worker classes and the HomeItem worker classes that needs additional explanation is the GetType virtual function first declared in HomeItemBasic. Since I have claimed that all the classes that participate in a polymorphic object implementation must have the same interface (so the user can treat them all the same), why am I declaring a new function in one of the worker classes that wasn't present in the base class?

## *What They Don't Know Won't Hurt Them*

That rule applies only to functions that are to be used by the user of the polymorphic object. The GetType function is intended for use only in the implementation of the polymorphic object, not by its users; therefore, it is not only possible but desirable to keep it "hidden" by declaring it inside one of the worker classes. Because the user never creates an object of any of the worker classes directly, declaring a function in one of those classes has much the same effect as making it a private member function. As we have already seen, hiding as many implementation details as possible helps to improve the robustness of our programs.

I should also mention the different data types for member variables in the HomeItem classes that have similar functions to those in the StockItem classes. In HomeItemBasic, we are using a long to hold a date, where we used a string in the DatedStockItem class. A sufficient reason for this change is that in the current class, we are getting the date from the user, so we don't have the problem of converting the system date to a storable value as we did with the implementation of the former class.[5] As for the double we're using to store the price information, that's a more sensible data type than short for numbers that may have decimal parts. I avoided using it in the earlier example only to simplify the presentation, but at this point I don't think it should cause you any trouble.

Aside from these details, this polymorphic object's definition is very similar to the one for the StockItem polymorphic object. The similarity between the interfaces (and corresponding similarity of implementations) of polymorphic objects is good news because it makes generating a new polymorphic object interface and basic implementation quite easy. It took me only a couple of hours to write the initial version of the HomeItem classes using StockItem as a

5. There's another reason as well. After I finished developing the StockItem class, I decided that it was more sensible to use a long anyway. That's why I added an exercise in Chapter 2 to replace the string date with a long.

starting point. What is even more amazing is that the test program (Figure 4.3) worked the very first time I ran it![6]

**FIGURE 4.3. The initial test program for the** HomeItem classes **(code\hmtst1.cc)**

```
// hmtst1.cc

#include <iostream.h>
#include <fstream.h>
#include "vector.h"
#include "hmit1.h"

int main()
{
  HomeItem x;
  HomeItem y;

  ifstream HomeInfo("home1.in");

  HomeInfo >> x;

  HomeInfo >> y;

  cout << "A basic HomeItem: " << endl;
  cout << x;

  cout << endl;

  cout << "A music HomeItem: " << endl;
  cout << y;
}
```

6. It took quite a few compiles before I actually had an executable, but that was mostly because I started writing this chapter and the HomeItem program on my laptop while on a trip away from home. Because I had a relatively small screen to work on and no printer, it was faster to use the compiler to tell me about statements that I needed to change.

I don't think that program needs much explanation. It is exactly the same as the corresponding StockItem test program in Figure 3.22 on page 139, with the obvious exception of the types of the objects and the name of the ifstream used to read the data. Figure 4.4 shows the result of running the above program.

**FIGURE 4.4. Results of running the first HomeItem test program (code\hmit1.out)**

```
A basic HomeItem:
Basic
Living room sofa
1600
19970105
Our living room sofa
Furniture

A music HomeItem:
Music
Relish
12.95
19950601
Our first album
CD
Joan Osborne
2
Right Hand Man
Ladder
```

Now that we've gone over the interfaces for the classes that cooperate to make a polymorphic HomeItem object, as well as the first test program and its output, we can see the initial implementation in Figure 4.5.

FIGURE 4.5. **Initial implementation of** HomeItem **manager and worker** classes **(code\hmit1.cc)**

```
// hmit1.cc

#include <iostream.h>
#include <iomanip.h>
#include <strstream.h>
#include <string.h>
#include <dos.h>
#include "string6.h"
#include "hmit1.h"
#include "hmiti1.h"


//friend functions of HomeItem

ostream& operator << (ostream& os, const HomeItem& Item)
{
 Item.m_Worker->Write(os);
 return os;
}

istream& operator >> (istream& is, HomeItem& Item)
{
 string Type;
 string Name;
 double PurchasePrice;
 long PurchaseDate;
 string Description;
 string Category;

 while (Type == "")
  {
  is >> Type;
  if (is.fail() != 0)
   {
   Item = HomeItem();
   return is;
```

```
    }
   }

  is >> Name;
  is >> PurchasePrice;
  is >> PurchaseDate;
  is >> Description;
  is >> Category;

  if (Type == "Basic")
   {
   Item = HomeItem(Name, PurchasePrice, PurchaseDate,
        Description, Category);
   }
  else if (Type == "Music")
   {
   string Artist;
   short TrackCount;
   is >> Artist;
   is >> TrackCount;
   vector<string> Track(TrackCount);
   for (short i = 0; i < TrackCount; i ++)
    {
    is >> Track[i];
    }
   Item = HomeItem(Name, PurchasePrice, PurchaseDate,
        Description, Category, Artist, Track);
   }
  else
   {
   cout << "Can't create object of type " << Type << endl;
   exit(0);
   }

  return is;
}


// HomeItem member functions
```

```
HomeItem::HomeItem()
: m_Count(0), m_Worker(new HomeItemBasic)
{
 m_Worker->m_Count = 1;
}

HomeItem::HomeItem(const HomeItem& Item)
: m_Count(0), m_Worker(Item.m_Worker)
{
 m_Worker->m_Count ++;
}

HomeItem& HomeItem::operator = (const HomeItem& Item)
{
 if (&Item != this)
  {
  m_Worker->m_Count --;
  if (m_Worker->m_Count <= 0)
   delete m_Worker;
  m_Worker = Item.m_Worker;
  m_Worker->m_Count ++;
  }
 return *this;
}

HomeItem::~HomeItem()
{
 if (m_Worker == 0)
  return;

 m_Worker->m_Count --;
 if (m_Worker->m_Count <= 0)
  delete m_Worker;
}

HomeItem::HomeItem(string Name, double PurchasePrice,
long PurchaseDate, string Description,
string Category)
```

```
: m_Count(0),
  m_Worker(new HomeItemBasic(Name, PurchasePrice,
  PurchaseDate, Description, Category))
{
  m_Worker->m_Count = 1;
}

HomeItem::HomeItem(int)
: m_Worker(0)
{
}

HomeItem::HomeItem(string Name, double PurchasePrice,
long PurchaseDate, string Description,
string Category, string Artist,
vector<string> Track)
: m_Count(0),
  m_Worker(new HomeItemMusic(Name, PurchasePrice,
  PurchaseDate, Description, Category, Artist, Track))
{
  m_Worker->m_Count = 1;
}


void HomeItem::Write(ostream& os)
{
  exit(1); // error
}

// HomeItemBasic member functions

HomeItemBasic::HomeItemBasic()
: HomeItem(1),
  m_Name(),
  m_PurchasePrice(0),
  m_PurchaseDate(0),
  m_Description(),
  m_Category()
{
```

```
}

HomeItemBasic::HomeItemBasic(string Name,
double PurchasePrice, long PurchaseDate,
string Description, string Category)
: HomeItem(1),
  m_Name(Name),
  m_PurchasePrice(PurchasePrice),
  m_PurchaseDate(PurchaseDate),
  m_Description(Description),
  m_Category(Category)
{
}

void HomeItemBasic::Write(ostream& os)
{
  os << GetType() << endl;
  os << m_Name << endl;
  os << m_PurchasePrice << endl;
  os << m_PurchaseDate << endl;
  os << m_Description << endl;
  os << m_Category << endl;
}

string HomeItemBasic::GetType()
{
  return "Basic";
}


// HomeItemMusic member functions

HomeItemMusic::HomeItemMusic(string Name,
double PurchasePrice, long PurchaseDate,
string Description, string Category,
string Artist, vector<string> Track)
: HomeItemBasic(Name,PurchasePrice,PurchaseDate,
  Description, Category),
  m_Artist(Artist),
```

```
  m_Track(Track)
{
}

void HomeItemMusic::Write(ostream& os)
{
  HomeItemBasic::Write(os);

  os << m_Artist << endl;

  int TrackCount = m_Track.size();
  os << TrackCount << endl;
  for (short i = 0; i < TrackCount; i ++)
    os << m_Track[i] << endl;
}

string HomeItemMusic::GetType()
{
  return "Music";
}
```

What does this first version of HomeItem do for us? Not too much; it merely allows us to read HomeItem objects from a file, display them, and write them out to a file. Although we've seen the implementation of similar functions in the StockItem class, it should still be worthwhile to discuss how these are similar to and different from the corresponding functions in the HomeItem classes. However, to avoid too much repetition we'll skip the functions that are essentially identical in these two cases, including the following functions for the base class, HomeItem:

1. operator <<;
2. the copy constructor;
3. the default constructor;
4. operator =;
5. the destructor;

6. the normal constructors that create worker objects with known initial data;
7. the "special" constructor that prevents an infinite regress when creating a worker object.

Here's a list of the functions we'll skip for the HomeItemBasic and HomeItemMusic classes:

1. the default constructor;
2. the copy constructor;
3. operator =;
4. the normal constructor;
5. the destructor.

The first HomeItem function we'll discuss is Write, shown in Figure 4.6.

**FIGURE 4.6.** HomeItem::Write **(from code\hmit1.cc)**

```
void HomeItem::Write(ostream& os)
{
  exit(1); // error
}
```

Calling this function is an error and will cause the program to exit. In case you're wondering why this is an error, you may be happy to know that Susan had the same question.

**Susan:** Why is calling HomeItem::Write an error?

**Steve:** Because this function exists solely for use by operator << in writing out the data for a derived class object. Therefore, if it is ever called for a HomeItem base class object, we know that someone has used the function incorrectly, and we leave the program before any more incorrect processing can occur.

The next function we need to look at is operator >>, shown in Figure 4.7.

**FIGURE 4.7. The** HomeItem **implementation of** operator >> **(from code\hmit1.cc)**

```
istream& operator >> (istream& is, HomeItem& Item)
{
 string Type;
 string Name;
 double PurchasePrice;
 long PurchaseDate;
 string Description;
 string Category;

 while (Type == "")
  {
  is >> Type;
  if (is.fail() != 0)
   {
   Item = HomeItem();
   return is;
   }
  }

 is >> Name;
 is >> PurchasePrice;
 is >> PurchaseDate;
 is >> Description;
 is >> Category;

 if (Type == "Basic")
  {
  Item = HomeItem(Name, PurchasePrice, PurchaseDate,
      Description, Category);
```

```
  }
else if (Type == "Music")
  {
  string Artist;
  short TrackCount;
  is >> Artist;
  is >> TrackCount;
  vector<string> Track(TrackCount);
  for (short i = 0; i < TrackCount; i ++)
    {
    is >> Track[i];
    }
  Item = HomeItem(Name, PurchasePrice, PurchaseDate,
       Description, Category, Artist, Track);
  }
else
  {
  cout << "Can't create object of type " << Type << endl;
  exit(0);
  }

return is;
}
```

This is quite similar in outline to the corresponding function in StockItem in that it reads data from an input source and creates a worker object of the correct type based on the value of one of the fields. However, this function does have a few noticeable differences from the StockItem version:

1. This function skips any empty lines that may be in the input file before reading the type of the object.
2. The type is specified explicitly as an extra field ("Basic" or "Music" in the current cases), rather than by the use of a special "0" value for the expiration date field, as in the DatedStockItem input file.

3. This function calls istream::fail to determine whether the program has attempted to read more information from the input file than it contains (or if any other error has occurred when trying to read from the input file). If such an error occurs, the operator >> function assigns a default-constructed HomeItem to the reference argument Item and returns to the calling function immediately.
4. The local variables Artist, TrackCount, and Track are created only when the function needs them (for a "Music" object) rather than at the beginning of the function as has been our practice until now.
5. In the case of a "Music" object, one of those local variables is a vector of strings.
6. The index variable i is also created only when it is needed, at the beginning of the for loop.

Susan had a question about the first of these differences.

**Susan:** Why would you want to put blank lines in the input file?

**Steve:** To make it easier to read. Because our StockItem input file couldn't have any blank lines in it, the data for each item started right after the end of the data for the previous item, which makes it hard for a human being to tell what the entries in the input file mean. Of course, the program doesn't care, but sometimes it's necessary for a person to look at the input file, especially when there's something wrong with it!

The reason for the second difference from the StockItem version of operator >> is fairly simple: All of the types of HomeItems share the basic data in the HomeItemBasic class, so we don't have any otherwise unused field that we can use to indicate which actual type the object belongs to; thus, we have to add another field to explicitly specify that type.

However, the other differences are a bit more interesting. First, part of the reason that we have to check for the input stream terminating (or "failing") here, when we didn't have to do that in the StockItem case, is that we're trying to skip blank lines between the data for successive objects. This means that when we reach the end of the file, we will have blank lines that we might try to read while looking for the next set of data; if there isn't any more data, we might run off the end of the file. I added this "blank line skipping" feature of operator >> to make the input files easier to read and write for human beings, but the way I originally implemented it had an unexpected side effect: The program looped forever if I gave it a bad file name. In fact, it always did this at the end of the file! Figure 4.8 is my original implementation; see if you can tell what's wrong with it.

**FIGURE 4.8. The (incorrect)** while **loop in the original implementation of** operator >>

```
while (Type == "")
 {
 s >> Type;
 }
```

This won't work if the file tied to s doesn't exist or if we've already reached the end of that file, because the line s >> Type; won't change the value of Type in either of those cases. Therefore, Type will retain its original value, which is "" (the empty string). Since the loop continues as long as s is the empty string, it becomes an endless loop and the program will "hang" (run forever). The solution is simple enough: Use fail to check if the stream is still working before trying to read something else from it.

Of course, if the stream isn't still working, we can't get any data to put into a HomeItem object; in that case, we set the reference argument Item to the value of a default-constructed HomeItem (so that the calling function can tell that it hasn't received a valid HomeItem) and return immediately.

Now that we've cleared that up, let's examine why it is more than just a convenience to be able to create new local variables at any point in a function.

### *Making All Local Stops*

There are a couple of reasons to create the local variable Track only after we detect that we're dealing with a "Music" object. First, it's relatively time-consuming to create a vector, especially one of a nonnative data type like strings, because each of those strings has to be created and placed in the vector before it can be used. But a more significant reason is that we don't know how large the vector needs to be until we have read the "track count" from the file. As you'll see later, it's possible (and even sometimes necessary) to change the size of a vector after it has been created, but that takes extra work that we should avoid if we can. Therefore, it is much more sensible to wait until we have read the count so that we can create the vector with a size that is just right to hold all of the track names for the CD, LP, or cassette.

Susan had a question about reading the track names in from the file.

**Susan:** I don't get how the code works to read in the track names from the file when there can be different numbers of tracks for each album.

**Steve:** That's what these lines are for:

```
s >> TrackCount;
vector<string> Track(TrackCount);
for (short i = 0; i < TrackCount; i ++)
 {
 s >> Track[i];
 }
```

First, we read the number of tracks from the file into the variable TrackCount. Next, we create a vector to hold that many strings (the track names). Finally, we use the loop to read all of the track names into the vector.

**Susan:** Okay, I get it.

The final reason to wait as long as possible before creating the vector of strings to hold the track names is that we don't need it at all if we're not creating a "Music" object, so any effort to create it in any other case would be a complete waste. Although we don't have to be fanatical about saving computer time, doing work that doesn't need to be done is just silly.

## *What Have* i *Started?*

The creation of an index variable such as i during the initialization of a for loop is also a bit more significant than it looks, because the meaning of this operation changed recently. Earlier versions of C++ had an inadvertent "feature" that was fixed in the final draft standard: A variable created in the initialization section of a for loop used to exist from that point until the end of the block enclosing the for loop, not just during the for loop's execution. This old rule was replaced by the more logical rule that the scope of a variable created in the initialization section of a for loop consists of the for loop's header and the controlled block of the for loop. Thus, the program in Figure 4.9 was illegal under the old rule because you can't have two local variables named i in the same scope and, under the old rule, the scopes of the two i's were overlapping. However, it is perfectly legal under the new rule because the scopes of the two i's are separate.[7]

**FIGURE 4.9. A legal program (code\fortest.cc)**

```
#include <iostream.h>

int main()
{
```

7. Unfortunately, as of this writing, not all compilers support this new feature, including some compilers that claim to be compliant with the standard. If you want your programs to compile under both the old and new rules, you will have to define your loop variables outside the loop headers.

```
for (short i = 0; i < 10; i ++)
 {
 cout << i << endl;
 }

cout << endl;

for (short i = 0; i < 10; i ++)
 {
 cout << 2 * i << endl;
 }
}
```

Susan had a question about creating a variable in the header of a for loop.

**Susan:** What does "for (short i=0" mean that is different from just "for (i=0"?

**Steve:** The former phrase means that we're creating a new variable called i that will exist only during the execution of the for loop; the latter one means that we're using a preexisting variable called i for our loop index.

**Susan:** Why would you want to use one of these phrases rather than the other?

**Steve:** You would generally use the first one because it's a good idea to limit the scope of a variable as much as possible. However, sometimes you need to know the last value that the loop index had after the loop terminates; in that case, you have to use the latter method so that i is still around after the end of the for loop.

## *Stereo Typing*

Before we get to the derived class member functions that have significant changes from the StockItem versions, I want to point out one of the oddities of using the value 0 in C++. Figure 4.10 shows an incorrect version of the HomeItemBasic default constructor.

**FIGURE 4.10. An incorrect default constructor for the** HomeItemBasic class

```
HomeItemBasic::HomeItemBasic()
: HomeItem(1),
  m_Name(),
  m_PurchasePrice(0),
  m_PurchaseDate(0),
  m_Description(0),
  m_Category(0)
{
}
```

What's wrong with this picture? The 0 values in the m_Description and m_Category member variable initializers. These are string variables, so how can they be set to the value 0?

The answer is that, as we've discussed briefly in Chapter 3, 0 is a "magic number" in C++. In this case, the problem is that 0 is a legal value for any type of pointer, including char*. Because the string class has a constructor that makes a string out of a char*, the compiler will accept a 0 as the value in a string variable initializer. Unfortunately, the results of specifying a 0 in such a case are undesirable; whatever data happens to be at address 0 will be taken as the initial data for the string. Therefore, we have to be very careful not to supply a 0 as the initial value for a string variable.

It's all very well to say "be careful", but that doesn't answer the question of how I found this problem in the first place. We'll cover that in Chapter 6, in the section "Nothing Ventured, Nothing Gained" on page 340.

Now that I've warned you about that problem, let's take a look at the other functions pertaining to the HomeItem manager and worker classes that differ from those in the StockItem classes. The first two of these functions are HomeItemBasic::GetType (Figure 4.11) and HomeItemMusic::GetType (Figure 4.12). Each of these functions returns a string representing the type of the object to which it is applied, which in this case is either "Basic" or "Music".

**FIGURE 4.11.** HomeItemBasic::GetType **(from code\hmit1.cc)**

```
string HomeItemBasic::GetType()
{
 return "Basic";
}
```

**FIGURE 4.12.** HomeItemMusic::GetType **(from code\hmit1.cc)**

```
string HomeItemMusic::GetType()
{
 return "Music";
}
```

In case it's not obvious why we need these functions, the explanation of the Write functions for the two worker classes should clear it up. Let's start with HomeItemBasic::Write (Figure 4.13).

**FIGURE 4.13.** HomeItemBasic::Write **(from code\hmit1.cc)**

```
void HomeItemBasic::Write(ostream& os)
{
 os << GetType() << endl;
 os << m_Name << endl;
 os << m_PurchasePrice << endl;
 os << m_PurchaseDate << endl;
 os << m_Description << endl;
```

```
  os << m_Category << endl;
}
```

This function writes out all the data for the object it was called for, which isn't too unusual. But what about that first output line, os << GetType() << endl;, which gets the type of the object to be written via the GetType function? Isn't the object in question obviously a HomeItemBasic?

## *Virtual Reality*

In fact, it may be an object of any of the HomeItem classes — say, a HomeItemMusic object — because the HomeItemBasic::Write function is designed to be called from the Write functions of other HomeItem worker classes. For example, it is called from HomeItemMusic::Write, as you can see in Figure 4.14.

**FIGURE 4.14.** HomeItemMusic::Write **(from code\hmit1.cc)**

```
void HomeItemMusic::Write(ostream& os)
{
  HomeItemBasic::Write(os);

  os << m_Artist << endl;

  int TrackCount = m_Track.size();
  os << TrackCount << endl;
  for (short i = 0; i < TrackCount; i ++)
    os << m_Track[i] << endl;
}
```

It would be redundant to make the HomeItemMusic::Write function display all the data in a HomeItemBasic object. After all, the HomeItemBasic version of Write already does that.

Susan wasn't convinced that reusing HomeItemBasic::Write was that important.

**Susan:** So who cares if we have to duplicate the code in HomeItemBasic::Write? It's only a few lines of code anyway.

**Steve:** Yes, but duplicated code is a prescription for maintenance problems later. What if we add another five or six data types derived from HomeItemBasic? Should we duplicate those few lines in every one of their Write functions? If so, we'll have a wonderful time tracking down all of those sets of duplicated code when we have to make a change to the data in the base class part!

Assuming this has convinced you of the benefit of code reuse in this particular case, we still have to make sure of one detail before we can reuse the code from HomeItemBasic::Write: The correct type of the object has to be written out to the file.

Remember, to read a HomeItem object from a file, we have to know the appropriate type of HomeItem worker object, which is determined by the type indicator (currently "Basic" or "Music") in the first line of the data for each object in the input file. Therefore, when we write the data for a HomeItem object out to the file, we have to specify the correct type so that we can reconstruct the object properly when we read it back in later. That's why we use the GetType function to get the type from the object in the HomeItemBasic::Write function: If the HomeItemBasic::Write function always wrote "Basic" as the type, the data written to the file wouldn't be correct when we called HomeItemBasic::Write to write out the common parts of any HomeItem worker object. As it is, however, when HomeItemBasic::Write is called from HomeItemMusic::Write, the type is correctly written out as "Music" rather than as "Basic", because the GetType function will return "Music" in that case.

The key to the successful operation of this mechanism, of course, is that GetType is a virtual function. Therefore, when we call GetType from HomeItemBasic::Write, we are actually calling the appropriate GetType function for the HomeItem worker object for which HomeItemBasic::Write was called (i.e., the object pointed to by this). Because each of the HomeItemBasic worker object types has its own version of GetType, the call to GetType will retrieve the correct type indicator.

By this point, Susan was apparently convinced that using HomeItemBasic::Write to handle the common parts of any HomeItem object was a good idea, but that led to the following exchange.

**Susan:** Why didn't we do this with the StockItem classes?

**Steve:** Because I wrote separate Write functions for the different StockItem classes.

**Susan:** You should have done it this way.

**Steve:** Yes, you're right, but I didn't think of it then. I guess that proves that you can always improve your designs!

After we account for this important characteristic of the Write functions, the rest of HomeItemMusic::Write is pretty simple, except for one function that we haven't seen before: size, which is a member function of vector.[8] This function returns the number of elements of the vector, which we can then write out to the output file so that when we read the data back in for this object, we'll know how big to make the vector of track information.

We have covered the member functions of the first version of our HomeItem polymorphic classes, so now let's add a few more features. Obviously, it would be useful to be able to search through all of the items of a given type to find one that matches a particular description. For example, we might want to find a HomeItemMusic object (such as a CD) that has a particular track on it.

Susan had a question about our handling of different types of objects.

---

8. Actually, there is a different size for each different type of vector — vectors of strings, vectors of shorts, vectors of StockItems, and so on, all have their own size member functions. However, this is handled automatically by the compiler, so it doesn't affect our use of the size function.

**Susan:** I thought we weren't supposed to have to know whether we were dealing with a HomeItemMusic or a HomeItemBasic object.

**Steve:** Well, that depends on the context. The application program shouldn't have to treat these two types differently when the difference doesn't matter (e.g., when loading them from a disk file), but the user definitely will need to be able to distinguish them sometimes (e.g., when looking for an album that has a particular track on it). The idea is to confine the knowledge of these differences to situations where they matter rather than having to worry about them throughout the program.

As we saw in the StockItem situation, it's not feasible to have a member function of HomeItem that looks for a particular HomeItem, because a member function needs an object of its class to work on and we don't know which object that is when we're doing the search; if we did, we wouldn't be searching!

For that reason, we have to create another class we'll call HomeInventory. This class contains a vector of HomeItems, which the search functions examine whenever we look for a particular HomeItem.

Why do I say "search functions" rather than "search function"? Because there are several ways that we might want to specify the HomeItem we're looking for. One way, of course, would be by its name, which presumably would be distinct for each HomeItem in our list.[9] However, we might also want to find all the HomeItems in the Furniture category, or even all the HomeItems in the Furniture category that have the color "red" in their description, for interior decorating purposes.

To implement these various searches, we will need several search functions. A good place to start is with the simplest one, which searches for a HomeItem with a given name. We'll call this function

9. For the moment, I'm going to assume that each name that the user types in for a new object is unique. We'll add code to check this in one of the exercises.

FindItemByName. Let's take a look at the first version of the interface of the HomeInventory class, which includes this member function (Figure 4.15).

**FIGURE 4.15. The initial** HomeInventory class **interface (code\hmin2.h)**

```
#include "vector.h"

class HomeInventory
{
public:
   HomeInventory();

   short LoadInventory(ifstream& is);
   HomeItem FindItemByName(string Name);

private:
   vector<HomeItem> m_Home;
};
```

This is a pretty simple interface because it doesn't allow us to do anything other than load the inventory from a disk file into the vector called m_Home (LoadInventory) and find an item in that vector given the name of the item(FindItemByName). However, the implementation is a little less obvious, as suggested by the fact that there is no member data item to keep track of the number of elements in the m_Home vector. To see how this works, let's take a look at the implementation of the HomeInventory class (Figure 4.16).

**FIGURE 4.16. The initial implementation of** HomeInventory **(code\hmin2.cc)**

```
#include <iostream.h>
#include <fstream.h>
#include "vector.h"
#include "string6.h"
#include "hmit2.h"
#include "hmin2.h"
```

```
HomeInventory::HomeInventory()
: m_Home (vector<HomeItem>(0))
{
}

short HomeInventory::LoadInventory(ifstream& is)
{
   short i;

   for (i = 0; ; i ++)
    {
    m_Home.resize(i+5);

    is >> m_Home[i];
    if (is.fail() != 0)
      break;
    }

   m_Home.resize(i);
   return i;
}

HomeItem HomeInventory::FindItemByName(string Name)
{
   short i;
   bool Found = false;
   short ItemCount = m_Home.size();

   for (i = 0; i < ItemCount; i ++)
    {
    if (m_Home[i].GetName() == Name)
      {
      Found = true;
      break;
      }
    }

   if (Found == true)
```

```
    return m_Home[i];

   return HomeItem();
}
```

The first clue to how a HomeInventory object keeps track of the number of HomeItems it contains is the size we specify for the m_Home vector in the HomeInventory constructor: 0 elements. Clearly, this can't be the final size because we almost certainly want to keep track of more than zero items!

The question, of course, is how many items we are going to have. The way the input file is currently laid out, there isn't any way to know how many items we will have initially until we've read them all from the input file. For that matter, even after we have read them all, we may still want to add items at some other point in the program. Therefore, we have two choices when designing a class like this:

1. Establish a vector containing a fixed number of elements and keep track of how many of them are in use.

2. Resize the vector as needed to hold as many elements as we need, using the size member function to keep track of how large it is.

Until this point, we've taken option 1, mainly because it's easier to explain. However, I think it's time to learn how we can take advantage of the more flexible second option, including some of the considerations that make it a bit complicated to use properly.

We will go over the LoadInventory function (shown in Figure 4.16) in some detail to see how this dynamic sizing works (and how it can lead to inefficiencies) as soon as we have dealt with another question Susan had about how we decide whether to declare loop index variables in the loop or before it starts.

> **Susan:** Why are we saying short i; at the beginning of the function here instead of in the for loop?

**Steve:** Because we will need the value of i after the end of the loop to tell us how many items we've read from the file. If we declared i in the for loop header, we wouldn't be able to use it after the end of the loop.

With that cleared up, let's start with the first statement in the loop, m_Home.resize(i+1);. This sets the size of the vector m_Home to one more than the current value of the loop index i. Because i starts at 0, on the first time through the loop the size of m_Home is set to 1. Then the statement is >> m_Home[i]; reads a HomeItem from the input file into element i of the m_Home vector; the first time through the loop, that element is m_Home[0].

Actually, I oversimplified a little bit when I said that the line we just discussed "reads a HomeItem from the input file". To be more precise, it *attempts* to read a HomeItem from the input file. As we saw in our analysis of the operator >> function that we wrote to read HomeItems from a file, that operator can fail to return anything; in fact, failure is guaranteed when we try to read another HomeItem from the file when there aren't any left. Therefore, the next two lines

```
if (is.fail() != 0)
  break;
```

check for this possibility. When we do run out of data in the file, which will happen eventually, the break statement terminates the loop. Finally, the two lines

```
m_Home.resize(i);
return i;
```

reset the number of elements in the vector to the exact number that we've read successfully and return the result to the calling program in case it wants to know.

Susan had some questions about this process.

**Susan:** So, what we're doing here is setting aside memory for the HomeItem objects?

**Steve:** Yes, and we're also loading them from the file at the same time. These two things are connected because we don't know how much memory to allocate for the items before we've read all of them from the file.

## *Waste Not, Want Not*

This is definitely a legal way to fill up a vector with a number of data elements when we don't know in advance how many we'll have, but it isn't very efficient. The problem is in the way we are using the innocent-looking resize function: to resize the vector every time we want to add another element. Every time we resize a vector, it has to call new to allocate enough memory to hold the number of elements of its new size; it also has to call delete to release the memory it was using before. Thus, if we resize a vector 100 times (for example) to store 100 elements, we are doing 100 news and 100 deletes. This is a very slow operation compared to other common programming tasks such as arithmetic, looping, and comparison, so it is best to avoid unnecessary memory reallocations.

Susan had some questions about reallocating memory.

**Susan:** I don't understand this idea of reallocating memory.

**Steve:** When we create a vector, we have to say how many elements it can hold so that the code that implements the vector type knows how much room to allocate for the information it keeps about each of those elements. When we increase the number of elements in the vector, the resize member function has to increase the size of the area it uses to store the information about the elements. The resize member function handles this by allocating another piece of memory big enough to hold the information for all of the elements in the new size, copying all the information it previously held into that new space, and then freeing the original piece of memory. Therefore, every time we change the size of a vector, the resize function has to do an allocation, a copy, and a deallocation. This adds up to a lot of extra work that is best avoided if we don't have to do it all the time.

**Susan:** Okay. Does this reallocation occur every time the user tries to look something up in the inventory?

**Steve:** No, just when we're adding an item or reading items from the file.

## *You Can Get What You Need*

As long as we don't know how many elements we will need until we read them all in, we can't get rid of reallocations entirely. However, we can reduce them significantly by doing them every so often rather than every time we read one element from the file. For example, we could resize the m_Home vector before reading every fifth element rather than before every element, producing the code in Figure 4.17.

**FIGURE 4.17. Another possible implementation of** LoadInventory **(from code\hmin2a.cc)**

```
short HomeInventory::LoadInventory(ifstream& is)
{
  short i;

  for (i = 0; ; i ++)
   {
   if (i % 5 == 0)
     m_Home.resize(i+5);

   is >> m_Home[i];
   if (is.fail() != 0)
     break;
   }
```

```
    m_Home.resize(i);
    return i;
  }
```

There's only one change between the previous version of this function and the current one: The two lines

```
if (i % 5 == 0)
  m_Home.resize(i + 5);
```

replace the following line in the previous version:

```
  m_Home.resize(i + 1);
```

First, let's look at the meaning of the % symbol in the line if (i % 5 == 0). This is the *modulus operator*, which produces the remainder of a division operation. In this case, we are dividing i by 5 and taking the remainder; if that remainder is 0 (i.e., i is evenly divisible by 5), then the if statement will be true, so the next statement, m_Home.resize(i + 5);, will allocate five additional elements to the vector m_Home.

Let's analyze how these statements work in more detail. If i is 0, the remainder will be 0, so we will execute the call to resize, setting the size of m_Home to 0 + 5, or 5. When i has a value between 1 and 4, its remainder after division by 5 won't be 0, so we won't execute the resizing line. When i becomes 5 on the sixth time through the loop, the if statement will compute the remainder of dividing 5 by 5, which of course is 0, so the call to resize will be executed again. This time, it will set the number of elements of the vector to 5 + 5, or 10 altogether. Continuing in this way, we can see that the result will be to expand the vector by five elements every fifth time through the loop, as desired.

As clever as this might be, there is a much better solution to reducing the number of allocations, which we've already employed in a slightly different part of this program. If you'd like to try to figure it out yourself, stop here and think about it.

## A Smith and Wesson Beats Four Aces

Give up? Okay, here it is: When we create the file that contains the data for the HomeItem objects, we can start by writing the number of elements as the first line of the file. This is the solution we used to preallocate the m_Track vector that holds the track names for a "Music" HomeItem. The disadvantage of this solution is that it is harder to apply when the input file is generated directly by a human being, who is likely to make a mistake in counting the elements. However, this is not much of a drawback when we consider that the most common way to generate such a file in the real world is to create, edit, and delete items via a program. This program will read any pre-existing data file, allow modifications to the items from the file, and write out the updated data to the file so that it will be there the next time we start the program. Of course, such a program provides other facilities such as producing reports and searching for individual items, but as long as we're maintaining the whole database in memory, those functions don't have to worry about the structure of the file.

Susan had some questions about the inventory file.

**Susan:** What file are you talking about?

**Steve:** The file that holds the information about all of the HomeItem objects in the inventory.

**Susan:** How was that file created?

**Steve:** Either by writing it with a text editor or by adding objects using the AddItem function and then telling the program to write it out.

**Susan:** How does the program know where the data for each item starts?

**Steve:** Our implementation of operator >> knows how many fields there are for each object; when the data for one object is finished, the data for the next object must be coming up next in the file.

Figure 4.18 is the version of the LoadInventory function that uses a preset count of items at the beginning of the file.

FIGURE 4.18. **Yet another implementation of** LoadInventory **(from code\hmin3.cc)**

```
short HomeInventory::LoadInventory(ifstream& is)
{
  short i;
  short ElementCount;

  is >> ElementCount;

  m_Home.resize(ElementCount+1);

  for (i = 0; ; i ++)
   {
   is >> m_Home[i];

   if (is.fail() != 0)
    break;
  }

  if (i < ElementCount)
   {
   cerr << "Not enough items in input file" << endl;
   exit(1);
   }

  m_Home.resize(ElementCount);
```

```
  return i;
}
```

The first part of this should be fairly obvious: We are reading the number of elements from the file into a variable called ElementCount. However, the next statement might not be so obvious: It sets the size of the vector to one more than the number of items that we expect to read. Why do we need an extra element in the vector?

### *Everything Is More Complicated Than It Looks*

If we were to allocate exactly enough elements to store the data that we read from the file, we wouldn't be able to try to read one more element so that we could tell that we had reached the end of the file. The problem is that an attempt to use a vector element that doesn't exist produces an "invalid element number" error from the vector code, so we would never reach the statement that calls fail to find out that we are at the end of the file. For this reason, I've added one element to the number of items that we actually expect so that we can tell if we have reached the end of file on schedule.

Of course, after we have finished reading all the data and have reached the end of the file, we must make sure that we have read the number of items we expected. If we're short one or more items, we display an error and exit from the program; on the other hand, if the number of items is correct, we reset the size of the m_Home vector to that number and return to the calling function.

Susan had a question about the way the error message was displayed.

**Susan:** What's cerr?

**Steve:** That's another automatically created ostream object, like cout. The difference is that you can make the output from cout go to a different file in a number of ways, both in the program and outside it. However, doing that doesn't affect where cerr sends its data. In other words, even if you change where the "normal" output goes, cerr will still send its data to the screen where the user can see the messages.

So that explains how the error message for a short file is displayed. However, we still need to consider the other possibility: having more items in the file than were supposed to be there. Why is this important? Because if there were actually more items in the file and we continued processing the data without telling the user about this problem, the information for those remaining items would be lost when we rewrote the file at the end of the program; obviously, that would be a serious mistake. It's almost always better to program "defensively" when possible rather than to assume that everything is as it is supposed to be and that no one has made any errors in the data.

So what will happen if there are more items in the file than there were supposed to be? We get an error from the vector code, because we try to read into an element of the vector that doesn't exist. Therefore, that possibility is covered.

Ignoring the possibility of errors in the data is just one way to produce a system that is overly susceptible to errors originating outside the code. Such errors can also result from the program being used in unexpected ways or even from the seemingly positive situation of a program with an unexpectedly long service life.

This last situation is, unfortunately, not merely theoretical. In fact, it is the basis of a very widespread problem that we'll all be intimately familiar with in the near future: the Year 2000 problem.

## *Terror in the Year Zero*

Before I explain the Year 2000 problem in detail, let me set the stage with some history of computing. In the past, RAM and disk storage were much more expensive than they are today. For this reason, a very large number of programs written in the last 30 years employ a space-saving "shortcut" when dealing with dates. To be precise, these programs use a 2-digit number to represent the year portion of a date in the form "YYMMDD" (that is, two digits for the year, two for the month, and two for the day), which reduces the amount of RAM or disk storage compared to the amount needed to store the entire year in the form "YYYYMMDD". I'm sure this seemed like (and may have even been) a good idea at the time, but it has turned out to be a very expensive way to save money because, contrary to expectations at the time they were written, many of these programs are still in use and none of them will work much longer, if indeed they haven't already started to fail.[10] How will these programs fail? There are many possible ways, but I can think of a few types of system that are going to have serious problems if they aren't fixed soon:

1. financial systems such as those that calculate amounts due on credit card debt, which depend on the number of days since the last payment;
2. automated inventory systems that calculate the number of items to order based on criteria such as the average of the last six months' orders;
3. programmed maintenance schedules for automobiles, commercial building control systems, and the like, that control the availability of devices based on how long it has been since the last maintenance was done;
4. other such "embedded" controller systems that manage the flow of materials through plants, pipelines, electrical distribution networks, oil tankers, and the like.

To see how these calculations might be incorrect when the year 2000 rolls around, let's take the first one as a more detailed example. Suppose that we have a program that calculates the interest due on a credit card in the following (somewhat oversimplified) way:

10. Susan had a very imaginative idea as to how this problem could have been prevented: using Roman numerals for dates. If our programs used that way of representing dates, the approach of the year MM would be a nonevent!

1. Calculate the "day number" of the previous payment by the following procedure:[11]
   a. Multiply the year number when the previous payment was made by 365.
   b. Add the day of the month when the previous payment was made.
   c. Add the day number of the beginning of the month in which the previous payment was made — that is, the number of days in the year before the first day of that month. This number is 0 for January, 31 for February, 59 for March, and so on.
2. Calculate the day number of the current payment by the same procedure as above, substituting the correct values for the year number, day of the month, and day number of the beginning of the month.
3. Subtract the day number of the previous payment from the day number of the current payment. The result is the number of days between the previous payment and the current payment.

For example, if the last payment was on 991103 (November 3, 1999, in YYMMDD notation) and the current payment is on 991202 (December 2, 1999), we calculate the day number of the last payment as 99 * 365 (for the year part) + 3 (for the third day of the month) + 304 (for the number of days in the year before the first of November), which gives us a day number of 36442. Then we calculate the day number of the current payment as 99 * 365 (for the year part) + 2 (for the second day of the month) + 334 (for the number of days in the year before the first of December), which gives us a day number of 36471. Subtracting 36442 from 36471, we determine that the number of days between these two payments is 29, which is correct.

11. I know I'm disregarding leap year, but that would be just another complication that isn't needed to explain the Year 2000 problem.

Susan had a question about this algorithm.

**Susan:** What is this "day number" you're calculating?

**Steve:** Basically, it's the number of days since some "zero" date in the past. If we want to determine the number of days between two dates, probably the easiest way is to figure out how many days each of the dates is after a fixed date in the past (the "day number" of each date), then subtract the day number of the first date from that of the second date. This will tell us how many days separate the two dates we're interested in.

Now let's look at the next billing cycle, where the previous payment date will be 991202. Suppose that the next payment is on January 2, 2000, which will be represented as 000102. In that case, the day number of the last payment is 36471, as previously calculated for December 2, 1999. Then we calculate the day number of the current payment as 0 * 365 (for the year part) + 2 (for the day of the month) + 0 (for the number of days in the year before the first of January), for a day number of 2. Subtracting the 36471 from 2, we determine that the number of days between these two payments is . . . -36469. Somehow that doesn't seem right!

If the credit card company is lucky, the bills this program generates will be obviously idiotic. If it's not so lucky, they may appear reasonable but in fact will be wrong in some unpredictable way. Similar horrors will occur in the inventory control and automobile examples as well as others too numerous to count.

The people responsible for these defective programs can't really claim that these problems are beyond their control; after all, the fact that the year 2000 is coming has been known for quite some time.[12]

12. I have read that for this very reason insurance companies are specifically excluding claims for damage caused by Year 2000 problems. Apparently the idea is that you can't insure against a foreseeable problem that is caused by your own negligence.

Given this, surely the companies affected by this problem will have everything fixed by January 1, 2000. Won't they?

### *I'll Think About It Tomorrow*

I'm afraid that's not going to happen. The first reason is that in mid-1998, many companies haven't even started working on the problem! How did such a vital task get put off until too late? That's easy to explain. Pretend you are a reasonably competent manager working for Amalgamated Conglomerate. Here are some of the major characteristics of the project the company wants you to do:

1. Its success is absolutely essential to the survival of the company.
2. It is mind-numbingly boring, tedious work, which implies even higher turnover than usual in software projects.
3. It is completely invisible to the customer, who has undoubtedly requested a number of new features that will have to be postponed to work on this project.
4. The skills learned are completely worthless when the project is over.[13]
5. The deadline cannot be postponed by even one day.

Now I want a show of hands: Who would like to lead this project? Somehow, I don't think I'm likely to get very many volunteers.

But why should fixing these problems be so difficult? All we have to do is change the date fields to use four digits rather than two for the year portion of the date, and change all of the code that refers to those date fields. How hard can that be?

Much harder than if modern object-oriented software design had been used. The problem is that everyone wrote their own date calculation routines and used them throughout their programs, often

13. At least until we start our Year 10000 projects in 9997 or so.

without documenting how they worked or where they were used. Some of these programs are thirty years old, and the people who worked on them are long gone, if they're even still alive. The only way to fix these date problems is to go over the code, line by line, searching for any reference to dates.[14] Once each such reference is found, it has to be fixed.[15] Unfortunately, the chance of introducing a new error when fixing an old one is not negligible; in fact, it can be quite high. This means that extremely thorough and careful testing is needed to try to ensure that new errors haven't been introduced in this process.

Okay, so it's a lot of work. But these companies have had plenty of time to fix it, so why haven't they done it by now?

### *In the Long Run, We Are All Dead*

There are a number of excuses, but the truth of the matter is this: Although the company desperately needs these programs fixed, it's not in any individual manager's interest to be in charge of the project. And since there isn't any "company" to do it if the individual managers don't want to, it doesn't get done.

In my opinion, this situation has exposed a serious flaw in the corporate structure. Within a corporation, there is no market. This means that while the benefits of fixing this problem would have accrued to the entire company, the difficulties would have fallen on the individual managers who were running the projects. Therefore, the most sensible course of action from the point of view of the individual manager is to duck responsibility; with any luck, he or she

14. This is actually too optimistic, as it assumes that you have the source code to examine. In fact, many companies have lost the source code for some of their essential programs, so they will have an even worse time trying to figure out what has to be fixed, or even what the program is doing right now.

15. In the case of embedded controllers such as those in pipelines and oil tankers, even loading the new programs into the computers after the programs are fixed can be a nontrivial exercise, as they may be buried in inaccessible places. It may also be difficult or expensive to turn off the equipment long enough to make the change.

will have retired or at least moved to another company before the day of reckoning arrived.

Was there any way of preventing this outcome? Maybe, but it would have required managers to act as entrepreneurs rather than as employees. That is, if companies were organized as a number of autonomous groups who bought and sold one another's products, anyone who could fix bugs like the Year 2000 problem would be able to make a good living doing so. Because of the laws of supply and demand, the fewer people who wanted to work on such projects, the more money each would make. As a result, the rewards for fixing the problem would be commensurate with the difficulty and risk of taking on the project, so it's possible that we wouldn't be in the mess we're in today.

Of course, it wouldn't be much fun if the banking system collapsed, but that wouldn't be fatal (at least in the short run). But what about the "embedded systems" that control power, sewer, water, and the like? If they aren't fixed in time, the results will be much worse than getting a very confused bank statement.

What might happen from one or more embedded system failures? I can't predict the consequences in detail, but I think it's pretty obvious that big cities aren't likely to be very good places to live if the industrial infrastructure (power, water, telephone) isn't working.

Okay, so it might be pretty bad, but are there any benefits to be gained from this mess? I can think of some. Of course, one attractive prospect is the probable collapse of certain large, universally hated bureaucratic organizations under the weight of massive program failure. If that occurs, it will be worth the estimated $600 billion price tag for fixing the problem in companies around the world. It's also within the realm of possibility that this fiasco will encourage a serious reconsideration of the reward and penalty structure of whatever corporations, if any, are still in business after January 1, 2000.

As interesting and even vital as the Year 2000 problem may be, hasn't it taken us a bit afield from our task of learning how to design programs? I don't think so. If you're going to write programs that anyone is going to depend on, you should have a good understanding of how serious program failure can be as well as of some of the more common causes of such failure, even if they are outside the technical aspects of programming.[16]

## *Back to the Future*

I hope I've sufficiently impressed you with the possible consequences of program failure. Now let's get back to our regularly scheduled discussion. The next thing we will need, as I've suggested previously, is a way for the user to enter, modify, and delete information for home inventory items without having to manually create or edit a data file.

Susan thought I had something against data files. I cleared up her confusion with the following discussion.

> **Susan:** What's wrong with data files?
>
> **Steve:** Nothing's wrong with them. What's wrong is making the user type everything in using a text editor; instead, we're going to give the user the ability to create the data file with a data entry function designed for that purpose.
>
> **Susan:** Oh, so we're creating a database?
>
> **Steve:** You could say that. Its current implementation is pretty primitive, but could be upgraded to handle virtually any number of items if that turned out to be necessary.

Let's start with the ability to enter data for a new object, as that is probably the first operation a new user will want to perform.

---

16. For the best selection of references to online documents discussing the Year 2000 problem, visit Gary North's WWW site: www.garynorth.com. Another good resource is Ed Yourdon's book, *Time Bomb 2000* (ISBN 0130952842).

Figure 4.19 shows the new header file for the HomeInventory class, which includes the new AddItem member function.

**FIGURE 4.19. The next interface for the** HomeInventory class **(code\hmin4.h)**

```
#include "vector.h"

class HomeInventory
{
public:
   HomeInventory();

   short LoadInventory(ifstream& is);
   HomeItem FindItemByName(string Name);
   HomeItem AddItem();

private:
   vector<HomeItem> m_Home;
};
```

How did I decide on the signature of the AddItem member function? Well, it seems to me that the result of this function should be the HomeItem that it creates. As for the arguments (or lack thereof), the data for the new item is going to come from the user of the program via the keyboard (i.e., cin), so it doesn't seem necessary to provide any other data to the function when it is called in the program.

Susan wanted to make sure she knew what "user" meant in this context.

**Susan:** Is that the end user or the user of the HomeItem class?

**Steve:** Good question. In this case, it's the end user.

The implementation of this new function is shown in Figure 4.20.

**FIGURE 4.20. The AddItem member function of HomeInventory (from code\hmin4.cc)**

```
HomeItem HomeInventory::AddItem()
{
  HomeItem TempItem = HomeItem::NewItem();

  short OldCount = m_Home.size();

  m_Home.resize(OldCount + 1);

  m_Home[OldCount] = TempItem;

  return TempItem;
}
```

The first statement of this function, HomeItem TempItem = HomeItem::NewItem();, creates a new HomeItem object called TempItem.

Susan had some questions about that statement.

**Susan:** Why is TempItem a HomeItem?

**Steve:** Because that's the type of object we use to keep track of the items in our home inventory.

**Susan:** I don't get how HomeItem is a type. It should be an object.

**Steve:** A class defines a new type of object. A type like HomeItem could be compared to a common noun like "dog", whereas the objects of that type resemble proper nouns like "Spot". You wouldn't say that you have "dog", but you might say that you have "a dog named Spot". Similarly, you wouldn't say that your program has HomeItem, but that it has a HomeItem called (in this case) TempItem.

The initial value for TempItem is the return value of the call to HomeItem::NewItem();. The reason we have to specify the class of this function (HomeItem) is that it is a member function of the HomeItem class, not of the HomeInventory class. But what kind of function call is HomeItem::NewItem()? It obviously isn't a normal member function call because there's no object in front of the function name NewItem.

This is a static member function call. You may recall from Chapter 2 that a static member function is one for which we don't need an object. Our previous use of this type of function was in the Today function, which returns today's date; clearly, today's date doesn't vary between objects. However, this type of member function is also convenient in cases such as the present one, where we are creating an object from keyboard input and therefore don't have the object available for use yet.

Before we get started on the implementation of the static member function called NewItem, let's take a look at the new interface for the HomeItem class, which is shown in Figure 4.21.

**FIGURE 4.21. The new interface for** HomeItem **(code\hmit4.h)**

```
// hmit4.h

#include "string6.h"
#include "vector.h"

class HomeItem
{
friend ostream& operator << (ostream& os, const HomeItem& Item);
friend istream& operator >> (istream& is, HomeItem& Item);

public:
  HomeItem();
  HomeItem(const HomeItem& Item);
  HomeItem& operator = (const HomeItem& Item);
virtual ~HomeItem();

// Basic: Art objects, furniture, jewelry, etc.
```

```
  HomeItem(string Name, double PurchasePrice,
  long PurchaseDate, string Description, string Category);

// Music: CDs, LPs, cassettes, etc.
  HomeItem(string Name, double PurchasePrice,
  long PurchaseDate, string Description, string Category,
  string Artist, vector<string> Track);

virtual void Write(ostream& os);
virtual void FormattedDisplay(ostream& os);
virtual string GetName();

static HomeItem NewItem();

protected:
  HomeItem(int);

protected:
  HomeItem* m_Worker;
  short m_Count;
};
```

We'll get to some of the changes between the previous interface and this one as soon as we get through with the changes in the implementation needed to allow data input from the keyboard. The first part of this implementation is the code for HomeItem::NewItem(), which is shown in Figure 4.22.

**FIGURE 4.22. The implementation of** HomeItem::NewItem() **(from code\hmit4.cc)**

```
HomeItem HomeItem::NewItem()
{
  HomeItem TempItem;

  cin >> TempItem;

  return TempItem;
```

```
}
```

As you can see, this is a very simple function, as it calls operator >> to do all the real work; however, I had to modify operator >> to make this possible. Susan wanted to know what was wrong with the old version of operator >>.

**Susan:** Why do we need another new version of operator >>? What was wrong with the old one?

**Steve:** The previous version of that operator wasn't very friendly to the user who was supposed to be typing data at the keyboard. The main problem is that it didn't tell the user what to enter or when to enter it; it merely waited for the user to type in the correct data.

I fixed this problem by changing the implementation of operator >> to the one shown in Figure 4.23.

**FIGURE 4.23. The new version of** operator >> **(from code\hmit4.cc)**

```
istream& operator >> (istream& is, HomeItem& Item)
{
  string Type;
  string Name;
  double PurchasePrice;
  long PurchaseDate;
  string Description;
  string Category;
  bool Interactive = (&is == &cin);

  while (Type == "")
   {
   if (Interactive)
     cout << "Type (Basic, Music) ";
   is >> Type;
   if (is.fail() != 0)
     {
```

```
    Item = HomeItem();
    return is;
    }
  }

if (Interactive)
  cout << "Name ";
is >> Name;

if (Interactive)
  cout << "Purchase Price ";
is >> PurchasePrice;

if (Interactive)
  cout << "Purchase Date ";
is >> PurchaseDate;

if (Interactive)
  cout << "Description ";
is >> Description;

if (Interactive)
  cout << "Category ";
is >> Category;

if (Type == "Basic")
  {
  Item = HomeItem(Name, PurchasePrice, PurchaseDate,
      Description, Category);
  }
else if (Type == "Music")
  {
  string Artist;
  short TrackCount;

  if (Interactive)
    cout << "Artist ";
  is >> Artist;
```

```
    if (Interactive)
      cout << "TrackCount ";
    is >> TrackCount;

    vector<string> Track(TrackCount);
    for (short i = 0; i < TrackCount; i ++)
      {
      if (Interactive)
        cout << "Track # " << i + 1 << ": ";
      is >> Track[i];
      }
    Item = HomeItem(Name, PurchasePrice, PurchaseDate,
         Description, Category, Artist, Track);
    }
  else
    {
    cout << "Can't create object of type " << Type << endl;
    exit(0);
    }

  return is;
}
```

I think most of the changes to this function should be fairly obvious. Assuming that we are reading data from the keyboard (i.e., Interactive is true), we have to let the user know what item we want typed in by displaying a prompt message such as "Name: " or "Category: ".

Susan had an excellent question about the implementation of this function.

**Susan:** How does it know whether input is from a file or the keyboard?

**Steve:** By testing whether the istream that we're reading from is the same as cin.

This test is performed by the statement

```
bool Interactive = (&is == &cin);
```

which defines a variable of type bool called Interactive that is initialized to the value of the expression (&is == &cin). What is the value of that expression going to be?

### *Strong Like bool*

The value is the result of applying the comparison operator, ==, to the arguments &is and &cin. As always with comparison operators, the type of this result is bool, which is why the type of the variable Interactive is bool as well. As for the value of the result, in this case the items being compared are the addresses of the variables cin and is. If you look back at the header for operator >>, you'll see that is is a reference argument that is actually just another name for the istream being supplied as the left-hand argument to the operator >> function. Therefore, what we are testing is whether the istream that is the left-hand argument to operator >> has the same address as cin has (i.e., whether they are different names for the same variable); if so, we are reading data from the keyboard and need to let the user know what we want. Otherwise, we assume the data is from a file, so there is no need to prompt the user.[17] Once that bit of code is clear, the rest of the changes should be pretty obvious, as they consist of the code needed to display prompts when necessary. For example, the sequence:

```
if (Interactive)
  cout << "Type (Basic, Music) ";
```

17. You may wonder why we have to compare the addresses of these two variables and not simply their contents — that is, writing (is == cin) instead of (&is == &cin). The reason is that the expression (is == cin) compares whether the two streams is and cin are in the same "state"; i.e., whether both (or neither) are available for use, not whether they are the same stream. If this isn't obvious to you, you're not alone. Not only did I not figure it out right away but when I asked a C++ programmer with over 20 years experience in the language, he took two tries to decipher it.

writes the line "Type (Basic, Music)" to the screen if and only if the input is from cin — that is, if the user is typing at the keyboard. The other similar sequences do the same thing for the other data items that need to be typed in.

Susan still wasn't convinced of the necessity to rewrite operator >>, but I think I won her over.

**Susan:** But why should we have to change operator >> in the first place? Why not just write a separate function to read the data from the keyboard and leave operator >> as it was? Isn't object-oriented programming designed to allow us to reuse existing functions rather than modify them?

**Steve:** Yes, but it's also important to try to minimize the number of functions that do essentially the same function for the same data type. In the current case, my first impulse was to write a separate function so I wouldn't have to add all those if statements to operator >>. However, I changed that plan when I realized that such a new function would have to duplicate all of the data input operations in operator >>. This means that I would have to change both operator >> and this new function every time I changed the data for any of the HomeItem classes. Since this would cause a maintenance problem in future updates of this program, I decided that I would just have to put up with the if statements as the lesser of two evils.

**Susan:** I don't understand why this would cause a maintenance problem.

**Steve:** If we have more than one function that shares the same information, we have to locate all such functions and change them whenever that shared information changes. In this case, the shared information is embodied in the code that reads values from an istream and uses those values to create a HomeItem object. Therefore, if we were to change the information needed to create a HomeItem object, we would have to find and change every function that created such an object. In a large program, just finding the functions that were affected could be a significant task.

Another reason to use the same function for both keyboard and file input is that it makes the program easier to read if we use the same function (e.g., operator >>) for similar operations.

Besides changing operator >>, I've added a couple of new functions to the interface for HomeItem — namely, FormattedDisplay and GetName. The first of these functions, as usual for virtual functions declared in the interface of a polymorphic object, simply uses the virtual function mechanism to call the "real" FormattedDisplay function in the object pointed to by m_Worker. The code in the versions of this function in the HomeItemBasic and HomeItemMusic classes is almost identical to the code for Write, except that it adds an indication of what each piece of data represents. Knowing that, you shouldn't have any trouble following either of these functions, so I'm going to list them without comment in Figures 4.24 and 4.25.

**FIGURE 4.24.** HomeItemBasic::FormattedDisplay **(from code\hmit4.cc)**

```
void HomeItemBasic::FormattedDisplay(ostream& os)
{
  os << "Type: ";
  os << GetType() << endl;
  os << "Name: ";
  os << m_Name << endl;
  os << "Purchase price: ";
  os << m_PurchasePrice << endl;
  os << "Purchase date: ";
  os << m_PurchaseDate << endl;
  os << "Description: ";
  os << m_Description << endl;
  os << "Category: ";
  os << m_Category << endl;
}
```

**FIGURE 4.25.** HomeItemMusic::FormattedDisplay **(from code\hmit4.cc)**

```
void HomeItemMusic::FormattedDisplay(ostream& os)
{
 HomeItemBasic::FormattedDisplay(os);

 os << "Artist: ";
 os << m_Artist << endl;
 os << "Tracks: ";

 int TrackCount = m_Track.size();
 os << TrackCount << endl;
 for (short i = 0; i < TrackCount; i ++)
  os << m_Track[i] << endl;
}
```

Now that we've looked at FormattedDisplay, what about GetName? You might think that this is about as simple as a function can get, as its sole purpose is to return the value of the m_Name member variable. We'll see shortly how this function is used in the test program. Before we look at that, though, you should note that this function has a characteristic that we haven't run across before: It is a virtual function implemented in HomeItem and HomeItemBasic but not in HomeItemMusic. Why is this, and how does it work?

## *Leaving Well Enough Alone*

The answer is that, just as with a non-virtual function, if we don't write a new version for a derived class (in this case, HomeItemMusic), the compiler will assume that we are satisfied with the version in the base class (in this case, HomeItemBasic). Since the correct behavior of GetName (returning the value of m_Name) is exactly the same in both of these cases, there's no reason to write a new version of GetName for HomeItemMusic, and therefore we won't.

Figure 4.26 shows how we can use these functions to add an item from the keyboard. After adding the item to the inventory, this test program retrieves its name via the GetName function, uses FindItemByName to look it up by its name, and displays it. Just to make sure our new operator >> still works for file input, this test program also loads the inventory from an input file and displays one of the elements read from that file, as the previous test program did. Making sure we haven't broken something that used to work is called *regression testing*, and it's a very important part of program maintenance.[18]

**FIGURE 4.26. The test program for adding a HomeItem interactively (hmtst4.cc)**

```
#include <iostream.h>
#include <fstream.h>
#include "vector.h"
#include "string6.h"
#include "hmit4.h"
#include "hmin4.h"

int main()
{
   ifstream HomeInfo("home3.in");
   HomeInventory MyInventory;
   HomeItem TempItem;
   string Name;

   MyInventory.LoadInventory(HomeInfo);

   TempItem = MyInventory.AddItem();
   Name = TempItem.GetName();
   HomeItem test2 = MyInventory.FindItemByName(Name);
   cout << endl << "Here is the item you added" << endl;
   test2.FormattedDisplay(cout);
```

18. In fact, operator >> did *not* work correctly for file input the first time I tried it because I had made the mistake of testing the equality of the istreams is and cin rather than the equality of their addresses, as mentioned previously. So it's a good thing I thought to check that use of operator >>!

```
   HomeItem test1 = MyInventory.FindItemByName("Relish");
   cout << endl << "Here is an item from the file" << endl;
   test1.FormattedDisplay(cout);

   return 0;
}
```

Now we can add a new item and retrieve it, so what feature should we add next? A good candidate would be a way to make changes to data that we've already entered. We will call this new function of the Inventory class EditItem, to correspond to our AddItem function. Let's look at the new interface of the HomeInventory class, which is shown in Figure 4.27.

**FIGURE 4.27. The next version of the interface for** HomeInventory **(code\hmin5.h)**

```
//hmin5.h

#include "vector.h"

class HomeInventory
{
public:
   HomeInventory();

   short LoadInventory(ifstream& is);
   void DumpInventory();
   HomeItem FindItemByName(string Name);
   HomeItem AddItem();
   short LocateItemByName(string Name);
   HomeItem EditItem(string Name);

private:
   vector<HomeItem> m_Home;
};
```

You may have noticed that I've added a couple of other support functions besides the new EditItem function. These are DumpInventory, which just lists all of the elements in the m_Home vector (useful in debugging the program), and LocateItemByName, which we'll cover in the discussion of EditItem.

Susan had a question about the first of these support functions.

**Susan:** Why do we want to get rid of items with DumpInventory?

**Steve:** We don't want to. "Dump" is programming slang for "display without worrying about formatting". In other words, a dump function is one that gives "just the facts".

Figure 4.28 shows the test program for this new version of the home inventory application.

**FIGURE 4.28. The next version of the** HomeInventory **test program (code\hmtst5.cc)**

```
#include <iostream.h>
#include <fstream.h>
#include "vector.h"
#include "string6.h"
#include "hmit5.h"
#include "hmin5.h"

int main()
{
  ifstream HomeInfo("home3.in");
  HomeInventory MyInventory;
  HomeItem TempItem;
  string Name;

  MyInventory.LoadInventory(HomeInfo);

  TempItem = MyInventory.FindItemByName("Relish");
  cout << endl;
```

```
  TempItem.Edit();
  cout << endl;

  TempItem.FormattedDisplay(cout);
  cout << endl;

  return 0;
}
```

The test program hasn't gotten much more complicated, as you can see; it loads the inventory, uses the new EditItem function to modify one of the items, and then displays the changed item.

Susan had a couple of good questions about this program and some comments about software development issues.

> **Susan:** What happens if the program can't find the object that it's trying to look up?
>
> **Steve:** That's a very good question. In the present case, that should never happen because the input file does have a record whose name is "Relish". However, we should handle that possibility anyway by checking whether the returned item is null. We'll do so in a later version of the test program; the discussion of that issue is on page 339.
>
> **Susan:** I don't see why we need to write a whole new function called LocateItemByName. What's wrong with the one we already have, FindItemByName?
>
> **Steve:** Because FindItemByName returns a copy of the object but doesn't tell us where it came from in the m_Home vector. Therefore, if we used that function we wouldn't be able to put the object back when we were finished editing it.
>
> **Susan:** Why can't we leave the classes alone? It's annoying to have to keep changing them all the time.

**Steve:** I'm afraid that's the way software development works. Of course, I could make it more realistic by playing the role of a pointy-haired manager hovering over you while you're working.

**Susan:** No, thanks. I believe you.

**Steve:** Okay, we'll save that for our future management book, *Programmers Are from Neptune, Managers Are from Uranus*.

**Susan:** I can't wait.

After that bit of comic relief, let's take a look at the implementation of the new EditItem function, shown in Figure 4.29.

**FIGURE 4.29. The EditItem function of HomeInventory (from code\hmin5.cc)**

```
HomeItem HomeInventory::EditItem(string Name)
{
  short ItemNumber = LocateItemByName(Name);

  HomeItem TempItem = m_Home[ItemNumber];

  TempItem.Edit();

  m_Home[ItemNumber] = TempItem;

  return TempItem;
}
```

As you can see, this isn't too complicated. It calls LocateItemByName to find the element number of the Homeitem to be edited, copies that HomeItem from the m_Home vector into a temporary HomeItem called TempItem, calls the Edit function (which we'll get to shortly) for that temporary HomeItem, and then copies the edited HomeItem back into the same position in the m_Home vector. If you compare this function with AddItem (Figure 4.20 on page 248), you will notice a couple of differences. First, this function calls

LocateItemByName rather than FindItemByName. These two functions are exactly the same, except that LocateItemByName returns the element number of the found HomeItem in the m_Home vector rather than the HomeItem itself. This allows us to update the m_Home vector with the edited HomeItem when we are through editing it. Second, the call to Edit in this function is different from the call to NewItem in AddItem because Edit has an object to operate on whereas NewItem had to create a previously nonexistent object. Therefore, Edit is a normal (non-static) member function rather than a static member function like AddItem.

What about the implementation of this new Edit function? I have good news and bad news. The good news: Using it is pretty simple. The bad news: Implementing it led to a fairly extensive revision of the HomeItem classes. I think the results are worth the trouble; hopefully, you will come to the same conclusion when we are done. Let's start with the new interface for the HomeItem class.

## *'Tis a Gift to Be Simple*

Figure 4.30 is the latest, greatest version of the interface for the HomeItem class.

**FIGURE 4.30. The latest version of the** Homeitem class **interface (code\hmit5.h)**

```
// hmit5.h

#include "string6.h"
#include "vector.h"

class HomeItem
{
friend ostream& operator << (ostream& os,
  const HomeItem& Item);
```

```
friend istream& operator >> (istream& is, HomeItem& Item);

public:
  HomeItem();
  HomeItem(const HomeItem& Item);
  HomeItem& operator = (const HomeItem& Item);
virtual ~HomeItem();

// Basic: Art objects, furniture, jewelry, etc.
  HomeItem(string Name, double PurchasePrice,
  long PurchaseDate, string Description, string Category);

// Music: CDs, LPs, cassettes, etc.
  HomeItem(string Name, double PurchasePrice,
  long PurchaseDate, string Description, string Category,
  string Artist, vector<string> Track);

virtual void Write(ostream& os);
virtual short FormattedDisplay(ostream& os);
virtual string GetName();
static HomeItem NewItem();

virtual void Read(istream& is);
virtual void Edit();

protected:
  HomeItem(int);
virtual HomeItem* CopyData();

protected:
  HomeItem* m_Worker;
  short m_Count;
};
```

If you compare this interface with the previous version in Figure 4.21, you'll notice that I've added a few new member functions — namely, Edit, CopyData, and Read. We'll get to Read in due time, but we're going to start with HomeItem::Edit. Unlike a "normal" function in a polymorphic object, where the base class version simply passes the buck to the appropriate worker object, the base class version of Edit (Figure 4.31) is a bit more involved.

**FIGURE 4.31.** HomeItem::Edit **(from code\hmit5.cc)**

```
void HomeItem::Edit()
{
 if (m_Worker->m_Count > 1)
  {
  m_Worker->m_Count --;
  m_Worker = m_Worker->CopyData();
  m_Worker->m_Count = 1;
  }

 m_Worker->Edit();
}
```

The reason that HomeItem::Edit is different from most of the base class functions is that it has to deal with the *aliasing* problem: the possibility of altering a shared object, which arises when we use *reference counting* to share one copy of a worker object among a possibly large number of manager objects. This is much more efficient than copying the worker object whenever we copy the manager object, but it has one drawback: If more than one manager object is pointing to the same worker object, and any of those manager objects changes the contents of "its" worker object, all of the other manager objects will also have "their" worker object changed without their advice or consent. This can cause chaos in a large system.

Luckily, it's not that difficult to prevent, as the example of HomeItem::Edit shows. This function starts by executing the statement if (m_Worker->m_Count > 1), which checks whether this object has more than one manager. If it has only one, we can change it without causing difficulty for its other manager objects; therefore, we skip the code in the {} and proceed directly to the worker class Edit function. On the other hand, if this worker object does have more than one manager, we have to "unhook" it from its other managers. We do this by executing the three statements in the controlled block of the if statement.

First, the statement m_Worker->m_Count --; subtracts 1 from the count in the current worker object to account for the fact that this manager object is going to use a different worker object. Then the next statement, m_Worker = m_Worker->CopyData();, creates a new worker object with the same data as the previous worker object and assigns its address to m_Worker so that it is now the current worker object for this manager object. Finally, the statement m_Worker->m_Count = 1; sets the count of managers in this new worker object to 1 so that the reference-counting mechanism will be able to tell when this worker object can be deleted.

After these housekeeping chores are finished, we call the Edit function of the new worker object to update its contents.

Now let's take a look at the CopyData helper function. The first oddity is in its declaration: It's a protected virtual function. The reason that it has to be virtual should be fairly obvious: Copying the data for a HomeItem derived class object depends on the exact type of the object, so CopyData has to be virtual. However, that doesn't explain why it is protected.

The explanation is that we don't want users of HomeItem objects to call this function. In fact, the only classes that should be able to use CopyData are those in the implementation of HomeItem. Therefore, we make CopyData protected so that the only functions that can access it are those in HomeItem and its derived classes.

The only remaining question that we have to answer about editing a HomeItem object is how the CopyData function works. Because CopyData is inaccessible to outside functions and is always called for a worker class object within the implementation of HomeItem, the base class version of CopyData should never be called and therefore consists of an exit statement. Let's continue by examining the code for HomeItemBasic::CopyData ().

**FIGURE 4.32.** HomeItemBasic::CopyData()

```
HomeItem* HomeItemBasic::CopyData()
{
  HomeItem* TempItem = new HomeItemBasic(*this);
  return TempItem;
}
```

This isn't a terribly complicated function, but it does have one new construct: the use of *this as an argument. Because *this is C++ speak for "the object for which this function was called", the phrase new HomeItemBasic(*this); allocates memory for a HomeItemBasic object and then calls the copy constructor for the HomeItemBasic class to create that object and initialize it as a copy of the object for which CopyData was called. Next, the address of the resulting HomeItemBasic object is assigned to the HomeItem pointer called TempItem. Finally, TempItem is returned to the calling function, where it is used as the new value of m_Worker for a manager object.

Of course, HomeItemMusic::CopyData is identical to HomeItemBasic::CopyData except for the type of the new object being created, so I won't bother explaining it again.

## *Better Read Than Dead*

Now that we've cleared up the potential problem with changing the value of a shared worker object, we can proceed to the new version of operator >> (Figure 4.33), which uses Read to fill in the data in an empty HomeItem.

**FIGURE 4.33. The latest version of** operator >> **(from code\hmit5.cc)**

```
istream& operator >> (istream& is, HomeItem& Item)
{
  string Type;
  bool Interactive = (&is == &cin);
```

```
 while (Type == "")
  {
  if (Interactive)
    cout << "Type (Basic, Music) ";
  is >> Type;
  if (is.fail() != 0)
    {
    Item = HomeItem();
    return is;
    }
  }

 if (Type == "Basic")
  {
  // create empty Basic object to be filled in
  HomeItem Temp("",0.0,0,"","");
  Temp.Read(is);
  Item = Temp;
  }
 else if (Type == "Music")
  {
  // create an empty Music object to be filled in
  HomeItem Temp("",0.0,0,"","","",vector<string>(0));
  Temp.Read(is);
  Item = Temp;
  }
 else
  {
  cerr << "Can't create object of type " << Type << endl;
  exit(0);
  }

 return is;
}
```

The first part of this function, where we determine the type of the object to be created, is just as it was in the previous version (Figure 4.23). However, once we figure out the type, everything changes: Rather than read the data directly from the file or the user, we create an empty object of the correct type and then call a function called Read to get the data for us.

Susan had some questions about the constructor calls that create the empty HomeItemBasic and HomeItemMusic objects.

> **Susan:** Why do you have a period in the middle of one of the numbers when you're making a HomeItemMusic object?
>
> **Steve:** That's the initial value of the price field, which is a floating-point variable, so I've set the value to 0.0 to indicate that.
>
> **Susan:** What's a floating-point variable?
>
> **Steve:** One that can hold a number that has a fractional part as well as a number that has only a whole part.
>
> **Susan:** Okay, but why do you need all those null things (0 and "") in the constructor calls?
>
> **Steve:** Because the compiler needs the arguments to be able to figure out which constructor we want it to call. If we just said HomeItem Temp();, we would get a default-constructed HomeItem object that would have a HomeItemBasic worker object, but we want to specify whether the worker object is actually a HomeItemBasic or a HomeItemMusic. If the arguments match the argument list of the constructor that makes a HomeItem object with a HomeItemBasic worker object, then that's what the compiler will do; if they match the argument list of the constructor that makes a HomeItemMusic, it will make a HomeItem manager object witha HomeItemMusic worker object instead. That's how we make sure that we get the right type of empty object for the Read method to fill in.

One question not answered in this dialogue is what was wrong with the old method of filling in the fields in the object being created. That's the topic of the next section.

## *For Your Eyes Only*

The old method of creating and initializing the object directly in the operator >> code was fine for entering and displaying items, but as soon as we want to edit them, it has one serious drawback: The knowledge of field names has to be duplicated in a number of places. As we saw in the discussion of our recent changes to operator >>, this is undesirable because it harms maintainability. For example, let's suppose we want to change the prompt "Name: " to "Item Name: ". If this were a large program, it would be a significant problem to find and change all the occurrences of that prompt. It would be much better to be able to change that prompt in one place and have the whole program use the new one, as the new version of the program will allow us to do.

Susan had a question about changing prompts.

**Susan:** Why would you want to change the prompts? Who cares if it says "Name" or "Item Name"?

**Steve:** Well, the users of the program might care. Also, what if we wanted to translate this program into another language, like Spanish? In that case, it would be a lot more convenient if all of the prompts were in one place so we could change them all at once.

Before we get into the implementation of Read, however, we should look at the new version of the interface for the worker classes of HomeItem (Figure 4.34), which contains some new member functions as well as some constructs we haven't seen before.

**FIGURE 4.34. The latest version of the interface for the** HomeItem **worker** classes **(code\hmiti5.h)**

```
// hmiti5.h

class HomeItemBasic : public HomeItem
{
```

```
public:
  HomeItemBasic();

  HomeItemBasic(string Name, double PurchasePrice,
  long PurchaseDate, string Description, string Category);

virtual string GetName();
virtual void Read(istream& is);
virtual void Edit();

virtual void Write(ostream& os);
virtual string GetType();
virtual short FormattedDisplay(ostream& os);

virtual short ReadInteractive();
virtual short ReadFromFile(istream &is);
virtual bool EditField(short FieldNumber);

protected:
  enum FieldNum {e_Name = 1, e_PurchasePrice,
  e_PurchaseDate, e_Description, e_Category};

  string GetFieldName(short FieldNumber);
virtual HomeItem* CopyData();

protected:
  string m_Name;
  double m_PurchasePrice;
  long m_PurchaseDate;
  string m_Description;
  string m_Category;
};

class HomeItemMusic : public HomeItemBasic
{
public:
  HomeItemMusic(string Name, double PurchasePrice,
  long PurchaseDate, string Description, string Category,
```

```
   string Artist, vector<string> Track);

  HomeItemMusic& operator = (const HomeItemMusic& Item);

  virtual void Write(ostream& os);
  virtual string GetType();
  virtual short FormattedDisplay(ostream& os);

  virtual short ReadInteractive();
  virtual short ReadFromFile(istream &is);
  virtual bool EditField(short FieldNumber);

  protected:
   enum FieldNum {e_Artist = HomeItemBasic::e_Category + 1,
   e_TrackCount, e_TrackNumber};

   string GetFieldName(short FieldNumber);
  virtual HomeItem* CopyData();

  protected:
   string m_Artist;
   vector<string> m_Track;
  };
```

Before we get to the new functions, I should tell you about some details of the declaration and implementation of the concrete data type functions in this version of the HomeItem classes. As in previous header files for the worker classes of a polymorphic object, we don't have to declare the copy constructor, operator =, or the destructor for the first derived class, HomeItemBasic. Even so, we do have to declare and write the default constructor for this class so that we can specify the special base class constructor. This is necessary to avoid an infinite regress during the construction of a manager object. We also don't have to declare any of those functions or the default constructor for the second derived class, HomeItemMusic.

None of this is new. However, there is one oddity in the implementation of the HomeItemMusic class, which appears to result from a bug in the version of DJGPP that I'm using to compile the programs in this book. For some reason, if I don't define operator = for the HomeItemMusic class, I get a linker error telling me that there's an undefined reference in the compiler-generated operator = code. When I define my own version of HomeItemMusic::operator =, the linker error goes away. That's strange enough, but here's the really weird part: The interface file shown in Figure 4.34 doesn't even declare operator =, yet the compiler doesn't complain about the fact that I'm implementing an undeclared function! I posted a message on a couple of Usenet newsgroups about this problem, but haven't had any responses. For the present, we'll just have to accept this as one of those mysterious problems that sometimes plague software development (and developers).

Another thing I should mention is that the functions ReadInteractive, ReadFromFile, and EditField are defined in HomeItemBasic and HomeItemMusic, rather than in HomeItem, because they are used only within the worker class implementations of Read and Edit rather than by the users of these classes. To be specific, the new functions ReadInteractive and ReadFromFile are used in the implementation of Read, and we'll discuss them when we look at Read, whereas the new EditField function is similarly used in the implementation of the Edit function. As in other cases where we've added functions that are not intended for use by the user of the HomeItem class, I have not defined them in the interface of HomeItem. This is an example of *information hiding*, similar in principle to making data and functions private or protected. Even though these functions are public, they are defined in classes that are accessible only to the implementers of the HomeItem polymorphic object — us.

There's also a new protected function called GetFieldName defined in HomeItemBasic and HomeItemMusic: It is used to encapsulate the knowledge of the field name prompts in connection with the information stored in the two versions of FieldNum. This latter is a new kind of construct called an enum. Of course, this leads to the obvious question: What's an enum?

## *U Pluribus* enum

An enum is a way to define a number of unchangeable values, which are quite similar to consts. One of the differences between these two types of named values is relevant here: The value of each successive name in an enum is automatically incremented from the value of the previous name (if you don't specify another value explicitly). This is quite convenient for defining names for a set of values such as vector or array indexes for prompts, which is how we will use enums in our program.

Susan had some questions about enums, starting with the derivation of this keyword.

> **Susan:** What does enum mean? Is it short for something?
>
> **Steve:** Yes. An enum is called that because it gives names to an "enumeration", which is a list of numbers.
>
> **Susan:** Are you going to put the prompts in a vector?
>
> **Steve:** No, but you're close; they'll be in an array, for reasons that I'll explain at the appropriate point.

Let's start with the definition of HomeItemBasic::FieldNum, which is:

```
enum FieldNum {e_Name = 1, e_PurchasePrice,
e_PurchaseDate, e_Description, e_Category};
```

This defines an enum called FieldNum that consists of the named values e_Name, e_PurchasePrice, e_PurchaseDate, e_Description, and e_Category. The first of these is defined to have the value 1, and the others have consecutive values starting with 2 and continuing through 5. These values, by absolutely no coincidence, are the field numbers we are going to use to prompt the user for the values of the member variables m_Name, m_PurchasePrice, m_PurchaseDate, m_Description, and m_Category.

The definition of HomeItemMusic::FieldNum is similar, but the values could use some explanation. First, here's the definition:

```
enum FieldNum {e_Artist = e_Category + 1,
e_TrackCount, e_TrackNumber};
```

The only significant difference between this definition and the previous one (besides the names of the values) is in the way we set the value of the first data item: We define it as one more than the value of e_Category, which, as it happens, is the last named value in HomeItemBasic::FieldNum. We need to do this so that we can display the correct field numbers for a HomeItemMusic, which of course contains everything that a HomeItemBasic contains as well as its own added variables. The user of the program should be able to edit either of these types of variables without having to worry about which fields are in the derived or the base class part. Thus, we want to make sure that the field number prompts run smoothly from the end of the data entry for a HomeItemBasic to the beginning of the data entry for a HomeItemMusic. If this isn't clear yet, don't worry. It will be by the time we get through the implementation of Read and the other data entry functions.

Now, what about those protected GetFieldName functions? All they do is to return the prompt corresponding to a particular field number. However, they deserve a bit of scrutiny because their implementation isn't quite so obvious as their function. Let's start with HomeItemBasic::GetFieldName, which is shown in Figure 4.35.

**FIGURE 4.35.** HomeItemBasic::GetFieldName **(from code\hmit5.cc)**

```
string HomeItemBasic::GetFieldName(short FieldNumber)
{
 static string Name[e_Category+1] = {"","Name",
```

```
  "Purchase Price","Purchase Date", "Description",
  "Category"};

 if ((FieldNumber > 0) && (FieldNumber <= e_Category))
  return Name[FieldNumber];

 return "";
}
```

This function contains a static array of strings, one for each field prompt and one extra null string at the beginning of the array. To set up the contents of the array, we use the construct {"","Name", "Purchase Price","Purchase Date", "Description", "Category"};, which is an *array initialization list* that supplies data for the elements in an array.

We need that null string ("") at the beginning of the initialization list to simplify the statement that returns the prompt for a particular field, because the field numbers that we display start at 1 rather than 0 (to avoid confusing the user of the program). Arrays always start at element 0 in C++, so if we want our field numbers to correspond to elements in the array, we need to start the prompts at the second element, which is how I've set it up. As a result, the statement that actually selects the prompt, return Name[FieldNumber], just uses the field number as an index into the array of strings and returns the appropriate one. For example, the prompt for e_Name is "1. Name: ", the prompt for e_PurchasePrice is "2. Purchase Price: ", and so on.

There are two questions I haven't answered yet about this function. First, why is the array static? Because it should be initialized only once, the first time this function is called, and that's what happens with static data. This is much more efficient than reinitializing the array with the same data every time this function is called, which is what would happen if we didn't add the static modifier to the definition of the Name array.

The second question is why we are using an array in the first place — aren't they dangerous? Yes, they are, but, unfortunately, in this situation we cannot use a vector as we normally would. The reason is that the ability to specify a list of values for an array is built into the C++ language and is not available for user-defined data types such as the vector. Therefore, if we want to use this very convenient method of initializing a multi-element data structure, we have to use an array instead.

This also explains why we need the if statement: to prevent the possibility of a caller trying to access an element of the array that doesn't exist. With a vector, we wouldn't have to worry that such an invalid access could cause havoc in the program; instead, we would get an error message from the index-checking code built into vector. However, arrays don't have any automatic checking for valid indexes, so we have to take care of that detail whenever we use them in a potentially hazardous situation like this one.

There's one more point I should mention here. I've already explained that when we define an enum such as HomeItemBasic::FieldNum, the named values in that enum (such as e_Name) are actually values of a defined data type. To be precise, e_Name is a value of type HomeItemBasic::FieldNum. That's not too weird in itself, but it does lead to some questions when we look at a statement such as if ((FieldNumber > 0) && (FieldNumber <= e_Category)). The problem is that we're comparing a short called FieldNumber with a HomeItemBasic::FieldNum called e_Category. Is this legal, and if so, why?

## *Taking a* shortcut

Yes, it is legal, because an enum value will automatically be converted to an integer value for purposes of arithmetic and comparison. For example, you can compare an enum with a value of any integer type, add an enum to an integer value, or assign an enum to an integer variable, without a peep from the compiler. While this is less than desirable from the point of view of strong type checking, it can be handy in circumstances like the present ones. By the way, this *automatic conversion* doesn't completely eliminate type checking for enums; you can't assign an integer variable to an enum without the compiler warning you that you're doing something questionable, so there is *some* real difference between enums and integer types![19]

Finally, we're ready for the implementation of Read. As with HomeItem::Edit, the base class version of this function has to handle the possibility that we're reading data into a shared worker object, as shown in Figure 4.36.

**FIGURE 4.36.** HomeItem::Read **(from code\hmit5.cc)**

```
void HomeItem::Read(istream& is)
{
 if (m_Worker->m_Count > 1)
  {
  m_Worker->m_Count --;
  m_Worker = m_Worker->CopyData();
  m_Worker->m_Count = 1;
  }

 m_Worker->Read(is);
}
```

I won't bother going over the *anti-aliasing* code again, as it is identical to the corresponding code in HomeItem::Edit. Instead, let's move right along to Figure 4.37, which shows the worker version of this function, HomeItemBasic::Read. Before reading on, see if you can guess why we need only one worker version of this function rather than one for each worker class.

19. The subject of automatic conversions among the various built-in types in C++ is complex enough to require more coverage than I can provide here. However, by a remarkable coincidence, I've signed a contract to write a book that covers that topic as well as a number of other unobvious features of C++. The main thrust of the book will be how to prevent these features of the language from causing trouble in your programs. This book, tentatively entitled *Shining C++*, should be available late in 1999 or early in 2000 (if the Year 2000 crisis doesn't get us first).

**FIGURE 4.37.** HomeItemBasic::Read **(from code\hmit5.cc)**

```
void HomeItemBasic::Read(istream& is)
{
 if (&is == &cin)
  ReadInteractive();
 else
  ReadFromFile(is);
}
```

The reason we need only one worker class version of this function is that its only job is to decide whether the input is going to be from the keyboard (cin) or from a file, and then to call a function to do the actual work. The class of the worker object doesn't affect the decision as to whether the input is from cin or a file, and the functions it calls are virtual, so the right function will be called for the type of the worker object. This means that the HomeItemMusic version of this function is identical, so we can rely on inheritance from HomeItemBasic to supply it and therefore don't have to write it ourselves.

By the same token, the code for Read doesn't tell us much about how reading data for an object actually works; for that we'll have to look at the functions it calls, starting with Figure 4.38, which shows the code for HomeItemBasic::ReadInteractive.

**FIGURE 4.38.** HomeItemBasic::ReadInteractive **(from code\hmit5.cc)**

```
short HomeItemBasic::ReadInteractive()
{
 short FieldNumber = e_Name;

 cout << FieldNumber << ". ";
 cout << GetFieldName(FieldNumber) << ": ";
 FieldNumber ++;
 cin >> m_Name;
```

```
  cout << FieldNumber << ". ";
  cout << GetFieldName(FieldNumber) << ": ";
  FieldNumber ++;
  cin >> m_PurchasePrice;

  cout << FieldNumber << ". ";
  cout << GetFieldName(FieldNumber) << ": ";
  FieldNumber ++;
  cin >> m_PurchaseDate;

  cout << FieldNumber << ". ";
  cout << GetFieldName(FieldNumber) << ": ";
  FieldNumber ++;
  cin >> m_Description;

  cout << FieldNumber << ". ";
  cout << GetFieldName(FieldNumber) << ": ";
  FieldNumber ++;
  cin >> m_Category;

  *this = HomeItemBasic(m_Name, m_PurchasePrice,
  m_PurchaseDate, m_Description, m_Category);

  return FieldNumber;
}
```

This isn't too complicated, but there are a few tricky parts, starting with the statement short FieldNumber = e_Name;. Why are we using a short value (FieldNumber) to keep track of which field number we are using when we have an enum type called FieldNum that can apparently be used for this purpose?

We have to use a short for this purpose because, as I noted earlier, we can't assign an integer value to an enum without the compiler complaining. Although we aren't directly assigning an integer value to FieldNumber, we are incrementing it by using the ++ operator. This operator, as you may recall, is shorthand for "add one to the previous value of the variable and put the new value back in the variable". The first part of that operation is allowed with an enum variable because such a variable is automatically converted to an integer type when it is used for arithmetic. However, the second part prevents us from using an enum variable because it tries to assign the integer result of the addition back to the enum, and that violates the rule against assigning an enum an integer value.[20]

Susan had a question about the rules for using enums.

**Susan:** I understand that we can't do arithmetic operations on an enum. What I don't understand is *why*.

**Steve:** It's to try to prevent errors in using them. An enum consists of a number of named values. As long as we stick to the rules for using enum values, the compiler can tell whether we're using them correctly. For example, because e_TrackNumber is the highest value defined in the FieldNum enum, if we were to try to refer to the value e_TrackNumber + 1, the compiler could tell that we were doing something illegal. However, if we could add a number to an enum *variable*, the compiler wouldn't be able to tell if we were doing something illegal because the value of the variable wouldn't be known until run time.

**Susan:** I still don't get it. I need an example.

**Steve:** That's a reasonable request. Okay, let's suppose that we used an enum instead of a short and tried to add 1 to it. If we created a local variable of type FieldNum and tried to add 1 to it via the statement FieldNumber = FieldNumber + 1;, we would get a warning message something like Figure 4.39.

20. Of course, it is theoretically possible simply to ignore the compiler warning and use the enum for arithmetic anyway, but I don't write programs that way. Once we start ignoring compiler warnings because "we know what we're doing", it's entirely too easy to ignore a warning that is really serious.

**FIGURE 4.39. A warning message about** enum **usage (code\enum.err)**

```
In method 'short int HomeItemBasic::ReadInteractive()':
warning: conversion from 'int' to 'enum HomeItemBasic::FieldNum'
```

**Susan:** Okay, I guess that makes sense. So how do we get around this compiler warning stuff?

**Steve:** By using a short variable instead of an enum. We can use an enum value to initialize the short variable, then increment the short to keep track of the field number that we're on.

Now that we've presumably cleared up that point, most of the rest of this function is pretty simple; it consists primarily of a number of sequences that are all quite similar. Let's take a look at the first of these sequences, which handles the name of the object.

First, we display the field number for the current field via the statement cout << FieldNumber << ". ";. Next, we retrieve and display the field name for the current field via the next statement, cout << GetFieldName(FieldNumber) << ": ";. Then we increment the field number to set up for the next field via the statement "FieldNumber ++;". Finally, we request the value for the variable corresponding to the name of the object via the last statement in the sequence, cin >> m_Name;.

Of course, the sequences that handle the other fields are almost the same as this one, differing only in the name of the variable we're assigning the input value to. However, as simple as this may be, it raises another question: Why are we repeating almost the same code a number of times rather than using a function? The problem is that these sequences aren't similar enough to work as a function; to be exact, the type of the variable to which the data is being assigned is different according to which field we're working on. For example, m_Name is a string, m_PurchasePrice is a double, and m_PurchaseDate is a long. Therefore, we would need at least three different functions that were almost identical except for the type of data they returned, which wouldn't be worth the trouble. Instead, we'll just put up with the duplication.

The only other statement that will need significant study is the following one:

```
*this = HomeItemBasic(m_Name, m_PurchasePrice,
m_PurchaseDate, m_Description, m_Category);
```

What can this possibly mean?

## *this Must Be the Place*

There are two parts to that statement: the constructor call on the right of the = and the construct "*this" on the left of the =. The constructor call is easier to explain: It constructs a HomeItem object with the contents specified by the arguments to the constructor. In the present case, those arguments are the values that we've just read in from the keyboard. After that object is constructed, we assign it to . . . what?

I hope you remember that "this" is the address of the object for which a member function was called. The purpose of this ReadInteractive function is to assign a new value to its object, which is accomplished by of this statement, so the appearance of this in the statement shouldn't be too surprising. The burning question, of course, is "What does * mean in this context?"

The answer is "The object pointed to by whatever is after the *". In this case, that means we can translate "*this" as "the object pointed to by this", which of course is just the object for which the current function was called. In other words, the statement we're analyzing assigns the result of the constructor call to the object for which this function (HomeItemBasic::ReadInteractive) was called. Since this is the purpose for which ReadInteractive was written, we must be almost done. In fact, we are; the only remaining statement is return FieldNumber;, which lets the calling function know what field number is the next to be handled. As we'll see, this return value is needed when this function is called from a derived class function such as HomeItemMusic::ReadInteractive to tell the calling function which fields it has to handle itself and which ones have been dealt with.

Susan didn't care for this idea very much, so we talked it over.

**Susan:** I hate this, and *this is even worse! What is it?

**Steve:** Remember, this is the address of the object for which the member function was called. The * before a pointer means "the object to which the following pointer points", so *this means "the object to which the this pointer points", which is the object for which the member function was called.

**Susan:** I still don't understand what this refers to.

**Steve:** Well, suppose we call the function ReadInteractive by the following statement: x.ReadInteractive();. In that case, what would be the value of *this during the execution of ReadInteractive?

**Susan:** Would it be x?

**Steve:** Exactly right!

Now let's take a look at HomeItemBasic::ReadFromFile (Figure 4.40), which, as its name suggests, reads data from a file and uses it to assign a value to a HomeItemBasic object.

**FIGURE 4.40.** HomeItemBasic::ReadFromFile **(from code\hmit5.cc)**

```
short HomeItemBasic::ReadFromFile(istream& is)
{
 is >> m_Name;
 is >> m_PurchasePrice;
 is >> m_PurchaseDate;
 is >> m_Description;
 is >> m_Category;
```

```
  *this = HomeItemBasic(m_Name, m_PurchasePrice,
  m_PurchaseDate, m_Description, m_Category);
}
```

As you can see, this is much simpler than the previous function. However, it does basically the same thing; the difference is merely that it deals with a file rather than a user, which makes its job much easier. This illustrates a maxim known to all professional programmers: Having to deal with users is the most difficult part of writing programs!

We've examined all the functions that make up the implementation of Read for the HomeItemBasic class. Now it's time to take a look at HomeItemBasic::Edit, which is the function called by HomeItem::Edit to edit existing data in a HomeItemBasic worker object. As in the case of Read, this function doesn't do anything class-specific, but hands all the dirty work over to virtual functions that will do the right thing for their objects. Therefore, we need only one copy of Edit, which will call the appropriate functions depending on the type of the object we're actually editing. Figure 4.41 shows the code for this function, HomeItemBasic::Edit.

**FIGURE 4.41.** HomeItemBasic::Edit **(from code\hmit5.cc)**

```
void HomeItemBasic::Edit()
{
  short FieldNumber;

  FormattedDisplay(cout);
  cout << endl;

  cout << "Please enter field number to be changed: ";
  cin >> FieldNumber;
  cout << endl;

  EditField(FieldNumber);
}
```

There's nothing terribly complicated about this function, largely because it uses FormattedDisplay and EditField to do most of the work. First, it calls FormattedDisplay to display the current value of the object in question, then it asks for the number of the field to be changed, and finally it calls EditField to do the actual modification for that field.

Susan had a question about the field number.

**Susan:** Is the field number the element number in the vector of HomeItems?

**Steve:** No, it's the number of the individual field that we're going to change in the HomeItem that we're editing.

Let's start by looking at the new version of HomeItemBasic::FormattedDisplay (Figure 4.42).

**FIGURE 4.42.** HomeItemBasic::FormattedDisplay **(from code\hmit5.cc)**

```
short HomeItemBasic::FormattedDisplay(ostream &os)
{
 short FieldNumber = e_Name;

 os << "Type: " << GetType() << endl;

 os << FieldNumber << ". ";
 os << GetFieldName(FieldNumber) << ": ";
 FieldNumber ++;
 os << m_Name << endl;

 os << FieldNumber << ". ";
 os << GetFieldName(FieldNumber) << ": ";
 FieldNumber ++;
 os << m_PurchasePrice << endl;

 os << FieldNumber << ". ";
 os << GetFieldName(FieldNumber) << ": ";
```

```
  FieldNumber ++;
  os << m_PurchaseDate << endl;

  os << FieldNumber << ". ";
  os << GetFieldName(FieldNumber) << ": ";
  FieldNumber ++;
  os << m_Description << endl;

  os << FieldNumber << ". ";
  os << GetFieldName(FieldNumber) << ": ";
  FieldNumber ++;
  os << m_Category << endl;

  return FieldNumber;
}
```

This is almost identical to the HomeItemBasic version of ReadInteractive. The differences are these:

1. It writes its output to the ostream specified by its argument, os, rather than to cout, as HomeItemBasic::ReadInteractive does.
2. It doesn't prompt the user for input.

Now let's look at the code for the HomeItemBasic version of the EditField function (Figure 4.43).

**FIGURE 4.43.** HomeItemBasic::EditField **(from code\hmit5.cc)**

```
bool HomeItemBasic::EditField(short FieldNumber)
{
  bool result = true;

  switch (FieldNumber)
   {
   case e_Name:
   cout << FieldNumber << ". ";
   cout << GetFieldName(FieldNumber) << ": ";
   cin >> m_Name;
```

```
        break;

        case e_PurchasePrice:
        cout << FieldNumber << ". ";
        cout << GetFieldName(FieldNumber) << ": ";
        cin >> m_PurchasePrice;
        break;

        case e_PurchaseDate:
        cout << FieldNumber << ". ";
        cout << GetFieldName(FieldNumber) << ": ";
        cin >> m_PurchaseDate;
        break;

        case e_Description:
        cout << FieldNumber << ". ";
        cout << GetFieldName(FieldNumber) << ": ";
        cin >> m_Description;
        break;

        case e_Category:
        cout << FieldNumber << ". ";
        cout << GetFieldName(FieldNumber) << ": ";
        cin >> m_Category;
        break;

        default:
        cout << "Sorry, that is not a valid field number." << endl;
        result = false;
        break;
        }

    return result;
}
```

This code probably looks a little odd. Where are all the if statements needed to select the field to be modified based on its field number? That would be one way to code this function, but I've chosen to use a different construct designed specifically to select one of a number of alternatives: the switch statement. This statement is functionally equivalent to a number of if/else statements in a row, but is easier to read and modify. Its syntax consists of the keyword switch followed by a *selection expression* in parentheses that specifies the value that will determine the alternative to be selected. The various alternatives to be considered are enclosed in a set of curly braces and are marked off by the keyword case followed by the (constant) value to be matched and a colon. In the current situation, the selection expression is FieldNumber, whose value will be compared with the various *case labels* inside the curly brackets of the switch statement. For example, if the value of FieldNumber is equal to e_Name, the section of code following case e_Name: will be executed.

We use the break statement to indicate the end of the section of code to be executed for each case. We've already seen the break statement used to terminate a for loop, and it works in much the same way here: It breaks out of the curly braces containing the code for the switch statement. It's also possible to terminate the code to be executed for a given case by executing a return statement to exit from the function. If we have already accomplished the purpose of the function, this is often a convenient alternative.

There's one more item I should mention: the default keyword, which begins a section of code that should be executed in the event that the value of the selection expression doesn't match any of the individual cases. This is very handy to catch programming errors that result in an invalid value for the selection expression. If we don't use default, the switch statement will essentially be skipped if there is no matching case, and that probably isn't the right thing to do. Therefore, it's a good idea to use default to catch such an error whenever you use a switch statement.

In the current situation, we're using the default code to display an error message and return the value false to the calling function so that it will know that its attempt to edit the object didn't work.

However, if you have been following along very carefully, you'll notice that the function that calls this one, Edit, doesn't bother to check the return value from EditField, so it wouldn't notice if this error ever occurred. Such an omission doesn't cause any trouble here because the user has already been notified that his edit didn't work. Unfortunately, however, the very common problem of forgetting to check return values isn't always so benign. In fact, it's serious enough that several features have been added to C++ just to make it possible to ensure that errors aren't ignored accidentally, but we won't get to discuss those features, collectively called *exception handling*, in this book.

## *Facing the Music*

We've now covered all the new member functions in HomeItemBasic, so it's time to take a look at the functions implemented in HomeItemMusic. Thankfully, there aren't as many of these. For one thing, GetName, Read, and Edit don't have to be overridden in HomeItemMusic because they do most of their work by calling virtual functions anyway. Two more functions in this class, Write and GetType, haven't changed since we first saw them in hmit1.cc, so we don't have to go over them again. HomeItemMusic::FormattedDisplay, on the other hand, has changed since we examined it in hmit4.cc, so it would be a good idea to look it over quickly (Figure 4.44).

**FIGURE 4.44.** HomeItemMusic::FormattedDisplay **(from code\hmit5.cc)**

```
short HomeItemMusic::FormattedDisplay(ostream &os)
{
  short FieldNumber = HomeItemBasic::FormattedDisplay(os);

  short TrackCount = m_Track.size();

  os << FieldNumber << ". ";
  os << GetFieldName(FieldNumber) << ": ";
  FieldNumber ++;
  os << m_Artist << endl;
```

```
  os << FieldNumber << ". ";
  os << GetFieldName(FieldNumber) << ": ";
  FieldNumber ++;
  os << TrackCount << endl;

  for (short i = 0; i < TrackCount; i ++)
   {
   os << FieldNumber << ". ";
   os << GetFieldName(FieldNumber) << i + 1 << ": ";
   FieldNumber ++;
   os << m_Track[i] << endl;
   }

  return FieldNumber;
}
```

This function isn't very different from its counterpart in HomeItemBasic, but there are a couple of points worth mentioning. First, of course, it calls HomeItemBasic::FormattedDisplay to display the part of the data contained in the base class part of the object. Then it assigns the return value from that call to a local variable called FieldNumber, which it uses to keep track of the current field it is displaying. Why do we want to use the return value from that function to initialize our current field variable rather than a const value, as we did in the base class?

## *Maintaining Our Position*

We do this to reduce the difficulty of maintaining this program. If we use the return value from HomeItemBasic::FormattedDisplay, we won't have to make any changes in the derived class function if the HomeItemBasic class eventually has more data added to it; the starting field number in HomeItemMusic:FormattedDisplay will automatically be the right value as long as the modifications to the HomeItemBasic::FormattedDisplay function have been made correctly.

Therefore, we have to make such a change only in one place rather than in two, as we would if we used a const value in the derived class function.

Susan wanted a bit more detail on this issue.

**Susan:** What kind of change would you make that might mess up the field numbers?

**Steve:** Let's suppose that we had six fields in the HomeItemBasic class, which of course would be numbered 1 through 6. In that case, the added fields in HomeItemMusic would start at 7. However, if we added another field to the HomeItemBasic class, then the number of the first field in the HomeItemMusic class would change to 8. All of this would have to be handled manually if we used a constant value to specify where we wanted to start in the HomeItemMusic class. However, as long as we use the return value from the HomeItemBasic version of FormattedDisplay, any such adjustments will happen automatically.

**Susan:** But the user might get confused if the field that used to be #5 suddenly became #6.

**Steve:** True, but there isn't much we can do about that, assuming that the new field was really necessary. All we can do is make sure that the numbers will still be in the right order with no gaps.

I should also mention that the field name prompt for track names is "Track #" followed by the track number. Because we don't want to confuse the user by starting at 0, we add 1 to the value of the loop index before we use it to construct the field name prompt. This ensures that the first track number displayed is 1, not 0. Remember, users don't normally count from 0, and we should humor them; without them, we wouldn't have anyone to use our programs!

Now let's take a look at HomeItemMusic::ReadInteractive (Figure 4.45).

**FIGURE 4.45.** HomeItemMusic::ReadInteractive **(from code\hmit5.cc)**

```
short HomeItemMusic::ReadInteractive()
{
 short TrackCount;

 short FieldNumber = HomeItemBasic::ReadInteractive();

 cout << FieldNumber << ". ";
 cout << GetFieldName(FieldNumber) << ": ";
 FieldNumber ++;
 cin >> m_Artist;

 cout << FieldNumber << ". ";
 cout << GetFieldName(FieldNumber) << ": ";
 FieldNumber ++;
 cin >> TrackCount;
 m_Track.resize(TrackCount);

 vector<string> Track(TrackCount);
 for (short i = 0; i < TrackCount; i ++)
  {
  cout << FieldNumber << ". ";
  cout << GetFieldName(FieldNumber) << i + 1 << ": ";
  FieldNumber ++;
  cin >> Track[i];
  }

 *this = HomeItemMusic(m_Name, m_PurchasePrice,
 m_PurchaseDate, m_Description, m_Category, m_Artist,
 Track);

 return FieldNumber;
}
```

Only one thing in this function might be a bit puzzling: Where do we get the values of the member variables m_Name through m_Category, which we use as arguments in the call to the constructor for HomeItemMusic near the end of the function? The answer is that they were input by the user during the execution of HomeItemBasic::ReadInteractive, which we called at the beginning of this function. Therefore, when we are ready to create the HomeItemMusic object containing all the data read from the user, we can combine all of those data items with the ones that we requested from the user in this function — namely, m_Artist and the track names in the local vector Track.

There are two more functions that we need to look at briefly. The first is HomeItemMusic::ReadFromFile, which is shown in Figure 4.46. Assuming that you understand the HomeItemBasic versions of ReadFromFile and ReadInteractive, this function should hold no secrets for you, so just take a look at it and make sure you understand it. Then let's move on.

**FIGURE 4.46.** HomeItemMusic::ReadFromFile (**from code\hmit5.cc**)

```
short HomeItemMusic::ReadFromFile(istream& is)
{
 short TrackCount;

 HomeItemBasic::ReadFromFile(is);

 is >> m_Artist;
 is >> TrackCount;

 vector<string> Track(TrackCount);
 for (short i = 0; i < TrackCount; i ++)
  {
  is >> Track[i];
  }

 *this = HomeItemMusic(m_Name, m_PurchasePrice,
 m_PurchaseDate, m_Description, m_Category, m_Artist, Track);
}
```

Finally, there's HomeItemMusic::EditField (Figure 4.47), which has a few points that we should consider before (finally!) ending this chapter.

**FIGURE 4.47.** HomeItemMusic::EditField **(from code\hmit5.cc)**

```
bool HomeItemMusic::EditField(short FieldNumber)
{
 if (FieldNumber < e_Artist)
  {
  return HomeItemBasic::EditField(FieldNumber);
  }

 short TrackCount = m_Track.size();

 switch (FieldNumber)
  {
  case e_Artist:
  cout << FieldNumber << ". ";
  cout << GetFieldName(FieldNumber) << ": ";
  cin >> m_Artist;
  return true;

  case e_TrackCount:
  cout << FieldNumber << ". ";
  cout << GetFieldName(FieldNumber) << ": ";
  cin >> TrackCount;
  m_Track.resize(TrackCount);
  return true;
  }

 if (FieldNumber > (e_TrackCount + TrackCount))
  {
  cout << "Sorry, that is not a valid field number." << endl;
  return false;
  }

 cout << FieldNumber << ". ";
```

```
  cout << GetFieldName(FieldNumber);
  cout << FieldNumber - e_TrackCount << ": ";

  cin >> m_Track[FieldNumber - e_TrackNumber];

  return true;
}
```

Let's start at the beginning, where we figure out whether the field the user wants to edit is handled by this function or by HomeItemBasic::Edit. If the field number is less than e_Artist, we know that this function isn't responsible for editing it, so we pass the editing task on to the HomeItemBasic version of EditField and return the return value from that function to our caller.

But suppose we have to handle the editing chore for the user's field here. In that case, we need to execute the proper code for the field the user wants to edit. If that field happens to be either the artist's name or the number of tracks, we handle it in the switch statement and return the value true to indicate success. However, handling the other fields (i.e., the track names) isn't quite as simple. If you compare HomeItemBasic::EditField (Figure 4.43) with the current function you'll notice that the switch statement in HomeItemBasic::EditField has a default case to handle the possibility that the field number is invalid, whereas the HomeItemMusic switch statement doesn't. Why is this?

Because a HomeItemMusic object can contain a variable number of track names in its m_Track member variable. This means that we can't tell at compile time how many fields are in the object we're going to edit, which in turn means that we have to wait until run time to figure out whether a particular field number is valid for a particular object. That's the purpose of the if statement

```
if (FieldNumber > (e_TrackCount + TrackCount))
```

which adds the number of tracks to the field number for the track count itself and then compares the result to the field number the user typed in. Since the track name fields immediately follow the track count field, if the user's field number is greater than that total, the field number is invalid. For example, if there's only one track, the maximum field number is e_TrackCount + 1; if there are two tracks, it is e_TrackCount + 2; and so on. If the field number the user typed is beyond the legal range, the code in the if statement displays a warning and returns the value false to the calling function to indicate that it was unable to update the object.

Assuming that the user typed in a legal field number, we continue with the code that prompts the user to type in the new name for the selected track:

```
cout << FieldNumber << ". ";
cout << GetFieldName(FieldNumber);
cout << FieldNumber - e_TrackCount << ": ";
```

This starts out by displaying the field number for the track to be edited followed by its field name ("Track #" followed by its track number). For example, if the starting field number for the track names is 8, the prompt for track 5 is "12. Track #5: ". Then the line

```
cin >> m_Track[FieldNumber - e_TrackNumber];
```

accepts the new value of the track name and stores it in the correct place in the m_Track member variable. Finally, the function returns true to indicate success.

## *Review*

We started out this chapter by considering the problem of keeping track of all the "stuff" that we accumulate in our homes. This happens to make a good project to illustrate the use of the C++ tools that we've already covered, as well as to introduce a few new tools along the way. It also has the fortunate characteristic that the finished program might actually be useful.

Once we selected a project, the next step was to figure out exactly what the program should do.[21] In this case, we wanted to be able to keep track of the type of object, date of acquisition, price, and description for every item in the home, as well as any additional information needed for specific types of objects. An example is the CD, for which the additional information is the name of the artist and those of the tracks.

This led to the more general question of how to divide the nearly infinite number of real-world objects that we might encounter into the categories represented by a necessarily limited number of possible types of program objects. For example, what should we do with LPs or cassette tapes? Because they are used for much the same purpose as music CDs are, I decided to put all of these objects in the same "Music" type. A CD-ROM, on the other hand, is probably best represented by a "software" type, even though it is physically identical to a music CD, because it is used differently and has different information associated with it. For example, a CD-ROM often has a serial number whereas a music CD doesn't.

Having made a decision on this matter, we were ready to start designing the interface that the user of the HomeItem classes will see, using the *manager/worker idiom* to implement a *polymorphic object* solution to our problem.

Once we looked at the first version of the interface for the HomeItem class, the most obvious observation was that it is very similar to the StockItem class from previous chapters. The main reason for that similarity is that both of these classes play the role of the manager class in a polymorphic object implementation. One manager class looks very much like any other because a manager

21. This may seem too simple even to mention, but the failure to define exactly what a particular program is supposed to do is a major cause of wasted money and effort, especially in large corporations.

object's main duties are to create, destroy, and otherwise handle its worker objects; those duties are similar no matter what the worker objects actually do.

For this reason, all of the "structural" functions in the manager classes for the StockItem and HomeItem types are almost identical except for the exact data types of arguments and return values. These structural functions include the operators << and >>, the default constructors, copy constructors, "normal" constructors, assignment operators, and destructors. They also include the "special" constructor used to prevent an infinite loop during construction of a worker object and the Write function used to create a human-readable version of the data for an object.

By contrast, the "regular" member functions of each of these manager classes are whatever is needed to allow the users of that class to get their work done. These functions differ signficantly from one polymorphic object implementation to another, as they are the most specific to the particular task of each class.

Upon examination, we saw that the same analogies apply to the worker classes for these two types as to the manager classes. The main difference between the StockItem worker classes and the first version of the HomeItem worker classes is that the HomeItem worker classes have a GetType member function that the StockItem worker classes don't have. This function allows the base class member data to be displayed with the correct tag indicating the exact type of the worker object being displayed, rather than requiring the duplication of code in the base and derived class output functions.[22]

Because this GetType function is used only within inside the implementation of the worker classes, it is first declared in HomeItemBasic rather than in HomeItem. This doesn't violate the principle that all objects of a polymorphic object type must have the same user interface, because GetType is not visible to the user of the

22. The use of a GetType member function to allow sharing of code for the base class member data display would probably have been a good idea for the StockItem classes as well, but I hadn't thought of it yet when I designed those classes.

HomeItem types and therefore doesn't change the user's view of these objects.

Next, we analyzed the first version of operator >> for the HomeItem classes. This function differs from the StockItem version of the same operator in a number of ways, the primary differences being its ability to skip blank lines in the input file, its deferred creation of variables until they are needed rather than all at the beginning of the function, and its use of an explicit type indicator ("Basic" or "Music") to determine the type of the worker object, rather than relying on the value of the expiration date field as the operator >> for StockItem did.

The most generally applicable of these differences is the deferred creation of variables, which is a good way to save execution time and make the program easier to follow. In this case, we didn't create a vector of track names until we had read the rest of the data for the object, including its type and track count; of course, a "Basic" object doesn't have the track count and track name fields anyway.

This implementation of operator >> also illustrates the new C++ feature that restricts the scope of a for index variable created in a for statement to the loop controlled by that for statement. Earlier versions of C++ allowed that variable to be accessed after the end of the for loop, an oversight that was corrected in the final proposed C++ standard.

Then we moved on to the HomeItemBasic::Write function, which uses the GetType function to determine which type of object it is writing to the ostream specified by its argument. The HomeItemBasic version of Write has to call GetType because the derived class function HomeItemMusic::Write calls this function to do most of the work; thus, the object for which HomeItemBasic::Write has been called may be a derived class object rather than a HomeItemBasic object. This means that HomeItemBasic::Write has to call the virtual function GetType to find out the actual type of the object being written so that it can write the correct type indicator to the output file along with the other data for the object. This is what makes it possible for us to reconstruct the object properly when we read the data back from the file.

When we got done with HomeItemBasic::Write, we continued by analyzing HomeItemMusic::Write. That function is pretty simple, except that it uses the size member function of the vector data type to find out how many tracks are in the vector so that it can write that track count, followed by all of the track names. This is necessary for us to reconstruct the "Music" object properly when we read its data from the file.

The next operation we undertook was to create a new HomeInventory class, which serves much the same function for HomeItems that the Inventory class does for StockItems: It allows us to create and keep track of a number of HomeItems and to search for a particular HomeItem.

The initial interface of this new HomeInventory class is also pretty simple, providing only the minimal set of operations we might want to use: loading the inventory from a disk file and searching for a particular item by name. After considering several ways to keep track of the number of elements in use, we decided on storing the number of elements in the input file and creating a vector of the correct size when we open the file. If we add new items to the vector, we keep track of that fact via its size member function.

This solution eliminates the waste of space or time of the other ways to determine the size of the vector when reading data from the input file, but it also has a twist of its own: the need to read the data into a temporary holding variable so we can detect the end of the input file without running off the end of the vector. This problem led to a discussion of the dangers of ignoring the possibility of errors in the data, as well as other sources of errors that lie outside the immediate scope of the code we write, including the Year 2000 problem.

After a discussion of the Year 2000 problem, we continued by creating the ability for the user to enter data for a new object by adding an AddItem member function to the HomeInventory class and a NewItem static member function to the HomeItem class. The latter needs to be a static member function because it creates a new HomeItem object by reading data from the keyboard; it doesn't have an existing HomeItem object to work on, so it can't be a regular member function.

The implementation of HomeItem::NewItem is quite simple: It uses operator >> to read data from the keyboard into a newly created HomeItem object and then returns it to the caller. However, this works only because we changed operator >> to be usable for keyboard input by having it determine whether the user is typing at the keyboard according to the identity of the input stream. If that stream is cin, the function displays prompts before each input operation; if not, the input operations are performed as they were previously.

We had to change operator >> rather than using it as previously implemented because adding another function for keyboard input would have required require us to duplicate the code that reads the data, causing maintenance problems when any of those input operations had to be modified.

Then we added versions of FormattedDisplay to both HomeItemBasic and HomeItemMusic, which provide output virtually identical to the output of operator << for objects of those two types, except that FormattedDisplay also displays labels indicating what the data items represent.

The next order of business was to discuss GetName, whose only notable characteristic is that even though it is a virtual function, it is not implemented in HomeItemMusic because the implementation in HomeItemBasic will work perfectly for a HomeItemMusic object. As with a nonvirtual function, if we call a virtual function for a derived class object that hasn't been defined in that class, the result will be to call the function in the nearest base class that defines the function — in this case HomeItemBasic::GetName.

Next we analyzed the test program hmtst4.cc, which includes the new AddItem and GetName functions added since the last test program. We used these functions to add a new item and retrieve it, as well as to retrieve an item loaded from the file (just to make sure that that still worked after all the changes we'd made).

In the next step, we added a mechanism to edit an object that already exists, via a new function called EditItem in the Inventory class and a corresponding function called Edit in the HomeItem class. We also added a helper function called LocateItemByName to the Inventory class to help us find an existing HomeItem to be edited.

We didn't have to change the test program very much from the previous version to accommodate this new ability to edit an existing object. However, we did have to modify the HomeItem classes significantly so that we could avoid keeping track of the field names in more than one function: This was intended to simplify maintenance later. One modification was the addition of a Read function that could fill in the data for an existing object rather than create the object directly in operator >>, as we had done until that point.

This revamping of the input mechanism required several new functions, which I added to HomeItemBasic and HomeItemMusic rather than to HomeItem, because they are used only as aids to the implementation of the new Read function. Included among these functions are ReadInteractive, ReadFromFile, EditField, and GetFieldName.

The last of these, GetFieldName, is particularly interesting on several counts. First, it uses a new construct, the enum, which is a way to define a number of constant values that are appropriate for naming array or vector indexes. Second, it uses a static array of strings to hold the field names for use in prompts. This array is static so that it will be initialized only once, during the first call to GetFieldName, rather than every time the function is called. The reason we're using an array instead of a vector is that it is (unfortunately) impossible in C++ to initialize a vector from a list of values; this special C++ facility is available only for arrays. Because we're using an array, we have to check for the possibility of a bad index rather than rely on the safety checks built into a vector; the program would fail in some mysterious way if we tried to access a nonexistent array element.

After some discussion of the properties of enums, including their ability to be converted to an integer type automatically when needed for arithmetic purposes, we continued with the implementation of Read, which merely decides whether the input is interactive and then calls the appropriate subfunction, ReadInteractive or ReadFromFile, accordingly. ReadInteractive, as its name implies, prompts the user for each field to be entered, using GetFieldName to retrieve the appropriate prompt for that field. ReadFromFile reads the same data but without displaying any prompts.

As soon as we have read all the data for an item, either interactively or from a file, either of the Read subfunctions finishes by calling the appropriate constructor to create an object containing that data and assigning the newly created object to *this. The latter expression means "the object pointed to by the this pointer" (the object for which the Read subfunction was called).

The other new function added to the HomeItem interface, Edit, first calls the updated version of FormattedDisplay to display the current data for the object to be edited, using GetFieldName to determine the prompt for each field to be displayed, and then calls EditField to request the new value for the field being modified. To simplify the code, this function uses a new construct, switch. This is essentially equivalent to a number of if...else if statements that select one of a number of possible actions.

After finishing the changes to HomeItemBasic, we examined the corresponding functions in HomeItemMusic, which use the HomeItemBasic base class functions to do as much of the work as possible. For this reason, the new HomeItemMusic functions added no great complexity except for the necessity of handling a variable number of data elements in the track name vector.

## *Exercises*

1. Implement the HomeItemComputer class as a derived class of HomeItemBasic to keep track of computers. The added fields should include serial number, amount of RAM, amount of disk space, a list of installed storage devices, and lists of installed ISA and PCI interface cards.

2. Implement the HomeItemSoftware class as a derived class of HomeItemBasic to keep track of computer software. The added fields should include the serial numbers of the software and computer on which it is installed. Can you devise a way to make sure that the latter serial number is the same as the serial number of a HomeItemComputer in the inventory?
3. Implement the HomeItemAppliance class as a derived class of HomeItemBasic to keep track of other electric and electronic appliances. The added fields should include the serial number of the appliance.
4. Can you think of a way to simplify the implementation of the classes in the above exercises by adding an additional class?
5. Implement the HomeItemBook class as a derived class of HomeItemBasic to keep track of books. The added fields should include author, publisher, publication date, number of pages, and ISBN (International Standard Book Number, a 10-character field that can contain the digits from 0 to 9 and the letter *X*).
6. Implement the HomeItemSet class as a derived class of HomeItemBasic to keep track of sets of identical items such as plates and flatware. The added fields should include the pattern name and number of items of each type.
7. Implement the HomeItemClothing class as a derived class of HomeItemBasic to keep track of clothes and shoes. The added fields should include owner's name and size.
8. Add code to the AddItem member function of the HomeInventory class to make sure that the new object being added has a name different from that of every object already in the inventory.

## *Conclusion*

At this point, we have a working, if rudimentary, set of HomeItem classes along with the HomeInventory class that manages the objects of these classes. Next, we're going to add some more facilities to the string class so that we can improve our application program enough to actually use it for keeping track of all the "stuff" we collect in everyday life.

CHAPTER 5

# Homeward Bound

In this chapter, we will begin to take the home inventory project to a stage where it will be a useful, if limited, application program that will allow you to keep track of your possessions. Of course, this doesn't mean that we will have completely finished this project; it's rare for a software application to be finished in the sense that nothing more can be done to improve it. In fact, the usual way to tell when you're done working on a project is that you have run out of time and have to put it into service, not that it does everything that you would like it to do. In this way, the home inventory project is quite representative of programming projects in general.

We'll get right to our improvements as soon as we get through some definitions as well as the objectives for the chapter.

## *Definitions*

The **preprocessor** is a part of the C++ compiler that deals with the source code of a program before the rest of the compiler ever sees that source code; thus, the name "preprocessor".

A **preprocessor directive** is a command telling the preprocessor to handle the following source code in a special manner.

A **preprocessor symbol** is a constant value similar to a const but is known only to the preprocessor, not to the rest of the compiler. The rules for naming preprocessor symbols are the same as those for other identifiers, but it is customary to use all uppercase letters in preprocessor symbols so that they can be readily distinguished from other identifiers.

The **#ifndef** preprocessor directive tells the preprocessor to check whether a particular preprocessor symbol has been defined. If not, the following source code is treated normally; if it has been defined, the following source code is skipped by the rest of the compiler as though it were not present in the source file.

The **#define** preprocessor directive defines a preprocessor symbol.

The **#endif** preprocessor directive terminates a section of source code controlled by a #ifndef or other conditional preprocessor directive.

An **include guard** is a mechanism to prevent a class definition from being included in a source code file more than once.

A **default argument** is a method of specifying a value for an argument to a function when the user of the function hasn't supplied a value for that argument. The valuc of the default argument is specified in the declaration of the function.

## *Objectives of This Chapter*

By the end of this chapter we will have

1. improved the string class to make it easy to search for a partially matching string;
2. learned how to use **include guards** to prevent a class interface from accidentally being defined more than once;
3. learned about **default arguments**, which reduce the amount of code we have to write for functions that can take a varying number of arguments;
4. learned about the **explicit** keyword, which gives us more control over how constructors will be used;
5. defined a **concatenation** operator that "adds" one string to the end of another one;
6. written a version of operator >> that can read a string of any length from the keyboard or a file;
7. learned something about the hazards of the "magic" value 0;
8. discovered just how difficult it is to anticipate how a program will be used, and how many bugs it contains, before seeing someone else try to use it;
9. seen how a seemingly simple request for an added feature in a program can be extremely difficult to fulfill.

## *Super-string Theory*

The strings we've been using in this book and in its predecessor, *Who's Afraid of C++?*, have been satisfactory for the uses we've made of them so far, but at this point we need some more functionality. We'll get to the implementation of the new functions as soon as we've taken care of some infrastructure details. Figure 5.1 shows the interface of the new string class that implements the new functions we'll need to finish our home inventory project.[1]

**FIGURE 5.1. The new string class interface (code\string7.h)**

```
#ifndef STRING7_H
#define STRING7_H

#include <iostream.h>
#include <string.h>

class string
{
friend ostream& operator << (ostream& os, const string& Str);
friend istream& operator >> (istream& is, string& Str);

public:
   string();
   string(const string& Str);
   string& operator = (const string& Str);
   ~string();

   string(char* p);
explicit string(short Length, char Ch=0);

   short GetLength();

   bool operator < (const string& Str);
   bool operator == (const string& Str);
   bool operator > (const string& Str);
   bool operator >= (const string& Str);
```

1. It took two chapters in *Who's Afraid of C++?* to examine the intricacies of the former version of the string class, but we don't have the space to go over it in that amount of detail here. Instead, we'll just cover the improvements I've added in this new version of the string class.

```
    bool operator <= (const string& Str);
    bool operator != (const string& Str);

    string operator + (const string& Str);
    short find_nocase(const string& Str);
    bool less_nocase (const string& Str);

private:
    short m_Length;
    char* m_Data;
};
#endif
```

## *Batteries Not #included*

The first change in this header file from the previous version, string6.h, doesn't have anything to do with adding new functionality to the string class. Instead, it is a means of preventing problems if we accidentally #include this header twice, using a mechanism generally referred to as an **include guard**. I'm referring to the two lines at the very beginning of the file and the last line at the end of the file. The first of these lines,

```
#ifndef STRING7_H
```

uses a **preprocessor directive** called #ifndef (short for "if not defined") to determine whether we've already defined a preprocessor symbol called STRING7_H. If this is the case, the compiler will ignore the rest of the file until it sees an #endif (which in this case is at the end of the file).

The next line,

```
#define STRING7_H
```

defines the same preprocessor symbol, STRING7_H, that we tested for in the previous line. Finally, the last line of the file,

```
#endif
```

ends the scope of the #ifndef directive.

> **Susan:** I don't get it. What is a preprocessor directive? For that matter, what is a preprocessor?
>
> **Steve:** The preprocessor used to be a separate program that was executed before the compiler itself, to prepare the source code for the compiler. Nowadays, the preprocessor is almost always part of the compiler, but it is still logically distinct. A preprocessor directive is a command to the preprocessor to manipulate the source code in some way.
>
> **Susan:** Why do we need the preprocessor anyway?
>
> **Steve:** We don't need it very much anymore. About the only functions it still serves are the processing of included header files (via the #include preprocessor directive) and the creation of the "include guard".
>
> **Susan:** About the preprocessor symbol: Why would you want several things all equal to (for example) 123?
>
> **Steve:** Because that makes the program easier to read than if you just said 123 everywhere you needed to use such a value. Giving a name to a number is now most commonly done via the const construct in C++, which replaces most of the old uses of preprocessor symbols, but we still need them to implement include guards so that we can prevent the C++ compiler itself from seeing the definition of a class more than once.

What is the point of all this? To solve a problem in writing large C++ programs: the possibility that we might #include the same header file more than once in the same source code file. This can happen because a source code file often uses #include to gain access to a number of interface definitions stored in several header files, more than one of which uses a common header file (like string7.h). If this were to happen without precautions such as an include guard, we would get an error when we tried to compile our program. The error message would say that we had defined the same class twice, which is not allowed. Therefore, any header file that might be used in a number of places should use an include guard to prevent such errors. Susan had some questions about this notion and why it should be needed in the first place.

> **Susan:** Why should it be illegal to define the same class twice?
>
> **Steve:** If we define the same class twice, which definition should the compiler use? The first one or the second one?
>
> **Susan:** I see how that might cause a problem, but what if the two definitions are exactly the same? Why would the compiler care then?
>
> **Steve:** For the compiler to handle that situation, it would have to keep track of every definition it sees for a class rather than just one. Because it's almost always an error to try to define the same class more than once, there's no reason to add that extra complexity to the compiler when we can prevent the problem in the first place.

Assuming that I've convinced you of the value of include guards, how do they work? Well, the #ifndef directive checks to see if a specific preprocessor symbol, in this case STRING7_H, has already been defined. If it has, then the rest of the #include file is essentially ignored. Let's suppose that STRING7_H hasn't been defined yet. In that case, we define that symbol in the next line and then allow the compiler to process the rest of the file.

So far this works exactly as it would if we hadn't added the include guard. But suppose that later, during the compilation of the same source file, another header file #includes string7.h again. In that case, the symbol STRING7_H would already be defined (because we defined it on the first access to string7.h). Therefore, the #ifndef would cause the compiler to skip the rest of the header file, preventing the string class from being redefined and causing an error.

Of course, the choice of the preprocessor symbol to be defined is more or less arbitrary, but there is a convention in C and C++ that the symbol should be derived from the name of the header file. This is intended to reduce the likelihood of two header files using the same preprocessor symbol in their include guards. If that happened and if both of these header files were #included in the same source file, the definitions in the second one to be #included would be ignored during compilation because the preprocessor symbol used by its include guard would already be defined. To prevent such problems, I'm following the (commonly used) convention of defining a preprocessor symbol whose name is a capitalized version of the header file's name, with the period changed to an underscore to make it a legal preprocessor symbol name. If everyone working on a project follows this convention (or a similar one), the likelihood of trouble will be minimized.

### *Construction Ahead*

The next change to the interface of string is the addition of a new constructor, whose signature is specified in the interface file as explicit string(short Length, char Ch=0);. We'll get to the reason for adding this constructor as soon as I explain a few details: what the construct char Ch=0 means in a function declaration, what the **explicit** keyword means, and why we need to specify it here. Let's start with the meaning of char Ch=0 in this context.

### *Default Is Mine*

This is another C++ feature that is new to us. It's called a *default argument*, and its purpose is to specify a value for an argument to a function when the user of the function doesn't supply a value for that argument. In this case, the construct "char ch=0" specifies that if the application programmer calls a string constructor with only a short argument, the string::string(short, char) constructor will be called, with the first argument set to the short value supplied in the constructor call and the second argument set to 0. On the other hand, if the application programmer calls a string constructor with two arguments, the first a short and the second a char, this string::string(short, char) constructor will also be called, but the first argument will be set to the short value supplied in the constructor call and the second argument will be set to the char value supplied in the constructor call.

We don't have to use default arguments if we don't want to; we can achieve the same effect by writing a separate function for each possible number of arguments supplied by the calling program. To see how this alternative works, let's start with Figure 5.2, which shows a simplified version of a string interface file that contains two overloaded string constructors that take the place of the one we're discussing.

**FIGURE 5.2. A simplified interface file for a** string class (**code\string7x.h**)

```
#ifndef STRING7X_H
#define STRING7X_H

#include <iostream.h>
#include <string.h>

class string
{
public:

  string(short Length);
  string(short Length, char Ch);

private:
  short m_Length;
  char* m_Data;
};
```

```
#endif
```

The implementation of the first constructor is shown in Figure 5.3.

**FIGURE 5.3. An alternate** string(short Length) **constructor (from code\string7x.cc)**

```
string::string(short Length)
: m_Length(Length + 1),
  m_Data(new char [m_Length])
{
   char Ch = 0;
   memset(m_Data,Ch,Length);
   m_Data[Length] = 0;
}
```

The implementation of the second constructor is the same as the implementation for the actual string::string(short Length, char Ch=0) constructor we are discussing (shown in Figure 5.5); the only difference is that the interface file doesn't specify a default value. As a result, we have to write two different functions to handle constructor calls with and without the second argument.

To recapitulate: Specifying the default argument as char Ch=0 for the second entry in the argument list of the constructor whose first argument is a short is exactly equivalent to writing two overloaded string constructors:

1. One with a single argument. This constructor, shown in Figure 5.3, uses a constant value 0 for the char value to be stored in the string, instead of the Ch argument.
2. One with two arguments of types short and char, neither having a default value. The code for this constructor is the same as the code for the constructor having a default value (Figure 5.5).

## *Warning: Explicit Material*

I hope this explains the notion of a default argument. Now let's get to the explicit keyword, which was added to C++ to allow class designers to solve a problem with constructors that resulted from a (usually convenient) feature of the language called **implicit conversion**. Under the rules of implicit conversion, a constructor that takes one argument (or that takes more than one argument but has default arguments for all arguments after the first one) is also a **conversion function** that is called automatically (or *implicitly*) where an argument of a certain type is needed and an argument of another type is supplied. In many cases, an implicit constructor call is very useful; for example, it's extremely handy to be able to supply a char* argument when a string (or a const string&) is specified as the actual argument type in a function declaration. The compiler allows this without complaint because we have a string constructor that takes a char* argument and can be called implicitly. However, sometimes we don't want the compiler to supply this automatic conversion because the results would be surprising to the user of the class. In some previous versions of C++, it wasn't possible to prevent the compiler from supplying the automatic conversion, but in the draft standard version we can use the explicit keyword to tell the compiler, in essence, that we don't want it to use a particular constructor unless we explicitly ask for it.

To see how this affects the way we write a program using one of these constructors, take a look at Figure 5.4, which illustrates the difference between an implicit and an explicit constructor call.

**FIGURE 5.4. An explicit constructor call vs an implicit one (code\strtstx.cc)**

```
// strtstx.cc

#include <iostream.h>
#include "string7.h"

main()
```

```
{
   string a;
   string b = "Test";

   a = string(5); // legal

   a = 5;         // illegal

   cout << a << endl;
}
```

The reason that the line marked "legal" is legal, given the definitions in string7.h, is that we are explicitly stating that we want to construct a string by calling a constructor (which happens to be string(short, char), with the second argument using the default value 0). By contrast, the line marked "illegal" will be rejected by the compiler; for this line to be legal, the string class defined in string7.h would have to have a constructor that could be called implicitly to create a string from the literal value 5. Although that interface file does indeed define a string constructor that can be called with one argument of the short type, we've added the explicit keyword to its declaration to tell the compiler that this constructor doesn't accept implicit calls. This is a safety measure that prevents a user from accidentally calling the string(short, char) constructor by providing a short argument to a function that expects a string. Because the user is very unlikely to want a short value such as 5 silently converted to a string of 5 null bytes, as the string(short,char) constructor would do in this case, making this constructor explicit will reduce unpleasant surprises.

But why have we defined this string constructor at all? We'll get to that as soon as we take a look at the code for this new constructor, shown in Figure 5.5.[2]

---

2. Please note that the default value for the second argument, or even the fact that it has a default value, is not visible in the implementation of this constructor. That information is present only in the interface file.

**FIGURE 5.5. The** string(short, char) **constructor for the** string class **(from code\string7.cc)**

```
string::string(short Length, char Ch)
: m_Length(Length + 1),
  m_Data(new char [m_Length])
{
   memset(m_Data,Ch,Length);
   m_Data[Length] = 0;
}
```

This function creates a new string that can hold a specified number of chars, then sets them all to the value of the second argument (or 0 if no second argument was supplied) via the memset function. Then it sets the last char to the null byte 0, as we always do when constructing a string so that the C string functions can recognize it as a valid C string (assuming that it contains no other null bytes). We need this new constructor for the next function we're defining, operator + (Figure 5.7).[3] But before we get into the implementation of the operator + function, perhaps we should consider what the meaning of + might be for a string in the first place.

## *Adding Insult to Injury*

While the ability to read and write strings is very important, there are other operations that the string class needs to support if it is to be useful in the real world. One of these is **concatenation**, which is just a fancy word for "adding one string onto the end of another one". For example, if we have someone's first and last names as separate strings, it might be handy to be able to tack the last name to the end of the first name so we can store the entire name as one string. While we could use strstreams, that is a very inefficient way to accomplish a

3. We'll also be using this constructor later to create strings of blanks for formatting item listings, in the section "Categorical Imperative" on page 412.

common operation. The reason we have to worry about this in the first place is that there isn't any built-in concatenation operation for strings C++ (mostly because the string class isn't a native type). However, this is a common enough operation that a convention has been developed to use the + sign to indicate it. This symbol is also used in languages such as Java and Basic for the same operation, so C++ isn't too unusual in this regard. At any rate, it's time for us to see how we would use the + to concatenate strings in C++ (Figure 5.6).

**FIGURE 5.6. Using** operator + **for** string **concatenation (code\strtst7a.cc)**

```
#include <iostream.h>
#include "string7.h"

int main()
{
   string x;
   string y;

   cout << "Please enter your first name: ";
   cin >> x;

   cout << "Please enter your last name: ";
   cin >> y;

   z = x + " ";
   z = z + y;

   cout << "Hello, " << z;

   return 0;
}
```

This program asks the user to type in his or her first name and then last name. Once the first and last names have been typed in, the statement z = x + " "; uses the + to concatenate a space onto the end of the first name; then the statement z = z + y; uses another + to concatenate the last name onto the result of the first operation.[4] Finally, the program greets the user by saying "Hello, " followed by the user's name.

Now that we've seen how we can use this new operator, let's take a look at how it is implemented (Figure 5.7).

**FIGURE 5.7. The implementation of** operator + **for the** string class **(from code\string7.cc)**

```
string string::operator + (const string& Str)
{
   short length = m_Length - 1;
   short strlength = Str.m_Length - 1;

   string tempstring(length + strlength);

   memcpy(tempstring.m_Data, m_Data, length);

   memcpy(tempstring.m_Data+length, Str.m_Data, strlength);

   return tempstring;
}
```

This function starts by initializing a couple of variables called length and strlength. The value of length is initalized to the number of chars in the left-hand argument to operator + (i.e., the string pointed to by this, which is x in the expression "z + y"). Similarly, the value of strlength is initialized to the number of chars in the right-hand argument to operator + (i.e., the input argument Str, which is y in the expression "z + y"). In both cases, we exclude the trailing null byte from the count. Once these variables are initialized, the function creates a new string variable called tempstring having a length equal to the sum of these two lengths, which will be used to hold the

4. In case you were wondering whether we should also write a version of operator += for the string class, the answer is that such an operator could be quite useful. That's why I've made it an exercise.

concatenated value. All of the chars in tempstring are set to null bytes because it is created by the string(short,char) constructor with the second argument equal to 0 by default.

The next step is to use memcpy to copy the data from the left-hand argument (z in the expression "z + y") to the data area of this new string. The next line, memcpy(tempstring.m_Data+length, Str.m_Data, strlength);, copies the data from the right-hand argument (y in the expression "z + y") to the data area of tempstring beginning immediately after the end of the data from the left-hand argument. The result of all this is a string containing the original contents of the left-hand argument followed by the original contents of the right-hand argument to operator +.

Susan had some questions about the implementation of this function.

**Susan:** Why is the length –1?

**Steve:** Because we don't want to copy the null byte at the end of the data. The string constructor will add a null at the end of the new string.

**Susan:** What would happen if we left off the null byte at the end of a string?

**Steve:** All of our code would still work. The problem would be if we wanted to use some of the C string functions or look at our strings with a debugger. The debugger knows how to display C strings but not our own kind of strings; however, as long as we add the null byte at the end of the data area, the debugger can display the data as though it were a C string.

**Susan:** OK, I get that. Now I have a request. Please change the name of the length variable to left_length and the name of the other variable to right_length.

> **Steve:** That might be a good idea, but it's too late; to be consistent, I'd have to change a lot of other places that use the same convention. With the explanation here, the readers should be able to figure out what the code means.

## *Inner Peace*

While the ability to concatenate strings is useful in many applications, I have a specific reason to add it now: It's needed in the reimplementation of operator >> for the string class. The prior version of operator >> couldn't handle strings of more than 256 characters, which was adequate for our use with StockItem objects because they don't have any fields that are likely to grow beyond that length. However, it's entirely possible that a description field for a HomeItem object might be a whole paragraph, and having a fixed maximum size for string input would therefore be a hindrance to proper use of the HomeItem class.

> **Susan:** Why would anyone want to type in such a long description when they couldn't change it if they made a mistake?

> **Steve:** That's a very good point. The solution is to add the ability to edit an existing description field. We won't have time to do that in this book, but I can always add it as an exercise! Also, the old version of the operator >> wouldn't behave very well if it tried to read a string that was longer than 79 characters; it would just leave the extra characters in the input file without any notice of the error being given to the user. Therefore, it's important to fix this problem.

Even though it might not be convenient for the user of the program to use very long descriptions, I've improved the implementation of operator >> to be able to read strings containing any number of characters. Figure 5.8 shows this new implementation.

**FIGURE 5.8. The new implementation of** operator >> **(from code\string7.cc)**

```
istream& operator >> (istream& is, string& Str)
{
   const short BUFLEN = 80;

   char Buf[BUFLEN];
   string Str1;
   string Str2;

   if (is.peek() == '\n')
      is.ignore();
   memset(Buf,0,BUFLEN);
   is.get(Buf,BUFLEN,'\n');
   Str2 = Buf;

   while ((is.fail() == 0) && (is.peek() != '\n'))
      {
      Str1 = Str1 + Str2;
      memset(Buf,0,BUFLEN);
      is.get(Buf,BUFLEN,'\n');
      Str2 = Buf;
      }

   Str = Str1 + Str2;

   return is;
}
```

This function is complicated enough to deserve some detailed discussion. After defining some variables, including Buf (the buffer that will hold the chars being read from the input stream), we check to see if the first char is a newline. If so, we ignore it so that we can safely mix numeric and string input.[5] Next, we use memset to fill Buf

5. This is explained in detail in the discussion of the original version of the string class in *Who's Afraid of C++?*

with null bytes before we read data into it so that we it will be able to determine where the data ends. Then we use the istream::get member function to read a maximum of BUFLEN–1 chars from the input istream into the buffer. To complete this part of the operation, we set the temporary string variable Str2 to the contents of Buf. At this point, we have a string called Str2 that contains the first part of the string, which will be the entirety of the string if all the chars to be read would fit into Buf (i.e., the string is less than 80 chars long).

Susan had some questions about this function.

**Susan:** Why do we need to fill the buffer with null bytes?

**Steve:** Because we don't know where it has been. That is, we don't know what data might be lying around in a buffer that we have allocated on the stack. Remember the uninitialized variable problems we had in the past?

**Susan:** Ugh. Don't remind me. Anyway, why do we need this function again?

**Steve:** To read data from a stream into a string so we can use it in our program.

**Susan:** Where you say "the string is less than 80 chars long", don't you mean "80 chars or less"?

**Steve:** That's very perceptive of you, but in fact the original statement is correct. The maximum number of characters is BUFLEN–1 (79) rather than BUFLEN (80) because the get function always adds a null byte to the end of whatever it reads, so the C string functions can be used on the data that has been read. Therefore, we can't read BUFLEN characters into the buffer, because that would leave no room for the null byte.

The while loop that makes up the next part of the code handles the situation where the string is at least 80 chars. The condition in the while is (is.fail() == 0 && is.peek() != '\n'). The first part of this expression, is.fail() == 0, will be true if we haven't reached the end of the input file. If we have reached the end of the file, we're obviously finished with the input. Assuming that the istream hasn't failed yet, the second part of the expression, is.peek() != '\n', will be false if the next char in the istream is a newline. If so, we are finished because our input is defined to stop when we reach the end of a line. If the next char to be read isn't a newline, we must continue reading data for our string. The first operation inside the loop is to concatenate the data we have just read, in Str2, to the previous contents of our other temporary variable, Str1, which contains all of the input that we've read in previous executions of the while loop. The first time we go through the loop, of course, Str1 starts out empty. Next, we use memset to clear Buf in preparation for reading some more data from the input istream, which we do in the next line. The last statement in the loop sets Str2 to the contents of Buf, which leaves us ready for the next iteration of the while loop.

Assuming that we haven't yet read all the chars for this string, the next execution of the while loop will start by adding the contents of Str2 (the data we read on the previous execution of the loop) to the contents of Str1 (the data we read before the previous execution of the loop). Then we execute the same steps as before to retrieve another part of the string's data.

Eventually, we will get to the end of the data for the string we are reading, at which time the while loop will terminate. At that point, Str1 and Str2 contain the final data for the string Str, so we concatenate Str2 to the end of Str1 and set Str to the result. Finally, we return the updated istream object to the caller for possible use in further input operations.

## *Location, Location, Location*

Now we're ready to discuss the next new string member function in this version of the string class: find_nocase. We need this function to determine whether a given string contains a particular sequence of characters. For example, if we have a string containing the value "red, blue, and green", describing the colors of a sofa, we want to be able to determine whether the letters "b", "l", "u", and "e" appear consecutively in that string. If they do, it is sometimes also useful to know where that sequence of characters starts in the string. To allow us to obtain this information, we have to add a new member function to our string class. Because this function finds a sequence of chars in a string, its name should be something like find. Because it is going to be case-insensitive (e.g., RED, Red, and red will all be considered equal), we'll call it find_nocase.[6]

What do I mean by "case-insensitive"? That when this function looks for a sequence of chars within a string, it considers upper- and lower-case letters as equivalent. We will employ this function in the HomeInventory class functions that will enable us to, for example, search through the home inventory for all HomeItem objects containing the word "purple" in their description fields. Before we look at how this is implemented, let's see how it can be used (Figure 5.9).

**FIGURE 5.9. Using** string::find_nocase **(code\strtst7b.cc)**

```
#include <iostream.h>
#include "string7.h"

int main()
{
   string x = "purple";
   string y = "A purple couch";
   short where;
```

6. I made this function case-insensitive after watching Susan's attempt to use a version of the HomeInventory example program that used a case-sensitive searching function. This illustrates why it is absolutely necessary to watch a (hopefully representative) user of a program actually try it before making the assumption that it is "ready for prime time".

```
    where = y.find_nocase(x);
    cout << "The string " << x <<
      " can be found starting at position " <<
      where << " in the string " << endl;
    cout << y << "." << endl;

    where = x.find_nocase("rp");
    cout << "The string 'rp' can be found starting at position " <<
      where << " in the string " << x << "." << endl;

    where = x.find_nocase("rpx");
    cout << "The string 'rpx' can be found starting at position " <<
      where << " in the string " << x << "." << endl;

    return 0;
}
```

This program starts out by defining some string variables called x and y and initializing them to the values "purple" and "A purple couch", respectively. Then it defines a short value called where that will hold the result of each search for an included sequence of chars. The next line, where = y.find_nocase(x);, calls the find_nocase member function of the string class to locate an occurrence of the value "purple" in the string y, which has the value "A purple couch". The next three lines display the results of that search.

The other two similar sequences search the same string value (in y) for the literal values "rp" and "rpx", respectively, and display the results of these searches. The first of these is very similar to the previous search for the word "purple", but serves to point out that we don't have to search for a word — any sequence of characters will do.

The last sequence, however, is somewhat different because we are searching for a literal value ("rpx") that is not present in the string we're examining ("A purple couch"). The question, of course, is what value the find_nocase function should return when this happens. Perhaps the most obvious possibility is 0, but that is unfortunately not appropriate because it violates the C and C++ convention that the first position of a string is considered position 0. Therefore, find_nocase returns the value –1 to indicate that the desired value has not been found in the string being examined.

Now that we've seen how to use it, let's take a look at the implementation of find_nocase, which is shown in Figure 5.10.

**FIGURE 5.10. The implementation of** string::find_nocase **(from code\string7.cc)**

```
short string::find_nocase(const string& Str)
{
   short i;
   short length = m_Length-1;
   short strlength = Str.m_Length-1;

   for (i = 0; i < length-strlength+1; i ++)
    {
    if (strnicmp(m_Data+i,Str.m_Data,strlength) == 0)
      return i;
    }

   return -1;
}
```

This starts out the same way as operator + does: by defining some variables called length and strlength to hold the actual number of chars in the string we're going to examine (i.e., the one pointed to by this) and in the argument string Str, which contains the text for which we're searching, respectively; in both cases the counts exclude the terminating null byte. To make the discussion simpler, let's call the string that might contain the desired value the *target string* and the argument string the *search string*.

Now we get to the heart of the function: the loop that uses strnicmp to compare each possible section of the target string with the search string we're looking for. On the first time through the loop, the value of i is 0; therefore, strnicmp(m_Data+i,Str.m_Data,strlength) compares strlength bytes from the beginning of the target string to the same number of bytes in the search string. If the two sets of bytes are equal, the result of the comparison is 0, in which case we have found what we were looking for, and so we exit the loop.

On the other hand, if the result of the comparison is not 0, we have to keep looking. The next step is to increment the value of the loop index i. The second time through the loop, the value of i is 1, so the expression strnicmp(m_Data+i,Str.m_Data,strlength) compares strlength bytes starting at the *second* byte of the target string with the same number of bytes starting at the beginning of the search string. If this comparison is successful, we stop and indicate success; if not, we continue executing the loop until we find a match or run out of data in the target string.

Let's look at an example in more detail. Suppose we are searching through the target string "A purple couch", looking for the search string "purple". The first time through the loop, we compare the first 6 bytes in the target string to the 6 bytes in the search string. Since the first byte of the target string is 'A' and the first byte of the search string is 'p', strnicmp returns a non-zero value to let us know that we haven't yet found a match. Therefore, we have to re-execute the loop. The second time through, we start the comparison at the second byte of the target string and the first byte of the search string; the second byte of the target string is a space, which isn't the same as the 'p' from the search string, so strnicmp returns a non-zero value to let us know that we still haven't found the search string. The third time through the loop, we start the comparison at the third byte of the target string and (as always) the first byte of the search string. Both of these have the value 'p', so strnicmp continues by comparing the fourth byte of the target string with the second byte of the search string. Those also match, so strnicmp continues to compare the rest of the bytes in the two strings until it gets to the end of the search string. This time they all match, so strnicmp returns 0 to let us know that we have found the search string.

Of course, the other possibility is that the search string isn't present in the target string. In that case, strnicmp won't return 0 on any of these passes through the loop, so eventually i will exceed its limit, causing the loop to stop executing. However, there's one thing I haven't explained yet: how we calculate the maximum number of times that we have to execute the loop. If we look at the for loop, we see that the continuation expression is i < length – strlength + 1. Is this the right limit for i, and if so, why?

Well, if the target string is the same length as the search string, then we know that we have to execute the loop only once because there's only one possible place to start comparing two strings of the same length — at the beginning of both strings. If we start i at 0 on the first time through the loop, it will be 1 at the beginning of the second time through the loop, so length – strlength + 1 gives the correct limit (of 1) if length and strlength have the same value. This demonstrates that the expression length – strlength + 1 is correct for the case where the search and target strings are the same length. Now, what about the case where the target string is 1 byte longer than the search string? In that case, there is one extra position in which the search string could be found — namely, starting at the second character of the target string. Continuing with this analysis, each additional character in the target string beyond the length of the search string adds one possible position in which the search string might be found in the target string, and therefore adds 1 to the number of times we might have to go through the loop. Since adding 1 to the value of length will add 1 to the value of the expression length – strlength + 1, that expression will produce the correct limit for any value of length and strlength.

There's one more function in the string class that we need to discuss: less_nocase. Its code is shown in Figure 5.11.

**FIGURE 5.11. The less_nocase function (from code\string7.cc)**

```
bool string::less_nocase(const string& Str)
{
   short Result;
   short CompareLength;

   if (Str.m_Length < m_Length)
      CompareLength = Str.m_Length;
   else
```

```
        CompareLength = m_Length;

    Result = strnicmp(m_Data,Str.m_Data,CompareLength);

    if (Result < 0)
        return true;

    if (Result > 0)
        return false;

    if (m_Length < Str.m_Length)
        return true;

    return false;
}
```

This function is exactly the same as the normal operator < function in the string class, except that it uses the strnicmp function rather than the memcmp function used in operator <.[7] We haven't discussed the strnicmp function yet, but it's quite similar to memcmp, with two differences:

1. strnicmp ignores case in its comparison, so that (for example) RED, Red, and red all compare as equal.
2. strnicmp is a C string function rather than a C memory manipulation function like memcmp, so it stops when it encounters a null byte.

The first of these characteristics of strnicmp is the reason that we have to use strnicmp rather than memcmp, which is case-sensitive. The second characteristic isn't an advantage when dealing with strings, which can theoretically contain null bytes. However, this isn't

7. As with the other pre-existing functions in the string class, we won't go over the implementation of the operator < function because it is covered in detail in *Who's Afraid of C++?*

a problem in the less_nocase function, as that function applies only to ASCII text, which doesn't contain null bytes anyway.

## *Home, Sweet Home*

Now that we have finished discussing our new, improved string class, let's get back to using it to add capabilities to our home inventory project. First on the list is the ability to find an item by searching for a sequence of chars in its description. Before we see how this is implemented, let's take a look at how it is used. Figure 5.12 shows the new application program that uses this feature.

FIGURE 5.12. **The latest home inventory application program (code\hmtst6.cc)**

```
#include <iostream.h>
#include <fstream.h>
#include "vector.h"
#include "string7.h"
#include "hmit6.h"
#include "hmin6.h"

int main()
{
   ifstream HomeInfo("home3.in");
   HomeInventory MyInventory;
   HomeItem TempItem;
   string Name;
   string Description;

   MyInventory.LoadInventory(HomeInfo);

   TempItem = MyInventory.FindItemByName("Relish");
   cout << endl;

   TempItem.Edit();
```

```
    cout << endl;

    TempItem.FormattedDisplay(cout);
    cout << endl;

    cout << "Please enter a search string: ";
    cin >> Description;

    TempItem = MyInventory.FindItemByDescription(Description);

    if (TempItem.IsNull())
      cout << "Sorry, I couldn't locate that item." << endl;
    else
      TempItem.FormattedDisplay(cout);
    cout << endl;

    return 0;
}
```

This program starts out just as the previous one did, by loading the inventory from the home3.in input file, looking up the entry whose name is "Relish", and displaying it for editing. Once the user has finished editing the entry, we get to the new part: reading a search string from the user and searching for that item in the inventory by the new FindItemByDescription member function of HomeInventory. Let's go through the changes needed to implement this new feature, starting with the new version of the HomeInventory interface, shown in Figure 5.13.

**FIGURE 5.13. The latest version of the HomeInventory interface (hmin6.h)**

```
//hmin6.h

#include "vector.h"

class HomeInventory
{
```

```
public:
  HomeInventory();

  short LoadInventory(ifstream& is);
  void DumpInventory();
  HomeItem FindItemByName(const string& Name);
  HomeItem AddItem();
  short LocateItemByName(const string& Name);
  HomeItem EditItem(const string& Name);

  HomeItem FindItemByDescription(const string& Partial);
  short LocateItemByDescription(const string& Partial);

private:
  vector<HomeItem> m_Home;
};
```

The only new functions added to this interface since the last version (see Figure 4.27) are the two "ItemByDescription" functions that parallel the "ItemByName" functions we implemented previously. However, there's another modification in this and the other new interface files: I've changed all the value arguments of nonnative types to const references, because passing such arguments by const reference is more efficient than passing them by value but just as safe, because it's impossible to accidentally change the calling function's variables through a const reference. For this reason, this is usually the best method of passing arguments of user-defined types. Variables of native types, on the other hand, are most efficiently passed by value because they do not require copy constructors or other overhead when passed in that way, as objects of user-defined types do.

Susan had a question about passing arguments.

**Susan:** Why does it matter whether an argument is native or user-defined?

**Steve:** Passing a native variable by value (i.e., copying it) is efficient because it's a simple "bunch of bits"; there's no need to worry about pointers and the like. On the other hand, copying a user-defined variable requires a lot more work because the compiler has to call the copy constructor for that type of variable.

Now let's take a look at the first of the two new functions, HomeInventory::FindItemByDescription, shown in Figure 5.14.

**FIGURE 5.14.** HomeInventory::FindItemByDescription **(from code\hmin6.cc)**

```
HomeItem HomeInventory::FindItemByDescription(
 const string& Partial)
{
  short i;
  string Description;
  bool Found = false;
  short ItemCount = m_Home.size();

  for (i = 0; i < ItemCount; i ++)
   {
   Description = m_Home[i].GetDescription();
   if (Description.find_nocase(Partial) >= 0)
    {
    Found = true;
    break;
    }
   }

  if (Found == true)
   return m_Home[i];

  return HomeItem();
}
```

This function is very similar to FindItemByName, so I won't go over it in excruciating detail. The main difference between the two is that FindItemByDescription uses the new find_nocase function to locate an occurrence of a search string named Partial in the description of each HomeItem object in the m_Home vector. To do this, it retrieves the description from a HomeItem object, using the GetDescription member function, and stores it in a string called (imaginatively enough) Description. Then it calls find_nocase to see if there is an occurrence of Partial in the Description string. If so, it leaves the loop and returns the object whose description contained the contents of the Partial argument; otherwise, it executes the loop again. This continues until it either finds a match or runs out of items to examine. In the latter case, it returns a null HomeItem to indicate that it couldn't find what the user was looking for.

However, this latter possibility means that we need an IsNull member function in the HomeItem class so that the calling program can tell whether it has received a null HomeItem. To see this and the other (relatively minor) changes to the HomeItem interface, let's take a look at the new version of that interface, which is shown in Figure 5.15.

**FIGURE 5.15. The new version of the** HomeItem **interface (code\hmit6.h)**

```
// hmit6.h

#include "string7.h"
#include "vector.h"

class HomeItem
{
friend ostream& operator << (ostream& os,
  const HomeItem& Item);

friend istream& operator >> (istream& is, HomeItem& Item);

public:
  HomeItem();
  HomeItem(const HomeItem& Item);
  HomeItem& operator = (const HomeItem& Item);
virtual ~HomeItem();
```

```
// Basic: Art objects, furniture, jewelry, etc.
  HomeItem(const string& Name, double PurchasePrice,
  long PurchaseDate, const string& Description,
  const string& Category);

// Music: CDs, LPs, cassettes, etc.
  HomeItem(const string& Name, double PurchasePrice,
  long PurchaseDate, const string& Description,
  const string& Category, const string& Artist,
  const vector<string>& Track);

virtual void Write(ostream& os);
virtual short FormattedDisplay(ostream& os);
virtual string GetName();
virtual string GetDescription();
virtual bool IsNull();
static HomeItem NewItem();

virtual void Read(istream& is);
virtual void Edit();

protected:
  HomeItem(int);
virtual HomeItem* CopyData();

protected:
  HomeItem* m_Worker;
  short m_Count;
};
```

Susan had a couple of questions about this new version of the interface.

> **Susan:** Why didn't you put the destructor at the end of the interface? After all, it is the last function to be executed.

**Steve:** I always put the "concrete data type" functions together at the beginning of the public section of the interface. That makes them easier to find.

**Susan:** Why aren't the constructors virtual if the destructor is?

**Steve:** Constructors can't be virtual, because the whole point of a virtual function is to allow the program to use the actual type of an object to determine which function is called. When we call a constructor to create an object, the object doesn't exist yet, so there would be no way to determine which virtual function should be called.

As with the HomeInventory class, I've changed all the string arguments to const string& to improve efficiency by preventing excessive copying. I've done the same with the Track argument to the HomeItemMusic normal constructor; it's now a const vector<string>& rather than a vector<string>, as in the previous version of the header. I've also added two new functions: GetDescription and IsNull. As usual, the HomeItem versions of these functions merely call the corresponding virtual function in the worker object and pass the results back to the calling function. As for the HomeItemBasic version of GetDescription, this function just returns the current value of the m_Description field in its object, so we don't have to bother analyzing it. IsNull is pretty simple too, but we should still take a look at its implementation, shown in Figure 5.16.

**FIGURE 5.16.** HomeItemBasic::IsNull **(from code\hmit6.cc)**

```
bool HomeItemBasic::IsNull()
{
 if (m_Name == "")
  return true;

 return false;
}
```

The idea here is that every actual HomeItem has to have a name, so any object that doesn't have one must be a null HomeItem. Therefore, we check whether the name is null. If so, we have a null item, so we return true; otherwise, it's a real item, so we return false to indicate that it's not null.

Of course, we don't have to reimplement IsNull in HomeItemMusic because we can use the HomeItemBasic version of this function should we need to check whether a HomeItemMusic object is "real" or null.

### *Nothing Ventured, Nothing Gained*

There's only one more point I want to mention before we leave the HomeItemBasic code. After I started using the new version of the string class, I got a compiler error in the constructor for HomeItemBasic. This was hard to understand because surely I hadn't changed anything in the string class that should cause it to stop working in situations where it had previously been operating properly. The problem turned out to be a slight oddity in the coding of the member initialization list in a previous version of the HomeItemBasic code. We discussed this code in Chapter 4 in the section entitled "Stereo Typing", but at that time I deferred the explanation of how I found the error. For reference, Figure 5.17 is another listing of the code that gave me the problem after I changed to the new string class.

**FIGURE 5.17. A slightly odd default constructor for HomeItem (from code\hmit2.cc)**

```
HomeItemBasic::HomeItemBasic()
: HomeItem(1),
  m_Name(),
  m_PurchasePrice(0),
  m_PurchaseDate(0),
  m_Description(0),
```

```
  m_Category(0)
{
}
```

As I mentioned previously, it's the 0 value for m_Description and m_Category that caused the problem. Those are string variables, but the compiler didn't complain when I initialized them with a value of 0. The reason is that 0 is a "magic number" in C and C++: Among its other special characteristics, it is an acceptable value for any type of pointer. In this example, the compiler considered it as a char*, so the string::string(char*) constructor was being called to initialize the strings m_Description and m_Category to the value of the "char*" 0. This didn't would not work very well, as the data stored at address 0 is unlikely to be anything we want to use. Therefore, it's a good thing that the compiler caught this in hmit6.cc. But why did this error suddenly surface when I changed to the new string class, when the compiler was happy to take a 0 previously?

The trigger was the new constructor that we added to implement the string concatenation function — the one that makes a string from a short value. Because 0 is a legal short as well as a legal char*, the compiler couldn't tell which of these I wanted and therefore gave an error message for each occurrence of this mistake — one message for the description field and one for the category field. Figure 5.18 shows the error messages.

**FIGURE 5.18. Error messages triggered by accidental use of 0 to initialize a** string (code\hmit6a.err)

```
hmit6a.cc: In method 'HomeItemBasic::HomeItemBasic()':
hmit6a.cc:208: call of overloaded constructor 'string(int)' is ambiguous
string7.h:14: candidates are: string::string(const string &)
string7.h:18:                 string::string(char *)
string7.h:19:                 string::string(short int, char)
hmit6a.cc:208: in base initialization for class 'string'
hmit6a.cc:208: call of overloaded constructor 'string(int)' is ambiguous
string7.h:14: candidates are: string::string(const string &)
string7.h:18:                 string::string(char *)
```

```
string7.h:19:             string::string(short int, char)
hmit6a.cc:208: in base initialization for class 'string'
```

What's the moral of this story? I'm not sure, other than "Watch out for 0". Of course, I will make sure to cover the various ramifications of this "feature" of C++ in my book on how to write better C++ programs, tentatively entitled *Shining C++*.[8]

## *Putting It All Together*

When first writing this part of this chapter, I thought that we had already covered everything needed to build a real application program that would allow the user to create, update, and find items in the database with reasonable ease and convenience. The main program for my first attempt at this was called hmtst7.cc. When Susan tried it out and then read the code, it had quite an effect on her, as indicated in this letter she wrote to her sister.

> **Susan:** I had another revelation over programming last night. After having read 250 pages of this book, Steve showed me the program. It is a Home Inventory program that we are writing for the book. Annie, it is the smallest little program that you can imagine. Just in DOS, and it is so simple. But I have just spent weeks tearing my hair out trying to understand how it all comes together, it is so damn complicated, and JUST SO HARD.
>
> Then Steve shows me the program [running] and IT LOOKS LIKE NOTHING! I could not believe it. I just see this little menu on the screen and yet I know what is behind it. At least 1500 lines

8. You may wonder why this error occurred even though we defined the string(short, char) constructor to be explicit, which means that it shouldn't be considered in an expression that seems to refer to it implicitly. The answer is that a member initialization expression is considered an explicit constructor call, and so even constructors that are labeled as explicit are considered as possible matches for such an expression.

> of code including 7 different header files. If you saw this program [run] you would laugh. It is just so basic. But if you saw what went into it you would die. It is nothing less than pure genius. As I told Steve yesterday it is like having a steak dinner but having not to just cook the meat, but having to go kill the cow. He corrected me, it is like having to make the gun first to kill the cow and invent fire and a grill to cook it.
>
> You have to write everything, I mean all of it. That includes the meaning for = and all the other operators. Unbelievable. Then I looked at Windows 95 and said, then "What the Hell is in this?" Steve said "About 5 million lines of code." Computers look like they are technological miracles. And they are. But behind them is nothing but sheer, old fashioned, genius of man. And it is all hard work. It looks like a miracle but there is no magic.

If you wish, you can try the program yourself, but I won't be reproducing the code here because it turned out that it was far from finished. You see, as stunned as Susan may have been by the complexity of this program, she wasn't too amazed to tell me what was wrong with it and how it could be improved. Here's her "wish list", along with my responses.

## *First Test Session: Change Requests and Problem Reports*

1. Presenting the menu options in different colors.

   Can't be done with C++ input/output functions.

2. Showing the list of names below the menu rather than above.
3. Putting the menu in the center of the screen rather than at the top.

   These two changes became irrelevant after I redesigned the program to use the screen more efficiently.

4. Sorting the items by name rather than by the order in which they were originally entered.

Done, via a new HomeInventory::SortInventoryByName member function (but see later comments on problems with this function).

5. Being able to move to the next matching item if there is more than one (on a partial field match).

   Wrote several HomeInventory member functions to assist in handling multiple matching entries (for more details, see "handling more entries than will fit on the screen", below).

6. Removing an item.

   Done.

7. Making a list of categories and displaying it when adding a new item.

   Not done, for reasons indicated below.

While watching Susan use the program, I came up with my own list of problems that needed to be fixed and some other improvements in addition to the ones she mentioned above.

8. The error message for an invalid entry is poorly formatted.

   Added functions for error reporting.

9. An error in entering a numeric value isn't handled properly.

   Same as above.

10. There's no indication to the user as to how the date or amount fields are supposed to be entered (YYYYMMDD and a number with a decimal point but no $ or comma, respectively).

    Added a note in the input prompt indicating proper data entry format.

11. An invalid date entry (i.e., other than a valid YYYYMMDD date) should be detected and reported to the user.

    Added code to check for this problem: The date must be at least 19000101 (but see later discussion of problems with this solution).

12. The user should be able to determine how many items are in the inventory.

    Added a line at the top of the menu indicating how many elements are currently in the inventory.

13. Allowing the user to select an item from a list of all items that meet some criterion (e.g., name, description).

    Added selection functions as noted above for this purpose.

14. Handling a list containing more entries than will fit on the screen at one time.

    Wrote a selection function in a new HomeUtility class to allow scrolling through any number of items.

15. Continuing rather than aborting when an error is detected.

    Handled most of these problems by improved error checking in the code; further problems surfaced later and were noted where they occurred.

16. Saving the data during the execution of the program.

    Not handled in this version of the program.

17. Backing up the old database before writing over it.

    Not done; left as an exercise.

18. If the user asks to delete an item, the program should ask, "Are you sure?"

    Done.

Amazingly, the hardest one of these turned out to be the "list of categories". In fact, I didn't implement this at all because it would have required a fairly significant reconstruction of the structure of classes in the program. The problem with this seemingly simple request is that the category list would have to be generated in the HomeInventory member function (because each HomeItem has only one category value out of all those in use, not the entire list). However, the list would need to be used in the HomeItem classes because that's where the user needs to specify the category and therefore where the list would be useful. Getting the data from the HomeInventory object to the appropriate HomeItem object would be difficult because the existing HomeItem functions don't have any facilities for doing this. While there are ways to solve such problems, they would take us too far afield to be worth the trip in this particular case, since the category listing is not absolutely essential to the usability of the program.

After finishing the above revisions to the program, I renamed the main program hmtst8.cc, compiled all of the files to produce hmtst8.exe, and tested it myself until I was satisfied that it worked. Then I had Susan give it another test. I fully expected that she would be happy with the new functionality and would find the program pretty much bullet-proof. Here are my notes from that second test session, along with my determination of the cause of the problem or question.

## *Second Test Session: Change Requests and Problem Reports*

1. Adding a new Music item with a bad date such as "1997/02/15" (instead of 19970215) caused the program to abort with a fatal error.

This was caused by my forgetting to check the return value of the HomeItemBasic version of the input function when calling it from the corresponding HomeItemMusic function.

2. The sorting algorithm used to put the items into alphabetical order sorts lowercase letters after uppercase ones. It should ignore case.

   This problem was caused by the use of <, which is case-sensitive, to compare strings. I fixed this by adding a less_nocase function to the string class and using that function in the sorting algorithm instead of <.

3. If the user typed in an item number that was not valid, the program exited with an illegal vector element error message.

   I added code to check whether the item number was valid and to ignore an invalid number rather than end the program.

Susan had some other comments and questions after using this version of the program.

**Susan:** The Music items should be listed separately from the other items.

**Steve:** What if you want to see all the items in your inventory? That may not seem to make sense with CDs and furniture, but what about when we add the clothing, appliance, and other types?

**Susan:** I don't want them jumbled together.

**Steve:** Well, we could add separate functions for showing things of each type, but I'm not sure how valuable the discussion of all those functions would be. I know, I'll make it an exercise!

**Susan:** Okay. Now, I noticed that if you type in something illegal (like a bad date) you have to start over again rather than being able to fix it right there.

**Steve:** Yes, that's true. It would make another good exercise to add the ability to continue entering data for the same item after an error. Thanks for the suggestion!

**Susan:** As long as I don't have to do it. I also have some other questions about the dates. What if I got something by inheritance and it was originally bought before 1900? Also, what if I don't know the date when I bought something? Can I type in ???????<g>

**Steve:** I'll make the starting date 1800 rather than 1900. As for using question marks to mean "I don't know": that won't work because the input routine is checking for a numeric value. However, I'll change it so you can use 0 to mean "I don't know when I got it". How's that?

**Susan:** That's okay. However, I noticed one more thing. It would let me type 19931822 (the 22nd day of the 18th month of 1993). Shouldn't it check for legal dates?

**Steve:** Yes, that would be a good . . . exercise!

After making all these changes, I recompiled and tested the program, then gave it to Susan to see what she could do with (or to) it. Here are my notes of that trial along with how I handled the points that came up.

### *Third Test Session: Change Requests and Problem Reports*

1. On a screen with only 25 lines, it was pretty easy to overflow the available space when editing a long item. This resulted in a very messy display.

   I changed the program to clear the screen before editing an item. Now the entire screen was available to display the item rather than the main menu being on the screen all the time.

2. If the user typed something other than just hitting the ENTER key after a message that said "ENTER to continue", the other keystrokes were interpreted as menu selections.

   I added code to ignore any keystrokes preceding an ENTER in that situation.

3. When the user typed an invalid item number, the program just ignored it rather than giving any indication of an error.

   I added code to display an "invalid item number" message in such a situation.

4. The routine that asked for an item number didn't handle backspaces correctly.

   I changed the routine to fix that problem.

5. If there weren't any items matching the user's selection criterion, the selection area was blank with no other indication of what had happened.

   I added code to provide a "No items found" error message.

6. The "category" field was pretty useless, as it couldn't be used for selecting items.

   I added a "select by category" menu item, which displays the category as well as the name of the item.

In addition to these changes, this version of the program also implemented a "crash protection" feature, which automatically saves the latest version of the database in a separate file every time a change is made to any item or an item is added or deleted. This might be a problem in terms of performance if the database gets to be very large, but I think it's worth it overall; without such a feature, the user could spend an hour or two typing in data and then have a power failure (or a program bug for that matter) and lose all that work.

Another item that might be useful (especially with long descriptions), but isn't essential in getting the program to work, is the ability to edit a text field without typing it all in again. That's the topic of another exercise at the end of this chapter.

After making all of these changes and testing them to make sure they seemed to work, I went back to the well one more time. Here are the results of this go-round.

### *Fourth Test Session: Change Requests and Problem Reports*

1. If Susan typed in a category that didn't exist, the program aborted with a "virtual memory exceeded" error.

    The problem here turned out to be my attempt to format the category listing header. If the header was longer than the actual category names, the code calculated a negative number of characters of padding. Then it tried to create a `string` of that number of spaces by calling the `string` constructor that takes a `short` number of characters. When this constructor called the `new` operator to allocate the space for the padding, it passed the negative number of characters along to `new`. However, `new` doesn't expect to get a negative argument as the number of objects to create, and so it interpreted that negative value as a very large positive number. When it tried to allocate that number of characters, the underlying memory allocation routines couldn't handle the request and terminated the program after giving that error message. I fixed this by correcting the formatting logic so that the program wouldn't ask for a negative amount of padding.

2. The code to display an error if there were no items found wasn't working.

    I changed the "wait for CR" code to fix this.

3. The name and category header wasn't lined up properly with the actual name and category entries for item numbers greater than 9 (i.e., more than one digit).

    I changed the formatting of the selection function to fix the width of the item number at 5 digits rather than as variable according to the size of the item number. This made it much easier to line the header up with the data.

Susan had another suggestion to make the program easier to use, as well as a question about the category listing function.

> **Susan:** How about letting the user type the date in with the slashes, as YYYY/MM/DD?
>
> **Steve:** That would make a good exercise too.
>
> **Susan:** How does the category listing function know where to put the categories on the screen?
>
> **Steve:** It goes through the items once to figure out how long the names are and once to do the formatting. Thus, by the time it does the formatting, it knows how long the longest item name is. We'll go over exactly how that works when we get to that function, SelectItemFromCategoryList (Figure 6.25 on page 412).

After making all the changes indicated above, I had Susan try it once more, with the following results.

### *Fifth Test Session: Change Requests and Problem Reports*

1. There wasn't any way to cancel the "Add item" operation if the user decided not to do that after starting the operation.

    I added code to allow ENTER to cancel the "Add item" operation.

2. Susan wanted to know how she could use the "Find item by category" operation if she didn't remember which category she was looking for.

   Here is one of the rare times when a program has a desired feature that the programmer didn't think to add explicitly. As it happens, all you have to do is hit ENTER when you are asked for the category name, and it will include items from all categories. I changed the prompt to inform the user about this feature. Since this serendipitous feature also works when the user is asked for a description or name, I changed those prompts as well.

After all these changes, I finally had a program that seemed to work properly according to a representative user's expectations for it. We'll start our analysis of this final version of the home inventory program shortly, but first we should take a look at the development process that I've just described.

## *Round and Round We Go*

Most books on programming present the software development process as a linear progression from the beginning to the end of a project with no detours on the way. However, this is a very misleading picture of what is actually an iterative process: Every actual project requires a lot of feedback from users. It also requires considerable time spent correcting errors that may have been overlooked in previous revisions or introduced while adding new features (or even fixing old bugs). The whole process often involves one step back (or sideways) for each several steps forward.

In fact, even the picture I just presented of the incremental implementation of the home inventory program up to this point is over-simplified. I left out a number of occasions on which designing and implementing a new feature took several attempts, including adding further infrastructure support (e.g., the less_nocase function in the string class).

This may seem odd. After all, programming is not a "soft" subject; for any given program, it should be fairly easy to decide whether it works or it doesn't.[9] The error in this analysis is that even relatively simple programs (such as the one we've spent so much time on) are complex constructs that display a wide range of behavior. Given this complexity, determining whether a given program "works" is anything but trivial; otherwise, I wouldn't have needed Susan to test the program after I finished my own testing. In fact, on virtually every occasion when I had her test a new version of the program in which I had made significant changes, she found some anomaly that necessitated further work. This is anything but unusual; in fact, some large software companies send out thousands of copies of each of their major programs to be tested before they release them, in the hope of finding most of the bugs before the paying customers find them (and get upset). Of course, those programs are much more complicated than the little one we've been developing, but the principle is the same: If a program hasn't been tested, it will have bugs.[10]

Luckily, by using the techniques I've illustrated, it's possible to produce programs that should have fewer bugs, and bugs that are less difficult to find.[11] Hopefully, the program that we'll finish in the next

9. Actually, this is not true in theory. It was proven many years ago that it is impossible in the general case even to determine whether a particular program will run forever or stop, given a particular set of input, by any mechanical means. This is the famous "halting problem" of Alan Turing. In practice, however, it is usually possible to determine whether a meaningful program works correctly, although this may be quite difficult to do.

10. According to a very well known principle called "Murphy's Law", even if a program has been tested, it will still have bugs.

11. By the way, if you find any bugs in this or any of the other sample programs, which is certainly possible despite my (and Susan's) testing, please let me know so I can fix them for the next printing of this book.

chapter won't have many bugs left by the time we get through with it. First, though, it's time for some review of what we've done so far.

## *Review*

We started this chapter by improving the string class that we inherited from *Who's Afraid of C++?*, which we needed to do so that we could add some new functionality to the home inventory program. Before we added any new functions to this class, the first modification we made was to add an **include guard**, which is a means of preventing the C++ compiler from seeing the same class definition more than one time for a given source code file. Implementing the include guard required us to look at some very old parts of C++ dating back to the early days of C: the **preprocessor** and its **preprocessor symbols**. The preprocessor was originally a separate program that was executed before the compiler itself, but nowadays it is often physically part of the compiler. Most of its features are no longer needed in C++, but we still need it to create an include guard as well as to handle included header files — its most common use these days.

Once we finished with that discussion, we examined another C++ feature that we hadn't seen before: the **default argument**. This gives us the ability to specify a value for an argument when the user of a function doesn't supply one. By using a default argument, we were able to write one constructor for the string class that could create a string of a specified number of characters, which would all be set to a given character value. If the user of this constructor did not specify the character value he or she wanted, the constructor would set all the characters to null; if the user specified a particular character value, the constructor would of course use that one. Using default arguments is optional; we could have written two different constructors to accomplish the same goal, but it is less work to write one constructor. This also reduces the total amount of source code in the system, which should improve reliability.

The next topic of discussion was the **explicit** keyword, which allows us to specify that a particular constructor should be called only when we explicitly ask for it. Unless we specify this keyword when we create a constructor with only one required argument, that constructor can be called automatically whenever we specify an actual argument of one type and we need an argument of a different type. For example, if we have a non-explicit constructor for the string class that takes a short argument, then any place where a string is required as an argument, we can supply a short value instead — the constructor will be called automatically to convert the short to a string. While this can be a very handy facility (as in the case of supplying a char* argument where a string argument was expected), it can also be very hazardous where it does something that the user doesn't expect. In the case of the string(short) constructor, somehow I doubt that anyone would expect a value of 5, for example, to be converted to a string of five null bytes! To prevent this, we made that constructor explicit so that this would not occur without the user's being aware of it.

After dealing with that new keyword, we went over the implementation of the new constructor for the string class. Then we examined exactly why we needed it in the first place: to allow us to implement a concatenation operator for the string class. We used operator + as the notation for this new operation, which might seem odd at first sight. However, this is a very common way to express the idea of tacking one string onto the end of another, and has been adopted as such in the C++ standard library, so we might as well use it here too.

The next question we tackled was why we need the ability to concatenate strings at this point in the project. The reason is that it allows us to improve the implementation of operator >> for strings. The problem with the previous version of this operator was that it could not handle strings of arbitrary length but was limited to those of 79 characters or less. Because it was possible that some fields in the home inventory data (especially the description) might be quite long, it was important for us to improve this operator so that it could handle strings of any length. To do this, we needed the ability to concatenate two strings.

After analyzing the code in operator >> that handles long strings in a number of sections, we continued to the next new member function in the string class: find_nocase. This function looks for a sequence of chars within a particular string, an ability that we need to implement the functions that allow the user to find items whose descriptions or other fields contain a specified sequence of characters. During the discussion of this function, we ran across a new C library function called strnicmp, which compares two C strings without considering the case of the characters in them. This is an important feature to provide because the user may not remember the case of the word for which he or she is looking.

The next and final new member function in the string class is less_nocase. It is exactly like the normal operator < function in the string class, except that it uses the strnicmp function to do the comparison so that upper- and lower-case characters will be compared without regard to considering their case. This was necessary in the implementation of the sorting routine in SortInventoryByName.

After finishing the discussion of the find_nocase function, we looked at an example program that illustrates the use of one of the newly added "find" functions, FindItemByDescription, which, as its name suggests, searches for an item whose description field contains a particular sequence of characters. After a brief description of this new example program, we started to tackle the latest version of the HomeInventory class, hmin6.h. Besides adding the new member functions needed to support searching for items by name or description, I took this opportunity to change the argument-passing conventions of all of the member functions that previously used value arguments of user-defined types to use const references instead. This is usually the best way to pass arguments of user-defined types because it avoids the necessity of making a copy of the argument. Arguments of native types, on the other hand, typically are best passed by value, as copying them is not very expensive.

Next, we discussed FindItemByDescription, which is very similar to the previously defined FindItemByName, except that it uses the new find_nocase function to search for an item that matches the user's partial description.

At this point, we were ready to look at the next version of the HomeItem interface, hmit6.h, which differs from the previous version of this interface in a few minor ways. First, I changed all the arguments of user-defined types to use const references rather than pass-by-value, just as I did with the HomeInventory class. I also added two new functions, GetDescription and IsNull. Neither of these functions is at all complicated, so we passed over them quickly.

At this point, I mentioned a compile-time error that surfaced in the normal constructor for the HomeItemBasic class. I had a bit of trouble figuring out why I should get an error just from using a new version of the string class when I had merely added a couple of new functions to that class. It turned out that the constructor in question was written incorrectly; it was trying to initialize a string variable with the value 0. The compiler was willing to accept the value 0 as a char*, so it automatically applied the string constructor that creates a string from a char* value. Once we defined another constructor that accepted a short argument, however, the value 0 could be interpreted as either a char* or a short value, so the compiler complained that our initialization expression was ambiguous. This saved us from a potentially nasty bug because we certainly wouldn't want to try to use whatever random data might be at memory address 0 to initialize a string variable!

After dealing with that compiler issue, I fondly believed that I had all the pieces to complete the home inventory project. Therefore, I wrote what I thought would be the final version of the program and submitted it to my beta tester, Susan, for her approval. I was quite surprised to discover that we still had a long way to go. After she had taken a look at the program, both in execution and in source code, we embarked on a voyage of discovery to find and fix errors and inconveniences, and to find ways to improve the functioning of the program. The next 10 pages or so of the chapter consisted of a repeated cycle of the following steps:

1. Susan's trying the program while I watched;
2. my fixing the problems she discovered and adding new features that would make the program easier to use.

Most of the changes I made fell into three main categories: fixing errors (including improved error handling), cosmetic changes (such as position of items on the screen), and improvements to the functioning of the program (such as allowing the user to select items by category). There were also a few changes that I didn't make because they would have required effort out of proportion to their importance in the functioning of the program. Instead, I left them as exercises, which you will see at the end of the next chapter, after we have gone over the code of the final version of the program.

## *Exercises*

1. Write a version of operator += for the string class. This function should concatenate its right-hand argument to its left-hand argument.
2. Draw a picture of the functioning of the concatenation operator for strings when it is concatenating the value "Steve" onto a string containing the value "Hello, ". Please note that there is a space before the second quotation mark in the latter value.
3. Draw a picture of the functioning of the operator >> function for strings when it is reading data for a string of 85 characters.
4. Draw a picture of the operation of the find_nocase function when it is searching for the value "purple" in a string with the value "A purple couch".

## *Conclusion*

In this chapter, we brought our home inventory project from humble beginnings to the threshold of greatness. In the process, we learned about a number of features of C++ that we hadn't needed before. In the next chapter, we'll finish the job that we started so many pages ago.

CHAPTER 6

# *Stealing Home*

In this chapter, we will take the home inventory program to the stage of actual usability. I hope that in this process you will develop a better notion of how much work it takes to create even a relatively simple program that solves its users' problems in a natural and convenient way. We'll get started as soon as we cover some definitions and objectives.

## *Definitions*

A **cursor** is an abstract object that represents the position on the screen where input or output will occur next.

The **global name space** is a name for the set of identifiers that is visible to all functions without a class name being specified.

## *Objectives of This Chapter*

By the end of this chapter we will have

1. learned how to use a class to group a number of functions together even if they don't have any associated data;
2. learned how to write an "endless" loop to execute a section of code an indefinite number of times;
3. learned how to check numeric input for validity and give the user a reasonable error message if that input is invalid;
4. learned how to obtain keyboard input without having to wait for the user to hit the ENTER key;
5. learned how to write output on the screen at a particular position;
6. learned how to clear the screen or an individual line on the screen;
7. learned how to display part of the inventory list on the screen, scrolling the rest of the list on and off the screen as necessary;
8. learned how to use the string concatenation operator to aid in the formatting of data;
9. learned how to compare and sort string data without regard for case;
10. learned how to print data on the printer, including the use of the "form feed" character to ensure that any further data sent to the printer will start on a new page;
11. learned how to delete an item from thc invcntory list;
12. improved our home inventory program sufficiently that a user could employ it to keep track of his or her possessions.

## *The Final Voyage*

Now let's get to the detailed analysis of the final version of the home inventory program. We'll start with the main() function of this program, which is shown in Figure 6.1.

**FIGURE 6.1. The main() function of the final version of the home inventory main program (from code\hmtst8.cc)**

```
int main()
{
 ifstream HomeInfo("home.inv");
 HomeInventory MyInventory;
 char option;
 string answer;

 MyInventory.LoadInventory(HomeInfo);

 for (;;)
  {
  option = GetMenuChoice(MyInventory);

  if (option == Exit)
   break;
  else
   ExecuteMenuChoice(option,MyInventory);
  }

  HomeInfo.close();

  for (;;)
   {
   cout << "Save the changes you have made? (Y/N) ";
   cin >> answer;

   if ((answer == "Y") || (answer == "y"))
    {
    ofstream NewHomeInfo("home.inv");
```

```
        MyInventory.StoreInventory(NewHomeInfo);
        cout << "Inventory updated" << endl;
        break;
        }
      else if ((answer == "N") || (answer == "n"))
        {
        cout << "Changes cancelled" << endl;
        break;
        }
      else
        clrscr();
      }

    return 0;
}
```

This starts off much like the previous versions, by creating a HomeInventory object called MyInventory and loading it with data from an input file called home.inv. Then it enters an "endless" for loop that calls the GetMenuChoice function to find out what operation the user wants to perform, and finally then calls the ExecuteMenuChoice function to perform that operation.

We haven't yet used an "endless" loop, which is written as "for (;;)".[1] Since we have specified no initialization, modification, or continuation expression, such a loop will run until it is interrupted by a break or return statement. In this case, the break statement is executed when the user indicates that he or she is finished with the program by entering the code for "exit" in the GetMenuChoice function.

Once the user is done entering, modifying, and examining data, the second "endless" for loop asks the user whether any changes should be made permanent by being written out to the home.inv file. If the user answers "y" or "Y", the changes are written out; if the answer is "n" or "N", the changes aren't written out. In either case,

1. One possible pronunciation of this construct is "forever".

the "endless" loop is terminated, as is the program immediately afterward. If the user doesn't type a valid character, the program keeps asking the question until it gets an answer it likes.

So much for the bird's-eye view of the program. Now let's take a more detailed look at how it works. The first topic we'll examine is where that Exit value came from. This question is answered by the enum defined in Figure 6.2.

**FIGURE 6.2. The** MenuItem enum **(from code\hmtst8.cc)**

```
enum MenuItem {AddItem=1, SelectItemFromNameList,
 EditByPartialName, EditByDescription, EditByCategory,
 DeleteItemFromNameList, PrintNames, PrintAll, Exit
};
```

As you can see, this enum lists all of the possible menu choices from which the user can select. I've put it at the top of the hmtst8.cc source file because the values it defines are needed in more than one function in the main program, and that's the easiest way to make these values available to several functions.

Next, let's look at the GetMenuChoice function, shown in Figure 6.3.

**FIGURE 6.3. The** GetMenuChoice **function (from code\hmtst8.cc)**

```
char GetMenuChoice(HomeInventory& Inventory)
{
 short MenuColumn = 1;
 short MenuRow;
 short option;

 for (;;)
  {
  clrscr();

  cout << Inventory.GetCount() << " items in database." << endl;
```

```
cout << endl;

cout << AddItem << ". Add item" << endl;

cout << SelectItemFromNameList <<
  ". Select item name from list" << endl;

cout << EditByPartialName <<
  ". Edit item by partial name" << endl;

cout << EditByDescription <<
  ". Edit item by description" << endl;

cout << EditByCategory <<
  ". Edit item by category" << endl;

cout << DeleteItemFromNameList <<
  ". Delete item" << endl;

cout << PrintNames <<
  ". Print item names" << endl;

cout << PrintAll << ". Print data base" << endl;

cout << Exit << ". Exit" << endl;

cout << endl;

cout << "Please enter a number from " <<
  AddItem << " to " << Exit << ": ";

cin >> option;

if ((option >= AddItem) && (option <= Exit))
  break;
else
  HomeUtility::HandleError("Sorry, that's an invalid option.");
}
```

```
  clrscr();

  return option;
}
```

Most of this code is pretty simple, but there are a few new twists. To start with, we're using a screen control function that we haven't seen before: clrscr. This function clears the screen so that we can start writing text on it without worrying about what might already be there.

Once the screen has been cleared, we display each of the menu choices on the screen and ask the user to type in the number of the operation to be performed. Next, we check the entered number to make sure that it is one of the legal values. If it is, we break out of the "endless" loop, clear the screen again so that the function we're going to perform has a fresh canvas to paint on, and return the number of the operation the user selected. On the other hand, if the user has typed in an invalid value, we call a utility function called HomeUtility::HandleError that notifies the user of the error; then we continue in the "endless" loop until we get a valid answer to our question.[2]

Susan had some questions about this function, so we discussed it.

**Susan:** Is this GetMenuChoice function listing the choices on the screen?

**Steve:** Yes.

**Susan:** How does it know how to put the number of the selection in front of each one?

2. We'll get to the purpose and implementation of the HomeUtility class member functions in the section "Utility Room" on page 374.

**Steve:** That's how enum values are displayed by operator <<. That's why each line begins with one of the values from the MenuItem enum.

**Susan:** How did you know to use the clrscr function to clear the screen?

**Steve:** I read the documentation for the compiler.

**Susan:** But how did you know there even was such a function?

**Steve:** Because I've used it before.

**Susan:** Well, what if it was the first time you ever needed it?

**Steve:** Then I would either have to read a book (like this one) or ask somebody. It's just like learning about anything else.

Once we know which operation the user wants to perform, main calls the final function in the main program, ExecuteMenuChoice (Figure 6.4).

**FIGURE 6.4.** ExecuteMenuChoice **(from code\hmtst8.cc)**

```
void ExecuteMenuChoice(char option, HomeInventory& Inventory)
{
 short itemno;
 ofstream Printer("lpt1");
 string Name;
 string Description;
 string Category;

 switch (option)
  {
  case AddItem:
   {
   cout << "Adding item" << endl << endl;
```

```
  Inventory.AddItem();
  ofstream SaveHomeInfo("home.$$$");
  Inventory.StoreInventory(SaveHomeInfo);
  }
break;

case SelectItemFromNameList:
  cout << "Selecting item from whole inventory";
  cout << endl << endl;
  itemno = Inventory.SelectItemFromNameList();
  if (itemno != -1)
    {
    Inventory.EditItem(itemno);
    ofstream SaveHomeInfo("home.$$$");
    Inventory.StoreInventory(SaveHomeInfo);
    }
break;

case EditByPartialName:
  cout << "Selecting item by partial name";
  cout << endl << endl;
  cout << "Please enter part of the name of the item ";
  cout << "(or ENTER for all items): ";
  cin >> Name;
  cout << endl;
  itemno = Inventory.SelectItemByPartialName(Name);
  if (itemno != -1)
    {
    Inventory.EditItem(itemno);
    ofstream SaveHomeInfo("home.$$$");
    Inventory.StoreInventory(SaveHomeInfo);
    }
break;

case EditByDescription:
  cout << "Selecting item by partial description";
  cout << endl << endl;
  cout << "Please enter part of the description of the item ";
  cout << "(or ENTER for all items): ";
```

```
      cin >> Description;
      cout << endl;

      itemno =
        Inventory.SelectItemFromDescriptionList(Description);

      if (itemno != -1)
        {
        Inventory.EditItem(itemno);
        ofstream SaveHomeInfo("home.$$$");
        Inventory.StoreInventory(SaveHomeInfo);
        }
    break;

    case EditByCategory:
      cout << "Selecting item by partial category";
      cout << endl << endl;
      cout << "Please enter part or all of the category name ";
      cout << "(or ENTER for all categories): ";
      cin >> Category;
      cout << endl;

      itemno =
        Inventory.SelectItemFromCategoryList(Category);

      if (itemno != -1)
        {
        Inventory.EditItem(itemno);
        ofstream SaveHomeInfo("home.$$$");
        Inventory.StoreInventory(SaveHomeInfo);
        }
    break;

    case DeleteItemFromNameList:
      cout << "Deleting item" << endl << endl;
      itemno = Inventory.SelectItemFromNameList();
      if (itemno != -1)
        {
        string Query;
```

```
          cout << "Are you sure you want to delete item ";
          cout << itemno + 1 << " (Y/N)? ";
          cin >> Query;
          if (Query.find_nocase("Y") == 0)
            {
            Inventory.DeleteItem(itemno);
            ofstream SaveHomeInfo("home.$$$");
            Inventory.StoreInventory(SaveHomeInfo);
            }
          }
        break;

        case PrintNames:
          Inventory.PrintNames(Printer);
        break;

        case PrintAll:
          Inventory.PrintAll(Printer);
        break;
        }
    }
```

While this function is fairly long, there's nothing terribly complex about it. After declaring some variables, the rest of the function consists of a switch statement. Each of the cases of the switch executes whatever operation the user selected during the execution of the GetMenuChoice function. Most of these are very similar, as you'll see.

As soon as we take care of an initial question from Susan, we'll take a look at each of these cases in order.

**Susan:** What's a case?

**Steve:** It's the part of a switch statement that executes the code for one of the possibilities. Basically, the switch and case statements are like a bunch of if/else statements but easier to read and modify. Take a look at Figure 6.4 on page 368 for an example of how it works.

1. The AddItem case displays a message telling the user what operation is being performed and calls the AddItem member function of the Inventory object to add the item. Finally, the (modified) inventory is saved to a "backup" file called home.$$$. The purpose of this file is to prevent disaster should the power fail or the system crash during a lengthy editing session. Because the inventory is written out to the home.$$$ file whenever any change is made, the user can recover the work that might otherwise be lost in case of any kind of system failure. After this is done, the processing for this step is complete, so the break statement exits from the switch statement and the ExecuteMenuChoice function returns to the main program.
2. The SelectItemFromNameList case displays a message telling the user what operation is being performed and calls the SelectItemFromNameList member function of the Inventory object to determine which inventory item the user wants to edit. If the user doesn't select an item to be edited, the result of this call will be the value –1, in which case the editing step is omitted and the ExecuteMenuChoice function returns to the main program. However, if the user does select an item to be edited, the EditItem member function of the Inventory object is called with the index of that item. When that function has finished execution, the inventory is saved as in AddItem.

Susan had some more questions at this point.

**Susan:** Why is the result –1?

**Steve:** Because 0 is a valid index; remember, we're programming in C++, and 0 is the index of the first item in the inventory list.

**Susan:** How about using 99?<g>

**Steve:** What an original idea! That would work fine until we had 99 items; unfortunately, then we would have an Item100 problem.

3. The EditByPartialName case displays a message telling the user what operation is being performed, asks the user to type in part of the name of the item to be edited, and calls the SelectItemByPartialName member function of the Inventory object to determine which inventory item the user wants to edit. The rest of this function is the same as the previous case, which makes sense because the only difference in the purpose of these two sections of code is how the user selects the item.

Susan, with her keen eye for detail, spotted a small discrepancy in this section of code, which led to the following discussion.

**Susan:** Why is the name of the case different from the name of the function?

**Steve:** That's a good question. It really should be the same, but I changed the program several times and forgot to resynchronize the two names. Because it doesn't affect the functioning of the program, I'm going to leave it as is.

4. The EditByDescription case is exactly the same as the previous case, except that it asks the user for part of the description rather than the name and calls SelectItemFromDescriptionList, rather than SelectItemByPartialName, to select the item to be edited.
5. The EditByCategory case is exactly the same as the previous two, except that it asks the user for the category name, rather than the item name or description, and calls SelectItemFromCategoryList to select the item to be edited.
6. The DeleteItemFromNameList case is a bit different from the previous cases. It starts by allowing the user to select the item to be deleted from the entire inventory. Then it asks the user to

confirm the deletion of that item, just to be sure that nothing gets deleted accidentally. Then it calls the DeleteItem member function of the Inventory object to do the actual deletion. Finally, it writes the changed inventory to the backup file.

Susan had a couple of comments about this case and its corresponding function.

**Susan:** You know, these long names look like German words: a whole bunch of words all strung together.

**Steve:** I do believe you're right!

**Susan:** Anyway, I like the confirmation. It's better to be safe rather than to accidentally delete an item when you didn't mean to.

**Steve:** I agree. Of course, we don't have a "mass delete" option, so an accident can't do unlimited damage, but I'd rather be safe than sorry.

7. The PrintNames and PrintAll cases are much simpler than the previous ones because they don't allow the user to select which items will be included in the printed list. The user can print either the names of all the items in the inventory or all the data for all the items. Of course, even though the program is useful without a fancier printing capability, there might be occasions where printing data for part of the inventory would be very handy. Therefore, I've added an exercise to improve these facilities.

## *Utility Room*

That takes care of the main program. Now let's take a look at the HomeUtility class, starting with its interface, which is shown in Figure 6.5.

**FIGURE 6.5. The** HomeUtility **interface (code\hmutil1.h)**

```
//hmutil1.h

#ifndef HMUTIL1_H
#define HMUTIL1_H

#include <iostream.h>
#include "vector.h"
#include "string7.h"

class HomeUtility
{
public:

static void IgnoreTillCR();
static void HandleError(const string& Message);
static bool CheckNumericInput();
static bool CheckDateInput(long Date);
static short GetNumberOrEnter(bool AllowArrows=false);
static void ClearRestOfScreen(short StartingRow);
static short SelectItem(vector<short>& Number,
  vector<string>& Name);
enum KeyValue {e_Return = -1, e_Up = -2, e_Down = -3};
};

#endif
```

This class is different from any of the others we've seen so far, as it consists entirely of public static member functions and a public enum. You may reasonably wonder why this is even a class at all; why not just make these functions global?

The reason is to avoid polluting the *global name space*. That is, it's entirely possible that another programmer might write a function called HandleError, and we want to make sure that the code we write can coexist with code that uses such common names. By creating a class to hold these functions that would otherwise be global, we are preventing clashes with other functions that might have the same names.[3]

How did I decide which functions should go into this class rather than anywhere else? My criterion was that the function could be used in more than one other class, so that it would most reasonably belong in a commonly accessible place such as a utility class.

You might not be surprised that Susan had some questions about this issue. Here is our discussion.

> **Susan:** Why are you creating a class that doesn't have any data? I don't get it.
>
> **Steve:** It's an ecological issue. If we create global functions, especially ones with names that other programmers might want to use, it's like dumping garbage in the ocean where it can affect others. In fact, the practice of creating global functions without a good reason is widely referred to as "polluting the global name space", because such functions interfere with other programmers' use of the same names. Remember, there can be only one global function with a given name and parameter list, so we should create such functions only when absolutely necessary.[4]
>
> **Susan:** OK, but why should these functions be in this class? How did you decide which ones should be here?

---

3. Actually, we don't need to create a class just to segregate these functions from the global name space; there's a new C++ feature called namespaces for exactly that purpose. However, I'd rather avoid introducing yet another concept and matching syntax as long as it's not strictly necessary, which it isn't in this case.

4. By an interesting coincidence, after first writing this paragraph I had exactly this problem when trying to reuse some old code I had written. This old code defined global names that conflicted with another library that the user of this code also needed. I fixed this by changing the names, but having kept them out of the global name space would have prevented the problem in the first place.

**Steve:** A function belongs in the utility class if it is used in several other classes. We certainly don't want to copy it into each of those classes: that wouldn't be very object-oriented!

Now that we know why we need the functions in the HomeUtility class, let's take a look at the first one, IgnoreTillCR, which is shown in Figure 6.6.

**FIGURE 6.6.** HomeUtility::IgnoreTillCR **(from code\hmutil1.cc)**

```
void HomeUtility::IgnoreTillCR()
{
 cin.ignore(10000,'\n');
}
```

This is a simple function that just calls the ignore function of the istream class to ignore a maximum of 10,000 chars in cin or up to the first newline (or "carriage return") character, whichever comes first. In fact, it's so simple that you might wonder why I even bothered making it a function, since cin.ignore(10000,'\n'); is actually shorter than HomeUtility::IgnoreTillCR().

That is true, but the reason I made this a function wasn't to reduce typing but to localize the knowledge of how it works in one place. That way, if I decided to use a different mechanism to ignore excess data, I could change just this one function rather than trying to find every place that I had used the ignore function for that purpose.

Susan had some questions about this function.

**Susan:** Why do we need this function again?

**Steve:** It ignores any extra characters that the user might type in before hitting the ENTER key. Otherwise, those characters will be interpreted as commands after the ENTER is pressed.

**Susan:** OK, but why 10,000?

**Steve:** Why not? After all, they're free.

Next, we have HomeUtility::HandleError, which is the common error-handling function used in the rest of the program whenever we simply want to display an error message, wait for the user to hit ENTER, and then continue with the program. The code for HandleError is shown in Figure 6.7.

**FIGURE 6.7.** HomeUtility::HandleError **(from code\hmutil1.cc)**

```
void HomeUtility::HandleError(const string& Message)
{
 cout << endl;
 cout << Message << endl;
 cin.clear();
 IgnoreTillCR();
 cout << "Please hit ENTER to continue." << endl;
 cin.get();
}
```

This is a simple function too. It starts by moving the cursor to the next line on the screen (so the user can tell where the error message begins). Then it displays the message, using the cin.clear() function call to clean up any errors that might have occurred in the cin input stream and calling IgnoreTillCR() to ignore any random characters that might be left in cin from the user's last input. Next, it displays the message "Please hit ENTER to continue" and waits for the user to hit a key, which is accepted via the cin.get() function call.

Susan had a couple of comments and questions about this function too.

**Susan:** So, you have to clean up the garbage in the input stream before you can use it again?

**Steve:** Yes, we have to reset the status of the stream before we can read from it again. This prevents a program from continuing to read garbage from the stream without realizing it.

**Susan:** What error message does this function display?

**Steve:** Whatever error message the calling function specifies.

**Susan:** Oh, I see. It's generic, not specific to a particular situation.

**Steve:** Yes, that's exactly right.

The next utility function is HomeUtility::CheckNumericInput, which is called after the user has typed in a numeric value. The code for this function is shown in Figure 6.8.

**FIGURE 6.8.** HomeUtility::CheckNumericInput **(from code\hmutil1.cc)**

```
bool HomeUtility::CheckNumericInput()
{
 string garbage;
 bool result = true;

 if (cin.peek() != '\n')
  {
  cin.clear();
  cin >> garbage;
  string Message = "Illegal data in numeric value: ";
  Message = Message + garbage;
  HandleError(Message);
  result = false;
  }

 return result;
}
```

While this is a bit more complex than the functions we've looked at so far in this class, it's not really that hard to follow. After declaring some variables, the code starts by calling the peek function of cin to see whether the next character in that istream is a newline ('\n') character. If it is, we can tell that the user has typed in a valid number, so we don't have to deal with an error. How do we know this?

## *Number, Please*

We know this because the versions of operator >> that read numeric (short, int, long, float, or double) values stop when they get to a character that doesn't belong in a number. In the current case, we've asked the user to type in a number, after which he or she is supposed to hit ENTER. If the user has indeed typed in a valid numeric value, all of the characters up to (but not including) the ENTER key will already have been used by operator >> in computing the new value of the numeric variable to the right of the >>. Therefore, the next character in the input stream should be the ENTER (which is represented in C and C++ by the newline character, '\n'). However, if the user has typed some character that doesn't belong in a number, that character will be the next character in the input stream after operator >> finishes reading the value for the numeric variable to its right. Therefore, if the next character isn't a newline, we know the user typed in something illegal.

If that happens, we should let the user know exactly what the illegal characters were. Therefore, after we call the clear function to clear the error status of the istream, the next statement, cin >> garbage, uses operator >> to read the rest of the characters in the input line into a string called garbage, which will end up holding everything from the first illegal character up to but not including a newline. Then we construct the whole error message by concatenating the illegal characters to the end of the message "Illegal data in numeric value: ". Finally, we call HandleError to display the message and wait for the user to press ENTER.

Susan wanted to go over this in more detail.

**Susan:** Let me see if I understand this. If the user typed in illegal characters, the input operation would stop at that point?

**Steve:** Right.

**Susan:** Would that cause an error message?

**Steve:** No, not by itself; it just sets an error condition in the input stream. It's up to us to produce the error message, and that's what we're doing here.

**Susan:** So the garbage characters have been left in cin?

**Steve:** Yes. That's why we have to call clear before we can use cin again.

## *Making a List, Checking It Twice*

The next function is HomeUtility::CheckDateInput, which is shown in Figure 6.9.

**FIGURE 6.9.** HomeUtility::CheckDateInput **(from code\hmutil1.cc)**

```
bool HomeUtility::CheckDateInput(long Date)
{
 bool result = CheckNumericInput();

 if (result == false)
  return false;

 if ((Date < 18000101) && (Date != 0))
  {
  string Message = "Date must be either 0 (if unknown)";
  Message = Message + " or a number in the form YYYYMMDD";
  Message = Message + "\n";
  Message = Message + "which is on or after 18000101";
```

```
    Message = Message + " (January 1st, 1800)";
    HandleError(Message);
    result = false;
    }

  return result;
}
```

This isn't a very complicated function either. It starts by calling CheckNumericInput to make sure that the "date" the user typed in is at least a numeric value. If the input value fails that test, CheckDateInput returns the bad news to the calling function in the form of a false return value. If the input value is a valid number, the second if statement checks whether it is in the range that I've decided to allow (after consultation with Susan): on or after January 1, 1800, or 0. The latter is needed to handle the very real possibility that Susan pointed out: The user may not know when the object was acquired. If the date fails this test, we return false to indicate that it's invalid; otherwise, the return value is true.

Even though I had discussed the range of legal dates with Susan, she had a couple of additional questions about this notion.

**Susan:** Why do we need a limit on the date at all?

**Steve:** For error reduction. The chance that the user has had the object for more than a couple of hundred years is smaller than the chance that the user typed the date in incorrectly. At least, that's the way I figure it.

**Susan:** What about collectors who may have some extremely old objects?

**Steve:** Well, that is certainly possible. However, the field we're discussing here represents the date that the user acquired the object, not how old the object is. That might very well be a useful piece of information, especially for collectibles, so I'll add an exercise to include such a field in a collectibles type.

## Enter Here

The next function we're going to examine in the HomeUtility class, GetNumberOrEnter (Figure 6.10), is somewhat more complicated than the ones we've been looking at so far. That's because it deals with getting input from the user one keystroke at a time.

**FIGURE 6.10.** HomeUtility::GetNumberOrEnter **(from code\hmutil1.cc)**

```
short HomeUtility::GetNumberOrEnter(bool AllowArrows)
{
 int key;
 char keychar;
 short FoundItemNumber;

 cout.flush();

 for (;;)
  {
  key = getkey();
  keychar = key;

  if (key == K_Return)
   return e_Return;

  if (AllowArrows)
   {
   if (key == K_Up)
    return e_Up;
   if (key == K_Down)
    return e_Down;
   }

  if ((key < '0') || (key > '9'))
   continue;

  cout << keychar;
  cout.flush();
```

```
    FoundItemNumber = key - '0';

    for (;;)
     {
     key = getkey();
     keychar = key;

     if (key == K_BackSpace)
      {
      cout << keychar;
      cout.flush();
      cout << ' ';
      cout << keychar;
      cout.flush();
      FoundItemNumber /= 10;
      continue;
      }

     if (key == K_Return)
      {
      cout << keychar;
      cout.flush();
      return FoundItemNumber;
      }

     if ((key < '0') || (key > '9'))
      continue;

     cout << keychar;
     cout.flush();

     FoundItemNumber = FoundItemNumber * 10 + (key - '0');
     }
  }
}
```

The first thing to note about this function is its argument, which is a bool called AllowArrows. If you look at the definition of the interface for the HomeUtility class (Figure 6.5 on page 375), you'll notice that this argument has a default value, which is false. The purpose of this argument is to determine whether the up and down arrow keys will be accepted as valid inputs; if the argument is false, they will be ignored, whereas if the argument is true and the user presses one of these keys, the function will return a code indicating which one. As you'll see, accepting the arrow keys will be useful in the last member function in this class, SelectItem.

The function starts by declaring some variables called key, keychar, and FoundItemNumber. The first of these is an int, which is a type we haven't used very much because it varies in size from one compiler to another. However, in this case I'm going to use an int variable to hold the return value from a function called getkey, which is the function that returns the key code for a key that has been pressed by the user. Since getkey is defined to return an int value, that's the appropriate type for a variable that holds its return value.

This getkey function is a leftover from C, but it is very useful all the same because it allows us to get input from the user without having to wait for him for her to hit ENTER. Under most circumstances, it's much easier to use the >> operator to get input from the user via the keyboard, but that approach has a serious limitation: It prevents us from giving the user immediate feedback. Such feedback is essential if we are going to allow the user to access varying segments of a large quantity of information in an intuitive manner, as you'll see when you try the program. Forcing the user to hit ENTER before getting any feedback would be very inconvenient, and we have to worry about how easy our programs are to use if we want happy users. Therefore, I've written this GetNumberOrEnter function to allow the user to receive immediate gratification when using our home inventory program.

This might be a good time for you to try the program out for yourself so you can see what I'm talking about. To do this, first compile it by changing to the \whosadv\code directory and typing RHIDE hmtst8. When RHIDE starts up, hit Ctl-F9 to compile the program and start it running; once it is finished, you can hit ENTER to dismiss the ending message and use Alt-X to exit back to DOS. Try out the program for a while and see how you like it before coming back to the discussion. Pay special attention to the "select" and "edit" functions, which allow you to see some of the items in the list, and use the up and down arrows to see more of the list. That behavior is implemented partly by GetNumberOrEnter and partly by the SelectItem function.

Now that we've seen how this function is used, let's get back to its implementation; as I've already mentioned, this is a somewhat complicated function, because it has to deal with the intricacies of reading data from the keyboard one character at a time. First, we call flush to make sure that any characters that have been written to cout have actually been sent to the screen. Then we start the "endless" loop that will allow the user to type as many keys as necessary to enter the data item. Why do I say "data item" rather than "number"? Because the user can type keys that aren't numbers at all, including the up or down arrow to select a different entry in the list of items that appears on the screen.

Susan had a question about this flush function.

> **Susan:** I don't remember seeing this flush function before. What does it do?
>
> **Steve:** Ordinarily, characters that are written to a stream are not sent immediately to the output device to which the stream is attached, because that is extremely inefficient. Instead, the characters are collected in an output buffer until there are enough of them to be worth sending out; this technique is called *buffering*.[5] However, in this case we have to make sure that any characters that

5. This buffering technique is also applied to input. Rather than read one character at a time from an input file, the operating system reads a number of characters at a time and gives them to the program when it asks for them. This greatly improves the efficiency of reading from a file; however, it is much less useful when reading data from the keyboard, as the user doesn't know what to type before we provide a prompt.

were supposed to be displayed have been displayed already, because we are going to be taking characters from the user and displaying them immediately. Any leftover characters would just confuse the user.

Now let's continue with the analysis of the code in this function. The first statement inside the "endless" loop is key = getkey();. This statement calls a C function called getkey, which waits for the user to type a key and then reads it. The value of the getkey function is the ASCII code for the key the user hit. Therefore, that statement should be relatively simple to understand.

## *Secret Decoder Ring Not Required*

However, the same is not true of the statement keychar = key;. Why would we want to assign one variable the same value as that of another? Because of the way that getkey works. Unlike normal cin input, getkey input is "silent"; that is, keys that are pressed by the user do not produce any visible results by themselves, so we have to display each character on the screen as the user types it. But to display a character on the screen via cout, the variable or expression to be displayed must have the type char, whereas the variable key is an int. If we were to write the statement, cout << key;, the program would display the ASCII numeric value for the key the user pressed. Needless to say, this would not be what the user expected; therefore, we have to copy the key value from an int variable to a char variable before we display it so that the user sees something intelligible on the screen.

Susan thought such cryptic output might have some use. Also, she wanted to know what would happen if the key value wouldn't fit.

**Susan:** If we displayed the ASCII value instead of the character, it would be sort of a secret code, wouldn't it?

**Steve:** Sort of, although not a very secure one. However, it would be fairly effective at confusing the user, which wouldn't be good.

**Susan:** OK. Now, about copying the value from an int to a char: A char is smaller than an int, right? What if the value was too big?

**Steve:** The answer is that it would be chopped off. However, in this case we're safe because we know that any key the user types will fit in a char.

The next order of business in this function is to check whether the user has hit the ENTER key. If so, we simply return the enum value e_Return to the calling function to inform it that the user has hit the ENTER key without typing a value.

Assuming that the user has not hit the ENTER key so far, we check the AllowArrows argument to see whether the arrow keys are allowed at this time. If they are, we check to see if either the up arrow or the down arrow has been hit. If it has, we return the appropriate code to tell the calling function that this has occurred so it can scroll the display if necessary.

The next statement after the end of the arrow-handling code is an if statement that checks whether the key that we are handling is in the range '0' to '9'. If the key is outside that range, we use the continue statement to skip back to the beginning of the outer for loop, essentially ignoring any such key. However, if the key is within the numeric digit range, we proceed by using the operator << to send it to the screen. Then we use the flush function of the cout object to ensure that the key has actually been displayed on the screen.

By this point, we have seen the first digit of the value, so we continue by setting FoundItemNumber to the numeric value of that digit, which can be calculated as the ASCII value of the key minus the ASCII value of '0'.

## The Rest of the Story

Now we're ready to enter the inner for loop that gathers all the rest of the numeric digits of the number. This starts with the same "endless" condition, (;;), as the outer loop because we don't know how many times it will have to be executed. Therefore, rather than specify the loop count in the for statement, we use a return statement to exit from the loop as soon as the user presses ENTER.

The first two statements in this inner loop are exactly the same as the first two statements in the outer loop, which should not be a surprise as they serve exactly the same function — to get the key from the user and copy it into a char variable for display. However, the next segment of code is different, because once the user has typed at least one digit, another possibility opens up — editing the value by using the backspace key to erase an erroneous digit. That's the task of the next part of the code, which was a bit more difficult to develop than you might think. The problem is that simply echoing the backspace key to the screen, as we do with other keys, does not work properly because it leaves the erroneous digit visible on the screen. Even after we solve this problem, however — by writing a space character on the screen to erase the erroneous digit and backing up again to position the cursor at the correct place for entering the new digit — we have another problem to deal with. Namely, we have to correct the value of the FoundItemNumber variable to account for the erased digit. This requires only that we divide the previous value of that variable by 10 because the remainder will be discarded automatically by the integer division process, effectively eliminating the contribution of the erased digit. Once we have taken care of these details, we are finished with this particular keystroke, so we use a continue statement to proceed to the next execution of the loop.

The next possibility to be handled is that of the ENTER key. When we see that key, we display it on the screen, which of course causes the cursor to move to the next line. Then we return the value of the FoundItemNumber variable to the calling function, which ends the execution of this function.

By this point in the function, we shouldn't be seeing anything but a digit key. Therefore, any key other than a digit is ignored, as we use the continue statement to skip further processing of such a key.

We're almost done. The last phase of processing is to display the digit key we have received and use it to modify the previous value of the FoundItemNumber variable. The new value of the FoundItemNumber is 10 times the previous value plus the value of the new digit, and that's exactly how the last statement in this function calculates the new value.

## *I Can See Clearly Now*

I'm sure you'll be happy to hear that the next function we will discuss is a lot simpler than the one we just looked at. This is the ClearRestOfScreen function, which is shown in Figure 6.11. It is used in the final function in the HomeUtility class, SelectItem, to clear the part of the screen that function uses for its item display.

**FIGURE 6.11.** HomeUtility::ClearRestOfScreen **(from code\hmutil1.cc)**

```
void HomeUtility::ClearRestOfScreen(short StartingRow)
{
  short i;

  for (i = StartingRow; i < ScreenRows(); i ++)
    {
    gotoxy(1,i);
    clreol();
    }

  gotoxy(1,StartingRow);
}
```

Even though this function isn't terribly complicated, it is the first one we've seen that uses the screen-handling functions from the conio library.

The first of these functions is the gotoxy function, which moves the cursor to the column (X) and row (Y) specified by its arguments. The first argument is the column number, which for some reason doesn't follow the standard C and C++ convention of starting with 0 but starts at 1. The same is true of the row number, which is the second argument to the function.

The second C library function that we haven't seen before is the clreol function, which erases everything on a given line of the screen from the cursor position to the end of the line. We call this function for each line from StartingRow to the end of the screen.

Before we can clear the screen one line at a time, however, we need to know when to stop. That's why we need to call the other C library function in this function: ScreenRows. As its name suggests, it returns the number of rows on the screen.

Susan had a few questions about this function.

**Susan:** What is conio?

**Steve:** It stands for "console I/O".

**Susan:** How do you pronounce gotoxy?

**Steve:** It's pronounced "go-to-X-Y".

Now that we've seen how ClearRestOfScreen works, I should tell you why we need it: to allow the SelectItem function to keep its working area clear of random characters. Of course, it could be used in other situations, but that's how we're using it here.

## *The Final Frontier*

The final function in the HomeUtility class is SelectItem, whose code is shown in Figure 6.12.

**FIGURE 6.12. The** HomeUtility::SelectItem **function (from code\hmutil1.cc)**

```
short HomeUtility::SelectItem(vector<short>& Number,
 vector<string>& Name)
{
   short FoundItemNumber;
   int Row;
   int Column;
   int RowCount = ScreenRows();
   short ItemCount = Name.size();

   ScreenGetCursor(&Row,&Column);
   Row ++;

// Max number of rows in scroll area is 1/2 rows on screen

   int RowsAvail = RowCount / 2;

// For testing, max rows is 5
   RowsAvail = 5;
// End test code

   if (RowsAvail > ItemCount)
     RowsAvail = ItemCount;

   if (RowsAvail == 0)
     {
     HandleError("No items found.");
     return 0;
     }

   short offset = 0;
   for (;;)
     {
```

```
ClearRestOfScreen(Row);

for (short i = offset; i < offset + RowsAvail ; i++)
  cout << setw(5) << Number[i] + 1 << ".  " << Name[i] << endl;

cout << endl;

cout << "Type item number to select or ENTER to end." << endl;

if (ItemCount > RowsAvail)
  cout << "Hit down arrow or up arrow to scroll." << endl;

cout << endl;

FoundItemNumber = GetNumberOrEnter(true);
if (FoundItemNumber == e_Return)
  return 0;

if (FoundItemNumber == e_Up)
  {
  if (ItemCount > RowsAvail)
    {
    offset --;
    if (offset < 0)
      offset = 0;
    }
  continue;
  }

if (FoundItemNumber == e_Down)
  {
  if (ItemCount > RowsAvail)
    {
    offset ++;
    if (offset >= Name.size()-RowsAvail)
      offset = Name.size()-RowsAvail;
    }
  continue;
  }
```

```
        for (short i = 0; i < ItemCount; i ++)
          {
          if (FoundItemNumber == Number[i]+1)
            return FoundItemNumber;
          }

        IgnoreTillCR();
        cout << FoundItemNumber <<
          " is an invalid entry. Hit ENTER to continue." << endl;
        IgnoreTillCR();
        return 0;
        }
}
```

This function, as its name indicates, is the heart of the item selection process. Its arguments are the Number vector, which contains the indexes into the inventory list of the particular items from which the user is selecting, and the Name vector, which contains the names of these items and sometimes other information about them (e.g., the category in which each item is found).

The first operation to be performed in this function is determining how many lines there are on the "screen"; I have put the word "screen" in quotes because what we are actually concerned with is only the DOS window in which our program is running, not the actual physical screen of the monitor. The reason that the number of lines on the screen is important is that we may want to calculate the number of items to be displayed in the "scroll area" (the area where we will be displaying all or part of the list of items) based on the amount of space available on the screen. For testing purposes, I have set the maximum number of items to be displayed to 5. I actually like it that way, but you can easily change it to see more items at one time.

Susan had some questions about the way we're handling the screen.

**Susan:** So, you even have to tell the program how big the screen is? Doesn't it know anything?

**Steve:** You have to realize that the same program may run on different machines that are set up differently. Even if everyone were running Windows 95, some people have their DOS windows set for 25 lines, some for 50 lines, and probably others I haven't seen. It's not very difficult to handle all these different possibilities just by calling the ScreenRows function.

**Susan:** OK. Now about changing the number of lines in the scroll area: How do you do that?

**Steve:** By deleting the line in the program that sets RowsAvail to 5, it will use half the screen for the scroll area.

**Susan:** Oh, I thought there was an option when you ran the program.

**Steve:** You're a programmer now. You can do that yourself.

The next operation is to determine the number of entries in the list of items we're going to display, which we can do by calling the size member function of the Name argument. Of course, we could just as well call the size member function of Number, because that argument has to have the same number of elements as Name has: If they have different numbers of elements, the calling function has made a serious error!

After finding out how many items we are going to handle, the next operation is to determine the current position of the cursor so that we can position the "scroll area" properly below the heading that was displayed by the calling function. To find the current position of the cursor, we call another C function, ScreenGetCursor. This function requires two arguments, both of which are addresses of variables. The first argument is the address of a variable (in this case Row) that will receive the current row number. The second is the address of a variable (in this case Column) that will receive the current column number.[6] As soon as we have determined the current cursor row, we increment the Row variable to skip a row between the heading and the beginning of the scroll area.

The next segment of code figures out how many items to display at one time; the current version of this function, as I've already mentioned, ignores this calculation and sets the number of items to 5. This makes my (and Susan's) testing more effective because most of the complexity of this routine is in the code that deals with the possibility of having to scroll the items onto and off the screen. This code is used only when there are more items than will fit in the limited space allocated for listing them, so if we have fewer items than will fit on the screen, the code that scrolls the list is not used. Code that is never used is never tested and therefore must be assumed not to work.[7]

Once we have decided how many items to list at once and have assigned the appropriate value to the RowsAvail variable, we then check whether the number of items we can display (as specified in that variable) is greater than the total number of items we need to display (as specified by the ItemCount variable). If this is the case, we set the total number to be displayed to the latter value.

If there are no items to be displayed, the user has requested a set of items that doesn't exist, so we call the HandleError routine to tell the user about this situation, and return to the calling function.

Assuming that we have some items to display, we are ready to start displaying them. First, we initialize a variable called offset, which keeps track of what part of the whole list is currently being displayed in the scroll area. It begins at 0 because we start by displaying the first portion of the list, which consists of the number of

6. The reason we have to pass addresses of variables to this function, rather than using reference arguments, is that this is a C function, and C does not have reference arguments.

7. Of course, as the well-known Murphy's Law implies, even code that has been tested is likely not to work.

items that will fit in the scroll area. Of course, if all of the items fit in the scroll area, they will all be displayed.

Once we have initialized offset, we enter the "endless" for loop that displays the elements and asks the user for input until he or she selects something. This for loop begins by calling the ClearRestOfScreen function to clear everything on the screen beyond the current cursor location.

The next two lines of code constitute the for loop that displays the items that are currently in the scroll area. The formatting of this display is somewhat interesting, at least to me, because it took me several tries to get it right. The elements of the display line include the item number, which is one more than the index of the item being displayed (to account for the first index being 0) and the item name. Initially, I simply accepted the default formatting for the item number and the name. However, as soon as the item numbers exceeded 9, I discovered that the names no longer lined up properly because the extra character in the two-digit item number pushed the name over one extra position. To solve this problem, I decided to use the setw manipulator to force the size of the item number to five digits; because the item number is a short, the program is limited to 32,767 items, so five digits will be sufficient.

Susan was surprised to hear that I had overlooked this, which led to the following exchange.

> **Susan:** I thought you left bugs in the program on purpose so I would find them.
>
> **Steve:** No, as a matter of fact, I thought it was working every time I gave it to you to test (all five times). I suppose that illustrates the eternal optimism of software developers!

After displaying the items along with their corresponding item numbers, one on each line, we display the message "Type item number to select or ENTER to end." Then, if we have more items than will fit in the scroll area, we display another message telling the user about the availability of the up and down arrow keys for scrolling.

Next, we call the GetNumberOrEnter function to get the item number from the user. Note that the argument to that function is true, which means that we want the function to accept the up and down arrows so that the user can hit those keys to tell us to scroll the item list either up or down. Of course, if all the items fit in the scroll area, hitting either of those keys will have no visible effect on the list.

Once we have received the value returned by the GetNumberOrEnter function, we examine it. If it is the value e_Return, the user has decided not to select any of the items. Therefore, we return the value 0 to indicate this situation.

However, assuming that the user hit something more than just the ENTER key, we have to check what the exact return value was. If it was the value e_Up or e_Down, and if we have more items than will fit in the scroll area, we change the value of the offset variable accordingly. Of course, we have to be careful not to try to display items whose indexes are before the beginning or beyond the end of the Name vector; the code that handles both of the arrow keys ensures this doesn't happen.

Finally, if we get past the handling of the arrow keys, we must have gotten a numeric value from the user. Therefore, we check that the value the user typed is actually an entry in the Number vector. Assuming that this is the case, we return that value to the calling function.

However, if the user entered an item number that is not found in the Number vector, we create an error message and display it. Finally, we return the value 0 to indicate to the calling function that the user did not make a valid selection.

## *Checking the Inventory*

That concludes our tour of the HomeUtility class. Now it's time to look at the changes to the next class, HomeInventory. We'll start with the latest version of the header file, hmin8.cc, which is shown in Figure 6.13.

**FIGURE 6.13. The latest header file for the** HomeInventory class **(code\hmin8.h)**

```
//hmin8.h

#include "vector.h"
#include "string7.h"

class HomeInventory
{
public:
   HomeInventory();

   short LoadInventory(ifstream& is);
   void DumpInventory();
   HomeItem AddItem();
   HomeItem EditItem(short Index);
   vector<short> LocateItemByDescription(const string& Partial);

   vector<short> LocateItemByCategory(const string& Partial);
   vector<short> LocateItemByPartialName(const string& Partial);
   void PrintNames(ostream &os);
   void PrintAll(ostream &os);
   void StoreInventory(ofstream& ofs);
   void DisplayItem(short Index);

   void SortInventoryByName();
   short GetCount();
   short SelectItemByPartialName(const string& Partial);
   short SelectItemFromNameList();
   short SelectItemFromDescriptionList(const string& Partial);
```

```
    short SelectItemFromCategoryList(const string& Partial);
    void DeleteItem(short Index);

private:
    vector<HomeItem> m_Home;
};
```

As you will see if you compare this version of the HomeInventory class interface to the previous one we examined (hmin6.h in Figure 5.13), I've deleted three functions from this interface — namely, FindItemByDescription, FindItemByName, and LocateItemByName. The first of these is no longer used in the application program, which instead uses its relative, LocateItemByDescription. The other two functions are no longer necessary because they have been superseded by the new LocateItemByPartialName, which can do everything that the old functions could do and a lot more besides.

This new version of the HomeInventory class also includes changes to existing functions. Let's take them in order of their appearance in the header file, starting with the LoadInventory function. The only difference between this version and the previous one is that the new version sorts the inventory by calling the new SortInventoryByName function after loading it. I'll provide a brief explanation of how the sort function works when we get to it. I haven't bothered to reproduce the LoadInventory function here just to show you the one added line.

The next function that was changed is the AddItem function, whose new implementation is shown in Figure 6.14.

**FIGURE 6.14. The latest version of AddItem (from code\hmin8.cc)**

```
HomeItem HomeInventory::AddItem()
{
    HomeItem TempItem = HomeItem::NewItem();

    if (TempItem.IsNull())
```

```
    return TempItem;

   short OldCount = m_Home.size();

   m_Home.resize(OldCount + 1);

   m_Home[OldCount] = TempItem;

   SortInventoryByName();

   return TempItem;
}
```

As you can see, this version of the function checks whether the newly created item is null, using the new IsNull member function of the HomeItem class. If that turns out to be the case, it returns that null item to the calling function rather than adding it to the inventory. This new version also sorts the inventory after adding an item, just as the new version of the LoadInventory function does.

Now we're up to the EditItem function, the new version of which is shown in Figure 6.15.

**FIGURE 6.15. The new version of the EditItem function (from code\hmin8.cc)**

```
HomeItem HomeInventory::EditItem(short Index)
{
   bool NameChanged = false;

   HomeItem TempItem = m_Home[Index];

   TempItem.Edit();

   if (TempItem.GetName() != m_Home[Index].GetName())
    NameChanged = true;

   m_Home[Index] = TempItem;

   if (NameChanged)
```

```
    SortInventoryByName();

   return TempItem;
}
```

The main difference between this version of EditItem and the previous version is that this one checks to see whether the name of the item has been changed. If this is the case, EditItem calls the SortInventoryByName function to ensure that the inventory list is still in order by the names of the items.

The next function we'll examine is LocateItemByDescription, whose new implementation is shown in Figure 6.16.

**FIGURE 6.16. The latest implementation of** LocateItemByDescription **(from code\hmin8.cc)**

```
vector<short> HomeInventory::LocateItemByDescription(
 const string& Partial)
{
   short ItemCount = m_Home.size();
   string Description;
   short FoundCount = 0;

   for (short i = 0; i < ItemCount; i ++)
    {
    Description = m_Home[i].GetDescription();
    if (Description.find_nocase(Partial) >= 0)
      FoundCount ++;
    }

   vector<short> Found(FoundCount);

   FoundCount = 0;

   for (short i = 0; i < ItemCount; i ++)
    {
    Description = m_Home[i].GetDescription();
    if (Description.find_nocase(Partial) >= 0)
```

```
      Found[FoundCount++] = i;
    }

  return Found;
}
```

This function is quite different from its previous incarnation; even its interface has changed. That's because it now locates all the items that match the description specified in its argument, not just the first one. Therefore, it must return a vector of indexes rather than only one. Also, because we don't know how many items will be found before we look through the list, we don't know how large the result vector will be on our first pass. I've solved that by using two passes, with the first pass devoted to finding the number of matching items and the second pass devoted to storing the indexes of those items in the result vector. One other construct that we haven't seen before is the use of the increment operator in the line Found[FoundCount++] = i;. When this operator is used inside another expression, its value is the old value of the variable being incremented. In this case, the value of the expression FoundCount++ is the value that the variable FoundCount had before being incremented. After that value is used, the variable is incremented so that it will be greater by one the next time it is referred to.

Besides modifying the previously noted functions, I've also added quite a few functions to this interface to implement all the new facilities this new version of the program provides. Let's take them one at a time, starting with LocateItemByCategory, which is shown in Figure 6.17.

**FIGURE 6.17.** HomeInventory::LocateItemByCategory **(from code\hmin8.cc)**

```
vector<short> HomeInventory::LocateItemByCategory(
 const string& Partial)
{
  short ItemCount = m_Home.size();
  string Category;
```

```
   short FoundCount = 0;

   for (short i = 0; i < ItemCount; i ++)
    {
    Category = m_Home[i].GetCategory();
    if (Category.find_nocase(Partial) >= 0)
      FoundCount ++;
    }

   vector<short> Found(FoundCount);

   FoundCount = 0;

   for (short i = 0; i < ItemCount; i ++)
    {
    Category = m_Home[i].GetCategory();
    if (Category.find_nocase(Partial) >= 0)
      Found[FoundCount++] = i;
    }

   return Found;
}
```

As you can see, this is almost identical to the function we've just examined, LocateItemByDescription. The only difference is that we're searching for items whose category matches the user's specification rather than items whose description matches that specification.

I'm not going to waste space by reproducing the code for the LocateItemByPartialName function, which is again almost identical to the two functions we've just looked at. The difference, of course, is that the field it examines for a match is the item's name rather than its description or category.

The next function we will examine is PrintNames, which is shown in Figure 6.18.

**FIGURE 6.18. The** PrintNames **function (from code\hmin8.cc)**

```
void HomeInventory::PrintNames(ostream& os)
{
  short ItemCount = m_Home.size();

  for (short i = 0; i < ItemCount; i ++)
   {
   os << m_Home[i].GetName() << endl;
   }

  os << '\f' << endl;
  os.flush();
}
```

This function isn't very complicated. It merely steps through all the items in the inventory and sends the name of each one to the output stream. One minor point of interest is that to ensure that any further data sent to the printer starts on a new page, I've added a "form-feed" character, represented as '\f', to the end of the output data. After sending that character to the printer, the function ends with a call to the flush function of the ostream object we are sending the data to.

Susan had a couple of questions about this function.

**Susan:** What is a form-feed?

**Steve:** It is a character that makes the printer go to a new page. It's called that because in olden days printers used continuous-form paper. When you finished printing on one form, you had to send a "form-feed" character to the printer so that it would advance the paper to the beginning of the next form. Today, most printers use cut-sheet paper, but the name has stuck.

**Susan:** How do we know that the form-feed character has been sent to the printer? Isn't it buffered?

**Steve:** That's exactly why we have to call the flush function, which ensures that the form-feed has actually been sent to the printer.

The next function is PrintAll. This, as shown in Figure 6.19, is exactly like the previous function, except that it displays all the data for each item rather than just its name.

**FIGURE 6.19. The PrintAll function (from code\hmin8.cc)**

```
void HomeInventory::PrintAll(ostream& os)
{
  short ItemCount = m_Home.size();

  for (short i = 0; i < ItemCount; i ++)
   {
   os << m_Home[i] << endl;
   }

  os << '\f' << endl;
  os.flush();
}
```

Now we're up to the StoreInventory function, whose code is shown in Figure 6.20.

**FIGURE 6.20. The StoreInventory function (from code\hmin8.cc)**

```
void HomeInventory::StoreInventory(ofstream& ofs)
{
  short i;
  short ElementCount = m_Home.size();

  ofs << ElementCount << endl << endl;

  for (i = 0; i < ElementCount; i ++)
   {
   ofs << m_Home[i];
```

```
        ofs << endl;
        }
    }
```

As you can see from the code in this function, it is almost identical to the code for the previous one. The main differences follow:

1. It writes the number of items to the file before starting to write the items (so that we can tell how many items are in the file when we read it back later).
2. It doesn't write a form-feed character to the file after all the items are written because we aren't printing the information.

The similarity between this function and PrintAll shouldn't come as too much of a surprise. After all, storing the inventory data is almost the same as printing it out; both of these operations take data currently stored in objects in memory and transfer it to an output device. The iostream classes are designed to allow us to concentrate on the input or output task to be performed rather than on the details of the output device on which the data is to be written, so the operations needed to write data to a file can be very similar to the operations needed to write data to the printer.

Susan had some questions about this function.

**Susan:** What is ofs?

**Steve:** It stands for output file stream, because we are writing the data for the items to a file via an ofstream object.

**Susan:** Why is it good that writing data to a file is like writing data to the printer?

**Steve:** This characteristic of C++, called *device independence*, makes it easier to write programs that use a number of different types of output (or input) device, as they all look more or less the same. Having to treat every device differently is a major annoyance to the programmer in languages that don't support device independence.

Now let's take a look at the next function, DisplayItem, whose code is shown in Figure 6.21.

**FIGURE 6.21. The** DisplayItem **function (from code\hmin8.cc)**

```
void HomeInventory::DisplayItem(short Index)
{
  m_Home[Index].FormattedDisplay(cout);
}
```

This is quite a simple function, as it calls the FormattedDisplay function of the HomeItem class to do all the work of displaying the data for a particular item in the inventory. As you can see, this function always writes the data to the screen.

## *A Better Sort of Function*

The next function we will look at is SortInventoryByName, whose code is shown in Figure 6.22.

**FIGURE 6.22. The** SortInventoryByName **function (from code\hmin8.cc)**

```
void HomeInventory::SortInventoryByName()
{
  short ItemCount = m_Home.size();
  vector<HomeItem> m_HomeTemp = m_Home;
  vector<string> Name(ItemCount);
  string HighestName = "zzzzzzzz";
  string FirstName;
  short FirstIndex;

  for (int i = 0; i < ItemCount; i ++)
```

```
    Name[i] = m_Home[i].GetName();

  for (int i = 0; i < ItemCount; i ++)
    {
    FirstName = HighestName;
    FirstIndex = 0;
    for (int k = 0; k < ItemCount; k ++)
      {
      if (Name[k].less_nocase(FirstName))
        {
        FirstName = Name[k];
        FirstIndex = k;
        }
      }
    m_HomeTemp[i] = m_Home[FirstIndex];
    Name[FirstIndex] = HighestName;
    }

  m_Home = m_HomeTemp;
}
```

I won't go into detail on the "selection sort" algorithm used in this function because I've already explained it in gory detail in *Who's Afraid Of C++?*. The only difference between this implementation and the one in that book is that here we're using the less_nocase function rather than operator < to compare the string variables so that we can sort without regard to case. However, the basic idea of this algorithm is that we go through the inventory looking for the item that has the "lowest" name (i.e., the name that would be earliest in the dictionary). When we find it, we copy it to an output list, and then mark it so that we won't pick it again. Then we repeat this process for each item in the original list of names. This is not a particularly efficient sorting algorithm, but it is sufficient for our purposes here.

The next function, GetCount, is extremely simple. Its sole purpose is to return the number of items in the inventory so that the main program can display this information on the screen, and its implementation consists of returning the value obtained from the size member function of the inventory object. Therefore, I won't waste space reproducing it here.

The next function in the header file, SelectItemByPartialName, is more interesting. Take a look at its implementation, which is shown in Figure 6.23.

**FIGURE 6.23. The** SelectItemByPartialName **function (from code\hmin8.cc)**

```
short HomeInventory::SelectItemByPartialName(
 const string& Partial)
{
  vector<short> Found = LocateItemByPartialName(Partial);

  vector<string> Name(Found.size());

  for (short i = 0; i < Found.size(); i ++)
    Name[i] = m_Home[Found[i]].GetName();

  short Result = HomeUtility::SelectItem(Found,Name) - 1;

  return Result;
}
```

This function starts by using the LocateItemByPartialName function to get a list of all the items whose names match the string specified by the calling function in the argument called Partial (the string the user typed in to select the items to be listed). Once LocateItemByPartialName has returned the vector of indexes of matching items, SelectItemByPartialName continues by extracting the names of those items and putting them in another vector called Name. Once the names and indexes have been gathered, we're ready to call HomeUtility::SelectItem, which will take care of the actual user interaction needed to find out which item the user really wants to edit. The result of the SelectItem function is an item number, which starts at 1[8]; however, the result of the SelectItemByPartialName function is an index into the inventory list, which is zero-based, as usual in C++.

Therefore, we have to subtract 1 from the result of the SelectItem function before returning it as the index into the inventory list.

By this point, Susan had become absorbed in the role of software developer, if the following exchange is any indication:

> **Susan:** Why are we coddling the users? Let them start counting at 0 like we have to.
>
> **Steve:** Many developers take exactly that approach. However, the users are our customers, and they will be a lot happier (and likely to buy more products from us) if we treat them well.

The next function we'll look at is SelectItemFromNameList, whose code is shown in Figure 6.24.

**FIGURE 6.24. The SelectItemFromNameList function (from code\hmin8.cc)**

```
short HomeInventory::SelectItemFromNameList()
{
  short ItemCount = m_Home.size();

  vector<short> Found(ItemCount);

  for (int i = 0; i < ItemCount; i ++)
    Found[i] = i;

  vector<string> Name(Found.size());

  for (short i = 0; i < Found.size(); i ++)
    Name[i] = m_Home[i].GetName();

  short Result = HomeUtility::SelectItem(Found,Name) - 1;

  return Result;
}
```

8. Or the value 0, which means that the user didn't select anything.

This is very similar to the previous function, except that it allows the user to choose from the entire inventory, as there is no selection expression to reduce the number of items to be displayed. Therefore, instead of calling a function to determine which items should be included in the list that the user will pick from, this function makes a list of all of the indexes and item names in the inventory, then calls the SelectItem function to allow the user to pick an item from the whole inventory list.

The next member function listed in the hmin8.h header file is SelectItemFromDescriptionList. I won't reproduce it here because it is virtually identical to the SelectItemByPartialName function, except of course that it uses the description field rather than the item name field to determine which items will end up in the list the user selects from. This means that it calls LocateItemByDescription to find items, rather than LocateItemByPartialName, which the SelectItemByPartialName function uses for that same purpose.

## *Categorical Imperative*

The next function in the header file, SelectItemFromCategoryList (Figure 6.25), is more interesting, if only because it does some relatively fancy formatting to get its display to line up properly.

**FIGURE 6.25. The** SelectItemFromCategoryList **function (from code\hmin8.cc)**

```
short HomeInventory::SelectItemFromCategoryList(
 const string& Partial)
{
  vector<short> Found = LocateItemByCategory(Partial);

  vector<string> Name(Found.size());
  vector<string> Category(Found.size());
  string Padding;
  short PaddingLength;
```

```
short MaxLength = 0;

for (short i = 0; i < Found.size(); i ++)
  {
  Category[i] = m_Home[Found[i]].GetCategory();
  Name[i] = m_Home[Found[i]].GetName();
  if (Name[i].GetLength() > MaxLength)
    MaxLength = Name[i].GetLength();
  }

for (short i = 0; i < Found.size(); i ++)
  {
  PaddingLength = MaxLength - Name[i].GetLength();
  Padding = string(PaddingLength,' ');
  Name[i] = Name[i] + Padding + "    " + Category[i];
  }

MaxLength += 7; // allow for item number in item display line
string Heading = "Item #  Name";
short HeadingLength = Heading.GetLength();
if (MaxLength > HeadingLength)
  PaddingLength = MaxLength - HeadingLength;
else
  PaddingLength = 0;
Padding = string(PaddingLength,' ');
Heading = Heading + Padding + "    Category";
cout << Heading << endl << endl;

short Result = HomeUtility::SelectItem(Found,Name) - 1;

return Result;
}
```

This function starts out pretty much like the other "select" functions — calling a "locate" function to gather indexes of items that match a particular criterion, which in this case is the category of the item. However, once these indexes have been gathered, instead of simply collecting the names of the items into a vector, we also must determine the length of the longest name, so that when we display the category of each item after its name, the category names will line up evenly. To make this possible, we have to "pad" the shorter names to the same length as the longest name. The code to do this is in the two lines of the for loop that gathers the names and categories:

```
if (Name[i].GetLength() > MaxLength)
    MaxLength = Name[i].GetLength();
```

If the current name is longer than the longest name so far, we update that MaxLength variable to the length of the current name. By the time we reach the end of the list of names, MaxLength will be the length of the longest name.

In the next for loop, we calculate the amount of padding each name will require, based on the difference between its length and the length of the longest name. Then we use the string(short, char) constructor to create a string consisting of the number of spaces that will make the current name as long as the longest name. As soon as we have done that, we add the padding and the category name. Then we are finished with the preparation of the data for the SelectItem function.

However, we still have more work to do before we call that function because we want to display a heading on the screen to tell the user what he or she is looking at. That's the task of the next section of the code. It starts out by adding 7 to the MaxLength variable to account for the length of the item number field.[9]

Next, we start constructing the heading line, starting with the literal value "Item # Name". To make the category heading line up over the category names in the display, wc havc to pad the heading

9. I should mention here that it is not a good idea to use "magic" numbers in programs. These are numbers that do not have any obvious relationship to the rest of the code. A good general rule is that numbers other than 0, 1, or other self-evident values should be defined as const or enum values rather than as literal values like '7'. However, I have commented this value in the code, so the next programmer should not have too much trouble figuring out what it does.

line to the length of the longest name, if necessary. This will be needed if the heading is shorter than the length of the longest name plus the allowance of 7 characters for the item name.[10] Once we have calculated the length of that padding (if any), we construct it and add it to the end of the heading so far. Then we add the "Category" heading to the heading line. Now the heading is finished, so we write it to cout. Finally, we call SelectItem to allow the user to select an item, and return the result of that call to the calling function.

This function was the stimulus for a discussion of software development issues between Susan and me.

**Susan:** That sure is a lot of work just to handle item names of different lengths. Wouldn't it be simpler to assume a certain maximum size?

**Steve:** We'd still have to pad all the names before tacking the category on; the only simplification would be in the creation of the header, so it wouldn't really make the function much simpler.

**Susan:** What would happen if we had such a long name or category that the line wouldn't fit on the screen?

**Steve:** That's a very good question. In that case, the display would be messed up. However, I don't think that's very likely because the user probably wouldn't want to type in such a long name or category.

10. By the way, neglecting the possibility that the heading is already long enough is what caused the "virtual memory exceeded" error message in an earlier version of this program. The problem was that the length of the padding was calculated as a negative value. However, operator new can't handle negative values, considering them to be very large positive values. Therefore, when I asked it to allocate (for example) -3 characters of memory, it tried to give me approximately 4 billion bytes. That exceeds the maximum amount this compiler can handle, so I got an error message.

**Susan:** Okay. Now I have another question. If we were printing a report of all these items and categories, would each page line up differently from the others if it had a longer or shorter name length?

**Steve:** Well, so far we haven't implemented a report like that. However, if we did, each page would line up the same on any particular report because we go through the whole list to find the longest name. On the other hand, if we ran the report several times down with different data, it is possible that the longest name would be of a different length in each report, so the columns wouldn't line up the same between reports.

**Susan:** So there really isn't any cut and dried way to make these decisions?

**Steve:** No, I'm afraid not. That's why they pay me the (relatively) big bucks as a software developer. I have to laugh whenever I see ads for "automatic bug-finder" software, especially when it claims to be able to find design flaws automatically. How does it know what problem I'm trying to solve?

The final function in this class is DeleteItem, whose code is shown in Figure 6.26.

**FIGURE 6.26. The** DeleteItem **function (from code\hmin8.cc)**

```
void HomeInventory::DeleteItem(short Index)
{
  short ItemCount = m_Home.size();

  for (short i = Index; i < ItemCount-1; i ++)
   m_Home[i] = m_Home[i+1];

  m_Home.resize(ItemCount-1);
}
```

This is a simple function. Starting at the item to be deleted, it moves all of the items after that point one position closer to the beginning of the inventory list and then reduces the size of the list by one. This effectively eliminates the selected item from the inventory.

## *Homing In*

Now it's time to return to the HomeItem class. Luckily, the changes here are much smaller than the changes to the HomeInventory class. In fact, only one new function as been added to the HomeItem interface since the last version we looked at, hmit6.h. That function is GetCategory, whose base class version simply calls the derived class function of the same name, which merely returns the value of the m_Category variable in the item. We've seen enough of this type of function, so we won't bother going over it further.

However, some of the functions have changed in implementation, so we should take a look at them. We'll start with the only function declared in hmit8.h whose implementation has changed: operator >>, the code for which is shown in Figure 6.27.

**FIGURE 6.27. The new** operator >> **implementation (from code\hmit8.cc)**

```
istream& operator >> (istream& is, HomeItem& Item)
{
 string Type;
 bool Interactive = (&is == &cin);
 HomeItem Temp;

 Item = HomeItem();

 while (Type == "")
  {
  if (Interactive)
   {
   cout << "Type (Basic(B), Music(M)) ";
```

```
    cout << "or hit ENTER to exit: ";
    is >> Type;
    if (Type == "")
      return is;
    }
  else
    is >> Type;

  if (is.fail() != 0)
    return is;
  }

if (Type.find_nocase("B") == 0)
  {
  // set type of Temp to Basic object, to be filled in
  Temp = HomeItem("",0.0,0,"","");
  }
else if (Type.find_nocase("M") == 0)
  {
  // set type of Temp to Music object, to be filled in
  Temp = HomeItem("",0.0,0,"","","",vector<string>(0));
  }
else
  {
  string Message = "Bad object type: ";
  Message = Message + Type;
  HomeUtility::HandleError(Message);
  return is;
  }

Temp.Read(is);
Item = Temp;

if (is.fail() != 0)
  HomeUtility::HandleError("Couldn't create object");

return is;
}
```

This function isn't too different from the last version we saw (Figure 4.33). The differences are as follows:

1. We are allowing the user to hit ENTER to exit from this function without having to define a new item. This is useful when the user decides not to create a new item after selecting the "Add Item" function.

2. We are requiring only the first letter of the type rather than the whole type name. We are also allowing either upper- or lower-case versions of the type letter.

3. We are using the HandleError function to display the error message indicating that the object type was invalid.

4. If the data for the object cannot be read from the input stream, we are displaying a message telling the user about that problem.

Now let's move on to the changes to the HomeItemMusic class implementation. We'll start with the Edit function, whose code is shown in Figure 6.28.

**FIGURE 6.28. The latest version of the** HomeItemBasic::Edit **function (from code\hmit8.cc)**

```
void HomeItemBasic::Edit()
{
  short FieldNumber;
  bool result;

  FormattedDisplay(cout);
  cout << endl;

  cout << "Please enter field number to be changed " <<
    "or ENTER for none: ";

  FieldNumber = HomeUtility::GetNumberOrEnter();

  cout << endl;
```

```
  if (FieldNumber == -1)
    return;

  EditField(FieldNumber);
}
```

This function differs from the previous version (Figure 4.41) only in its improved flexibility and error checking. Rather than simply asking the user to enter a field number and then assuming that the field number entered is valid, we use the GetNumberOrEnter function to allow the user to enter a field number or to just hit the ENTER key to indicate that he or she has decided not to edit a field after all. Once we have received the return value from the GetNumberOrEnter function, we check to see whether it is the special value -1, which indicates that the user has decided not to enter a number but has just hit the ENTER key. If this is the case, we simply return to the calling function without calling EditField to do the actual field modification. Otherwise, we call EditField to modify the selected field and return when it is finished.

The next function in the HomeItemBasic class we will cover is ReadInteractive, whose code is shown in Figure 6.29.

**FIGURE 6.29. The newest version of** HomeItemBasic::ReadInteractive **(from code\hmit8.cc)**

```
short HomeItemBasic::ReadInteractive()
{
  double PurchasePrice;
  long PurchaseDate;
  bool result;

  short FieldNumber = e_Name;

  cout << FieldNumber << ". ";
  cout << GetFieldName(FieldNumber) << ": ";
```

```
FieldNumber ++;
cin >> m_Name;

cout << FieldNumber << ". ";
cout << GetFieldName(FieldNumber) << " (xxx.xx with no $ or ,): ";
FieldNumber ++;
cin >> PurchasePrice;
result = HomeUtility::CheckNumericInput();
if (result == true)
  m_PurchasePrice = PurchasePrice;
else
  {
  m_Name = "";
  return 0;
  }

cout << FieldNumber << ". ";
cout << GetFieldName(FieldNumber) << " (YYYYMMDD): ";
FieldNumber ++;
cin >> PurchaseDate;
result = HomeUtility::CheckDateInput(PurchaseDate);
if (result == true)
  m_PurchaseDate = PurchaseDate;
else
  {
  m_Name = "";
  return 0;
  }

cout << FieldNumber << ". ";
cout << GetFieldName(FieldNumber) << ": ";
FieldNumber ++;
cin >> m_Description;

cout << FieldNumber << ". ";
cout << GetFieldName(FieldNumber) << ": ";
FieldNumber ++;
cin >> m_Category;
```

```
  *this = HomeItemBasic(m_Name, m_PurchasePrice,
  m_PurchaseDate, m_Description, m_Category);

  return FieldNumber;
}
```

The only difference between this version of the ReadInteractive function and the one in Figure 4.38 is its improved error checking and feedback to the user. In addition to checking the validity of numbers and dates entered by the user, this new version also tells the user what sort of input is expected. In particular, it tells the user to type in the purchase price without using a $ or comma — it's entirely possible that the user might not realize that using these symbols would cause a problem in interpreting the value. This version also tells the user to type the date in the form YYYYMMDD rather than in a more familiar format such as MM/DD/YY. After telling the user how to enter these data items, it tries to check that the values entered for those items are reasonable. This is a much safer approach than assuming that these values must be all right, as the previous version of the function did.

The changes to the next function we will cover, EditItem (Figure 6.30), are very similar to those in the previous function. To be precise, they consist of more error checking. These changes should be obvious enough that we don't have to discuss them.

**FIGURE 6.30. The new version of the HomeItemBasic::EditItem function (from code\hmit8.cc)**

```
bool HomeItemBasic::EditField(short FieldNumber)
{
 bool result = true;
 double PurchasePrice;
 long PurchaseDate;

 switch (FieldNumber)
  {
  case e_Name:
```

```
cout << FieldNumber << ". ";
cout << GetFieldName(FieldNumber) << ": ";
cin >> m_Name;
break;

case e_PurchasePrice:
cout << FieldNumber << ". ";
cout << GetFieldName(FieldNumber) << ": ";
cin >> PurchasePrice;
result = HomeUtility::CheckNumericInput();
if (result == true)
  m_PurchasePrice = PurchasePrice;
break;

case e_PurchaseDate:
cout << FieldNumber << ". ";
cout << GetFieldName(FieldNumber) << ": ";
cin >> PurchaseDate;
result = HomeUtility::CheckDateInput(PurchaseDate);
if (result == true)
  m_PurchaseDate = PurchaseDate;
break;

case e_Description:
cout << FieldNumber << ". ";
cout << GetFieldName(FieldNumber) << ": ";
cin >> m_Description;
break;

case e_Category:
cout << FieldNumber << ". ";
cout << GetFieldName(FieldNumber) << ": ";
cin >> m_Category;
break;

default:
cout << endl;
HomeUtility::HandleError("Sorry, that is not a valid field number");
result = false;
```

```
    break;
    }

  return result;
}
```

The two functions in the HomeItemMusic class, ReadInteractive and EditField, that have changed from the previous versions follow the changes that we have just looked at very closely, so I will list them without further comment.

**FIGURE 6.31. The latest version of HomeItemMusic::ReadInteractive (from code\hmit8.cc)**

```
short HomeItemMusic::ReadInteractive()
{
  short TrackCount;
  bool result;

  short FieldNumber = HomeItemBasic::ReadInteractive();

  // Check whether Basic input worked. If not, forget it.
  if (FieldNumber == 0)
    return 0;

  cout << FieldNumber << ". ";
  cout << GetFieldName(FieldNumber) << ": ";
  FieldNumber ++;
  cin >> m_Artist;

  cout << FieldNumber << ". ";
  cout << GetFieldName(FieldNumber) << ": ";
  FieldNumber ++;
  cin >> TrackCount;
  result = HomeUtility::CheckNumericInput();
  if (result == true)
    m_Track.resize(TrackCount);
  else
```

```
    {
    m_Name = "";
    return 0;
    }

  vector<string> Track(TrackCount);
  for (short i = 0; i < TrackCount; i ++)
    {
    cout << FieldNumber << ". ";
    cout << GetFieldName(FieldNumber) << i + 1 << ": ";
    FieldNumber ++;
    cin >> Track[i];
    }

  *this = HomeItemMusic(m_Name, m_PurchasePrice,
  m_PurchaseDate, m_Description, m_Category, m_Artist,
  Track);

  return FieldNumber;
}
```

**FIGURE 6.32. The latest version of** HomeItemMusic::EditField **(from code\hmit8.cc)**

```
bool HomeItemMusic::EditField(short FieldNumber)
{
  if (FieldNumber < e_Artist)
    {
    return HomeItemBasic::EditField(FieldNumber);
    }

  bool result;

  short TrackCount = m_Track.size();

  switch (FieldNumber)
    {
    case e_Artist:
```

```
    cout << FieldNumber << ". ";
    cout << GetFieldName(FieldNumber) << ": ";
    cin >> m_Artist;
    return true;

    case e_TrackCount:
    cout << FieldNumber << ". ";
    cout << GetFieldName(FieldNumber) << ": ";
    cin >> TrackCount;
    result = HomeUtility::CheckNumericInput();
    if (result == true)
      m_Track.resize(TrackCount);
    return result;
    }

  if (FieldNumber > (e_TrackCount + TrackCount))
    {
    HomeUtility::HandleError("Sorry, that is not a valid field number");
    return false;
    }

  cout << FieldNumber << ". ";
  cout << GetFieldName(FieldNumber);
  cout << FieldNumber - e_TrackCount << ": ";

  cin >> m_Track[FieldNumber - e_TrackNumber];

  return true;
}
```

## *Are We Having Fun Yet?*

If nothing else, I hope that this exercise has given you a better appreciation of the difficulty of programming a solution to even an apparently simple problem in the real world. After reviewing what we've covered in the chapter, we'll get to some exercises that will give you an even better idea of how much work programming can be![11]

## *Review*

We started this chapter with our work cut out for us: The program was performing as intended, so we just had to go over exactly how it worked. We started with the new main function, which consists of two consecutive "endless" loops (loops that execute until a particular criterion is met). The first loop keeps executing as long as the user is still entering, modifying, or examining the data in the inventory. When the user is finished, the only remaining question is whether he or she wants to save the changes, so the code in the second loop is designed to find the answer to that question and either save or discard the changes as desired.

The main work of the program is done inside the first loop, which consists of a call to the GetMenuChoice function to find out which operation the user wants to perform, followed by a call to the ExecuteMenuChoice function to execute that operation. When the user selects the "exit" operation, this loop terminates and allows the second loop to start execution.

The GetMenuChoice function is fairly simple, but it uses some functions we hadn't seen previously, including the clrscr function, which clears the screen, the GetCount function, which returns the number of items in the inventory, and the HandleError function of the HomeUtility class.

Once the GetMenuChoice function has determined which operation the user wants to perform, the ExecuteMenuChoice function takes over to execute it. It does this with a switch statement that

11. I'm sure you're just brimming with excitement at that thought, but please try to hold yourself back until you have read the review, so you don't lose track of what we've already covered in this chapter.

contains one case for each possible operation. All of these cases are fairly similar. The main task of each of them is to request any information that might be required from the user, to display a heading telling the user what operation is in progress, and then to call a function in the Inventory class to do the actual work. If the operation results in a change to the database, the resulting inventory is saved in a backup file so that it can be recovered in the event of a power failure or other crash. Because of the similarity of the code in each of these cases, we won't review them further. Instead, we will proceed to the functions of the HomeUtility class, starting with a very simple function, IgnoreTillCR. As its name suggests, this function ignores characters until it gets to a "carriage return"[12], which is generated when the ENTER key is struck. The next function is HandleError, which is used to display an error message and wait for the user to hit ENTER.

The next function in this class is CheckNumericInput, which is intended to be called after every numeric input operation. It determines whether the previous input operation was successful by looking to see whether the next character waiting in the input stream is a newline. If so, all of the characters up to that point have been accepted by the input operator as part of a numeric value, which means that the user didn't type anything that shouldn't be in a number. In that case, the function returns the value true to its caller to indicate success. However, if the next character in the input stream isn't a newline, the user must have included some inappropriate character(s) in the input. In that case, this function displays the leftover characters and returns the value false to the calling function to inform it of the error.

The next function we discussed is HomeUtility::CheckDateInput, which first calls CheckNumericInput to make sure that the user hasn't inserted any odd characters into the date value being typed in. Then it checks the value of the date to make sure that it is believable: Our definition of that characteristic is on or after January 1st, 1800, or 0.

12. This character is also known as "newline".

Of course, 0 is not a valid date; however, we need some way for the user to say, "I don't know when I acquired this object", and 0 is as good a way as any to say that.

The next function in the HomeUtility class, GetNumberOrEnter, is considerably more complicated than the other functions in that class, as it has the more complex task of taking input from the user one keystroke at a time. This function actually has two "modes" of operation. In the first mode, it accepts only digits, ENTER, and the backspace key, which is used for correcting errors; in the second mode, it also accepts the up and down arrow keys — this mode is used when the user wants to select an item from a list via the SelectItem function. While going through this function, we ran into several new constructs, the most significant being the getkey function (left over from C) that allows us to read one key from the keyboard without having to wait for the user to hit the ENTER key, as is necessary when we use the standard C++ stream input functions. In addition to getkey, we also discussed the symbols that represent the special keys, such as backspace and newline; these keys have to be handled differently from the "normal" digit keys in this function. We also saw that it is necessary to copy the key value from an int to a char variable before displaying it on the screen if we want it to come out in the proper format. Sending an int to cout via operator << will display the numeric value of the int, which in this case would not be informative to the user who is expecting to see the key he or she just pressed!

After we covered the details of this GetNumberOrEnter function, including the way in which it handles the backspace key so that the user can back up and change the value of the number, we moved on to the relatively simple HomeUtility::ClearRestOfScreen function, which is used by SelectItem to erase the part of the screen it uses to display its list of items. Even though this ClearRestOfScreen function isn't very complicated, it deserved some discussion because it was the first one where we used several of the screen-handling functions from the conio (console I/O) library: gotoxy, clreol, and ScreenRows. The gotoxy function, as its name suggests, allows us to position the "cursor" (the place where the next character will be written on the screen) to a particular X and Y coordinate: X is the column number and Y is the row number. Unusually for C or C++, this function starts counting at 1; that is, the first row and first column are numbered 1 rather than 0. The clreol function erases some or all of the characters on the line where the cursor is currently located, from the cursor's position rightward to the end of the line. The ScreenRows function tells us the number of lines on the screen, which we need so we will know where to stop clearing lines.

HomeUtility::SelectItem, the next function we discussed, is responsible for allowing the user to select from a list of items. It has two arguments: Number, a vector of indexes into the inventory list of the items to be displayed, and Name, a vector of textual information about each of those items. The latter vector always includes the names of the items and sometimes contains additional information about them (e.g., the category under which each item is found).

The first thing we do in this function is determine the number of lines on the "screen" in the DOS window in which our program is running, as well as how many lines have already been used by the calling program. The former information is accessible via the GetScreenRows function, which we've already discussed; the latter information is available via the GetCursor function, which tells us the row and column where the cursor is currently positioned. We can use this information and the number of items to be displayed to determine how much screen area we will devote to the "scroll area", which is where we display the listing of data items from which the user selects an individual item to be edited.[13]

Once we have decided how many lines we will use for the scroll area, we check how many items the calling function has provided. If this is less than the number of lines allocated for the scroll area, we

13. In the version of the program on the CD at the back of the book, the maximum size of the scroll area is fixed at 5, as this makes debugging the program easier. However, you are free to change that so it will use more of the screen. Personally, I like it the way it is.

reduce the size of the scroll area to match. If there are no items in the input vector, we give an error message to the user telling him or her that information.

After we know how many items we will display at one time, we start by displaying the first part of the item list. Once we have cleared the portion of the screen where we will display the list, we display each of the elements in this part of the list, using fixed-width formatting for the item number to ensure that all of the item names line up correctly. After displaying the list, we ask the user to type in one of the listed item numbers, via GetNumberOrEnter. Besides an item number, the user can hit the up or down arrow to ask us to scroll the item list up or down. The user can also hit the ENTER key to end input or the backspace key to correct an erroneous entry. If the user simply hits ENTER, or erases all the digits that were typed in by using the backspace key, we get a return value from GetNumberOrEnter that indicates this. In that event, we return the value 0 to our calling function to indicate that the user hasn't selected an item.

On the other hand, if the user hasn't simply hit ENTER, we have to check the return value from GetNumberOrEnter to see what the user has done. If that return value is one of the arrow keys, we adjust the portion of the list to be displayed and continue. Otherwise, we must have received an actual numeric value from the user. In that case, we check that this value is a valid entry in the list of item numbers from which the user was selecting. If so, we are finished, and we return that value to the calling function. If it is not an item number from the list, we tell the user about this error and return 0 to the calling function to indicate that the user has not made a valid selection.

After dealing with that final function in the HomeUtility class, we moved on to the changes in the HomeInventory class. These changes weren't too extensive, primarily consisting of better error checking and sorting of the inventory list by the name of the item. Other changes included the ability of the "locate" functions to return a vector of item indexes rather than just one, the addition of functions to locate items by their category fields, and the ability to print items or item names. The most complicated function in this new version of the class, besides the sorting function, is SelectItemFromCategoryList, because it uses some fairly fancy formatting to get the category information to line up correctly. The main complexity is caused by the necessity to pad the item names to a consistent length so that the category information will start in the same column on the screen for each item no matter how long its name may be. Because we don't know how long the longest name will be until we have examined all the names, we have to make two passes through the list. The first pass finds the length of the longest name, and the second pass pads each name to that length. Once we have done this, we add the category name for each item to the end of the entry for that item. After we have created and displayed the heading, we call the SelectItem function to allow the user to select one of the items.

The final function in the HomeInventory class that we discussed is DeleteItem, which deletes an item from the inventory list. Starting at the item to be deleted, it moves all of the items after that point one position closer to the beginning of the inventory list; then it reduces the size of the list by one. This effectively eliminates the selected item from the inventory.

The changes to the HomeItem class were relatively small. We modified the implementation of operator >> to allow the user to hit ENTER to avoid entering an item, to allow the user to enter only the first letter of the type rather than having to type "Basic" or "Music", and to improve error handling. The changes in the HomeItemBasic and HomeItemMusic classes consisted of simple improvements to error handling and flexibility in user input, so they didn't require any additional discussion.

## *Exercises*

1. Add the ability to edit an existing description field. Which classes will have to be changed to do this?

2. Before writing over the old version of the data base at the conclusion of the program, copy that file to another name so that the user can go back to it if necessary.
3. At present, the ExecuteMenuChoice function always saves the inventory in the backup file after calling AddItem. This is not necessary if the user didn't actually add a new item. Fix the code so that this unnecessary operation is avoided.
4. Add the ability for the user to see only items of a given type, such as "Basic" or "Music", rather than having to see all types together in one list.
5. Change the data entry function so that the user can correct an entry and continue entering data for an item even after making an error.
6. Add validation of dates so that invalid dates such as 19970231 are not accepted.
7. Allow the user to type dates with or without slashes so that 1997/02/28 will be the same as 19970228.
8. Add the ability for the user to print selected items according to category, description, and the like.
9. Explain why hitting the ENTER key when asked for a category produces a list including all categories.
10. Implement the HomeItemCollectible class as a derived class of HomeItemBasic to keep track of objects such as coins or stamps. The added fields should include date of creation, condition, artist, and any other appropriate fields.

## *Conclusion*

If you've made it this far, congratulations! You have truly begun to understand the complexities of C++ in particular and software development in general. At this point, you should be able to read almost any book on software development in C++ with profit and understanding.

CHAPTER 7

# *Tying up Loose Ends*

## *Where Am I, Anyway?*

Now that you've reached the end of this book, some questions have probably occurred to you. For example:

1. Am I a programmer now?
2. What am I qualified to do?
3. Where do I go from here?
4. Is that all there is to C++?

The answer to the first three questions, as usual with such open-ended topics, is "It all depends". Of course, I can give you some general answers. Let's start with questions 1 and 2.

If you have done all of the exercises in this book, you certainly have earned the right to call yourself a programmer — you've read quite a bit of code and have written some nontrivial programs. But, of course, this doesn't mean that you're a professional programmer. No book (or series of two books) can turn a novice into a professional —

in any field. That takes a lot of hard work, and although you've undoubtedly worked hard in understanding this book and applying your understanding to the exercises, you still have a lot to learn about programming.

Questions 3 and 4 are also closely related. You now have enough background that you should be able to get some benefit from a well-written book about C++ that assumes you are already acquainted with programming; that would be a good way to continue. As for whether we've covered everything about C++, the answer is unequivocal: absolutely not. Including the prerequisites for this book, I would estimate that you are now familiar with perhaps 10% of the very large, complicated, and powerful C++ language; however, that 10% is the foundation for the rest of your learning in this subject. Most books try to cover every aspect of the language and, as a result, cannot provide the deep coverage of fundamentals. I've worked very hard to ensure that you have the correct tools to continue your learning.

Good luck with your future exploration of C++.

# *Glossary*

## *Special Characters*

**&** has a number of distinct meanings. When it precedes the name of a variable without following a type name, it means "the address of the following variable". For example, &Str means "the address of the variable Str". When & follows a type name and precedes a variable name, it means that the variable being declared is a reference — that is, another name for a preexisting variable. In this book, references are used only in argument lists, where they indicate that the variable being defined is a new name for the caller's variable rather than a new local variable.

% is the "modulus" operator, which returns the remainder after dividing its left-hand argument by its right-hand argument.

< is the "less than" operator, which returns the value true if the expression on its left has a lower value than the expression on its right; otherwise, it returns the value false. Also see *operator <* in the index.

**=** is the assignment operator, which assigns the value on its right to the variable on its left. Also see *operator =* in the index.

**>** is the "greater than" operator, which returns the value true if the expression on its left has a greater value than the expression on its right; otherwise, it returns the value false. Also see *operator >* in the index.

**[** is the left square bracket; see *square brackets* for usage.

**]** is the right square bracket; see *square brackets* for usage.

**{** is the left curly brace; see *curly braces* for usage.

**}** is the right curly brace; see *curly braces* for usage.

**!=** is the "not equals" operator, which returns the value true if the expression on its left has a value different from the expression on its right; otherwise, it returns the value false. Also see *operator !=* in the index.

**&&** is the "logical AND" operator. It produces the result true if the expressions on both its right and left are true; if either of those expressions is false, it produces the result false. However, this isn't the whole story. There is a special rule in C++ governing the execution of the && operator: If the expression on the left is false, then the answer must be false and the expression on the right is not executed at all. The reason for this *short-circuit evaluation rule* is that in some cases you may want to write a right-hand expression that will only be legal if the left-hand expression is false.

**++** is the increment operator, which adds 1 to the variable to which it is affixed.

**+=** is the "add to variable" operator, which adds the value on its right to the variable on its left.

**-=** is the "subtract from variable" operator, which subtracts the value on its right from the variable on its left.

**//** is the comment operator; see *comment* for usage.

**<<** is the "stream output" operator, used to write data to an ostream. Also see *operator* << in the index.

**<=** is the "less than or equal to" operator, which returns the value true if the expression on its left has the same or a lower value than that of the expression on its right; otherwise, it returns the value false. Also see *operator* <= in the index.

**==** is the "equals" operator, which returns the value true if the expression on its left has the same value as that of the expression on its right; otherwise, it returns the value false. Also see *operator* == in the index.

**>=** is the "greater than or equal to" operator, which returns the value true if the expression on its left has the same or a greater value than that of the expression on its right; otherwise, it returns the value false. Also see *operator* >= in the index.

**>>** is the "stream input" operator, used to read data from an istream. Also see *operator* >> in the index.

**[ ]** is used after the delete operator to tell the compiler that the pointer for which delete was called refers to a group of elements rather than just one data item. This is one of the few times when we have to make that distinction explicitly rather than leaving it to context.

|| is the "logical OR" operator. It produces the result true if at least one of the two expressions on its right and left is true; if both expressions are false, it produces the result false. However, there is a special rule in C++ governing the execution of the || operator: If the expression on the left is true, then the answer must be true and the expression on the right is not executed at all. The reason for this *short-circuit evaluation* rule is that in some cases you may want to write a right-hand expression that will only be legal if the left-hand expression is false.

A **#define** statement is a *preprocessor directive* that defines a *preprocessor symbol.* While this statement can be used to define constant values for general use, it has been mostly superseded except as part of the *include guard* mechanism.

An **#endif** statement is a *preprocessor directive* that terminates a section of conditional code. It is used in this book as part of the *include guard* mechanism.

An **#ifdef** statement is a *preprocessor directive* that begins a section of conditional code.

An **#ifndef** statement is a *preprocessor directive* that tells the preprocessor to check whether a particular *preprocessor symbol* has been defined. If not, the following source code is treated normally. However, if the specified preprocessor symbol has been defined, the following source code is skipped by the rest of the compiler as though it were not present in the source file. The #ifndef statement is used in this book as part of the *include guard* mechanism.

An **#include** statement is a *preprocessor directive* that has the same effect as that of copying all of the code from a specified file into another file at the point where the #include statement is written. For example, if we wanted to use definitions contained in a file called iostream.h in the implementation file test.cc, we could insert the include statement #include <iostream.h> in test.cc rather than physically copying the lines from the file iostream.h into test.cc.

## *A*

An **access specifier** controls the access of nonmember functions to the member functions and variables of a class. The C++ access specifiers are public, private, and protected. See *public*, *private*, and *protected* for details. Also see *friend*.

**Access time** is a measure of how long it takes to retrieve data from a storage device, such as a hard disk or RAM.

**Address**; see *memory address*.

An **algorithm** is a set of precisely defined steps guaranteed to arrive at an answer to a problem or set of problems. As this implies, a set of steps that might never end is not an algorithm.

**Aliasing** is the practice of referring to one object by more than one "name"; in C++, these names are actually pointers.

The **aliasing problem** is a name for the difficulties that are caused by altering a shared object.

An **application program** is a program that actually accomplishes some useful or interesting task. Examples include inventory control, payroll, and games.

An **application programmer** (or *class user*) is a programmer who uses native and class variables to write an application program. Also see *library designer*.

An **argument** is a value supplied by one function (the *calling function*) that wishes to make use of the services of another function (the *called function*). There are two main types of argument: *value arguments*, which are copies of the values from the calling function, and *reference arguments*, which are not copies but actually refer to variables in the calling function.

An **argument list** is a set of argument definitions specified in a function declaration. The argument list describes the types and names of all the variables the function receives when it is called by a calling function.

An **array** is a group of elements of the same type — for example, an array of chars. The array name corresponds to the address of the first of these elements; the other elements follow the first one immediately in memory. As with a vector, we can refer to the individual elements by their indexes. Thus, if we have an array of chars called m_Data, m_Data[i] refers to the ith char in the array. Also see *pointer*, *vector*.

An **array initialization list** is a list of values used to initialize the elements of an *array*. The ability to specify a list of values for an array is built into the C++ language and is not available for user-defined data types such as the vector.

The **ASCII code** is a standardized representation of characters by binary or hexadecimal values. For example, the letter "A" is represented as a char with the hexadecimal value 41, and the digit 0 is represented as a char with the hexadecimal value 30. All other printable characters also have representations in the ASCII code.

An **assembler** is a program that translates *assembly language* instructions into *machine instructions*.

An **assembly language** instruction is the human-readable representation of a *machine instruction*.

**Assignment** is the operation of setting a variable to a value. The operator that indicates assignment is the equal sign, =. Also see *operator* = in the index.

An **assignment operator** is a function that sets a preexisting variable to a value of the same type. There are three varieties of assignment operators:

1. For a variable of a native type, the compiler supplies a native assignment operator.
2. For a variable of a class type, the compiler generates its own version of an assignment operator (a compiler-generated assignment operator) if the class writer does not write one.
3. The class writer can write a member function to do the assignment; see *operator* = in the index.

An **assignment statement** such as $x = 5;$ is not an algebraic equality, no matter how much it may resemble one. It is a command telling the compiler to assign a value to a variable. In the example, the variable is $x$ and the value is $5$.

The **auto storage class** is the default *storage class* for variables declared within C++ functions. When we define a variable of the auto storage class, its memory address is assigned automatically upon entry to the function where it is defined; the memory address is valid for the duration of that function.

**Automatic conversion** is a feature of C++ that allows an expression of one type to be used where another type is expected. For example, a short variable or expression can be provided when an int expression is expected, and the compiler will convert the type of the expression automatically.

## *B*

**Base class**: see *inheritance*.

A **base class initializer** specifies which base class constructor we want to use to initialize the base class part of a derived class object. It is one of the two types of expression allowed in a *member initialization list*. Also see *inheritance*.

The **base class part** of a derived class object is an unnamed component of the derived class object whose member variables and functions are accessible as though they were defined in the derived class, so long as they are either public or protected.

A **batch file** is a text file that directs the execution of a number of programs, one after the other, without manual intervention. A similar facility is available in most operating systems.

A **binary** number system uses only two digits, 0 and 1.

A **bit** is the fundamental unit of storage in a modern computer; the word *bit* is derived from the phrase *binary digit*. Each bit, as this suggests, can have one of two states: 0 and 1.

A **block** is a group of statements considered as one logical statement. It is delimited by the curly braces, { and }. The first of these symbols starts a block, and the second one ends it. A block can be used anywhere that a statement can be used and is treated exactly as if it were one statement. For example, if a block is the controlled block of an if statement, all of the statements in the block are executed if the condition in the if is true, and none is executed if the condition in the if is false.

A **bool** (short for Boolean) is a type of variable whose range of values is limited to true or false. This is the most appropriate return type for a function that uses its *return value* to report whether some condition exists, such as operator <. In that particular case, the return value true indicates that the first argument is less than the second, while false indicates that the first argument is not less than the second.

**Brace**; see *curly braces.*

A **break statement** is a loop control device that interrupts the processing of a loop whenever it is executed within the controlled block of a loop control statement. When a break statement is executed, the flow of control passes to the next statement after the end of the controlled block.

A **buffer** is a temporary holding place where information is stored while it is being manipulated.

**Buffering** is the process of using a buffer to store or retrieve information.

A **byte** is the unit in which data capacities are stated, whether in RAM or on a disk. In modern computers, a byte consists of eight bits.

## *C*

A **C function** is one that is inherited from the *C library.* Because C does not have a number of features that have been added in C++, such as *function overloading* and *reference arguments*, C functions must often be called in different ways from those we use when calling a C++ function.

The **C library** is a collection of functions that were originally written for users of the C programming language. Because C++ is a descendant of C, these functions are often still useful in C++ programs.

A **C string** is a literal value representing a variable number of characters. An example is "This is a test.". C strings are surrounded by double quotes ("). Please note that this is *not* the same as the C++ string class.

A **cache** is a small amount of fast memory where frequently used data is stored temporarily.

**Call**; see *function call* or *call instruction*.

A **call instruction** is an *assembly language* instruction used to implement a *function call*. It saves the *program counter* on the stack and then transfers execution from the *calling function* to the *called function*.

A **called function** is a function that starts execution as the result of a *function call*. Normally, it returns to the *calling function* via a *return statement* when finished.

A **calling function** is a function that suspends execution as a result of a *function call*; the *called function* begins execution at the point of the function call.

The **carriage return** character is used to signal the end of a line of text. Also see *newline* in the index.

A function is said to be **case-sensitive** if upper- and lower-case letters are considered to be distinct.

A function is said to be **case-insensitive** if upper- and lower-case letters are considered equivalent. See *less_nocase* in the index.

A **char** is an *integer variable* type that can represent either one character of text or a small whole number. Both signed and unsigned chars are available for use as "really short" *integer variables*; a signed char can represent a number from -128 to +127, whereas an unsigned char can represent a number from 0 to 255. (In case you were wondering, the most common pronunciation of char has an "a" as in "married", while the "ch" sounds like "k". Other pronunciations include the standard English pronunciation of "char" as in overcooking meat, and even "car" as in "automobile".)

A **char*** (pronounced "char star") is a pointer to (i.e., the memory address of) a char or the first of a group of chars.

**Child** class: see *inheritance.*

**cin** (pronounced "see in") is a predefined *istream*; it gets its characters from the keyboard.

A **class** is a user-defined type; for example, string is a class.

A **class designer** is a programmer who designs classes. Also see *application programmer.*

A **class implementation** tells the compiler how to implement the facilities defined in the *class interface*. It is usually found in a implementation file, which the compiler on the CD-ROM in the back of this book assumes has the extension .cc.

A **class interface** tells the user of the class what facilities the class provides by specifying the class's public member functions. It also tells the compiler what data elements are included in objects of the class, but this is not logically part of the interface. A class interface is usually found in a *header file* — that is, one with the extension .h.

The **class membership operator**, **::**, indicates which class a function belongs to. For example, the full name of the default constructor for the string class is string::string().

**class scope** describes the visibility of *member variables* — that is, those defined within a class. These variables can be accessed by any *member function* of that class; their accessibility to other functions is controlled by the *access specifier* in effect when they were defined in the *class interface*.

A **comment** is a note to yourself or another programmer; it is ignored by the compiler. The symbol // marks the beginning of a comment; the comment continues until the end of the line containing the //. For those of you with BASIC experience, this is just like REM (the "remark" keyword) — anything after it on a line is ignored by the compiler.

**Compilation** is the process of translating source code into an object program, which is composed of machine instructions along with the data needed by those instructions. Virtually all of the software on your computer was created by this process.

A **compiler** is a program that performs compilation.

A **compiler-generated function** is supplied by the compiler because the existence of that function is fundamental to the notion of a *concrete data type*. The compiler will automatically generate its own version of any of the following functions if they are not provided by the creator of the class: the *assignment operator*, the *copy constructor*, the *default constructor*, and the *destructor*.

A **compiler warning** is a message from the compiler informing the programmer of a potentially erroneous construct. While a warning does not prevent the compiler from generating an *executable program*, a wise programmer will heed such warnings, as they often reveal hazardous coding practices.

**Compile time** means "while the compiler is compiling the source code of a program".

**Concatenation** is the operation of appending a string to the end of another string. Also see *operator +* in the index.

A **concrete data type** is a class whose objects behave like variables of native data types. That is, the class gives the compiler enough information that objects of that class can be created, copied, assigned, and automatically destroyed, just as native variables are.

The keyword **const** has two distinct meanings as employed in this book. The first is as a modifier to an argument of a function. In this context, it means that we are promising not to modify the value of that argument in the function. An example of this use might be the function declaration `string& operator = (const string& Str);`. The second use of const in this book is to define a data item similar to a variable, except that its value cannot be changed once it has been initialized. For this reason, it is mandatory to supply an initial value when creating a const. An example of this use is `const short x = 5;`.

A **constructor** is a *member function* that creates new objects of a (particular) class type. All constructors have the same name as that of the class for which they are constructors; for example, the constructors for the string class have the name string. A constructor that takes only one required argument is also a *conversion function.*

A **continuation expression** is the part of a for statement computed before every execution of the controlled block. The block controlled by the for will be executed if the result of the computation is true but not if it is false. See *for statement* for an example.

The **continue** keyword causes execution of a for loop to continue to the next iteration without executing any further statements in the current iteration.

A **controlled block** is a block under the control of a loop control statement or an if or else statement. The controlled block of a loop control statement can be executed a variable number of times, whereas the controlled block of an if or else statement is executed either once or not at all.

**Controlled statement**; see *controlled block.*

A **conversion function** is a *member function* that converts an object of its class to some other type, or vice versa. Also see *implicit conversion.*

A **copy constructor** makes a new object with the same contents as an existing object of the same type.

**cout** (pronounced "see out") is a predefined ostream; characters sent to it are displayed on the screen.

**CPU** is an abbreviation for Central Processing Unit. This is the "active" part of your computer, which executes all the *machine instructions* that make the computer do useful work.

The **curly braces { and }** are used to surround a *block*. The compiler treats the statements in the block as one statement.

A **cursor** is an abstract object that represents the position on the screen where input or output will occur next.

## *D*

**Data** refers to the pieces of information that are operated on by programs. Originally, "data" was the plural of "datum"; however, the form "data" is now commonly used as both singular and plural.

A **day number** is an integer value representing the number of days between two dates.

A **debugger** is a program that controls the execution of another program so that you can see what the latter program is doing. The RHIDE development environment on the CD-ROM in the back of this book includes a debugger that will allow you to examine the execution of your programs.

A **dedicated register** is a register such as the *stack pointer* whose usage is predefined rather than determined by the programmer, as in the case of *general registers* such as `eax`.

A **default argument** is a method of specifying a value for an argument to a function when the user of the function doesn't supply a value for that argument. The value of the default argument is specified in the declaration of the function.

A **default constructor** is a *member function* that is used to create an object when no initial value is specified for that object. For example, string::string() is the default constructor for the string class.

The **default** keyword is used with the switch statement to specify an action to be performed when none of the case statements match the selection expression of the switch.

The **delete** operator is used to free memory previously used for variables of the *dynamic storage class*. This allows the memory to be reused for other variables.

**Derived class**: see *inheritance*.

A **destructor** is a *member function* that cleans up when an object expires; for an object of the auto storage class, the destructor is called automatically at the end of the function where that object is defined.

A **digit** is one of the characters used in any positional numbering system to represent all numbers starting at 0 and ending at one less than the base of the numbering system. In the decimal system, there are ten digits, 0 through 9, and in the hexadecimal system, there are sixteen digits, 0 through 9 and "a" through "f".

A **double** is a type of *floating-point variable* that can represent a range of positive and negative numbers, including fractional values. With most current C++ compilers, including DJGPP, these numbers can vary from approximately 4.940656e–324 to approximately 1.79769e+308 (and 0), with approximately 16 digits of precision.

**Dynamic memory allocation** is the practice of assigning memory locations to variables during execution of the program by explicit request of the programmer.

Variables of the **dynamic storage class** are assigned memory addresses at the programmer's explicit request. This storage class is often used for variables whose size is not known until run time.

**Dynamic type checking** refers to checking the correct usage of variables of different types during execution of a program rather than during compilation; see *type system* for further discussion.

**Dynamic typing** means delaying the determination of the exact type of a variable until run time rather than fixing that type at compile time, as in static typing. Please note that dynamic typing is not the same as *dynamic type checking*; C++ has the former but not the latter. See *type system* for further discussion.

## *E*

An **element** is one of the variables that make up a vector or an *array*.

The keyword **else** causes its *controlled block* to be executed if the condition in its matching if statement turns out to be false at run time.

An **empty stack** is a stack that currently contains no values.

**Encapsulation** means hiding the details of a class inside the *implementation* of that class rather than exposing them in the *interface*. This is one of the primary organizing principles of *object-oriented programming*.

An **end user** is the person who actually uses an application program to perform some useful or interesting task. Also see *application programmer*, *library designer*.

The **ENTER** key is the key that generates a *newline* character, which tells an *input* routine that the user has finished entering data.

**Envelope** class; see *manager/worker idiom.*

An **enum** is a way to define a number of unchangeable values, which are quite similar to consts. The value of each successive name in an enum is automatically incremented from the value of the previous name (if you don't specify another value explicitly). The term enum is short for "enumeration", which is a list of numbers.

**Executable**; see *executable program.*

An **executable program** is a program in a form suitable for running on a computer; it is composed of *machine instructions* along with data needed by those instructions.

The **explicit** keyword tells the compiler not to call a specified constructor unless that constructor has been called explicitly. This prevents such a constructor from being called to perform an *implicit conversion.*

## *F*

The keyword **false** is a predefined value representing the result of a conditional expression whose condition is not satisfied. For example, in the conditional expression x < y, if x is not less than y, the result of the expression will be false. Also see bool.

A **fencepost error** is a logical error that causes a loop to be executed one more or one fewer time than the correct count. A common cause of this error is confusing the number of elements in a *vector* or *array* with the index of the last element. The derivation of this term is by analogy with the problem of calculating the number of fence sections and fenceposts that you need for a given fence. For example, if you have to put up a fence 100 feet long and each section of the fence is 10 feet long, how many sections of fence do you need? Obviously, the answer is 10. Now, how many fenceposts do you need? 11. The confusion caused by counting fenceposts when you should be counting segments of fence (and vice versa) is the cause of a fencepost error. To return to a programming example, if you have a vector with 11 elements, the index of the last element is 10, not 11. Confusing the number of elements with the highest index has much the same effect as that of the fencepost problem. This sort of problem is also known, less colorfully, as an *off-by-one error.*

**Field**; see *manipulator.*

A **float** is a type of *floating-point variable* that can represent a range of positive and negative numbers, including fractional values. With most current C++ compilers, including DJGPP, these numbers can vary from approximately 1.401298e−45 to approximately 3.40282e+38 (and 0), with approximately 6 digits of precision.

A **floating-point variable** is a C++ approximation of a mathematical "real number". Unlike mathematical real numbers, C++ floating-point variables have a limited range and precision depending on their types. See the individual types *float* and *double* for details.

A **for** statement is a loop control statement that causes its controlled block to be executed while a specified logical expression (the continuation expression) is true. It also provides for a starting expression to be executed before the first execution of the controlled block and for a modification expression to be executed after every execution of the controlled block. For example, in the for statement for (i = 0; i < 10; i ++), the initialization expression is i = 0, the continuation expression is i < 10, and the modification expression is i ++.

A **form-feed** character, when sent to a printer, causes the paper to be advanced to a new page.

The keyword **friend** allows access by a specified class or function to private or protected members of a particular class.

A **function** is a section of code having a name, optional *arguments*, and a *return type*. The name makes it possible for one function to start execution of another one via a *function call*. The arguments provide input for the function, and the return type allows the function to provide output to its *calling function* when the return statement causes the *calling function* to resume execution.

A **function call** (or *call* for short) causes execution to be transferred temporarily from the current function (the *calling function*) to the one named in the function call (the *called function*). Normally, when a called function is finished with its task, it returns to the calling function, which picks up execution at the statement after the function call.

A **function declaration** tells the compiler some vital statistics of the function: its name, its *arguments*, and its *return type*. Before we can use a function, the compiler must have already seen its function declaration. The most common way to arrange for this is to use a #include statement to insert the function declaration from a *header file* into an *implementation file*.

**Function header**; see *function declaration*.

**Function overloading** is the C++ facility that allows us to create more than one function with the same name. So long as all such functions have different *signatures*, we can write as many of them as we wish and the compiler will be able to figure out which one we mean.

## G

A **general register** is a register whose usage is determined by the programmer, not predefined as with dedicated registers such as the *stack pointer*. On an Intel CPU such as the 486 or Pentium, the 16-bit general registers are ax, bx, cx, dx, si, di, and bp; the 32-bit general registers are eax, ebx, ecx, edx, esi, edi, and ebp.

A **get pointer** holds the address of the next byte in the input area of an istream — that is, where the next byte will be retrieved if we use >> to read data from the stream.

**Global scope** describes the visibility of variables defined outside any function; such variables can be accessed by code in any function. It also describes the visibility of functions defined outside any class.

The **global name space** is a name for the set of identifiers visible to all functions without a class name being specified. Adding identifiers to the global name space should be avoided when possible, as such identifiers can conflict with other similar identifiers defined by other programmers.

A **global function** is a function that has *global scope*.

A **global variable** is a variable that has *global scope*.

## H

**Hardware** refers to the physical components of a computer — the ones you can touch. Examples include the keyboard, the monitor, and the printer.

A **header file** is a file that contains *class interface* definitions and/or *global* function declarations. By convention, header files have the extension .h.

The **heap** is the area of memory where variables of the *dynamic storage class* store their data.

**Hex** is an abbreviation for hexadecimal.

A **hexadecimal** number system has sixteen digits, 0 through 9 and "a" through "f".

## *I*

An **identifier** is a user-defined name; both function names and variable names are identifiers. Identifiers must not conflict with keywords such as if and for; for example, you cannot create a function or a variable with the name for.

An **if** statement is a statement that causes its *controlled block* to be executed if the logical expression specified in the if statement is true.

An **ifstream** (pronounced "i f stream") is a stream used for input from a file.

**Implementation**; see *class implementation.*

An **implementation file** contains *source code statements* that are turned into *executable code* by a *compiler.* In this book, implementation files have the extension .cc.

An **implicit conversion** is one that occurs without the programmer's explicit request. Also see *explicit.*

**Include**; see #include statement.

An **include guard** is a mechanism used to prevent the same class definition from being included in the same source code file more than once.

To **increment** a variable means to add 1 to its value. This can be done in C++ by using the increment operator, ++.

An **index** is an expression used to select one of a number of elements of a vector or an *array*. It is enclosed in square brackets ([ ]). For example, in the expression a[i+1], the index is the expression i+1.

An **index variable** is a variable used to hold an index into a vector or an *array*.

**Inheritance** is the definition of one class as a more specific version of another previously defined class. The newly defined class is called the *derived* (or sometimes the child) class, while the previously defined class is called the *base* (or sometimes the parent) class. In this book, we use the terms *base* and *derived*. The derived class inherits all of the *member variables* and *regular member functions* from the base class. Inheritance is one of the primary organizing principles of *object-oriented programming*.

**Initialization** is the process of setting the initial value of a *variable* or *const*. It is very similar to *assignment* but not identical. Initialization is done only when a variable or const is created, whereas a variable can be assigned to as many times as desired. A const, however, cannot be assigned to at all, so it must be initialized when it is created.

**Input** is the process of reading data into the computer from the outside world. A very commonly used source of input for simple programs is the keyboard.

**Instruction**; see *machine instruction*.

An int (short for *integer*) is a type of *integer variable*. While the C++ language definition requires only that an int be at least as long as a short and no longer than a long, with most current C++ compilers this type is equivalent to either a short or a long, depending on the compiler you are using. A 16-bit compiler such as Borland C++ 3.1 has 16-bit (2-byte) ints that are the same size as shorts. A 32-bit compiler such as DJGPP (the compiler on the CD-ROM that comes with this book) has 32-bit (4-byte) ints that are the same size as longs.

An **integer variable** is a C++ representation of a whole number. Unlike mathematical integers, C++ integers have a limited range, which varies depending on their types. See the individual types char, short, int, and long for details. The type bool is sometimes also considered an integer variable type.

**Interface**; see *class interface*.

**Interface file**; see *header file*.

**Internal polymorphism**; see *polymorphic object*.

**I/O** is an abbreviation for "input/output". This refers to the process of getting information into and out of the computer. See *input* and *output* for more details.

**iostream.h** is the name of the *header file* that tells the compiler how to compile code that uses predefined stream variables like cout and cin and operators like << and >>.

An object of a *derived class* is said to have an "**isA**" relationship with its *base class* if the derived class object can be substituted for a base class object. In C++, objects of publicly derived classes have this relationship with their base classes.

An **istream** is a stream used for input. For example, cin is a predefined istream that reads characters from the keyboard.

## *K*

A **keyword** is a word defined in the C++ language, such as if and for. It is illegal to define an *identifier* such as a variable or function name that conflicts with a keyword; for example, you cannot create a function or a variable with the name for.

## *L*

**Letter class**; see *manager/worker idiom.*

A **library** (or library module) contains the object code generated from several *implementation files*, in a form that the *linker* can search when it needs to find general-purpose functions.

A **library designer** is a programmer who creates classes for *application programmers* to use in writing application programs.

The **linker** is a program that combines information from all of the *object files* for our program, along with some previously prepared files called *libraries*, to produce an *executable program.*

**Linking** is the process of creating an executable program from *object files* and *libraries.*

A **literal value** is a value that doesn't have a name, but instead represents itself in a literal manner. Some examples are 'x' (a char literal having the ASCII value that represents the letter "x") and 5 (a numeric literal with the value 5).

**Local scope** describes the visibility of variables defined within a function; such variables can be accessed only by code in that function.[1]

A **local variable** is a variable that has *local scope.*

A **logical expression** is an expression that takes on the value true or false rather than a numeric value. Some examples of such an expression are x > y (which will be true if x has a greater value than y and false otherwise) and a == b (which will be true if a has the same value as b, and false otherwise). Also see *bool.*

A **long** is a type of *integer variable* that can represent a whole number. With most current C++ compilers, including DJGPP, a long occupies 4 bytes of storage and therefore can represent a number in either the range —2147483648 to 2147483647 (if signed) or the range 0 to 4294967295 (if unsigned).

A **loop** is a means of executing a *controlled block* a variable number of times depending on some condition. The statement that controls the controlled block is called a loop control statement. This book covers the while and for loop control statements. See *while* and *for* for details.

1. In fact, a variable can be declared in any block, not just in a function. In that case, its scope is from the point where it is declared until the end of the block where it is defined. However, in this book all local variables have function scope, so omitting this distinction simplifies the discussion without invalidating the analysis.

A **loop control statement** is a statement that controls the *controlled block* in a loop.

## *M*

**Machine address**; see *memory address.*

**Machine code** is the combination of *machine instructions* and the data they use. A synonym is *object code*.

A **machine instruction** is one of the fundamental operations that a *CPU* can perform. Some examples of these operations are addition, subtraction, or other arithmetic operations; other possibilities include operations that control what instruction will be executed next. All C++ programs must be converted into machine instructions before they can be executed by the CPU.

A **machine language program** is a program composed of *machine instructions.*

A **magic number** is a number that does not have any obvious relationship to the rest of the code. A good general rule is that numbers other than 0, 1, or other self-evident values should be defined as const or enum values rather than as literal values such as '7'.

**Manager object**; see *manager/worker idiom*, *polymorphic objects.*

The **manager/worker idiom** (also known as the envelope/letter idiom) is a mechanism that allows the effective type of an object to be determined at run time without requiring the user of the object to be concerned with pointers. It is used to implement *polymorphic objects* in C++.

A **manipulator** is a member function of one of the iostreams classes that controls how output will be formatted without necessarily producing any output of its own. Manipulators operate on *fields*; a field can be defined as the result of one << operator.

A **member function** is a function defined in a *class interface*. It is viewed as "belonging" to the class, which is the reason for the adjective "member".

A **member initialization expression** is the preferred method of specifying how a *member variable* is to be initialized in a *constructor*. Also see *inheritance*.

A **member initialization list** specifies how *member variables* are to be initialized in a *constructor*. It includes two types of expressions: *base class initializers* and *member initialization expressions*. Also see *inheritance*.

A **member variable** is a variable defined in a *class interface*. It is viewed as "belonging" to the class, which is the reason for the adjective "member".

**Memberwise copy** means to copy every *member variable* from the source object to the destination object. If we don't define our own *copy constructor* or *assignment operator* for a particular class, the *compiler-generated* versions will use memberwise copy.

A **memory address** is a unique number identifying a particular byte of *RAM*.

A **memory hierarchy** is the particular arrangement of the different kinds of storage devices in a given computer. The purpose of using storage devices having different performance characteristics is to provide the best overall performance at the lowest cost.

A **memory leak** is a programming error in which the programmer forgot to delete something that had been dynamically allocated. Such an error is very insidious because the program appears to work correctly when tested casually. The usual way to find these errors is to notice that the program runs apparently correctly for a (possibly long) time and then fails because it runs out of available memory.

A **modification expression** is the part of a for statement executed after every execution of the *controlled block*. It is often used to increment an *index variable* to refer to the next element of an *array* or vector; see *for statement* for an example.

**Modulus operator**; see *%*.

A **month number** is an integer value representing the number of months between two dates.

## *N*

A **nanosecond** is one-billionth of a second.

A **native data type** is one defined in the C++ language, as opposed to a *user-defined data type* (class).

The **new operator** is used to allocate memory for variables of the *dynamic storage class*; these are usually variables whose storage requirements may not be known until the program is executing.

The **newline** character is the C++ character used to indicate the end of a line of text.

**Nondisplay character**; see *nonprinting character.*

A **nonmember function** is one that is not a member of a particular class being discussed, although it may be a *member function* of another class.

A **nonnumeric variable** is a variable that is not used in calculations like adding, multiplying, or subtracting. Such variables might represent names, addresses, telephone numbers, Social Security numbers, bank account numbers, or driver's license numbers. Note that even a data item referred to as a number and composed entirely of the digits 0 through 9 may be a nonnumeric variable by this definition; the question is how the item is used. No one adds, multiplies, or subtracts driver's license numbers, for example; these numbers serve solely as identifiers and could just as easily have letters in them, as indeed some of them do.

A **nonprinting character** is used to control the format of our displayed or printed information, rather than to represent a particular letter, digit, or other special character. The *space* is one of the more important nonprinting characters.

A **non-virtual** function is one that is not declared with the virtual keyword. This means that the compiler can decide at compile time the exact version of the function to be executed when it is referred to via a base class pointer or base class reference.

A **normal constructor** is a *constructor* whose arguments supply enough information to initialize all of the member fields in the object being created. Also see *constructor*.

A **null byte** is a byte with the value 0, commonly used to indicate the end of a *C string*. Note that this is not the same as the character "0", which is a normal printable character having the ASCII code 48.

A **null object** is an object of some (specified) class whose purpose is to indicate that a "real" object of that class does not exist. It is analogous to a *null pointer.* One common use for a null object is as a *return value* from a *member function* that is supposed to return an object with some specified properties but cannot find such an object. For example, a null StockItem object might be used to indicate that an item with a specified UPC cannot be found in the inventory of a store.

A **null pointer** is a *pointer* with the value 0. This value is particularly suited to indicate that a pointer isn't pointing to anything at the moment, because of some special treatment of zero-valued pointers built into the C++ language.

A **null string** is a string or *C string* with the value "".

A **numeric digit** is one of the digits 0 through 9.

A **numeric variable** is a variable that represents a quantity that can be expressed as a number, whether a whole number (an *integer variable*) or a number with a fractional part (a *floating-point variable*), and that can be used in calculations such as addition, subtraction, multiplication, or division. The integer variable types in C++ are char, short, int, and long. Each of these can be further subdivided into signed and unsigned versions. The signed versions can represent both negative and positive values (and 0), whereas the unsigned versions can represent only positive values (and 0) but provides greater ranges of positive values than the corresponding signed versions do. The floating-point variable types are float and double, which differ in their range and precision. Unlike the integer variable types, the floating-point types are not divided into signed and unsigned versions; all floating-point variables can represent either positive or negative numbers as well as 0. See *float* and *double* for details on range and precision.

## *O*

An **object** is a variable of a class type, as distinct from a variable of a *native type*. The behavior of an object is defined by the code that implements the class to which the object belongs. For example, a variable of type string is an object whose behavior is controlled by the definition of the string class.

**Object code**; see *machine code*. This term is unrelated to C++ objects.

An **object code module** is the result of compiling an *implementation file* into *object code*. A number of object code modules are combined to form an *executable program*. This term is unrelated to C++ objects.

**Object file**; see *object code module*. This term is unrelated to C++ *objects*.

**Object-oriented programming** is an approach to solving programming problems by creating *objects* to represent the entities being handled by the program, rather than by relying solely on *native data types*. This has the advantage that you can match the language to the needs of the problem you're trying to solve. For example, if you were writing a nurse's station program in C++, you would have objects that represent nurses, doctors, patients, various sorts of equipment, and so on. Each of these objects would display the behavior appropriate to the thing or person it represents.

**Off-by-one error**; see *fencepost error*.

An **ofstream** (pronounced "o f stream") is a *stream* used for output to a file.

An **op code** is the part of a *machine instruction* that tells the *CPU* what kind of instruction it is and sometimes also specifies a *register* to be operated on.

An **operating system** is a program that deals with the actual *hardware* of your computer. It supplies the lowest level of the software infrastructure needed to run a program. By far the most common operating system for Intel CPUs, at present, is MS-DOS (which is also the basis for Windows 95), followed by OS/2 and Windows NT.

The keyword **operator** is used to indicate that the following symbol is the name of a C++ operator we are redefining, either globally or for a particular class. For example, to redefine =, we have to specify operator = as the name of the function we are writing, rather than just =, so that the compiler does not object to seeing an operator when it expects an identifier.

An **ostream** is a stream used for *output*. For example, cout is a predefined ostream that displays characters on the screen.

**Output** is the process of sending data from the computer to the outside world. The most commonly used source of output for most programs is the screen.

A member function in a derived class is said to **override** the base class *member function* if the derived class function has the same *signature* (name and argument types) as that of the base class member function. The derived class member function will be called instead of the base class member function when the member function is referred to via an object of the derived class. A member function in a derived class with the same name but a different signature from that of a member function in the base class does not override the base class member function. Instead, it "hides" that base class member function, which is no longer accessible as a member function in the derived class.

## *P*

**Parent class**; see *inheritance*.

A **pointer** is essentially the same as a *memory address*. The main difference is that a memory address is "untyped" (i.e., it can refer to any sort of variable) whereas a pointer always has an associated data type. For example, char* (pronounced "char star") means "pointer to a char". To say "a variable points to a memory location" is almost the same as saying "a variable's value is the address of a memory location". In the specific case of a variable of type char*, to say "the char* x points to a *C string*" is essentially equivalent to saying "x contains the address of the first byte of the C string". Also see *array*.

A **polymorphic object** is a C++ *object* that presents the appearance of a simple object that displays *polymorphism* without exposing the user of the object to the hazards of pointers. The user does not have to know any of the details of the implementation, but merely instantiates an object of the single visible class (the *manager class*). That object does what the user wants with the help of an object of a *worker class*, which is derived from the manager class. Also see *manager/worker idiom*.

**Polymorphism** is the major organizing principle in C++ that allows us to implement several classes with the same interface and to treat objects of all these classes as though they were of the same class. Polymorphism is a variety of *dynamic typing* that maintains the safety factor of *static type checking*, because the compiler can determine at compile time whether a function call is legal even if it does not know the exact type of the object that will receive that function call at run time. "Polymorphism" is derived from the Greek *poly*, meaning "many", and *morph*, meaning "form". In other words, the same behavior is implemented in different forms.

To **pop** is to remove the top value from a stack.

The **preprocessor** is a part of the C++ compiler that deals with the source code of a program before the rest of the compiler ever sees that source code; thus, the name "preprocessor".

A **preprocessor directive** is a command telling the preprocessor to handle the following source code in a special manner.

A **preprocessor symbol** is a constant value similar to a const, but it is known only to the preprocessor, not to the rest of the compiler. The rules for naming preprocessor symbols are the same as those for other identifiers, but it is customary to use all upper-case letters in preprocessor symbols so that they can be readily distinguished from other identifiers.

The keyword **private** is an *access specifier* that denies *nonmember functions* access to *member functions* and *member variables* of its class.

Creating a class via **private inheritance** means that we are not going to allow outside functions to treat an object of the derived class as an object of the base class. That is, functions that takes a base class object as a parameter will not accept a derived class object in its place. None of the public *member functions* and public data items (if there are any) in the base class will be accessible in a privately derived class object. Contrast with *public inheritance*.

A **program** is a set of instructions specifying the solution to a set of problems, along with the data used by those instructions.

The **program counter** is a *dedicated register* that holds the address of the next instruction to be executed. During a *function call*, a *call instruction* pushes the contents of the program counter on the stack. This enables the *called function* to return to the *calling function* when finished.

**Program failure** can be defined as a situation in which a program does not behave as intended. The causes of this are legion, ranging from incorrect input data to improper specification of the problem to be solved.

**Program maintenance** is the process of updating and correcting a program once it has entered service.

**Programming** is the art and science of solving problems by the following procedure:

1. Find or invent a general solution to a set of problems.
2. Express this solution as an algorithm or set of algorithms.
3. Translate the algorithm(s) into terms so simple that a stupid machine like a computer can follow them to calculate the specific answer for any specific problem in the set.

*Warning*: This definition may be somewhat misleading, since it implies that the development of a program is straightforward and linear, with no revision. This is known as the "waterfall model" of programming, since water going over a waterfall follows a preordained course in one direction. However, real-life programming doesn't usually work this way; rather, most programs are written in an incremental process as assumptions are changed and errors are found and corrected.

The keyword **protected** is an *access specifier.* When present in a *base* class definition, it allows *derived* class functions access to member variables and functions in the *base* class *part* of a derived class object, while preventing access by other functions outside the base class.

The keyword **public** is an *access specifier* that allows *nonmember functions* access to *member functions* and *member variables* of its class.

Creating a class via **public inheritance** means that we are going to let outside functions treat an object of the derived class as an object of the base class. That is, any function that takes a base class object as a parameter will accept a derived class object in its place. All of the public *member functions* and public data items (if there are any) in the base class are accessible in a derived class object as well. Contrast with *private inheritance.*

**Push** means to add another value to a stack.

A **put pointer** holds the address of the next byte in the output area of an ostream — that is, where the next byte will be stored if we use << to write data into the stream.

## *R*

**RAM** is an acronym for Random Access Memory. This is the working storage of a computer, where data and programs are stored while we're using them.

A **reference argument** is another name for a variable from a *calling function* rather than an independent variable in the *called function.* Changing a reference argument therefore affects the corresponding variable in the calling function. Compare with *value argument.*

The **reference-counting idiom** is a mechanism that allows one object (the "reference-counted object") to be shared by several other objects (the "client objects") rather than having to make a copy for each of the client objects.

A **register** is a storage area that is on the same chip as the *CPU* itself. Programs use registers to hold data items that are actively in use; data in registers can be accessed within the time allocated to instruction execution rather than the much longer times needed to access data in *RAM.*

**Regression testing** means running a modified program and verifying whether previously working functionality is still working.

A **regular member function** is any member function that is not in any of the following categories:

1. constructor,
2. destructor,
3. the assignment operator, operator =.

A *derived class* inherits all regular member functions from its *base class.*

A **retrieval function** is a function that retrieves data that may have been previously stored by a **storage function** or that may be generated when needed by some other method such as calculation according to a formula.

A **return address** is the *memory address* of the next *machine instruction* in a *calling function*. It is used during execution of a *return statement* in a *called function* to transfer execution back to the correct place in the calling function.

A **return statement** is used by a *called function* to transfer execution back to the *calling function*. The return statement can also specify a value of the correct *return type* for the called function. This value is made available to the calling function to be used for further calculation. An example of a return statement is `return 0;`, which returns the value 0 to the calling function.

A **return type** tells the compiler what sort of data a *called function* returns to the calling function when the *called function* finishes executing. The return value from main is a special case; it can be used to determine what action a batch file should take next.

A **return value** is the value returned from a *called function* to its *calling function*.

**RHIDE** is the Integrated Development Environment developed by Robert Höhne. It is included on the CD-ROM in the back of this book.

**ROM** is an abbreviation for *Read-Only Memory*. This is the permanent internal storage of a computer, where the programs needed to start up the computer are stored. As this suggests, ROM does not lose its contents when the power is turned off, as contrasted with RAM.

**Run time** means "while a (previously compiled) program is being executed".

The **run-time type** of a variable is the type that variable has when the program is being executed. In the presence of *polymorphism*, this type may differ from the type with which the variable was declared at *compile time*.

## *S*

A **scalar variable** has a single value (at any one time); this is contrasted with a vector or an *array*, which contains a number of values, each of which is referred to by its *index*.

The **scope** of a variable is the part of the program in which the variable can be accessed. The scopes with which we are concerned are local, global, and class; see *local scope*, *global scope*, and *class scope* for more details.

A **selection expression** is the part of a switch statement that specifies an expression used to select an alternative section of code.

A **selection sort** is a sorting algorithm that selects the highest (or lowest) element from a set of elements (the "input list") and moves that selected element to another set of elements (the "output list"); the next highest (or lowest) element is then treated in the same manner. This operation is repeated until as many elements as desired have been moved to the output list.

A **short** is a type of *integer variable* that can represent a whole number. With most current C++ compilers, including DJGPP, a short occupies 2 bytes of storage and therefore can represent a number in either the range -32768 to 32767 (if signed) or the range 0 to 65535 (if unsigned).

The **short-circuit evaluation rule** governs the execution of the || and && operators. See *||* and *&&* for details.

A **side effect** is any result of calling a function that persists beyond the execution of that function other than its returning a *return value*. For example, writing data to a file is a side effect.

The **signature** of a function consists of its name and the types of its *arguments*. In the case of a *member function*, the class to which the function belongs is also part of its signature. Every function is uniquely identified by its signature, which is what makes it possible to have more than one function with the same name. This is called *function overloading*.

A **signed char** is a type of *integer variable*. See char for details.

A **signed int** is a type of *integer variable*. See int for details.

A **signed long** is a type of *integer variable*. See long for details.

A **signed short** is a type of *integer variable*. See short for details.

A **signed variable** can represent either negative or positive values. See char, short, int, or long for details.

**Slicing** is the partial assignment that occurs when a derived class object is assigned to a base class variable. This term is used because in such an assignment only the base class part of the derived class object is assigned while the other fields are "sliced off".

**Software** refers to the nonphysical components of a computer, the ones you cannot touch. If you can install it on your hard disk, it's software. Examples include a spreadsheet, a word processor, and a database program.

**Source code** is a program in a form suitable for reading and writing by a human being.

**Source code file**; see *implementation file*.

**Source code module**; see *implementation file*.

The **space character** is one of the *nonprinting characters* (or nondisplay characters) that control the format of displayed or printed information.

**Special constructor**; see *polymorphic object*.

The **square brackets**, **[** and **]**, are used to enclose an *array* or *vector index*, which selects an individual element of the array or vector. Also see [ ].

A **stack** is a data structure with characteristics similar to those of a spring-loaded plate holder such as you might see in a cafeteria. The last plate deposited on the stack of plates will be the first one removed when a customer needs a fresh plate; similarly, the last value deposited (pushed) onto a stack is the first value retrieved (popped).

The **stack pointer** is a *dedicated register*. It is used to keep track of the address of the most recently pushed value on the stack.

A **starting expression** is the part of a for statement that is executed once before the *controlled block* of the for statement is first executed. It is often used to initialize an *index variable* to 0 so that the index variable can be used to refer to the first element of an array or vector. See *for statement* for an example.

A **statement** is a complete operation understood by the C++ compiler. Each statement ends with a semicolon (;).

A **static member function** is a *member function* of a class that can be called without reference to an object of that class. Such a function has no *this pointer* passed to it on entry and therefore cannot refer to member variables of the class.

The **static storage class** is the simplest of the three *storage classes* in C++; variables of this storage class are assigned memory addresses in the *executable program* when the program is *linked.*

**Static type checking** refers to the practice of checking the correct usage of variables of different types during compilation of a program rather than during execution. C++ uses static type checking. See *type system* for further discussion. Note that this has no particular relation to the keyword static.

**Static typing** means determining the exact type of a variable when the program is compiled. It is the default typing mechanism in C++. Note that this has no particular relation to the keyword static, nor is it exactly the same as static type checking. See *type system* for further discussion.

**Stepwise refinement** is the process of developing an algorithm by starting out with a "coarse" solution and "refining" it until the steps are within the capability of the C++ language.

**Storage**; synonym for *memory.*

A **storage class** is the characteristic of a variable that determines how and when a memory address is assigned to that variable. C++ has three storage classes: static, auto, and dynamic. Please note that the term *storage class* has nothing to do with the C++ term class. See *static storage class*, *auto storage class*, and *dynamic storage class* for more details.

A **storage function** is a function that stores data for later retrieval by a *retrieval function*.

A **stream** is a place to put (in the case of an ostream) or get (in the case of an istream) characters. Some predefined streams are *cin* and *cout*.

A **stream buffer** is the area of memory where the characters put into a stream are stored.

The **string class** defines a type of object that contains a group of chars; the chars in a string can be treated as one unit for purposes of assignment, I/O, and comparison.

A **strstream** is a type of stream that exists only in memory rather than being attached to an input or output device. It is often used for formatting of data that is to be further manipulated within the program.

The **switch** statement is functionally equivalent to a number of if/else statements in a row, but is easier to read and modify. The keyword switch is followed by a *selection expression* (in parentheses), which specifies an expression that is used to select an alternative section of code. The various alternatives to be considered are enclosed in a set of curly braces following the selection expression, and are marked off by the keyword case followed by the (constant) value to be matched and a colon.

## *T*

**Temporary**; see *temporary variable*.

A **temporary variable** is automatically created by the *compiler* for use during a particular operation, such as a *function call* with an *argument* that has to be converted to a different type.

The keyword **this** represents a hidden argument automatically supplied by the *compiler* in every *member function* call. Its value during the execution of any member function is the address of the class object for which the member function call was made.

A **token** is a part of a program that the *compiler* treats as a separate unit. It's analogous to a word in English, while a *statement* is more like a sentence. For example, string is a token, as are :: and (, whereas x = 5; is a statement.

The keyword **true** is a predefined value representing the result of a conditional expression whose condition is satisfied. For example, in the conditional expression x < y, if x is less than y, the result of the expression will be true.

The **type** of an object is the class to which it belongs. The type of a *native variable* is one of the predefined variable types in C++. See *integer variable*, *floating-point variable*, and *bool* for details on the native types.

The **type system** refers to the set of rules the language uses to decide how a variable of a given type may be employed. In C++, these determinations are made by the *compiler* (*static type checking*). This makes it easier to prevent type errors than it is in languages where type checking is done during execution of the program (*dynamic type checking*). Please note that C++ has both static type checking and *dynamic typing*. This is possible because the set of types that is acceptable in any given situation can be determined at *compile time*, even though the exact type of a given variable may not be known until *run time*.

## *U*

An **uninitialized variable** is one that has never been set to a known value. Attempting to use such a variable is a logical error that can cause a program to act very oddly.

An **unqualified name** is a reference to a *member variable* that doesn't specify which object the member variable belongs to. When we use an unqualified name in a *member function*, the *compiler* assumes that the object we are referring to is the object for which that member function has been called.

An **unsigned char** is a type of *integer variable*. See *char* for details.

An **unsigned int** is a type of *integer variable*. See *int* for details.

An **unsigned long** is a type of *integer variable*. See *long* for details.

An **unsigned short** is a type of *integer variable*. See *short* for details.

An **unsigned** variable is an *integer variable* that represents only positive values (and 0). See *char*, *short*, *int*, and *long* for details.

The term **user** has several meanings in programming. The primary usage in this book is *application programmer*; however, it can also mean *library designer* (in the phrase *user-defined data type*) or even *end user*.

A **user-defined data type** is one that is defined by the user. In this context, user means "someone using language facilities to extend the range of variable types in the language", or *library designer*. The primary mechanism for defining a user-defined type is the *class*.

## *V*

A **value argument** is a variable of *local scope* created when a *function* begins execution. Its initial value is set to the value of the corresponding *argument* in the *calling function*. Changing a value argument does not affect any variable in the calling function. Compare with *reference argument*.

A **variable** is a programming construct that uses a certain part of *RAM* to represent a specific item of data we wish to keep track of in a program. Some examples are the weight of a pumpkin or the number of cartons of milk in the inventory of a store.

A **vector** is a group of variables that can be addressed by their position in the group; each of these variables is called an *element*. A vector has a name, just as a regular variable does, but the elements do not. Instead, each element has an *index* that represents its position in the vector.

Declaring a function to be **virtual** means that it is a member of a set of functions having the same *signatures* and belonging to classes related by *inheritance*. The actual function to be executed as the result of a given function call is selected from this set of functions dynamically (i.e., at run time) based on the actual type of an object referred to via a base class pointer (or base class reference). This is the C++ *dynamic typing* mechanism used to implement polymorphism, in contrast to the *static typing* used for *nonvirtual functions*, which are selected at compile time.

A **void return type specifier** in a *function declaration* indicates that the function in question does not return any value when it finishes executing.

The term **vtable** is an abbreviation for *virtual function address table*. It is where the addresses of all of the *virtual functions* for a given class are stored; every object of that class contains the address of the vtable for that class.

## *W*

A **while statement** is a *loop control statement* that causes its *controlled block* to be executed while a specified logical expression is true.

**Worker class**: see *polymorphic object.*

## *Y*

A **year number** is an integer value representing the number of years between two dates.

## *Z*

**Zero-based indexing** refers to the practice of numbering the elements of an *array* or vector starting at 0 rather than 1.

# About the Author

Steve Heller had always been fascinated by writing. In his childhood days in the 1950s and 1960s, he often stayed up far past his bedtime reading science fiction. Even in adulthood, if you came across him in his off-hours, he was more likely to be found reading a book than doing anything else.

After college, Steve got into programming more or less by accident; he was working for an actuarial consulting firm and was selected to take charge of programming on their time-sharing terminal because he was making much less than most of the other employees. Finding the programming itself to be more interesting than the actuarial calculations, he decided to become a professional programmer.

Until 1984, Steve remained on the consuming side of the writing craft. Then one day he was reading a magazine article on some programming-related topic and said to himself, "I could do better than that". With encouragement from his wife of the time, he decided to try his hand at technical writing. Steve's first article submission (to the late lamented *Computer Language Magazine*) was published, as were a dozen more over the next ten years.

But although writing magazine articles is an interesting pastime, writing a book is something entirely different. Steve got his chance at this new level of commitment when Harry Helms, then an editor for Academic Press, read one of his articles in *Dr. Dobb's Journal* and wrote him asking whether he would be interested in writing a book for AP. He answered, "Sure, why not?", not having the faintest idea of how much work he was letting himself in for.

The resulting book, *Large Problems, Small Machines*, received favorable reviews for its careful explanation of a number of facets of program optimization, and sold about 20,000 copies within a year after publication of the second edition, entitled *Efficient C/C++ Programming*.

By that time, Steve was hard at work on his next book, *Who's Afraid of C++?*, which was designed to make object-oriented programming intelligible to anyone from the sheerest novice to the programmer with years of experience in languages other than C++. To make sure that his exposition was clear enough for the novice, he posted a message on CompuServe requesting the help of someone new to programming. The responses included one from a woman named Susan, who ended up contributing a great deal to the book. In fact, about 100 pages consisted of email between Steve and Susan. Her contribution was wonderful, but not completely unexpected.

What was unexpected was that Steve and Susan would fall in love during the course of this project, but that's what happened. Since she lived in Texas and he lived in New York, this posed some logistic difficulties. The success of his previous book now became extremely important, as it was the key to Steve's becoming a full-time writer. Writers have been "telecommuting" since before the invention of the telephone, so his conversion from "programmer who writes" to "writer" made it possible for him to relocate to her area, which he promptly did.

Since his move to Texas, Steve has been hard at work on his writing projects, including *Introduction to C++*, a classroom text that covers more material in the same space as *Who's Afraid of C++?* (at the expense of the e-mail exchanges in the latter book), followed by *Who's Afraid of Java?*.

Steve and Susan were married in 1997.

# Index

**D**

## K



## L



## M



## N



## O